FORMAL GRAMMAR: THEORY AND IMPLEMENTATION
Edited by Robert Levine

The second volume in the series Vancouver Studies in Cognitive Science, this book is also the second in a set of conferences hosted by the Cognitive Science Programme at Simon Fraser University and devoted to the exploration of issues in cognition and the nature of mental representation. Comprising most of the conference papers, including the commentaries, as well as a number of invited papers, this collection reflects recent work in phonology, morphology, semantics, and neurolinguistics.

The speakers at the 1989 conference were asked to do two things – first, to address current research in their specific areas and, second, to try to assess the relationship between the formal content of linguistic theories and implementation of those theories. In this context the notion of implementation was construed fairly broadly and embraced not only machine-based applications such as generation, parsing, and natural language interface design, but also real-time aspects of human linguistic capability – in particular, learnability and the neural architecture which carries out whatever computations realize knowledge of language as biosphysical behaviour.

Not all the contributions focus on the theory/implementation interface; the interests represented are as varied as is the range of formalisms considered and they include categorial grammar, generalized phrase structure grammar, and the government-binding framework.

In combining linguistic theory and implementation this book makes an important contribution to bringing these disciplines together and allowing the reader to be aware of and benefit from the activities and results of both fields.

VANCOUVER STUDIES IN COGNITIVE SCIENCE

VOLUME 1   *Information, Language, and Cognition* (1990)
            Editor, Philip P. Hanson, Philosophy,
            Simon Fraser University

VOLUME 2   *Formal Grammar: Theory and Implementation*
            Editor, Robert Levine, Linguistics,
            Ohio State University

VOLUME 3   *Connectionism: Theory and Practice*
            Editor, Steven Davis, Philosophy,
            Simon Fraser University

formal grammar: theory and implementation

theory
and
implementation

edited by Robert Levine

New York   Oxford
OXFORD UNIVERSITY PRESS
1992

Oxford University Press

Oxford New York Toronto
Delhi Bombay Calcutta Madras Karachi
Petaling Jaya Singapore Hong Kong Tokyo
Nairobi Dar es Salaam Cape Town
Melbourne Auckland

and associated companies in
Berlin Ibadan

Published by Oxford University Press, Inc.
200 Madison Avenue, New York, New York 10016

Oxford is a registered trademark of Oxford University Press

Library of Congress Cataloging-in-Publication Data
Formal grammar : theory and implementation / edited by Robert Levine.
p.   cm. — (Vancouver studies in cognitive science : v. 2)
Papers from a Feb. 1989 conference hosted by the Cognitive Science
Programme at Simon Fraser University.   Includes bibliographical references.
ISBN 0-19-507314-2 (cloth). — ISBN 0-19-507310-X (ppr.)
1. Formalization (Linguistics)—Congresses.
2. Grammar, Comparative and general—Congresses.
3. Computational linguistics—Congresses.
4. Biolinguistics—Congresses. I. Levine, Robert, 1947- .
II. Simon Fraser University. Cognitive Science Programme.
III. Series. P128.F67F67 1992 415—dc20 91-23867

2 4 6 8 9 7 5 3 1

Printed in the United States of America
on acid-free paper

Contents

PREFACE

vii

CHAPTER 1

Learnability of Phrase Stucture Grammars   Janet Dean Fodor   3
Comment   Jean Mark Gawron   69

CHAPTER 2

Dynamic Categorial Grammar   Richard T. Oehrle   79
Comment   Pauline Jacobson   129

CHAPTER 3

Categorial Grammars, Lexical Rules, and the English Predicative
Bob Carpenter   168

CHAPTER 4

Implementing Government Binding Theories
Edward P. Stabler, Jr.   243
Comment   Verónica Dahl   276

CHAPTER 5

A Learning Model for a Parametric Theory in Phonology
B. Elan Dresher   290
Comment   Kenneth Church   318

CHAPTER 6

Some Choices in the Theory of Morphology   Arnold M. Zwicky   327

CHAPTER 7

Semantics, Knowledge, and NP Modification
Stephen Crain and Henry Hamburger   372

CHAPTER 8

On the Development of Biologically Real Models of Human
Linguistic Capacity   Mary-Louise Kean   402

CHAPTER 9

Properties of Lexical Entries and Their Real-Time Implementation
Lewis P. Shapiro   416

Preface

This volume is an outgrowth of the second conference, held in February 1989, in a series of conferences hosted by the Cognitive Science Programme of Simon Fraser University and devoted to the exploration of issues in cognition and the nature of mental representations. The conference theme was "Formal Grammar: Theory and Implementation," and followed what has become the standard format of the SFU Cognitive Science conferences: six main speakers (Elan Dresher, Mary-Louise Kean, Richard Oehrle, Ivan Sag, Edward Stabler, and Arnold Zwicky), each paired with a commentator (respectively, Kenneth Church, Lewis Shapiro, Pauline Jacobson, Janet Dean Fodor, Verónica Dahl, and Martin Kay). Of these presentations, all but the contributions of Sag and Kay are represented in this volume, along with invited papers by Robert Carpenter, Stephen Crain and Henry Hamburger, and Mark Gawron; they reflect work in phonology (Dresher, Church), morphology (Zwicky), semantics (Crain and Hamburger), neurolinguistics (Kean, Shapiro), and syntax (Fodor, Gawron; Oehrle, Jacobson; Carpenter; Stabler, Dahl). The notion of implementation was construed rather broadly in assembling the conference program, embracing not only machine-based applications such as generation, parsing, and natural language interface design, but real-time aspects of human linguistic capability – in particular, learnability and the neural architecture which carries out whatever computations realize knowledge of language as biophysical behaviour. The expectation was that the speakers, all of whom are primarily specialists in either theoretical or implementation fields, would address current research concern in their own area of expertise. But the further objective of the conference was that they would, wherever appropriate, attempt to assess the relationship between the formal content of linguistic theories and the implementation of those theories.

The juxtaposition of theory and implementation in the cognitive sciences is particularly natural in terms of the research paradigm inaugurated in vision research by David Marr. In much of his work Marr identified three distinct levels of representation which need to be explicitly distinguished in investigations of any cognitive system: the level of the computation itself – in effect, the identification and representation of the mathematical operations and structures corresponding to that cognitive system's knowledge objective; the level of the algorithm – the particular procedures and routines by which those structures and operations are calculated; and the level of hardware – the combination of biological mechanisms whose activities co-operate to yield a physical realization of the algorithm. Many linguists have been strongly influenced by Marr's model of cognitive science, and have tended to identify the contents of formal theories of language with the level of the computation; on this view, grammars are formal models of what is being calculated, and research in computational linguistics, psycholinguistics, and neurolinguistics will ultimately yield an account of how the mind organizes the contents of the formal theory into computationally realizable operations and how the brain instantiates these operations neurally. It is probably fair to say that among linguists who are anxious to situate their discipline comfortably within the larger framework of research in cognition, this picture of the relationship between theory and implementation is fairly widely held.

But such a view of the theory/implementation interface in linguistics seems somewhat too simple, in a number of respects. In recent years the relationship between theory formation on the one hand and computational application on the other has been particularly fruitful, and it is especially evident that methods and ideas arising in computational linguistics have fed back into the actual content of theories of grammar. For example, unification has been widely used by computational linguists during the past decade as an operation defining possible data structures given the existence of other, partially specified data structures. As such, it is most naturally treated as an algorithm, or class of algorithms, and Kasper and Rounds (1990) indeed define unification in just these terms. But unification is equivalently definable as a lattice-theoretic object, the least upper bound (or greatest lower bound, depending on how the lattice is defined) on a set of feature-value structures under an extension partial ordering, and has been applied under this interpretation in studies of the formal foundations of syntactic theory, as in Pollard and Sag (1987), Gazdar et al. (1988), and much other work. To take a second example, the first use of list-valued attributes, and operations on such lists, to record the syntactic valence of lexical heads appears in work by Shieber and others on the PATR-II implementation language (see Shieber et al. 1983) and is incorporated, with further developments and refinements, in purely theoretical research, particularly Head-Driven Phrase Structure Grammar. Again, much work in current categorial grammar stems from Ades and Steedman (1982), whose explicit aim was a formal theory directly reflecting on-line sentence-processing operations by making the structure-licensing principles of the grammar isomorphic with a pushdown-stack parsing routine. More generally, the development of logic programming systems, most notably those based on PROLOG, is closely paralleled in the increasing tendency for linguistic theories to take the form of declarative, constraint-based systems of principles, rather than derivation-licensing systems. Cases like these show that implementation is not merely the servant of formal grammar, dutifully expediting matters of execution after the major conceptual issues have been settled at a more abstract level of the Marr hierarchy; rather, the creative connection between theory and implementation runs in both directions.

Nonetheless, the fact that linguistic theory has increasingly come to share an algebraic foundation with implementation systems has not led linguists to take systematic account of implementability in making or evaluating proposals for the representation of natural language structure. In this respect, ease of application is no different from considerations involving on-line processing, computational complexity, or acquisition results; for the most part, linguists, like their colleagues in the natural and behavioural sciences, appear to be guided primarily by notions of generality and elegance. If learnability or computer implementation considerations seem to afford post hoc support for a · particular theoretical proposal, so much the better; but argumentation for a given rule or principle rarely appeals directly to such considerations. Fodor's paper is therefore noteworthy in making learnability considerations the central criterion for assessing the adequacy of a major theory of grammar – in this case Generalized Phrase Structure Grammar – and for revising the architecture of the theory to eliminate all language-parochial constraints and defaults. Learnability considerations are, of course, particularly suited to this mode of argumentation, because the generally accepted requirement that language learning has no access to negative data imposes substantial restrictions on the content of linguistic formalisms, and it is still far from clear to what extent other sorts of implementation consideration can play a comparable role in shaping such formalisms.

Not all the contributors focus on issues germane to the theory/implementation interface; the interests represented are varied, as is the range of formalisms considered, which include Categorial Grammar, Generalized Phrase Structure Grammar, and the Government-Binding framework. And it is also clear that the degree of convergence between implementation systems and theories of grammar is intrinsically limited; the two things are different, after all, and it would be quite unreasonable to expect that natural language grammars will be optimal in all respects from the point of view of implementation, or that formal grammar will ever directly reflect standard programming practice in computational linguistics. What is important is that investigators in linguistic theory and in implementation maintain an awareness of, and attempt to benefit as much as possible from, each other's activities and results.

It is a pleasure to acknowledge the support of the individuals and institutions who made this anthology possible, beginning with the contributors themselves. Generous financial support for the conference was provided by the Social Science and Humanities Research Council of Canada, the SFU Centre for Systems Science, and Simon Fraser University. Tom Perry of the Department of Linguistics and other members of the Cognitive Science group at SFU worked hard on-site to organize a successful conference and succeeded brilliantly. I thank my friends Donna Gerdts and Michael Hayward for lending invaluable assistance in expediting editorial communications in the preparation of the volume, and the staff of UBC Press, especially Jean Wilson, for their co-operation. Finally, I wish to express my particular appreciation and special thanks to Lindsay Burrell, who, as project assistant in the Department of Philosophy at Simon Fraser, was responsible for preparing MS-Word versions of all chapters prior to final typesetting, and to Steven Davis, the series editor of Vancouver Studies in Cognitive Science, with whom it was a true pleasure to collaborate in the organization of the conference and the publication of this volume.

Robert D. Levine

REFERENCES

Ades, A. and Steedman, M. (1982). On the order of words. *Linguistics and Philosophy* 4:517-58

Gazdar, G., Pullum, G.K., Klein, E., Carpenter, R., Hukari, T.E., and Levine, R.D. (1988). Category structures. *Computational Linguistics* 14:1-19

Kasper, R.T. and Rounds, W.C. (1990). The Logic of Unification in Grammar. *Linguistics and Philosophy* 13:35-58

Pollard, C. and Sag, I. (1987). *Information-Based Syntax and Semantics, Vol.1: Fundamentals*. Stanford: CSLI

Shieber, S., Uszkoreit, H., Robinson, J., and Tyson, M. (1983). The formalism and implementation of PATR-II. In *Research on Interactive Acquisition and Use of Knowledge*. Menlo Park, CA: SRI International Artificial Intelligence Center

CHAPTER ONE

Learnability of Phrase Structure Grammars*

Janet Dean Fodor

INTRODUCTION

Gazdar, Klein, Pullum, and Sag (1985) made it very clear in the introductory chapter of their book on Generalized Phrase Structure Grammar that what they were about to present was a linguistic theory, not a psychological theory of language use or language learning. They were prepared to acknowledge that some relationship between the two might be forged: "since a given linguistic theory will make specific claims about the nature of languages, it may well in turn suggest specific kinds of psycholinguistic hypotheses." But their estimate of actual progress to date in identifying and testing such hypotheses was quite glum. Though "Crain and Fodor . . . have argued that GPSG does have implications for psycholinguistic concerns, nonetheless, it seems to us that virtually all the work needed to redeem the promissory notes linguistics has issued to psychology over the past 25 years remains to be done" (p. 5). The present paper can be regarded as a bulletin from the front, where we have been hard at work these past few years, redeeming to the best of our ability. Our own part of the greater psycholinguistics program has been to try to determine whether Generalized Phrase Structure Grammar (GPSG) is compatible with what is known about human sentence processing and language acquisition.[1] Where it is not, we have tried to say what it would take to make it so.

The study of sentence parsing and production is concerned to a large extent with processes and procedures about which "pure" linguistics makes no claims. Its closest contact with linguistic theory concerns the properties of mental representations. How are sentence structures mentally represented by speaker/hearers? How is the grammar mentally represented? On these topics there have been a number of clever experiments, and energetic debates about the import of their findings. In the past few years there has been an investigation of whether sentences are assigned deep structure representations, and/or S-structure representations more abstract than traditional surface structures; there has been an investigation of how the mental grammar divides into modules (components); and an investigation of whether sentence representations include empty categories and, if so, which ones. I cannot cite all the individual studies here. The first two projects are reviewed in Fodor (1990); for a review of the third, which is still very much in progress, see Fodor (1989c). A fair summary, I think, would be that phrase structure grammar is not so far running ahead of any other linguistic theory in accounting for sentence processing findings, but it is not running behind, either.

The study of language acquisition offers an even richer domain of facts to challenge and shape linguistic theory. The progress that has been made has not derived primarily from empirical investigations of what real children learn when or how. Instead, a more intimate connection with linguistic theory is provided by the study of language learnability in principle. And here there has been one main driving idea: that children succeed in learning a natural language without benefit of systematic negative data (i.e., information about what is NOT a sentence of the language).[2] This is a familiar point by now and I won't belabour it. Its most important consequence is that while the learner's data can set a LOWER bound on the generative capacity of the grammar he establishes, it cannot set an UPPER bound.[3] Only his innate linguistic knowledge, that is, Universal Grammar (UG), can do that. It follows that we should be able to map out the contents of UG by observing what upper bounds learners do impose on their generalizations.

For this purpose we could study the interim generalizations and misgeneralizations made by children on the way to acquiring the adult language. But we also have an abundance of relevant data in adult languages themselves. Each language exhibits a host of generalizations which fall interestingly short of the ultimate "maximal" super-generalization that could just as well have been formulated by learners but for the restrictions imposed by UG. Every one of these partial generalizations in an adult language thus exhibits an upper bound which can help to delineate the content of UG. Of course, "pure" linguistics is in the business of characterizing UG also. But where it sets about the task by charting the universal properties of natural languages, learnability studies proceed instead by subtraction. Given the "no negative data" assumption, we know that a child learning Chinese (say) receives from his environment no more information about Chinese than a finite subset of its (shorter) sentences.[4] We also know that this child will end up knowing a great deal more than that: he will know, over an infinite domain, which strings are sentences of Chinese and which are not. To determine UG, we merely subtract the information in the learner's input from the information in his final grammar. (Fortunately these measures do not have to be absolutely exact; a lot can be learned about UG at this early stage of research by subtracting a GENEROUS estimate of the information in the input from a MODEST estimate of the information in the final grammar. As long as we err in this direction, we will only underestimate UG.)

So now we can ask: does what phrase structure theory has to say about UG square with what learnability considerations tell us about UG? And since science is a matter of getting as close to the truth as one can, there is also the comparative question: is there any other theory of UG that fits the learnability facts better? In one sense, of course, the subtraction of input information from final information is theory independent, so all theories should arrive at the same answer (barring errors of reasoning, and so forth) about what information is supplied by UG. However, different theories make very different claims about how this information is mentally encoded. And that can have different implications for how the innate information interacts with the information coming in from the environment. The nature of this interaction is crucial. Because of the lack of negative data to correct overgeneralizations, UG must interact with the learner's experiences of the language in such a way as to prevent overgeneralizations BEFORE they happen. Therefore it is not enough for a learner to know what the range of candidate grammars is. He also needs to know which of those candidate grammars it is safe for him to adopt in the face of a given input (also depending perhaps on what his prior grammar was).[5] The one thing that is certain is that he must not adopt just ANY grammar that is compatible with the current input. If he did, he might pick one which overgenerates, that is, which generates a language which properly includes the target language; and with no negative data to reveal to him that this was an error, he would have no reason to give up the incorrect grammar.

This, of course, is the problem of upper bounds, more commonly known as the subset problem, an inevitable corollary of the absence of negative data. Its moral is that a learner must have a selection criterion of some kind to guide his choice among grammars compatible with his available evidence, and that this selection criterion must obey the Subset Principle (Berwick 1985; Wexler & Manzini 1987), that is, it must never select a grammar which generates a language which is a proper superset of the language generated by some other grammar which is compatible with the available evidence.[6] It will be convenient, even if less precise, to make use of some abbreviations here. Let us use the term "subset grammar" to mean (NOT a grammar that is included in another grammar, but) a grammar which generates a language that is included in the language generated by another grammar; and correspondingly for the term "superset grammar." Then the Subset Principle says that the learner's selection criterion must always select a "subset grammar" rather than a "superset grammar" whenever there is a choice.

I will refer to the Subset Principle as condition C1. It is the most important but not the only condition that one might want to impose on the selection criterion. Let us use "I" to refer to a novel input which initiates a particular learning event, "G_i" to refer to the learner's grammar at the time that I is encountered, and "G_{i+1}" to refer to the grammar that the learner adopts in response to I.[7] Then one might hold that the selection criterion should be such that:

C2: G_{i+1} licences I. (Would prevent fruitless grammar changes.)

C3: $G_{i+1} = G_i$ if G_i licenses I. (Would prevent unnecessary grammar changes.)

C4: Generalization of C3: The difference between G_i and G_{i+1} should be as small as possible consistent with C2.

C5: $L(G_{i+1})$ (i.e., the language generated by G_{i+1}) should include $L(G_i)$. (Would prevent retrograde grammar change, loss of constructions previously mastered.)

The general effect of these conditions is to direct grammar choice in profitable directions, to minimize the amount of random trial and error before selection of the correct grammar, and thus to bring the model closer to a realistic account of actual language learning.[8] Conditions such as these have been discussed in the literature. For example, C3 characterizes the "error-driven learning" of Wexler and Culicover (1980); it is also related to the definition of "conservative learning" in Osherson, Stob, and Weinstein (1984). The particular conditions above are given as illustration. They may not be exactly the right ones; some of them have disadvantages as well as advantages.[9] But even conditions that are desirable may not be feasible, since their implementation may require reference to properties of grammars which are not accessible to the learner, or which the learner could establish only by unrealistically complex computations. A non-linguistic example: if you're buying diamonds at the corner jewellery store, it doesn't help at all to be told to select the ones that came from deepest in the mine, for that information is presumably unavailable; it also doesn't help much to know you should select stones that have been cut so that their surface area is exactly 1.53 times their height, for though that information is available in principle, it's unlikely that you could compute it in practice.

A linguistic example of this is provided by Wexler and Culicover (1980), who imposed condition C2 on grammar changes consisting of the ADDITION of a transformational rule, but not on changes consisting of DELETING a transformation. Why? They didn't say, but it's clear enough. In their model, a rule to be added is composed in response to the input. The learning mechanism starts with the deep structure of the input sentence (deduced from its meaning, which is given by the non-verbal context), then applies the relevant transformational rules in G_i, and then constructs whatever rule is necessary (if any) to make the final phrase marker of this G_i derivation match the input string I. Thus there is an implementation algorithm here to ensure that G_{i+1} generates I. But a rule to be deleted is selected at random, without regard for whether omitting it from the derivation will result in generation of I. This is presumably because it is too difficult to identify an APPROPRIATE rule to delete. It's not difficult to CHECK whether a candidate G_{i+1} generates I; that would require only re-running the derivation on the basis of G_{i+1} instead of G_i. But there is no obvious procedure based on the G_i derivation for FINDING a G_{i+1} that would have the desired effect on the derivation. The only way would be by trial and error: pick a rule to discard at random, run through the derivation without it, and if the surface string isn't I, try again. Since there may have been no rule in G_i whose elimination would result in I, there is no guarantee that this procedure will be successful.[10] And even when it is successful, the procedure is so cumbersome that it could very well outweigh the benefit of C2. So here we see that it is difficult to avoid random unprofitable steps (e.g., deletion of a needed rule) on the route to the right grammar, if grammars contain rules and if those rules interact in derivations in such a way that they don't stand in any simple, transparent relation to the structures generated.

Another example concerns the implementation of C1, the Subset Principle. Wexler and Manzini (1987) proposed that learners apply the Subset Principle by literally comparing languages (i.e., sets of sentences) and looking for subset relations among them. A grammar that is about to be adopted is checked to see that the language it generates does not properly include the language generated by any other grammar that could be chosen at that point.[11] But this is an extraordinarily onerous procedure, and it seems utterly implausible to suppose that children go through it every time they update their grammar (see Fodor 1989b, for discussion). Indeed, it is hardly plausible to suppose that learners concern themselves at all with the other sentences (the sentences other than I) generated by a candidate grammar. It might be argued that comparing sentence sets would be necessary to check for satisfaction of condition C5 above (no loss of generative power). But again the computations involved are surely prohibitive. It is generally agreed that a learner does not store prior inputs; so he would have to take his current G_i, establish the full language it generates, and then determine whether all of its sentences were generated by the candidate G_{i+1}. One wouldn't ask even a computer to go about the job this way if there were any alternative. Ideally there would be some simple and accessible relation between grammars which would serve as a flag for subset relations between their languages. We will see below that this varies considerably across different theories of grammars.

To summarize so far: because children learn reliably and efficiently without benefit of negative data, we know that they do not adopt grammars at random. They must rely on some selection criterion which obeys C1, the Subset Principle, and some other general conditions along the lines of C2-C5. For a realistic model of the acquisition process, we must assume that UG defines the class of possible grammars in such a way that the properties and relations relevant to these conditions are determinable in principle, and can be determined in practice without excessively complex computations. Whether or not a particular property of grammars is readily accessible, or is accessible at all, can vary from one theory of UG to another. Hence, whether an adequate selection criterion for learning is definable may also vary from one theory of UG to another.

In this paper I will argue that NO satisfactory selection criterion can be formulated for GPSG grammars of the kind characterized by Gazdar, Klein, Pullum, and Sag (1985) (GKPS). There is no selection criterion for GPSG which satisfies even the Subset Principle, yet alone any of the other desiderata suggested above. Therefore GPSG grammars are not learnable without systematic negative data. However, I will also show that the standard version of the theory can be modified in various ways, into what I will call LPSG (learnable phrase structure grammar), for which there IS a satisfactory and very natural selection criterion, namely, grammar simplicity. But before embarking on the technicalities of what it is about standard GPSG that makes it unlearnable, I want to set the scene by comparing briefly two other linguistic theories, Government Binding theory (GB), and the Standard Theory (ST) of Chomsky (1965), which occupy more or less opposite extremes on a continuum of transparency of the selection criterion. In GB it is utterly simple and direct. In ST it is quite obscure, for reasons I will explain. Thus these theories establish useful benchmarks against which other theories can be compared. As will become clear, GPSG falls very close to the dismal ST end of the scale.

OTHER THEORIES

Government Binding theory

To meet the learnability requirement, every theory of language must support a selection criterion which determines, directly or indirectly, a set of triples, $<G_i, I, G_{i+1}>$ as defined above, that is sufficient to guide learners to the correct grammar for any natural language that is indeed learnable under reasonable conditions. In the most transparent case possible, a linguistic theory would simply LIST all the legitimate triples. (By "list" here I don't mean that they must be ordered, just that they are individually specified.) Then there would be no accessibility problem, no complex calculations, no indeterminacy, but essentially just a table look-up. GB doesn't go quite this far, but it approaches quite closely.

GB doesn't list all possible grammars one by one; instead it states just once everything that is common to them all, and then it lists all the ways in which they differ. What is common to all grammars is encoded in the principles of GB; how they can differ is encoded in the parameters. Listing, of course, is not an economical way of representing information, and it is not even possible over an infinite domain. But GB maintains that there is only a finite number of possible languages, as long as attention is restricted to "core grammar" (see below); and some economy is achieved by the fact that cross-language differences are factored by the parameters into a relatively small number of orthogonal dimensions of variation.[12]

Now for the selection criterion. The only things for it to select between are the values of the various parameters. Since these are all explicitly represented, each one can have innately associated with it a suitable input trigger I, or set of such triggers. When a learner encounters a trigger sentence in his input, he can (should) set the parameter in question to the value with which the trigger is associated. To ensure satisfaction of the Subset Principle, any parameter values representing languages that stand in a subset/superset relation must be innately ordered, with the value for the subset language given priority over the value for the corresponding superset language;[13] and a learner must be allowed to move from a higher to a lower priority value only in the presence of a suitable trigger. And that's all there is to the GB selection criterion, except for some technical decisions about how triggers are to be characterized.

It is imaginable that triggers do not need to be explicitly specified because any input is an adequate trigger for any parameter value as long as it meets certain general conditions. Specifically, a trigger must be compatible with the parameter value that it is a trigger for (compatible in the sense that it is a sentence of the language that is generated by the grammar resulting from that parameter setting).[14] Also (to preserve the Subset Principle) a trigger for one parameter value must be an input which is NOT compatible with any other value of higher priority. This kind of general characterization of which constructions trigger which parameter values would be more economical in terms of innate representations in the language faculty than an explicit list would be, but it would be more demanding in terms of the amount of on-line calculation needed.[15] So it's not clear which model would be optimal on grounds of economy. But recent work by Robin Clark (1988, 1989) indicates that non-specification of triggers is not adequate in the case of natural language. Though satisfactory for choosing among alternative values of the same parameter, with the rest of the grammar held constant, it is NOT sufficient in cases of competition between different parameters. Clark gives examples which show that a mere compatibility condition on values and their triggers would allow one and the same input to be a trigger for more than one parameter. That is, there could be more than one parameter such that resetting it would allow the grammar to accommodate that input. Therefore there will be ambiguity with respect to which of those parameters should be reset in response to that input. The learner cannot be allowed to resolve the ambiguity by a random choice, because there is no guarantee that he will be able to recover if he makes the wrong guess. Clark shows that one wrong guess can result in a "garden path" in which one parameter after another is mis-set on the basis of the first mistake. The solution proposed by Clark is that the parameters are innately ordered so as to establish priorities that will resolve such ambiguities. But another solution is to assume that UG specifies particular triggers for some or all parameter values, which satisfy not only the conditions above but also a uniqueness condition, namely that no construction is the trigger for more than one parameter value (perhaps for a given G_i).

With some such revision, it appears that GB would have a successful selection criterion. It would make learning possible, by respecting the Subset Principle, and it would make learning feasible, by requiring no complex computations to determine the merits of competing grammars. Just how rapid the convergence on the correct grammar would be would depend on various other factors, such as whether all inputs were utilizable for learning,[16] and whether ALL parameter values were explicitly assigned a unique trigger, or only those that would otherwise result in garden paths. In the latter case a learner would still have some random choices to make, so there would still be some trial and error behaviour before convergence on the final grammar. But even so, compared with other frameworks the amount of non-deterministic floundering would be considerably reduced; and with sufficiently tight innate pre-programming it could be eliminated altogether.

The contrast with the Standard Theory is especially striking. ST notoriously failed to impose sufficiently narrow limits on the class of possible grammars. And it also failed to characterize the optimal, or the legitimate, G_i to G_{i+1} transitions, or to provide any adequate basis for doing so. It is also interesting that none of the intervening revisions of the Standard Theory did much better vis-à-vis learnability. The significant move, from a learnability point of view, was the shift from grammars that were open-ended collections of rules etc., to grammars (as in GB's parameter model) that are selected by a finite number of pre-established either/or choices.

The Standard Theory

An ST grammar was taken to be a collection of rules, constraints, surface filters, etc. Though some of these might be innate, much of the grammar was assumed to be constructed by each learner from scratch. UG provided guidance to the learner only in the form of a projective definition of the class of possible rules, filters, etc., from which he could draw the ingredients for building his grammar. Grammar building sounds like a great deal of work for learners, especially compared with a parameter model in which learners merely "set switches" to pick pre-constructed options. But this may not be a decisive objection, since we don't really know how hard learners do work inside their heads. A more serious problem for ST was that it was not clear that a learner could succeed in selecting the correct grammar however hard he worked at it.

ST did not assume specific triggers to determine the selection of grammars. Since it did not explicitly list the possible grammars, or even the possible grammar ingredients (rules, constraints, etc.), it had no way to associate each one with a distinguished set of triggering inputs. Because it gave a general, projective definition of possible grammars, it also had to provide a general, projective method for defining the legitimate $<G_i, I, G_{i+1}>$ triples. Let us set aside here the question of how ST learners could obey conditions like C2-C5, and concentrate solely on C1, the Subset Condition. What ST needed was a reliable GENERAL selection criterion, or evaluation measure, for determining a ranking of grammars in subset situations where the input could not decide the issue.[17, 18]

A common suggestion (in phonology as well as syntax) was that the evaluation measure is a formal symbol-counting simplicity metric over grammars, or over competing rules, etc. This was a basic assumption in *Aspects*, where progress on matters of explanatory adequacy was seen in terms of development of notational conventions such that grammars preferred by learners would be shorter grammars. But within a few years this picture of grammar evaluation had almost completely disappeared from the literature. With hindsight it is easy to see why: a simplicity metric gave consistently wrong results when applied to transformational rules.[19] Adult grammars, according to ST, contained transformations such as Passive, Extraposition, Raising, There-insertion, Pronominalization, and so forth. So it is rules such as these that the ST evaluation metric would have to prefer, given input, say, from English. But a simplicity metric would in fact always select something more general. For example, suppose a learner encountered a passive construction in his input, and construed it correctly as exhibiting movement of an NP from postverbal position to the front of its clause. For safe learning in accord with the Subset Principle, the learner should formulate a narrowly defined transformation sufficient to generate that construction type but no others. Given the range of possible rules in ST (for example, lexically governed, or with Boolean conditions appended, etc.), it would actually be an unwarranted leap for a learner even to infer from this input that ANY NP could move from after ANY verb to the front of ANY clause. But a simplicity metric would leap far further even than that. Since every restriction on a rule complicates its statement, the simplicity metric would favour an extremely general rule moving any category from any position to any position – in effect, the rule *Move* α of later versions of transformational theory. Children would never acquire the various more specific (more complex) ST transformations.[20]

Learnability concerns were central in the development of ST, clearly acknowledged in Chomsky's concept of explanatory adequacy, which is concerned with why the grammar for a language is as it is, that is, why learners formulate that grammar rather than some other. Development of an adequate evaluation metric was therefore a matter of importance for ST. Given that a simplicity metric would not do, a search was made for an evaluation measure based on something other than formal simplicity. But though there were some interesting proposals here and there, no sufficiently systematic measure ever seems to have been identified. This is really no wonder, because the arguments which show that simplicity is NOT an adequate evaluation measure for ST also show that what ST would need would be almost exactly the REVERSE of a simplicity ranking. And that would have been too implausible to swallow. While it isn't necessary to assume that learners always pick the simplest grammar that works, it is bizarre to suppose that they always pick the most complex one.

For this reason among many others, ST is no longer of interest. But because it will be important to the discussion of GPSG below, it is worth dwelling for a moment on WHY the rules of ST interacted so disastrously with a simplicity metric. As usual, the lack of systematic negative data is at the bottom of the problem, but two properties in particular of ST rules also share the blame. One is that ST transformations contained context restrictions. For any context sensitive rule, there is a simpler rule without the context restriction which (with other aspects of the grammar held constant) will generate a more inclusive language. Thus any positive datum that supports the context sensitive rule will also support the context free rule. A learner could choose between them only on the basis of simplicity, and simplicity selects the context free rule. So a CS rule in the target grammar could not be learned; it would always be rejected by learners in favour of the overgeneral CF rule. Note that this problem would apply equally to free-standing constraints or filters, not only to constraints that are part and parcel of particular rules. Since these are all negative characterizations of the language, only negative data could FORCE a grammar to contain them; and a simplicity metric would always prefer a grammar without them.[21, 22]

The second problem concerning ST rule selection arose a little later in the evolution of the theory, when syntactic feature notation became established. (For minor features and lexical categories in 1965, and more systematically for all syntactic categories in Chomsky 1970.) For any rule expressed in feature notation, there is a simpler rule containing fewer feature specifications which (with other aspects of the grammar held constant) will generate a more inclusive language. Thus any positive datum that supports the more complex and more restricted rule will also support the simpler and broader rule; and the simplicity metric will select the latter. So even a context free rule in the target grammar could not be learned if it were couched in feature notation; it would always be rejected by learners in favour of a highly schematic rule with fewer features, which would overgenerate. (I note in passing that *Move* α can be seen as an ST transformation that has been stripped of all its context restrictions and all its featural contrasts; the last one to go was the *Move NP* / *Move WH* contrast. By the arguments just given, *Move* α is the one and only learnable transfor-

mation. But then it is so contentless that it needs little or no learning;
all the work of acquisition has shifted to other aspects of the theory.)

I have observed so far that ST rules did not permit an effective
selection criterion for learning, because they were context sensitive
and because they contained feature specifications. As if that weren't
enough, ST suffered from a third acquisition problem, which was that
it was so rich in potential descriptive devices that ambiguities about
the correct description kept arising. Though the descriptive armamen-
tarium changed somewhat over the years, ST and its descendants
(EST, REST) allowed grammars to contain a variety of kinds of rules
and also an array of filters, rule ordering restrictions, derivational
constraints, and so forth. And since at least some of these were allowed to vary across languages, they needed to be learned. But just as
a GB learner might wonder which parameter to reset to accommodate
a new input, so also (and on a much greater scale) an ST learner might
wonder whether to add a new rule or a new lexical entry or to delete a
restriction in an old rule or to discard a filter, or to opt for some
combination of these or other descriptive alternatives. So a selection
criterion, or evaluation measure, couldn't just compare rules with
rules, or filters with filters. It would also have to evaluate all manner
of trade-offs and interactions between them, and establish somehow a
coherent ranking, consistent with the Subset Principle, of all the different possible mixtures that a grammar could contain.

In view of this it's not surprising that ST learning was not generally
pictured as a simple deterministic process of moving systematically
from one candidate grammar to another, driven by the input. Rather,
the learning mechanism was thought of as some kind of hypothesis
formation and testing (HFT) device, which could float a hypothesis
about the grammar, consider its merits, contemplate what further
inputs would be helpful in deciding if it was correct, and so forth.
However, even the best HFT models are very unwieldy. Those that
don't presuppose this kind of "little linguist" activity typically resort
instead to unrealistically long non-directed searches through the
whole domain of grammars. (See the review by Pinker 1979.) Neither
approach begins to explain the uniformity and effiency of natural
language acquisition. Wexler and Culicover's successful learning
model for ST grammars was a remarkable achievement in the circumstances. But they themselves described the learning mechanism they
presuppposed as psychologically quite unrealistic in many respects.
Certainly it did not embody a selection criterion that satisfied the
Subset Principle or most of the other desiderata above. Instead they
sidestepped the Subset Problem by assuming a universal base related
to meaning, only obligatory transformations, and uniqueness of deri-

vation from a given base structure. Between them, these assumptions provide the equivalent of negative data: a string could be determined to be ungrammatical if the meaning it would have to have was the same as that of an attested sentence.[23] Even so, the Wexler and Culicover learner would (except for the most improbable good luck) have had to engage in a staggering amount of semi-random trial and error behaviour in the course of finding the right grammar.

To summarize: ST lacked a suitable evaluation measure which would consistently select subset grammars. A simplicity metric gave exactly the wrong results; an anti-simplicity metric would have been psychologically implausible; and no other alternative seems to have been found which was free of these problems and also sufficiently general to apply to all choices between grammars that a learner might have to make. Eventually the search was abandoned. Since a selection criterion wouldn't interface correctly with ST grammars, the theory of grammars had to change instead. And it has kept on changing until at last, in GB parameter theory, it has arrived at a version in which it needs no projective evaluation measure at all. GB grammar choices are individually stipulated with no reliance on a general criterion. It cannot even be objected that the stipulated choices simulate an anti-simplicity criterion. Since all the alternatives are laid out in advance, there is really no sense in which one grammar (one setting of the parameter "switches") counts as any simpler or more complex than any other.[24]

In short, GB learning is more successful than ST learning was, primarily because GB learning does not rely on a general evaluation measure but instead lists all the options and ranks them explicitly. The explicit ranking approach has its own obvious disadvantages, however. In particular, listed options must be finite in number, and for plausibility they should be relatively few in number. This is why parameter theory is generally assumed to apply only to the "core" of a natural language; the rich variation exhibited in the "periphery" is held to be characterized in some other way. But of course, if peripheral facts must be DESCRIBED in some other way, then they must also be LEARNED in some other way. And so GB parameter theory presupposes TWO language learning devices: (i) the parameter setting device for the core, which is quite "mechanical" and guaranteed successful; and (ii) some other learning device for the periphery, presumably more traditional in design, that is, some sort of HFT mechanism with all the disadvantages just rehearsed in connection with ST.

It is interesting to contemplate whether an acquisition model could have both virtues, that is, the simple mechanical quality of GB switch-setting, and also the projectability of a general selection criterion so that it could apply across the FULL range of natural language constructions. Whether or not this is attainable is very much an open question at present. But I will argue that GPSG, when suitably modified, comes close to providing this sort of balance between simple mechanism and full coverage.

However, GPSG as it now stands (the GKPS model) is a learning disaster, of very much the same kind as ST. It is a rule-based theory (though principle-based too), and as such it can be shown to be much closer to the ST end of the scale than to the GB end in respects relevant to learnability. In particular, its grammars cannot reasonably be innately listed and so it needs a projective evaluation measure to impose the Subset Principle and adjudicate between grammars when more than one is compatible with the input. But a simplicity metric makes systematically wrong choices, and it is not clear that there is any credible alternative that will do better. However, as elsewhere in the theory of learnability, the way to solving acquisition problems may lie not in revision of the acquisition mechanisms but in revision of the linguistic assumptions. As I will show, some relatively small changes to GPSG, preserving its general character, will make a very large difference to learnability.

MAKING GPSG LEARNABLE

GPSG, though vastly different from ST in other respects, shares with ST the three main characteristics which make an adequate selection criterion difficult to come by. GPSG assumes that grammars are expressed in feature notation. It assumes that grammars contain language-specific constraints (though it does not allow context sensitive rules). And since it assumes that grammars contain both rules and constraints, it is prey to descriptive ambiguities about whether a new input should be accommodated by adding a rule or discarding a constraint. To reiterate the points made above for ST, the consequence of the first two properties is that a selection criterion based on simplicity would consistently select superset grammars instead of subset grammars; yet it is not clear what relation other than relative simplicity would apply broadly enough to rank all possible grammars. The consequence of the third property is that it is hard to think of any selection criterion at all that could point the learner in the most profitable direction for finding the right grammar and avoid massive trial and error.[25]

I will argue in this section that the advantages of a simplicity metric can be retained, and its disadvantages remedied, within a modified GPSG framework. This is of interest because it shows that the learnability problems that afflicted ST are not inherent in the learning of rule systems per se. Everything depends on what kinds of rules are assumed, and how they interact with other descriptive devices in grammars. In what follows I will give a partial characterization of LPSG, a learnable variant of GPSG, which differs from the standard (GKPS) variant in five ways:

1 No language-specific Feature Co-occurrence Restrictions (FCRs) or Feature Specification Defaults (FSDs).

2 The Specific Defaults Principle: UG must assign a specific (i.e., non-disjunctive) default value to every feature in every context, except where the value is universally fixed or is universally free.

3 Lexical (meta)rules do not preserve subcategorization features. Subcategorization (SUBCAT) features take as their values sets of categories rather than integers.

4 The Double M Convention: if a rule contains two (or more) optional marked feature specifications, only one marked value may be selected for the same local tree, unless the rule explicitly indicates that they may co-occur.

5 Linear Precedence (LP) statements characterize permitted orders of sister constituents, not required orders.

These proposed modifications are not all independent of each other, but for expository purposes I will isolate them as far as possible and discuss them separately. In this paper I will only have space to discuss the first two. Proposal (3) is discussed in Fodor (to appear). Proposal (5) is touched on briefly in Fodor and Crain (1990); some relevant arguments are given by Pinker (1984:ch. 4). In each case the motivation for the proposed revision is that it eliminates a bar to learnability. I don't know whether there are alternative revisions that would do as well or better. I would like to argue that all of these revisions are independently desirable on purely linguistic grounds, that is, that they lead to more satisfactory descriptions of natural language facts than before, but I'm not sure that this is so. I note, however, that part of (3) has been adopted, quite independently of acquisition considerations, by Pollard and Sag (1987) as a central aspect of Head Driven Phrase Structure Grammar (HPSG); and something approaching (5) has been argued by Uszkoreit (1986) to be necessary for the description of German.[26] Otherwise, all I'm prepared to defend at present is that these revisions to gain learnability do no significant damage to the descriptive achievements of standard GPSG.

My strategy for illustrating the non-learnability of standard GPSG grammars will be to consider a GPSG-learning child whose target language is Polish. I will show that, with respect to long distance extraction, this child would learn not Polish but English or even Swedish. There are several different ways in which this could come about. I will discuss two, which are remedied by modifications (1) and (2) above.

I have indicated in (1), below, the extraction facts that I will be assuming for Polish, English and Swedish. They are somewhat idealized, but not greatly so.

(1)

		Polish	English	Swedish
Extraction from matrix VP	Who do you like?	√	√	√
Extraction from object compl.	Who does John think that you like?	*	√	√
Extraction from WH-compl.	Who does John know whether you like?	*	*	√

For Polish examples see Cichocki (1983), Kraskow (ms.); for Swedish examples see Engdahl (1982). For simplicity, the discussion here will be limited to extraction in questions, and all complement clauses are to be assumed to be tensed.[27] I will also ignore bridge verbs; these are discussed in Fodor (to appear).[28] Finally, I will take the WH-island constraint to be an absolute constraint in English, ignoring dialectal variation and different degrees of acceptability for different extracted phrases and different kinds of WH-clause.

The fact that the restrictions on extraction vary across languages entails that some learning must occur. And the logic of the subset problem says that it is English and Swedish that must be learned. With respect to these extraction facts, Polish is a proper subset of English, which is a proper subset of Swedish. The stronger Polish constraints must therefore be established by UG, since they could not be gleaned from positive data. If the constraints were innate, positive data would be sufficient to allow them to be "un-learned" (eliminated) in the case of languages like English and Swedish, which have more generous extraction patterns. So Polish must be the learner's first hypothesis, then English, and then Swedish. If they were ranked in any other way, either Polish or English or both would be unlearnable.

These facts are no threat to GB. As we observed in the second section, it matters little to GB which way the subset relations lie, for the parameters and their values can be set up with whatever rankings are necessary to satisfy the Subset Principle. Let us assume that what underlies the facts in (1) is parameterization for the bounding nodes for Subjacency.[29] Then the initial value of the bounding nodes parameter will be the maximal set of bounding nodes, and the subsequent values will eliminate them one by one. Then learners can safely move from one value to the next on the basis of positive data. This is illustrated in (2), where I have thrown in Italian (Rizzi 1978) for good measure.[30]

(2)	Polish	English	Italian	Swedish
Bounding nodes for Subjacency	S, S', NP →	S, NP →	S', NP →	NP

It is considerably more difficult to map these subset relationships in GPSG. Assuming simplicity as the selection criterion, GPSG predicts that learners will begin by hypothesizing Swedish, and that they will therefore never learn Polish or English. One important reason why this is so is that GPSG uses language-specific Feature Co-occurrence Restrictions (FCRs) to capture the cross-language variation with respect to island constraints. FCRs are constraints. If they are language-specific they must presumably be learned. But with a simplicity criterion, and without systematic negative evidence, constraints cannot be learned.[31] And failure to learn constraints means learning Swedish (or whatever language is maximally generous with respect to extraction), regardless of what the target language is.

Language-specific constraints

The problem

In GPSG the WH-island constraint in English is expressed by a Feature Co-occurrence Restriction (FCR), shown in (3) (= GKPS's FCR 20).[32]

(3) FCR 20: ~([SLASH] & [WH])

This says that no node may carry both a SLASH feature and a WH feature. The category-valued feature SLASH is what GPSG uses to encode long distance dependencies of the kind that GB creates by WH-movement. The SLASH feature must appear on all nodes of the tree on the route from the sister of the antecedent phrase down to the trace. This is illustrated in (4), which shows extraction from a tensed non-WH complement clause. This extraction is grammatical in English and Swedish but not in Polish. (Note: [FIN] in (4) is an abbreviation of GKPS's [VFORM FIN] for finite verb forms; I shall include it in representations only where it is specifically relevant to the discussion.)

(4)

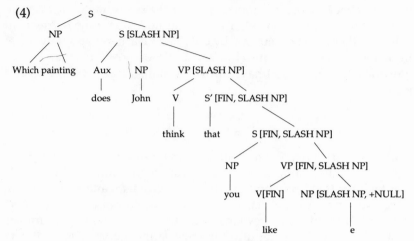

The FCR in (3) will prevent a SLASH feature from appearing on the highest node of a WH-clause; therefore there can be no continuous path of SLASH features relating the antecedent to the trace when there is a WH-island boundary on the route between them. This is illustrated in (5), which shows extraction from a tensed WH-complement clause. This extraction is grammatical in Swedish but not in English or Polish.

(5)

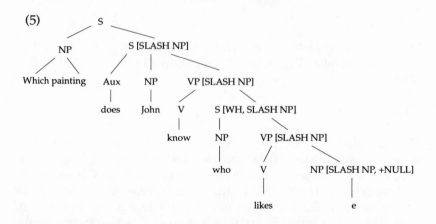

The FCR in (3) will be included in the grammars of English and Polish,[33] but not in the grammar of Swedish. (GKPS do not indicate which of their FCRs are intended to be universal, but I think we can safely assume that this one is not.) GKPS don't discuss languages with stricter island constraints than English, but the most natural way to extend their approach to Polish would be to suppose that its grammar contains an additional constraint on the distribution of SLASH. FCR (3) says that SLASH cannot co-occur with WH. For Polish we might consider the FCR in (6), which says that SLASH cannot co-occur with the features characteristic of a finite clause, namely [+SUBJ, FIN]. (Note: In GPSG both VP and S have the feature analysis [+V, -N, BAR 2]; they are differentiated only by the fact that VP is [-SUBJ] while S is [+SUBJ]].)

(6)   FCR: ~([SLASH] & [+SUBJ, FIN])

However, (6) is too strong for Polish, for it would disallow not only the subordinate S[FIN, SLASH NP] in (4), but also a S[FIN, SLASH NP] at the top of a slash node path. But the latter is not illegitimate in Polish. It occurs, for instance, in the Polish equivalent of (7), where the extraction is within a single clause and is acceptable.

(7)

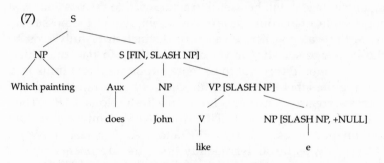

Deciding exactly how (6) ought to be revised leads into many other issues,[34] and it would be pointless to be distracted by them since LPSG must abandon this whole approach in any case. The general idea to be captured is that in Polish a SLASH feature cannot pass down THROUGH a finite S node. It does not do so in (7), which is acceptable in Polish, but it does in (4), which is not acceptable in Polish.

This no-passing-through-S constraint could be captured by either of the restrictions shown in (8).

(8)   (a)   *   (b)   *   [...SLASH X...]

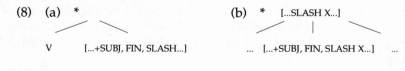

(8a) blocks S[FIN, SLASH] as sister to a verb (order of sisters irrelevant), though not as sister to the "filler" (the antecedent of the trace). (8b) blocks S[FIN, SLASH] if its slash feature has been passed down from its mother. These restrictions differ slightly in empirical consequences, but the difference will not be important here; see Fodor (to appear) for relevant discussion. For convenience I will assume (8a) in what follows. A minor complication here is that it is not clear that GPSG permits constraints like those in (8). They are not canonical FCRs, since they govern feature co-occurrence across two categories in a local tree. And though GPSG does admit cross-category constraints on feature distribution, they are all universal, for example, the Foot Feature Principle (FFP) and the Control Agreement Principle (CAP);[35] in GPSG only within-category constraints are language-specific. It is not clear whether GKPS assume this to be a principled correlation, or just an accident of the facts to which the theory has been applied so far. I am going to have to take it as an accident. In the long run it will be of no concern, since I shall argue that NO constraints can be language-specific. But until we reach that point, and to avoid begging any issues, it will be useful to acknowledge the possibility, at least in principle, of all four kinds of constraint, that is, the possibility that the within-category/cross-category distinction is fully crossed with the language-specific/universal distinction. To flag the difference, in case it should turn out to be more important than I think it is, I will reserve the label FCR for within-category constraints, and will call the cross-category constraints Local Tree Restrictions (LTRs). Then FCRs are just a limiting case of LTRs. And GKPS's "universal feature instantiation principles" such as FFP and CAP are just universal LTRs.[36] Certainly, as far as learnability goes, the arguments against language-specific constraints apply equally to FCRs and LTRs.[37]

To return now to the learning of the extraction facts in Polish, English, and Swedish: we see that in GPSG, the grammars of the three languages would differ in exactly the wrong way for learnability. As shown in (9), the Swedish grammar is the simplest because it lacks both constraints.

(9)	Polish	English	Swedish
FCR (3)	+	+	
LTR (8a)	+		

And also because it lacks the constraints, the Swedish grammar generates a superset of the constructions generated by the other grammars, so it cannot be rejected on the basis of the learner's evidence. Thus children exposed to Polish or English would learn Swedish instead.[38]

The solution

For learnability, the grammar of Swedish should be less favoured than the grammar of Polish. This would be so if Swedish, instead of having fewer constraints than Polish, had more rules than Polish. English would be in the middle, with more rules than Polish but fewer than Swedish. In other words, the learnability problem for extraction constraints, and for all other comparable examples of cross-language variation, would apparently be solved if GPSG were to give up language-specific constraints such as (3) and (8a), and substitute language-specific rules with exactly the opposite effect – in this case, rules PERMITTING extraction from object complements, or from WH-islands, rather than constraints PROHIBITING these extractions.

English would have a rule for extracting from finite subordinate clauses; Swedish would have this rule and a rule for extracting from WH-clauses; and Polish would have neither. This situation is sketched in (10). For the moment I am not committing myself to how these rules should be stated formally; that is the topic of the next section.[39]

(10)	Polish	English	Swedish
Rule (x): extraction from finite clause		+	+
Rule (y): extraction from WH-clause			+

The complexity relations among these grammars are now such that a simplicity metric will assure compliance with the Subset Principle. Polish will be the first hypothesis for learners, and English and Swedish learners would add the additional rules as they encountered positive evidence for them. So this rule-based approach is just a straightforward implementation of the commonsense view that English and Swedish speakers learn that they may extract from subordinate clauses, Swedish speakers learn that they may extract from WH-clauses too, and nobody extracts anything until they learn that they may.

Is there anything wrong with this commonsense view? Note that the overall complexity of grammars will not necessarily be any greater on the rule-based approach than on GPSG's constraint-based approach. There may be some slight difference in how many feature specifications grammars will contain,[40] but basically all that has happened is that the complexity has been redistributed: constraints in one language have been traded in for rules in another. There is also no obvious sense in which any generalization(s) have been lost by shifting from language-specific constraints to language-specific rules. So this looks to be a perfectly satisfactory solution to the acquisition problem created by language-specific FCRs in standard GPSG. However, tampering with one part of the theory can have repercussions elsewhere, and I will show now that LPSG cannot substitute rules for constraints without also revising aspects of the feature instantiation process, that is, the process by which rules license trees. But this we know is needed in any case, because GPSG rules are expressed in feature notation, and we have seen the disastrous effect that feature notation can have on learnability in the absence of negative evidence.

Feature notation

The problem

For learning without negative data, cross-language differences should be expressed by rules rather than by constraints. But to enforce this in GPSG as its stands would create havoc. Precisely because it has relied on FCRs to impose language-specific constraints, GPSG does not have rules that are suitable to do this work. Specifically, in the case of the extraction facts: GPSG uses the SAME rules to license extraction constructions as to license non-extraction constructions. It is impossible, therefore, for a GPSG grammar without language-specific FCRs to license a construction without also licensing extraction from it (unless that extraction is prohibited by a constraint in UG). Consider, then, our learner of Polish, who is attempting to learn conservatively, that is, to adopt only those rules that are motivated by his positive data. His data will include no extraction from finite complement clauses. So the grammar he arrives at ought to disallow extraction from finite complement clauses. But it won't.

What his grammar should disallow is the Polish equivalent of (4) above. But his grammar will already have everything needed to generate (4). All it takes is a top linking rule to introduce a highest SLASH feature, a bottom linking rule to cash the SLASH feature out as a trace, and the SLASH-passing rules to create the middle of the path. The top and bottom linking rules will get into the learner's grammar because they are needed for clause-bounded extraction constructions like (7), which are grammatical in Polish. And in GPSG the SLASH-passing rules are free, since they are identical with the corresponding basic rules for non-SLASH constructions. SLASH features are freely instantiated in GPSG, subject only to general constraints such as FCRs and LTRs (HFC, FFP, CAP). Thus consider a Polish-learning child who encounters in his input a verb phrase containing a finite complement clause. The relevant local tree is as in (11). To license this he must construct an appropriate rule, as in (12).[41] But once in his grammar, this rule would license not only (11) but also the ungrammatical (in

Polish) configuration (13), which mediates long-distance extractions through a finite embedded S. (Note: I have instantiated SLASH in (13) with NP as its value though other categories may extract too. Throughout this paper I will consider only NP extractions.)

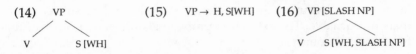

(11)   VP
      /   \
     V   S [FIN]

(12)   VP → H, S[FIN]

(13)   VP [SLASH NP]
      /   \
     V   S [FIN, SLASH NP]

Thus, however conservative his learning strategy, a Polish learner who encountered a clausal complement without extraction would immediately conclude that Polish permits extraction from clausal complements; the two facts would fall together indistinguishably in his mental representation of them. Similarly for extraction from WH-islands. A child encountering in his input a verb with a WH-complement, as in (14), would be moved to formulate the rule (15); then, by free instantiation of SLASH, rule (15) would generate the illicit local tree (16), which is the crucial link in extraction from a WH-island.

(14)   VP
      /   \
     V   S [WH]

(15)   VP → H, S[WH]

(16)   VP [SLASH NP]
      /   \
     V   S [WH, SLASH NP]

Thus learners of Polish and English, on encountering a subordinate WH-clause, could not help but infer that their target language permits extraction from WH-clauses.

The culprit here is not feature notation per se, but the assumption of free feature instantiation, that is, the assumption that any feature whose value is not explicitly stipulated in a rule may take either (any) of the values of that feature in the local trees that the rule licenses (subject to FCRs, etc.). Though it wasn't called feature instantiation in the old days, it was this very same convention that was the cause of the overgeneralizing tendency of feature notation in the Standard Theory. It is important to be precise about exactly WHY free instantiation has this effect, so that we can determine what might be done to restrain it. The exercise will be a delicate one, since in restraining feature instantiation we must take care not to undermine its whole point, which is to simplify grammars by omitting explicit feature specifications from rules wherever possible.

There is a very direct relationship between free instantiation and violations of the Subset Principle. Free instantiation of a feature not mentioned in a rule is damaging because it means that more than one local tree is licensed by the same rule. And the MORE features that are not mentioned in the rule, the MORE local trees are licensed by the rule.

So every time we simplify a rule by lopping off a feature specification, it generates a superset of the constructions it generated before. Thus neither simplicity considerations nor the learner's data would deter him from choosing a superset rule.

It will be helpful to set out a specific example. Suppose there is a rule R_a which does not specify a value for some (binary valued) feature F. And assume free instantiation for F, that is, that either [+F] or [-F] can be instantiated in a local tree licensed by R_a. Now consider a rule R_b which licenses just one of these two local trees, say the one with [-F]. R_b must presumably specify [-F] explicitly, in order to block instantiation of [+F]. So R_a is simpler than R_b. And R_a generates a superset of the local trees that R_b generates. Therefore only R_a will ever be hypothesized by learners, since it is both simpler and compatible with the same (positive) data. If R_b is the target rule, it will be unlearnable. In general: in standard feature notation with free instantiation, simpler grammars are "superset grammars" and more complex grammars are "subset grammars." This kind of positive correlation between simplicity and greater generative capacity is fatal for learning; by favouring superset grammars, it renders subset grammars unlearnable. The extraction problem is only one instance of this fundamental point.

Let me summarize so far. We wanted the grammars of English and Swedish to have to contain special rules to license their long distance extractions; the grammar of Polish would be simpler for lack of these rules. However, we CAN'T force English and Swedish to employ special rules, because they already HAVE rules, simpler ones, which will generate the same constructions. The rules they have are (17) and (18). (These might be subsumed under even more general schematic rules, but that is not important here.)

(17)   VP → H, S[FIN]
(18)   VP → H, S[WH]

The rules we would like to force them to have would be something along the lines of (19) for extraction from finite complement clauses and (20) for extraction from WH-categories; (19) would be rule (x) in (10) above, and (20) would be rule (y).

(19)   VP[SLASH NP] → H, S[FIN, SLASH NP]
(20)   VP[SLASH NP] → H, S[WH, SLASH NP]

But (17) and (18) subsume these more specific rules (19) and (20), so the latter would never be acquired. The situation across languages would be as in (21), with all three grammars identical. Thus the rule-based approach to cross-language variation that was sketched in (10) would be unachievable.

(21)	Polish	English	Swedish
(17) VP → H, S[FIN]	+	+	+
(18) VP→ H, S[WH]	+	+	+
Rule (x)=(19) VP[SLASH NP] → H, S[FIN, SLASH NP]			
Rule (y)=(20) VP[SLASH NP] → H, S[WH, SLASH NP]			

I should reiterate that this is how things would be IF we took standard GPSG and merely removed its language-specific constraints; it is NOT the way things are in standard GPSG. In GPSG the rules (17) and (18) license both extraction and non-extraction but there is no harm in their doing so. Under feature instantiation these rules overgenerate for English and Polish but the overgeneration is counteracted by language specific constraints (FCRs, LTRs) which limit the feature values that instantiation can supply. In LPSG, however, this is not possible because the language specific constraints cannot be learned. So LPSG is faced with a dilemma. To revert to the language specific constraints of GPSG would make grammars unlearnable. But without the language specific constraints of GPSG, the only rules that are learnable overgenerate. Either way, there looks to be no hope for Polish.

What is to be done? A radical solution would be to give up feature instantiation. I will argue below that that would be a cure worse than the disease. But before we panic about its disadvantages, let us at least be clear about how it would solve the extraction problem. I will work this through on a small scale, assuming feature instantiation as usual except only in the case of SLASH: I will assume that no SLASH feature may appear in a local tree unless its presence there is explicitly licensed by a rule, or is required by an LTR or FCR.

Under this assumption rules (17) and (18) will no longer license trees containing SLASH features. Thus they will not license extraction. Therefore the more complex rules (19) and (20) would be needed to license extraction. And these rules would now be learnable if extraction is exemplified in the input, since they would no longer be in competition with simpler rules that can do the same work. Hence LPSG could achieve the situation outlined in (10) after all. The mystery rules (x) and (y) in (10) CAN now be identified with (19) and (20) respectively. Swedish will have both, English will have only (19), and Polish will have neither. All three languages will have both of the basic (non-extraction) rules. This is summarized in (22). Note that though the basic rules in (22) LOOK just like (17) and (18) above, they have a much narrower interpretation now that we are assuming that SLASH cannot be freely instantiated.

(22)		Polish	English	Swedish
	VP → H, S[FIN]	+	+	+
	VP → H, S[WH]	+	+	+
Rule (x)=(19)	VP[SLASH NP] → H, S[FIN, SLASH NP]		+	+
Rule (y)=(20)	VP[SLASH NP] → H, S[WH, SLASH NP]			+

The relative complexities of the three grammars are now just as they should be, and all three will be learnable from positive data only.

Eliminating free instantiation of SLASH would thus solve the learning problem for extraction from subordinate clauses, by forcing languages which let SLASH pass down into some constituent to have a rule which says that it may. However, extraction is not the only learning problem, and SLASH is not the only guilty feature. Some broader rejection of free instantiation is needed for LPSG. How far would it have to go? To eliminate instantiation altogether would be suicidal because grammar size would explode. Every single feature value in every single local tree would have to be explicitly specified in a rule. The resulting rules would be complex, numerous, and just as uniluminating as those of traditional phrase structure grammars before syntactic feature notation was adopted. Feature notation with instantiation makes it possible to factor generalizations out of particular rules and state them just once in cross-constructional universal principles. In GPSG these principles embody aspects of X-bar theory, patterns of feature percolation, and other significant generalizations about how feature values are distributed in trees. Feature values that are predictable on the basis of these principles can be omitted from the statement of individual rules. Rules thus become quite schematic. Each rule contains just the residue of non-predictable features, those which are peculiar to the constructions it licenses. Thus feature notation serves the two essential (and related) functions of permitting generalizations to be captured, and reducing the size of grammars. Without this, phrase structure grammars could not be taken seriously as grammars of natural languages. Yet these advantages rest crucially on the possibility of omitting feature specifications from rules and instantiating them in trees. To give up feature instantiation is thus tantamount to giving up entirely on GSPG. But to retain feature instantiation is apparently to doom GPSG to unlearnability.[42]

The solution

Though the situation seems dire, there is a simple solution, one that is already implicit in the rule comparisons in (22). Notice that where [SLASH] and [WH] are NOT intended to appear in local trees, the rules in (22) say nothing about them. On the traditional interpretation of feature notation, not specifying a feature value in a rule meant that either (any) of its values was acceptable in a local tree licensed by the rule. But the interpretation of feature notation relevant to the SLASH features in (17)-(20) is such that not specifying a value for SLASH in a rule means that SLASH has no value in a local tree. This is not a logical necessity. We might have adopted the convention that when SLASH is not specified in a rule, its value in trees is NP. That would be to say that the default value for SLASH is NP. In fact the default that actually seems to be motivated is for SLASH to be absent.[43] Similarly for WH. In rule (19), for example, WH is not mentioned, and we are now construing that to mean that WH will not appear in the trees that the rule licenses. So we are presupposing here that the default for WH is to be absent. These judgements about default values embody the intuition that extraction constructions are more marked than non-extraction constructions, and that WH-constituents are more marked than non-WH constituents. The criteria for deciding what is marked and what is not are notoriously troublesome, and I have no space to discuss them here. (For recent reviews see Gair 1987; Klein 1990; Fodor & Crain, in prep.) But these particular judgements seem reasonable enough, and I will just assume them in what follows.[44] What we have seen is that assigning appropriate defaults to these features ensures that rules have the right relative complexities so that the rule-based approach to cross-language variation can work. Let us take a look now at exactly HOW default assignments solve the subset problem for rules in feature notation.

In the earlier example, rule R_a with no specification for feature F licensed trees with [+F] and trees with [-F], while rule R_b which specified [-F] licensed only trees with [-F]. Now let us add to the grammar a feature specification default (FSD) which assigns [+F] as the default for F. (This is arbitrary; the default could just as well have been [-F], with consequent changes in the discussion below.) Now R_a will license only [+F], and R_b will still license only [-F]. Since there is now no superset/subset relation between the two rules, positive data should be sufficient to choose between them. And that is so. Consider first the case where the learner's target language, hence his input, has [+F], the unmarked value. Then his grammar will give the correct results if he posits a rule which (redundantly) specifies [+F], and also if he posits the simpler rule with no specification for F. If for some reason (not simplicity!) he hypothesizes a rule with the specification [-F] it will be wrong, but his data will show him that it is wrong because it will fail to license the [+F] input. So the incorrect rule can be rejected in favour of one that does license the input. All that is required for this feedback mechanism to work is that the selection criterion be subject to condition C2 above (that is, that G_{i+1} licenses I);[45] then the learner will never accept a rule that licenses a marked value in response to an input with the unmarked value.[46] Now let's consider the case where the target language has the marked value [-F]. If the learner formulates a rule specifying [-F], his grammar will be correct. If instead he is enticed by simplicity into formulating a rule without any specification for F, it will generate [+F] by default, and so it will fail to match the [-F] input and by C2 will be rejected. So the learner will never accept a rule that licenses an unmarked value in response to an input with the marked value. Thus whichever direction he errs in, he will receive feedback and will be able to eliminate the error.

The effect of assigning a default to a feature is to prevent non-specification of that feature in a rule from licensing both (all) values of that feature in a tree. The default assignments ensure that every rule, even if it lacks overt specifications for its features, has specific CONSEQUENCES in terms of the local trees it licenses. And because its effects are specific, the learner can determine whether the rule is right or wrong. The indeterminacy of the choice between a subset rule and a superset rule is thus eliminated, so the simplicity metric does not need to be invoked by learners; the data are sufficient to select between candidate rules. Unfortunately, as the theory stands now a huge price is being paid for this determinacy of rule selection, namely that the grammar has to contain one rule for each local tree it licenses. The first comparison of rules R_a and R_b above showed that a one-to-many relation between rules and local trees creates a conspiracy between rule simplicity and rule generality which defeats the Subset Principle. This can be cured by assigning every feature a default value, since a rule in which a value is not specified will then license just one local tree – the one with the default value. (For convenience I make the temporary assumption here that the values of other features in the rule are fixed.) So now it is no longer the case that a rule becomes more and more general the more of its feature specifications we omit. It generates exactly the same number of distinct local trees, namely one, however many feature specifications we omit. The problem is that with one rule per local tree, there is no generalization in the grammar at all. If that's what LPSG grammars have to be like then they are obviously of no interest, and the fact that they are learnable is simply beside the point.

The next step in shaping up LPSG is thus to introduce some OTHER way in which a rule can capture a generalization, some other way of letting it license a number of similar local trees. In fact what is needed is nothing more exciting than the traditional parenthesis notation to indicate options, applied now to feature value specifications. A rule licensing the unmarked value for feature F has no value specified for F; a rule licensing the marked value for F will have [mF] specified, where the m (= marked) translates into either + or - or some other appropriate value as determined by the relevant FSD for that feature. For simplicity here I will assume that F is a binary feature with values + and -. A rule could license two local trees, one with [+F] and one with [-F], by specifying [(m)F], that is, by specifying that the marked value is optional. So [(m)F] in LPSG will express what feature omission used to express in a traditional feature notation system. But where feature omission CREATED a subset problem, the use of parentheses SOLVES the subset problem. The parentheses make EXPLICIT the disjunction that was implicit in the traditional feature notation. The consequence is that the disjunctive rule, which licenses more trees, is more complex than either of the rules it subsumes. The rule with parentheses is a "superset rule" but it is not dangerous, because the simplicity metric will disfavour it unless or until there is positive evidence for both of the constructions it licenses. At that point, but NOT BEFORE, a learner would collapse the two specific rules into one disjunctive rule schema, thus simplifying his grammar and capturing a generalization.

The significant shift from standard GPSG to LPSG is, thus, that in LPSG, every construction added to a language carries a cost in the grammar.[47] The extra cost can be very small. As long as learners systematically base their selections on relative grammar complexity, small differences can have a profound effect on the final shape of the grammar.[48]

I have argued that if learners had access to FSDs assigning a default value to every feature, all subset problems due to the use of feature notation would be eliminated. In fact, something slightly less than this would be sufficient to do the job. A feature does not need a default value for learnability if its values do not have to be learned. And there are two circumstances in which feature values don't have to be learned. One is where they are universally established, for example where UG has an FCR that fixes the value of F absolutely in some context. (Note that if UG determined the value of F in EVERY context, then feature F would be serving no contrastive purpose. So by "universally" here I don't mean "in all contexts" but rather "established by Universal Grammar.") The second case is where the value of a feature is universally free, that is, where UG determines that both (all) values of the feature are acceptable in some context. As illustration, consider the GKPS number feature [+/-PLU]. The value of this feature is limited by CAP, which requires [PLU] on an NP to agree with [PLU] on a projection of V, or by HFC which requires the N' and N" projected from an N to match it in number. In such contexts there is no need for a default feature assignment or for specification of the feature in rules. Now consider the number feature in contexts other than these. I assume that except where agreement principles are in force, the number of an NP is free in English and indeed in all languages. That is, I assume that no language has a verb which (apart from reasons of agreement) requires a singular direct object,[49] no language has a topicalization process which permits only plural NPs to be fronted, and so forth.[50] In such cases where UG guarantees that either (any) value is acceptable, the traditional interpretation of feature notation is perfectly satisfactory and should be retained. There is no need for a default value. Failure to specify a value for the feature can be construed as freely licensing either (any) value.

All of this is summed up in the Specific Defaults Principle listed above and repeated here.

> **The Specific Defaults Principle**: UG must assign a specific (that is, non-disjunctive) default value to every feature in every context, except where the value is universally fixed or is universally free.

This is a metacondition that UG must satisfy for learnability of any rule system cast in feature notation. It says that UG must assign a default value to every feature in every context such that the value of that feature in that context is free to vary in some language(s) but not in all. The fact that it is free to vary in some languages means that it can't be absolutely fixed innately. The fact that it is not free to vary in all languages means that some learners have to acquire grammars which fix its value. And we have seen that, at least on the assumptions about learners made here, they will not reliably acquire such grammars unless the feature has a default value to block free instantiation of either value, and thus avoid violations of the Subset Principle.[51]

Comparing LPSG and GPSG

It is clear that the Specific Defaults Principle benefits learners. But what does it do to grammars? In fact it has the merit of ensuring that many features, perhaps the majority, can be omitted from rules. A feature value needs to be specified in an LPSG rule if and only if its value (in context) is not universally fixed or universally free, and it is not the default value. Even so, LPSG rules will inevitably need more feature values specified than GPSG rules. This is because LPSG has given up free instantiation of NON-default values, which GPSG permitted and which was the source of its learnability problems. However, we have seen that LPSG can take advantage of feature omission for UG-determined cases, and can employ parentheses for collapsing related rules into general schemata; it also lacks all the language-specific FCRs and FSDs of GPSG. So the complexity difference between LPSG and GPSG grammars may not be very great.

Of course, the Specific Defaults Principle entails that LPSG needs more universal FSDs than GPSG had. But these extra FSDs won't add to the cost of particular grammars, for they must all be innate if they are to avoid creating as many learning problems as they cure. Like FCRs, FSDs are constraints: they require that features take certain values in certain contexts. Indeed they are identical with FCRs except only that they are weaker, since they can be overridden by rules and FCRs.[52] Because they are constraints, FSDs cannot be learned without negative data, any more than FCRs can. And so all FSDs in LPSG must be supplied by UG.

This is clearly not the case in GPSG. The FSDs proposed by GKPS are shown in (23):

(23) FSD 1: [-INV]
      FSD 2: ~[CONJ]
      FSD 3: ~[NULL]
      FSD 4: ~[NOM]
      FSD 5: [PFORM] ⊃ [BAR 0]
      FSD 6: [+ADV] ⊃ [BAR 0]
      FSD 7: [BAR 0] ⊃ ~[VFORM PAS]
      FSD 8: [NFORM] ⊃ [NFORM NORM]
      FSD 9: [INF, +SUBJ] ⊃ [COMP *for*]
      FSD 10: [+N, -V, BAR 2] ≡ [CASE ACC]
      FSD 11: [+V, BAR 0] ⊃ [AGR NP[NFORM NORM]]

I won't comment in detail on each of these (especially as other LPSG revisions will necessitate slight differences in their content). Most of these are reasonable enough candidates for universal defaults, but that this is not a deliberate policy in GPSG is shown by FSD 9, which is egregiously language-specific.[53]

LPSG obviously needs many more universal FSDs than are given here. (Or LTDs, Local Tree Defaults; see above. I won't keep making this distinction but will use the term FSD generically except where the difference is of interest.) The FSDs in (23) give defaults for only ten of the thirty features that GKPS employed for English. They give simple absolute defaults for INV, CONJ, NULL and NOM; and context-sensitive defaults for BAR, VFORM, NFORM, COMP, CASE, AGR. (The latter are context sensitive in that the default value is dependent on the value of some other feature in the category; for example, BAR has the default value 0 if the category has a value for PFORM or if it is [+ADV]; but BAR has no default – or it might be assigned some other default by some other FSD – when it co-occurs with other features.)[54] Note in particular that none of the FSDs in (23) mentions either SLASH or WH. SLASH does fall under a universal default principle. Since SLASH is a head feature, it falls under the Head Feature Convention (HFC) which assigns it a context-sensitive default value. HFC entails, for instance, that the default for SLASH on a VP is [SLASH NP] if the mother S has [SLASH NP]; that the default is [SLASH PP] on VP if the S has [SLASH PP]; that SLASH is default absent on the VP if the S has no SLASH feature; and so forth. (Note that this matching of mother and daughter features is ONLY a default, not an absolute constraint. An absolute HFC would require [SLASH NP] on V if the VP has [SLASH NP], but V[SLASH NP] (signifying a verb containing a WH-trace of category NP) is of course an impossible category; it is excluded by a universal FCR, which overrules HFC. Thus HFC is what I am calling a Local Tree Default (LTD).) Notice, however, that neither HFC nor any of the FSDs above provides a basic default for either SLASH or WH in GPSG. Thus nothing in GPSG encodes the fact that extraction constructions and WH-clauses are more marked than non-extraction constructions and non-WH-clauses. And that is what gets GPSG learners into trouble, as we saw above.[55] In LPSG there MUST be basic defaults for SLASH and WH. The additional FSDs we have been presupposing for LPSG are as in (24).

(24) FSD: ~[SLASH]
      FSD: ~[WH]

Like all defaults these can be overridden by rules which explicitly state that certain constituents have a WH or SLASH feature. They must also be overridden by FFP and HFC, which govern the percolation of SLASH features through trees. FFP is an absolute constraint and would be expected to outrank FSDs. That HFC, which is itself only a default, outranks the FSDs in (24) follows, I believe, from a general principle that context-sensitive defaults should always take precedence over context-free defaults. This would be the case if defaults were taken to be governed by an Elsewhere convention giving priority to more specific principles over less specific ones.[56]

It may prove to be a disadvantage of LPSG that it can permit no language-specific defaults which run against the trend of a universal default. For purposes of linguistic description, language-specific defaults have sometimes been proposed.[57] This is an important matter, and I cannot address it fully here. But it is worth observing that at least from the point of view of learnability, it is never necessary to assume a language-specific default. There would be pressure to do so only if (in some context) in some language, the universally marked feature value were MORE frequent (or more "natural" by some other criterion) than the universally unmarked value. But learning will be possible in LPSG even in such a situation, because the logic of the demonstration above that innate defaults make learning possible is completely symmetric. If the target value is unmarked and the learner guesses marked, his grammar doesn't violate the Subset Principle. If the target value is marked and he guesses unmarked, his grammar does not violate the Subset Principle. So from the point of view of learnability in principle, it doesn't matter WHICH value is marked and which is unmarked. A child could perfectly well acquire a language in which the marked value is very frequent. The only consequence would be that his eventual grammar would be more complex than if the marked value were rare. And he might be slower to arrive at the correct grammar. I assume that learners presuppose the unmarked value of every feature until they encounter relevant evidence, so they would reach the correct grammar sooner if the unmarked value were the target. Thus empirical observations about learning sequence might supplement linguistic criteria in helping to pin down the content of the innate FSDs.

Given the task of characterizing all natural languages, the more universal defaults that can be identified the better. More defaults mean more generalizations captured, and more feature specifications that can be omitted from language-specific rules. Context sensitive defaults are particularly useful, because they can extract subtler universal trends in feature distribution than does a single across-the-board default for a feature. For these purposes it is important to pick the right value as the default for each feature in each context. We have seen that to make learning possible, any default value would do. But for the purpose of capturing linguistic generalizations it matters which value is assigned as default. For example, in Fodor and Crain (in prep.) it is observed that though the default for the feature NULL is probably [-NULL] in most contexts, a [+NULL] default for categories of the type X[SLASH X] (equivalently A[SLASH A]) would capture a markedness version of the old A-over-A constraint; that is, it would entail that a language permitting extraction of a category A from within a phrase of category A is marked, and that such extractions are more marked than other extractions even in languages in which both are permitted. This seems to be descriptively correct for extraction of NP from NP in English, for example. GPSG has the simple FSD 3 in (23) above, that is, ~[NULL].[58] LPSG would keep that for the "elsewhere" case, and would add the context-sensitive (25).

(23)   FSD 3: ~[NULL]
(25)   FSD: X[SLASH X] $\supset$ [+NULL]

The new FSD in (25) asserts that it is more natural for a category such as NP[SLASH NP] or PP[SLASH PP] etc. to be null than to be non-null. If it is null, it is a WH-trace. If it is non-null, then it must lie somewhere on the path of slash nodes that links the antecedent with its trace. But a node NP[SLASH NP] on that path means that an NP is being extracted from an NP (*mutatis mutandis* for PP[SLASH PP], etc.), and this is exactly what the A-over-A constraint proscribes. By classifying (25) as an FSD rather than an absolute constraint, we allow that such extractions can be permitted by a grammar though they would carry a cost – the cost of an explicit [-NULL] specification in the licensing rule to override the [+NULL] default.

Thus some valuable descriptive mileage can be obtained from FSDs if defaults are assigned in a way that reflects linguistic estimates of markedness. And when nothing else decides the matter, it would at least help to streamline grammars if the default is taken to be whichever value of the feature occurs most frequently in that context. Then more often than not (for a binary feature) it will be unnecessary to mention the feature in the rule. These proportions of which features need to be mentioned and which can be omitted get better and better, the stronger the asymmetry of distribution of the two values. The cheapest situation to encode is where only the unmarked value of F occurs in the context. The most expensive situation to encode is where both values of F are acceptable in the context, though not universally so; then the grammar will need the explicitly disjunctive specification [(*m*)F]. But this means that grammars will be less costly the more sharply differentiated the marked and unmarked values are in their distribution. Keeping the marked value rare is the key to keeping the grammar simple. On the other hand, since only a feature that is NOT constrained by the grammar can carry information for communicative purposes, there must be some expressive pressure on a grammar to make feature contrasts available by means of disjunctive feature specifications in rules. The optimal balance between these opposing pressures of economy and communicative value can't be stipulated a priori. But there are a few empirical predictions that can be made. One is that asymmetries of occurrence are more likely for features that have defaults as a result of the Specific Defaults Principle, and are less likely for features which need no default because their values are universally free in context.[59] Note that GPSG, by contrast, predicts no tendency towards asymmetric frequency of occurrence for features like SLASH and WH since it assigns them no (simple) default. Another prediction of LPSG, even if it is not one that is easy to test, concerns the direction of language change. If and when languages change, not due to external influences but as an internal settling favouring greater simplicity, the asymmetries between marked and unmarked values for features which have defaults should increase but those for features without defaults should decrease.

To summarize: it appears that universal FSDs are at worst harmless linguistically, and at best are descriptively very useful. So there is no reason why LPSG should not adopt as many of them as learnability requires. They serve two linguistic functions, similar to those of FCRs though squishier. They capture non-absolute universal trends (such as A-over-A). And they simplify grammars by allowing many feature values, perhaps the majority, to be omitted from rules. The latter is particularly helpful to LPSG since, as we have seen, LPSG is forced to be more sparing than GPSG with respect to omission of BOTH values of a feature. Unlike FCRs, which are absolute constraints, FSDs can afford to be quite sweeping in their coverage because they can be overridden, at a price, for exceptional constructions. At the same time, since they are innate they are not subject to the simplicity metric and so can afford to map out quite intricate patterns of default feature distribution, sensitive to other features in the context. The rules of a particular grammar should then only have to specify feature values that are truly idiosyncratic to that language. In this respect (though they differ in many others) the few features that remain in rules serve much the same function as the parameters of GB; see Fodor and Crain (1990) for discussion.

I have not attempted to give a formal proof that these proposed revisions of GPSG will eradicate all violations of the Subset Principle. (I should say: all relevant violations of the Subset Principle. There are others that these revisions do not bear on, such as those which are covered by revisions (3)-(5) listed in the second section, above.) And I do not believe there is a general recipe, guaranteed to work in all cases, for converting a GPSG grammar into an LPSG grammar without loss of its descriptive generalizations. However, there is something that approaches this. Though I have been using the particular phenomenon of long-distance extraction for illustration, the problems

diagnosed and the solutions proposed have all been characterizable at
a quite abstract level. It is not that LPSG has had to give up one
particular rule or constraint in favor of some other particular rule or
constraint. Rather, it has had very generally to eliminate FCRs and
FSDs from particular grammars, and to add FSDs to UG. The net
effect would often be that a language-specific FCR in GPSG is traded
in for a universal FSD with essentially the same content in LPSG. For
example, the WH-island constraint, which was captured by an FCR in
the GPSG grammars of English and Polish, is expressed in LPSG by a
universal FSD (which, in Swedish, is overridden by a rule). Actually,
in this case the exchange of FCR for FSD is not quite transparent.
GKPS's FCR 20 (in (3) above) stipulates ~([SLASH] & [WH]). LPSG
could keep this as it stands but reinterpret it as an FSD. However, it
doesn't actually need this FSD because the simple FSDs in (24) will
suffice. These stipulate ~[SLASH] and ~[WH]. The first says that
whether or not a category has [WH], it should not have [SLASH]
unless its licensing rule specifically permits it to. The second says that
whether or not a category has [SLASH], it should not have [WH]
unless its licensing rule specifically permits it to. So obviously a category should not have both SLASH and WH unless these are both
licensed by the same rule (a relatively costly rule, since it has to
override two defaults).

The general tendency for language-specific FCRs in GPSG to translate into universal FSDs in LPSG suggests that the conversion from
GPSG to LPSG should go quite smoothly wherever a language-specific FCR in GPSG leans in a direction that can plausibly be regarded
as the universal default. However, if a language-particular constraint
inclines the other way, that is, if it excludes what is generally unmarked and tolerates what is generally marked, the situation could be
more problematic. As discussed above, a language-specific default is
not learnable. So in such a case some real revision of the GPSG analysis would be necessary, and there is no way of anticipating in the
abstract what form it would have to take. Perhaps the GPSG constraint could be "analysed away" in some fashion, by taking a quite
different look at the facts. But if it couldn't, or couldn't without loss of
interesting generalizations, LPSG would be in trouble. Obviously I
can't guarantee that this will never arise. But we can at least check
through all the FCRs that have been given in GPSG, to see which ones
are language-specific, and which of those (if any) run against the
universal grain.

In their description of English, GKPS give the following FCRs, not
sorted into universal and language-particular. The judgements in the
column on the right are my own, and they are quite rough and ready.

(26)   language-specific
FCR 1:   [+INV] ⊃ [+AUX, FIN]   √
FCR 2:   [VFORM] ⊃ [+V, -N]
FCR 3:   [NFORM] ⊃ [-V, +N]
FCR 4:   [PFORM] ⊃ [-V, -N]
FCR 5:   [PAST] ⊃ [FIN, -SUBJ]
FCR 6:   [SUBCAT] ⊃ ~[SLASH]
FCR 7:   [BAR 0] ≡ [N] & [V] & [SUBCAT]
FCR 8:   [BAR 1] ⊃ ~[SUBCAT]
FCR 9:   [BAR 2] ⊃ ~[SUBCAT]
FCR 10:   [+INV, BAR 2] ⊃ [+SUBJ]   √
FCR 11:   [+SUBJ] ⊃ [+V, -N, BAR 2]
FCR 12:   [AGR] ⊃ [-N, +V]   √
FCR 13:   [FIN, AGR NP] ⊃ [AGR NP[NOM]]   √
FCR 14:   [([+PRD] & [VFORM]) ⊃ ([PAS] V [PRP])   √
FCR 15:   [COMP] ≡ [+SUBJ]
FCR 16:   [WH, +SUBJ] ⊃ [COMP NIL]   √
FCR 17:   [COMP *that*] ⊃ ([FIN] V [BSE])   √
FCR 18:   [COMP *for*] ⊃ [INF]   √
FCR 19:   [+NULL] ⊃ [SLASH]
FCR 20:   ~([SLASH] & [WH])   √
FCR 21:   A' ⊃ ~[WH]   √
FCR 22:   VP ⊃ ~[WH]   √

Many of these FCRs (for example, FCRs 2-4, 7) are essentially defini-
tional of the features they contain. I assume that it is intended as
analytic, for instance, that a [BAR 0] category is a lexical major category, as FCR 7 requires. Though it's a rather fine dividing line, other
FCRs here appear to express basic empirical tenets of GPSG; for example, FCR 19 encodes the claim (assuming no other changes in the
theory) that the only empty category is WH-trace. However, roughly
half of the FCRs in (26) appear to be language-particular. To evaluate
the status of each of these would mean reviewing the whole GKPS
analysis of English, clearly out of the question here. But a few comments will illustrate the general approach.

The FCRs that LPSG must do without fall into a few groups. There
are FCRs 1 and 10, which have to do with the GKPS treatment of
subject auxiliary inversion. I believe that it is preferable, for completely independent reasons, to treat auxiliary inversion as verb topicalization, with auxiliary verbs individually subcategorized for occurrence in the topicalized construction (see Fodor & Crain, in prep.). On
that analysis there is no need for an AUX feature at all, or for any

language-specific FCRs to control it; all the peculiarities of English
with respect to inversion reside in its lexical entries.

Then there are FCRs 17 and 18 which (like FSD 9 above) concern
lexical selection and could, probably should, be recast as subcategorization restrictions on *that* and *for*. There are FCRs 12 and 13 which
concern agreement. For learnability, agreement must be the default in
all contexts where it is universally permitted; non-agreement must be
due to lack of morphological distinctions, or in exceptional cases to
the overriding of the syntactic default by feature specifications in
rules. Then FCR 12 to limit English agreement is unnecessary. Let us
assume the correctness of Keenan's (1974) proposed universal generalization that when agreement occurs, a function expression agrees
with its nominal argument. Then FCR 12 should be replaced in LPSG
by a universal FCR allowing only functors to agree, and a universal
FSD making it the default for any functor to agree. Similarly, FCR 13
can be replaced with a universal FSD establishing [NOM] as the unmarked case for an NP immediately dominated by S. (It should be
noted that the GPSG treatment of agreement has been considerably
revised in HPSG; see Pollard & Sag, to appear.)

Finally there are FCRs 16 and 20-22 that involve SLASH and WH.
FCR 16 is probably better deleted in any case; it expresses the generalization that questions and relative clauses alike lack an overt complementizer in English, but this fails to allow for a WH-question
introduced by the WH-complementizer *whether*. FCRs 20-22 have now
been traded in for universal defaults in LPSG. We have considered
FCR 20, the WH-island constraint, in detail. FCRs 21 and 22 concern
WH percolation in "pied piping" constructions (see note 32 above). In
LPSG, rather than constraints to block WH percolation through A'
and VP in a WH-focus phrase in English, there will be rules to permit
WH percolation through PP and NP. All of this needs to be set out in
detail. But at least this quick survey has uncovered no reason to think
that making GPSG learnable makes it less capable of characterizing
natural languages.

Adjustments

In such a closely interlocking system, no revision is without ramifications elsewhere. The LPSG shift from language-specific FCRs to universal FSDs overridden by language-specific rules creates a slight
disturbance in the balance between rules and feature instantiation
principles which I must now tidy up. In particular, the Foot Feature
Principle (FFP) needs to be adjusted to mesh properly with the new
style of rules. LPSG rules differ from GPSG rules, as we have seen, in

that they must specify ALL non-UG-predictable feature values, that is, all values that are not, in that context, universally fixed or free or the default.

The ID rules we have arrived at so far for extracting NP from a finite object clause and from a WH-clause are (19) and (20) respectively, repeated here.

(19)   VP[SLASH NP] → H, S[FIN, SLASH NP]
(20)   VP[SLASH NP] → H, S[WH, SLASH NP]

It is important for learnability that these rules contain explicit SLASH features, so that extraction carries a cost to discourage learners from anticipating its acceptability when their input has not yet evidenced it. But of course it isn't necessary for these rules to specify BOTH of a matched pair of slash features. One slash feature per rule would be enough to encode the acceptability of slash-passing through the clause boundary. If one SLASH were in the rule, the other could be derived from it by FFP. For simplicity I will now focus on (19), but similar points apply to (20). Rule (19) is redundant; it ought to be simplified to either (27) or (28), with FFP filling in the missing SLASH feature during feature instantiation. (Which of [27] and [28] is appropriate will be discussed below.)

(27)   VP[SLASH NP] → H, S [FIN]
(28)   VP → H, S[SLASH NP]

But there's a problem. FFP CAN'T fill in the missing SLASH feature, in either (27) or (28), unless we repeal the GPSG restriction that FFP (unlike HFC and CAP) applies only to instantiated features, not to features inherited from rules.[60]

In GPSG this restriction on FFP does no harm and does a little good. It does no harm because relatively few foot features are inherited from rules in GPSG. As we have seen, GPSG uses instantiation to introduce foot features such as SLASH which pass down through the middle portion of an extraction path. But LPSG must have all non-UG-predictable features specified in rules; and since the acceptability of foot features in passing rules differs among Polish, English, and Swedish, it is NOT universally predictable and must be specified in the rules. So in LPSG, unlike GPSG, most foot features are inherited, and if FFP didn't apply to inherited features it would have nothing to apply to, and the generalization it expresses would be lost. It would be better, then, for LPSG if FFP could be allowed to apply to ALL foot features regardless of whether they are instantiated or inherited. Then (27) or (28) could take the place of the redundant (19).

This, however, would be to give up the advantage of the restriction on FFP in GPSG, which has to do with top linking rules. In a top linking local tree for SLASH, such as (29a), there is a SLASH feature on the head daughter but none on the mother.

(29) (a)   S   (b) S → NP, H [SLASH NP]

          NP   S [SLASH NP]

What rule should license this tree? The natural candidate is (29b). But (29b) will license (29a) only if the SLASH on the daughter does NOT copy up to the mother. Thus a top linking rule has to "violate" FFP, and the theory must provide it with some way of doing so. One way would be for the rule to include an explicit ~[SLASH] specification on the mother, as in (30), to block instantiation of SLASH on the mother by FFP.

(30)   S~[SLASH] → NP, H[SLASH NP]

This would be to treat FFP as a default principle which gives in to explicit feature markings in rules. GKPS could have dealt this way with an exception to HFC (if they were prepared to employ "~" in rules; in fact they use it only in constraints). But for FFP they take a different route. They use rule (29b), just as it stands, and they stipulate that FFP doesn't apply to inherited features. This is more satisfactory than the approach represented by (30), not just because rule (29b) is simpler than (30), but because (29b) portrays top linking configurations as natural and straightforward, which they surely are, whereas (30) portrays them as exceptional, as flouting a general trend in feature distribution. However, we have seen that the GKPS solution using rule (29b) is NOT suited to LPSG, because LPSG wants FFP to apply to inherited features. So LPSG needs a different solution to the problem of top linking rules.

One possibility that is attractive is to have FFP apply to both instantiated and inherited features, but only to features on the mother. It would copy a feature down from the mother to a daughter, but never up from a daughter to the mother. Then rule (27) could do the SLASH-passing work of rule (19); and the top linking rule (29b) could remain as is. This approach has several advantages. First, a downward-copying FFP makes it costly to have a foot feature on a mother not matched by one on a daughter, but cheap to have a foot feature on a daughter not matched by one on the mother. Thus it captures the generalization that a trail of foot features does not normally terminate part-way down a tree (in the unmarked case it continues down to the lexical level where the feature is phonetically realized, either segmentally, e.g., as *self*, or as [+NULL]); but it IS perfectly normal for a trail of foot features to BEGIN part-way down a tree, rather than at the topmost node. The only exception to the unbroken downward flow of a foot feature is in constructions like (31), to which GKPS assign the structure (32a), generated by an exceptional ID rule (32b) (which itself is generated by the metarule STM2, but that is not relevant here; see GKPS:Ch. 7 for details).

(31)   Who does he think is clever?

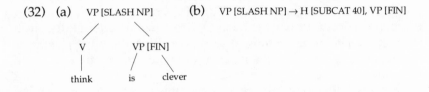

(32)   (a)   VP [SLASH NP]   (b)   VP [SLASH NP] → H [SUBCAT 40], VP [FIN]

What is exceptional about (32a) is that it contains no trace at all; the complement of *think* is just a finite VP, and the lowest SLASH feature in the tree is on the VP over *think*. With a downward-copying FFP applying to inherited features, as we are considering for LPSG, rule (32b) could not generate this local tree with no SLASH daughter. Instead, LPSG would have to employ a rule like (33) to generate (32a).

(33)   VP[SLASH NP] → V[SUBCAT 40], VP[FIN, ~SLASH]

FFP would have the status of a default principle, and it would be overridden by the explicit specification in (33) that there be no SLASH on the daughter. Note that (33) is more complex than GKPS's rule (32b); with its blocking feature on the VP daughter, (33) presents this subject gap construction as contravening a general trend. And this seems appropriate. Unlike "normal" bottom linking, in which SLASH is realized as a trace, the "disappearing SLASH" effect in these STM2 constructions does seem to be an exceptional phenomenon. So the fact that the revised FFP requires the marked rule (33) may be counted as a point in its favor.

A second advantage of the proposed downward-copying version of FFP is that it could be coalesced with HFC. FFP is now similar to HFC in that it too applies to inherited features, and it too can be overridden by specifications in rules. The two principles would be comparable if HFC were amended so that it applies only to features (inherited or instantiated) on mother categories. I believe there are no obstacles to this revision, no cases where HFC needs to apply to a feature on a daughter and copy it upwards onto the mother.[61] So HFC and the new FFP could be combined into a single downward-copying mechanism. The only difference remaining between them would concern which features they apply to (head or foot) and which daughter(s) they copy them onto: foot features are copied onto any one or more daughters, while head features are copied only onto the head. The "head" versus "foot" terminology coined by GKPS may conjure up a picture of head features being copied down from mother to daughter, while foot features are copied upward from daughter to mother. But what matters is not the metaphor but the direction of information flow through trees. The revised FFP/HFC says that information flow is asymmetrically downward for foot features as well as for head features, and there is nothing absurd about this; we must just check that it is compatible with the patterns of feature percolation observed in natural language.

For acquisition an important aspect of this asymmetric approach is that, unlike a symmetric system in which features are copied both up and down, it doesn't leave learners with a choice of whether to mark a SLASH feature on the mother or on a daughter in a SLASH-passing rule (for example, whether to adopt rule [27] or rule [28] above). All learners would uniformly mark the SLASH on the mother (except possibly in the case of lexical ID rules; see discussion below). This is important to the functioning of HFC. If learners could construct rules with SLASH specified on a daughter rather than on the mother, a marked rule specifying SLASH on a non-head daughter would be no more costly than an unmarked rule specifying SLASH on the head daughter. But if features only copy downward, then the unmarked rule would be well-behaved while the marked rule would have to contain TWO SLASH features: one on the mother, and one on the non-head daughter to override HFC. Thus here, too, the relative complexity of rules is appropriate if FFP/HFC copies only downward.

For all its merits, the revised FFP has one flaw. I have argued that downward feature percolation is nicely matched to the observed tendencies of SLASH paths in natural language. But there is one respect in which it is not. HFC copies a head feature down onto the head daughter if it can. It normally CAN do so in any local tree with a phrasal head (for example, specifier $+X^1$ constructions, adjunct $+X^1$ constructions, phrasal co-ordinations, etc.). Thus a rule with SLASH marked on its mother will have a unique outcome: a local tree with SLASH passing to the head daughter. (An exceptional construction with SLASH-passing to the non-head daughter could be learned from positive data; as we saw above, it would require a special feature specification in the rule to override HFC, and would thus not be anticipated by learners in the absence of relevant data. Another exceptional case would have SLASH passing to both daughters, to create a parasitic gap construction; but again, the rule would need a marked feature and would not be adopted without motivation.) So the Subset Principle is satisfied by downward copying to a head daughter. But now consider rules with a lexical head daughter. A SLASH feature cannot normally pass down to a lexical head (for example, V[SLASH NP] is not a coherent category). So HFC does not apply. But FFP requires that a SLASH on the mother pass down to at least one daughter, if it can. The problem is: which one?

A local tree with a lexical head often has more than one non-head daughter (for example, two NP arguments in a dative construction, or an NP and a PP, or a PP and an S, etc.). When HFC is inapplicable, there is no principle that determines which daughter may accept a SLASH from the mother. Thus it is predicted that extraction from one is just as good as extraction from another. What this amounts to is the claim that if a lexical item is a bridge for extraction, it is a bridge for extraction from ALL of its sisters; it cannot bridge extraction from one but not from another. I address the issue of lexical bridges for extraction in Fodor (to appear) and I argue there that though this generalization is largely true, it is not always true. And if there is even one exception to it in any natural language, then the proposed system with revised FFP/HFC will violate the Subset Principle. It will favor a rule that licenses two local tree types, over a rule that licenses only one. For instance, rule (34) would permit generation of both local trees in (35); yet sometimes (by hypothesis) only one of these local trees is in the target language.

(34) VP[SLASH NP] → V, PP, S

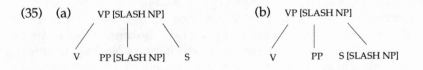

(35) (a)   VP [SLASH NP]

      V   PP [SLASH NP]   S

(b)   VP [SLASH NP]

      V   PP   S [SLASH NP]

To block one of (35a) or (35b) would require complicating the rule by addition of a ~[SLASH] marking on one daughter; but learners would have no motivation to adopt such a restriction, and so the language would be unlearnable.

There are some imaginable ways out of this problem. For example, there might possibly be a universal generalization determining which of the non-head daughters can accept a SLASH.[62] Or possibly, lexical learning, since it must be finite, is not so strictly ruled by the Subset Principle as syntactic learning is. Yet another possibility is that FFP/HFC copies features down from mother to daughter for non-lexical ID rules, but upward from daughter to mother for lexical ID rules. Then instead of (34) the grammar would have (36a) or (36b) or both.[63]

(36) (a) VP → V, PP[SLASH NP], S
      (b) VP → V, PP, S[SLASH NP]

I cannot now judge whether any of these possibilities is realistic. But I will end by sketching another alternative, which does not require that FFP copies only downward. It is of interest because of its relation to the approach proposed for HPSG by Pollard and Sag (ms.).

The Nonlocal Feature Principle, which is the HPSG descendent of FFP, applies to inherited as well as instantiated features, as we require for LPSG. Informally put, it requires SLASH (more generally: foot features) to copy both down and up, but upward copying applies only if the SLASH feature is not bound to its antecedent at that level in the tree. Thus Pollard and Sag solve the problem of top linking rules in an upward-copying system by offering the foot feature a choice: it can EITHER be copied up OR be bound.[64] Unfortunately, Pollard and Sag implement this idea by means of an ID rule for top linking which is unnecessarily complicated. Translated into LPSG terms (and limited again to NP antecedents), it would be as in (37).

(37) S → NP$_i$, H[INHERITED SLASH NP$_i$, TO-BIND SLASH NP$_i$]

There are now two types of SLASH feature: INHERITED SLASH is much like old SLASH, while TO-BIND SLASH is a SLASH feature that must be discharged within its local tree. Rule (37) is thus a top linking rule because the TO-BIND feature requires the SLASH to be bound to its sister; hence it will not copy up to the mother. But rule (37) achieves this only at the cost of an extra feature. In this respect it is like rule (30) above, repeated here, which used a blocking feature on the mother to achieve the same outcome, and which we rejected for failing to capture the naturalness of top linking.

(30) S~[SLASH] → NP , H[SLASH NP]

But the HPSG analysis can be stripped down into something simpler. Suppose we revert to the old SLASH feature, and to the old top linking rule (29b) above, repeated here with co-indexing added. (Until now I have not included indices on antecedents and the values of SLASH, but they are independently needed, and are important here for indicating the binding of a SLASH.)

(29b) S → NP$_i$, H[SLASH NP$_i$]

There are redundant aspects of rule (29b) that could be stripped off and supplied by defaults. All that is really needed is as in (38).

(38) S → NP$_i$, H[SLASH]

Because of HFC, the H in (38) will be realized as S, so that (38) licenses a "Chomsky-adjunction" structure, as in (39).

(39)

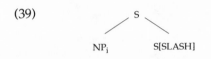

NP$_i$ S[SLASH]

Since "Chomsky adjunction" is characteristic of top linking, we can assume that the default is for this local tree to be fleshed out as a top linking construction. That is, the default is for the value of SLASH to be identical to the sister category, as in (40), and for there to be no matching slash feature on the mother.[65]

(40)

NP$_i$ S[SLASH NP$_i$]

This captures the Pollard and Sag idea that a foot feature doesn't copy upward if it finds its antecedent. What I have added is that for SLASH to find its antecedent does not require a special feature and a marked rule, but is the unmarked case (default) in a characteristic context.

Thus this upward-copying approach also appears to offer a satisfactory way of tidying up FFP to fit with the new restrictions on feature instantiation and inheritance in LPSG. Various details remain to be worked through here. For example: I have assumed a principle, call it P, which, like Pollard and Sag's Nonlocal Feature Principle, blocks the usual effect of FFP when a foot feature is bound. What exactly does P say? Does it PROHIBIT a matching foot feature on the mother? Or does it merely stop FFP from REQUIRING a matching feature on the mother, but permit one to occur there if otherwise licensed? In other words, are there any local trees similar to (40) but in which the mother does have a SLASH feature matching that of the head daughter? An example would be as in (41).

(41)

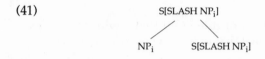

However, (41) would be subject to another constraint, the Strong Crossover Constraint, stated in (42) (where order of daughters is irrelevant).

(42)

This constraint says that an extraction antecedent must not be co-referential with any NP that is in the same local tree as one of the SLASH nodes on the path leading down to its trace; if it IS coreferential with such an NP, that NP must BE its trace. (Why there should be such a constraint is unclear but is of no concern here.) The Strong Crossover Constraint (42) excludes the local tree (41). The only version of (41) that is compatible with (42) is (43), where the SLASH now appears on BOTH daughters.[66]

(43)   S[SLASH NP$_i$]
                          ╱   ╲
             NP$_i$[SLASH NP$_i$]   S[SLASH NP$_i$]

This is a strange construction. The NP$_i$[SLASH NP$_i$] here must be null (to avoid an i-within-i violation), so (43) would be comparable to a GB construction with an intermediate trace in COMP linked to another trace in the lower clause. GPSG (or LPSG, HPSG) doesn't need such a construction, but also has no need to exclude it, I think. (It would provide an alternative route for extraction from a subordinate clause, but since the rule would be highly marked it would not be adopted freely by learners.) Thus I think principle P is another example of the "elsewhere" relation between defaults: a general principle (FFP) requires a foot feature to copy upward regardless of context, but it is overridden by a more specific principle (P) which requires a foot feature not to copy up in an "adjunction" context.

To summarize: The issue has been how best to tailor the old FFP to fit with the new requirements on including features in rules in LPSG. Some proposals have been discussed, and I shall leave the choice between them open. As far as learnability is concerned, it doesn't matter HOW we elect to modify FFP; all that's required is that it can be done somehow. The purpose of this section has been to encourage the hope that it can not only be done, but can also in the process contribute interestingly to the linguistic goal of capturing universal trends in feature distribution.

THE LEARNING MECHANISM

What a GPSG learner would have to learn, in addition to a lexicon, is ID rules, LP rules, and language-particular FCRs and FSDs. For LPSG we have had to clean away the language-particular constraints (FCRs and FSDs) because they are not learnable from positive data. So in LPSG only rules (and the lexicon) are learned. And an unexpected and very welcome consequence of this is that learning no longer needs to be by hypothesis formation and testing, because it no longer faces the ambiguity that results from an embarrassment of descriptive riches as in ST or GPSG with their mix of rules and constraints.

Faced with a new construction not described by his current grammar, an LPSG learner should first identify which local tree(s) in that construction are novel. Then he knows that for each one a new rule must be added to the grammar, or a current rule must be expanded in scope. Unlike an ST learner, or a GPSG learner, he doesn't have to choose between adding a rule and deleting a constraint. An LPSG learner also knows, since possible rules are very limited in format, that he must add either a new LP rule for ID configurations already generated,[67] and/or a new context-free ID rule. Unlike an ST learner, he does not have to choose between a base rule and a transformation, or between a transformation that moves A to the left and one that moves B to the right, and so on. Finally, since there is such a straightforward relation between ID rules and the local trees they license, an LPSG learner can essentially read the new rule off the new local tree that he has encountered in his input. Unlike an ST learner, he does not have to be creative and DEVISE a rule that will have the required effect on the derivation. The very worst he could possibly do is to take the novel local tree into his grammar in toto, and use it as his new rule.

(The fact that we conventionally write rules horizontally as A → B , C
and draw local trees as   A

/\

B C

is irrelevant, of course.) The resulting rule would be highly specific
and non-schematic, not at all economical. But then he could improve
matters by deleting from the rule all those feature specifications that
follow from his innate FCRs and FSDs. On the basis of HFC, he could
strip off all the head features on the head daughter, as long as they
aren't exceptional but do indeed mirror the head features on the
mother. On the basis of FFP, he could strip off all foot features on
daughters if they match one on the mother. (Or vice versa, depending
on whether foot features copy up or down.) On the basis of FCR 2 for
[VFORM], he could strip off [+V] and [-N] from maximal projections
of V;[68] and similarly for all the other universal FCRs. And on the basis
of the universal FSDs, he could strip off all the unmarked values of
features, such as the value NORM for the feature [NFORM] on an NP,
or the value ACC for the feature [CASE] on an NP daughter to VP,
and so forth.

The feature specifications that remain in his rule would be just
those peculiar to that particular construction in that particular language. He might be able to save the cost of many of these specifications too, by collapsing his new rule with one that's already in his
grammar. If, for example, an English learner were in the process of
acquiring rule (27) above from an encounter with a long distance
extraction construction, he could eliminate all but the SLASH feature
by using parentheses to combine (27) with the corresponding basic
rule; the result would be as shown in (44).

(44)   (27)   VP[SLASH NP] → H, S
                      VP → H, S
        _____
         VP[SLASH (NP)] → H, S

More generally, as discussed earlier, any pair of rules differing only
with respect to marked and unmarked values of the same feature can
be collapsed by means of parentheses around the marked value specification.

It appears, then, that though LPSG requires learners to learn rules,
as GPSG does and as ST and other pre-GB transformational theories
did, LPSG may nevertheless support a completely deterministic
learning procedure. I have only sketched the procedure here, and
there are several aspects of it that demand further scrutiny. For in-

stance, it needs to be shown that the various constraints and defaults which govern feature instantiation in sentence generation can be applied in a coherent sequence which allows some to override others in the correct way; and then it needs to be shown that this sequence can be reversed, without loss of information, in the process of deriving schematic rules from specific input trees in learning. (This cannot be taken for granted. It was found, for example, that the order of application of ST transformations in a derivation could not be reversed for purposes of sentence parsing without loss of determinism.) It would be unsatisfactory, for example, if [+F] were unmarked in the presence of [+G], [-F] were unmarked elsewhere, but the value of G could be eliminated from the learner's new rule before he had used it to establish whether the value of F was marked or unmarked, hence whether or not it could be stripped away also.

Also, it needs to be shown that the process of collapsing rules into general rule schemata by means of abbreviatory devices is orderly and information preserving. There are certainly some prima facie problems. These are discussed in Crain and Fodor (in prep). There is also the question of how a learner determines the proper analysis of a novel input which his grammar does not yet license. If he cannot assign his input the correct structure, he will not be able to read off the correct new rules. See Fodor (1989a) for some discussion that doesn't go nearly far enough. Note that this is a problem that every theory must deal with. Unlike the other matters addressed in this paper, it is not one that looks to be especially troublesome for a grammar-construction model of learning as opposed to a parameter setting model. One further point that I have not touched on here is the resilience of the learning mechanism in the face of misleading input. This too is a serious problem for all learning models; even if the Subset Principle is rigorously adhered to, a learner could end up with an overgenerating grammar on the basis of incorrect input, such as speech errors. This is addressed in Crain and Fodor (in prep.), where it is argued that as long as erroneous input does not keep reinforcing them, overshoots CAN be corrected in LPSG.[69]

If these various additional complications can be dealt with successfully, it appears that LPSG grammars are learnable by a very simple "mechanical" learning routine. This learning routine would work as well for the periphery of language as for the core; peripheral phenomena would simply call for more m values in rules. And though very different from parameter setting in its details, the LPSG learning routine would be fairly comparable in its practical advantages. Notice especially that it not only satisfies the Subset Principle, which has been our main concern, but also provides a practical basis for satisfying conditions C2-C5 (repeated here) and/or whichever others like them we deem desirable.

C1: $L(G_{i+1})$ is not a proper superset of $L(G_j)$ if G_j satisfies all other conditions that G_{i+1} is required to satisfy.
C2: G_{i+1} licenses I.
C3: $G_{i+1} = G_i$ if G_i licenses I.
C4: G_{i+1} is as much like G_i as possible consistent with C2.
C5: $L(G_{i+1})$ includes $L(G_i)$.

The procedure just outlined for acquiring a new rule builds up G_{i+1} on the basis of G_i and I. It guarantees that G_{i+1} will license I, since at absolute worst each novel local tree in I will serve as its own rule. If the feature stripping and rule collapsing processes work reliably, then the acquisition procedure will also ensure that G_{i+1} does not differ from G_i if G_i already licenses I, since feature stripping and rule collapsing will blend a redundant rule into the grammar with no trace. The procedure will also entail that the minimum is added to G_i to accommodate I. The only change in the grammar will be the addition of a rule, or part of a rule, for licensing each novel local tree in I. All UG-redundant specifications will have been stripped from such rules by the inverse-feature-instantiation process, and rule collapsing will have removed specifications that are redundant on the basis of within-language generalizations. Finally, it is guaranteed (with one minor exception; see note 46 above) that all sentences of $L(G_i)$ are preserved in $L(G_{i+1})$, since adding a rule to Gi cannot reduce the size of the language it generates. Thus the LPSG learning mechanism promises to converge with some efficiency on the correct grammar.

When Stephen Crain and I first began this investigation of the acquisition of GPSG grammars, the question was only whether learning is possible in principle, and the strongly anticipated answer was that it is not. But I think we were wrong. It now appears that a phrase structure system which is at least a close cousin of GPSG (and HPSG) is learnable in principle, and even more surprisingly that it is also learnable in practice, by a mechanism significantly more realistic than the kinds of hypothesis testing devices with which rule-based grammars have always seemed to be encumbered.

NOTES

* The work reported in this paper was done in collaboration with Stephen Crain. Some of the points made here are discussed more fully in our forthcoming book, *On the Form of Innate Linguistic Knowledge*.

1 Since our research on this topic began, GPSG has been overtaken by HPSG (Head-driven Phrase Structure Grammar, Pollard & Sag 1987). Since not all aspects of HPSG have yet been presented in print, and since GPSG is probably more widely known because of Sells (1985), I will take GPSG as the basis for discussion in the present paper. But I will mention HPSG specifically where the differences between the two theories are relevant to learnability issues.

2 Another important factor addressed in learnability studies is the complexity of the input needed for learning natural languages. See Wexler and Culicover (1980). Also note 69 below.

3 Throughout this paper I will use the pronouns "he," "him," and "his" to refer to the generic learner, to avoid the complexity of disjunctions such as "she or he."

4 I am abstracting here from the problem of ungrammatical input that provides misinformation about the language, and from other practical issues such as how a learner imposes structure on an input sentence, how accurately he can determine what it means, etc.

5 Note that I am not adopting here the idealization to instantaneous acquisition of Chomsky (1965) and other work; see Pinker (1981) for discussion. Modelling learning without this idealization might be easier, if, for example, it were assumed that the sequence of inputs helps direct a learner to the correct grammar; or it might be harder, if input order is random but the sequence of grammars hypothesized is not and needs to be explained. See discussion below.

6 The Subset Principle would be vacuously satisfied if no two natural languages stand in a proper subset/superset relationship. But this is surely false. At the other extreme, the Subset Condition of Wexler and Manzini (1987) says that the languages associated with the values of a GB parameter all stand in subset relations one to another. This is probably false, too.

7 For our purposes here, each I could be identified with an equivalence class of sentences of the language – all those with the same syntactic structure regardless of lexical choices. Also, as noted above, I am making the simplifying assumption, common in learnability work, that I is well-formed and has somehow been assigned its correct syntactic structure. To take this for granted is to set aside some interesting and difficult questions, which all learnability models must eventually confront. For discussion, see Wexler and Culicover (1980); Pinker (1984); Berwick (1985); Fodor (1989a).

8 Note that none of these conditions requires that for a given G_i and I, there

is a unique G_{i+1}. One might wish to add this condition, but it is not essential. For one thing, it is imaginable (though not commonly assumed) that a natural language has more than one "correct" grammar in a community. Even if not, the selection criterion could permit a free choice among alternative grammars, except in "subset situations," for there would be positive data that could lead a learner to change his grammar later if he had chosen the wrong one. Of course, the datum for discarding a wrong grammar might be too complex or too infrequent for learning to rely on it. And even if it were accessible, learning would presumably be more efficient if the selection criterion narrowed the choice of G_{i+1} as far as possible in all cases. The optimum would be a completely deterministic system, but that is not easy to achieve in all frameworks; see discussion below.

9 For example, C5 has the potential disadvantage that it would prevent "retreat" from overgeneralizations, though overgeneralization could occur, despite all cautions of the learner, because of speech errors in the input, etc. In any case, C5 is too strong; it would bring learning to a standstill if the input I happened to be incompatible with all G_{i+1} that generate a superset of $L(G_i)$. Such an input would signal a past error by the learner, and retreat could and should occur. So we might choose to replace C5 with a more flexible (but less easily implemented) version such as: G_{i+1} gives up the smallest possible number of sentences of $L(G_i)$ compatible with C2. C4 has the potential disadvantage of preventing "restructuring" of the grammar to achieve overall simplification. Restructuring might be more trouble than it is worth; see Fodor and Smith (1978), McCawley (1974). But if it is considered desirable to permit it, C4 might be replaced by a condition on G_{i+1} without regard for its relation to G_i, e.g., the condition that G_{i+1} should be as small as possible consistent with C2 and C5. This would permit large reductions in grammar size but only small increases.

10 A weakened version of C2 would permit the learner to ignore the input if no G_{i+1} which generates it can be found in some reasonable amount of time or effort; see Berwick (1985). This leeway might be desirable in a model like Wexler and Culicover's even for rule addition, since the only way to be sure that a learner can always construct a rule to map the output of the G_i derivation into I would be to permit a very broad class of possible transformations; but then the number of grammars that learners would have to search through would be huge.

11 Wexler and Manzini thereby gave up a valuable practical advantage of GB's parameter theory; see the second section below. Their reason for doing so was that the five values of the parameter they identified in the definition of *governing category* had to be assigned opposite rankings to satisfy the Subset Principle for anaphors and for pronominals. But even if

this claim is true, there are less extreme responses to it. For example, Wexler and Manzini argue on independent grounds that the parameter must be set not just once for the whole language but once for each pronoun and anaphor. So it could be proposed that the feature specifications [α anaphoric, β pronominal] on a lexical item control the direction in which the scale of values for its governing category is to be read.

12 In what follows I will ignore all potential complications stemming from the possible non-independence of parameters, in either the sense of Manzini and Wexler (1987) or the quite different sense of Fodor and Crain (1990).

13 In assuming that the values of a parameter must be ordered in UG, I am setting aside the possibility that subset relationships are established "online" by comparing languages; see the discussion in the previous section. I note also that to assume innate ordering does not presuppose precise evolutionary shaping of the language faculty to arrange the values in the required "subset order." If a "superset value" happened to precede a "subset value" in the innate sequence, then the latter would never be exemplified in a human language, and we would not know of its existence. So Nature could fix the sequence at random (though it must be identical for all learners). See Fodor (1989b) for discussion.

14 One might consider it to be one of the distinguishing marks of a trigger (distinguishing it from a typical input for a hypothesis-formation-and-testing learning device) that it may be arbitrarily related to the grammar change it induces, i.e., that the properties of the language that are exemplified in the trigger construction could be arbitrarily different from the properties of the language newly attributed to it by the change in grammar in response to the trigger. (See Atkinson 1987 for discussion.) However, this aspect of the theory of triggers cannot be pressed too far. If the trigger were NOT compatible with the parameter value, in the sense above, the bizarre situation would arise that the language could be learned only by exposure to a sentence of some other language. Though this is a logical possibility, I shall ignore it here.

15 Another connotation of the notion of a trigger is that the grammar change resulting from an encounter with the trigger input is made instantly without cogitation. A related point is that the acquisition device needs no access to the pairing between grammars and the languages they license (e.g., it does not need to be able to construct derivations). This aspect of the theory of triggers would be weakened if triggers were associated with parameter values by general criteria rather than by innate listing.

16 To avoid non-determinism it is necessary that only one value of one parameter is triggered by a given input, but the converse might or might not be true. That is, for a given parameter value there might or might not be more than one trigger (not just more than one sentence, but more than one

type of syntactic construction). The fewer the triggers per value, the simpler the representation of UG. The more triggers per value (up to the limits set by the non-determinism problem), the greater the chance that every learner will encounter one, and encounter it soon. But even with multiple triggers, it could still be the case that some constructions were not associated as triggers with any parameter value. This would be reasonable for rare or complex constructions. For accessible constructions it would be wasteful of potentially useful learning data, since a child's encounter with such a construction would not constitute a learning event. (Note that this would require a weakening of condition C2; see also note 10 above.)

17 Here, too, I am ignoring the proposal of Wexler and Manzini (see above) that a learner faced with two or more candidate grammars would examine the languages they licensed to see if one were a subset of the other.

18 I avoided the term "evaluation metric" in the general discussion above because of its traditional connotations, which make it seem incongruous as applied to GB parameter values. But specific details aside, I believe an evaluation metric in the traditional sense is identical with what I have been calling a selection criterion for learners.

19 It also gave wrong results when applied to the phonological rules of the period. The emphasis at the time was on how a simplicity metric could be used to encourage learners to generalize. Extraordinarily, considering how much attention was devoted to the issue, the fact that it would encourage learners to OVERgeneralize was apparently completely overlooked.

20 *Move* α is acceptable in a GB system where it interacts with parameters and lexical properties such as case and theta assignment that limit its effects. But *Move* α in place of Passive, Extraposition, Raising, etc., in ST would massively overgenerate since it would have nothing to hold it in check.

21 A constraint could of course be acquired if it were conjoined, innately and irremediably, to a rule learnable from positive data. Parameter theory offers a natural mechanism for this, if it permits more than one property of languages to be associated with the same parameter "switch." In other frameworks this is less easy to arrange but some such effects can be achieved indirectly (e.g., with pre-emptive relations between items or operations, as in the Uniqueness Condition or an Elsewhere Condition). See Fodor and Crain (1990) for some discussion.

22 Chomsky and Lasnik (1977) proposed a number of filters, and considered their status with respect to acquisition. In discussing the $*_{NP}[NP$ tense VP] filter for English, they noted that it is neither universal nor learnable without negative data. Their solution was to assume that the constraint (actually, a principle entailing it) was innate but that it could be eliminated on the basis of positive evidence. However, once constraints are eliminable, it is not clear what would prevent learners from eliminating them, to

simplify their grammars; they would then be trapped in irremediable overgeneration. (See also note 31 below.)

23 If indirect negative data ARE available to children, then the whole research project is radically changed. All conclusions drawn on the basis of the contrary assumption might be flawed; in particular, the arguments in this paper against the learnability of GPSG would be invalidated. However, see Fodor and Crain (1987), and Grimshaw and Pinker (1989), for reasons for doubting that learners do have reliable access to sufficient negative evidence, direct or indirect, to establish upper bounds on generalizations.

24 It would still be the case that one grammar was simpler to ACQUIRE than another, in the sense of requiring fewer revisions to arrive at; see Williams (1981). So the ordering of the values of a parameter could still be construed, if desired, as a markedness ranking.

25 If the division of labour between rules and constraints in GPSG is principled, then LPSG could adopt it as part of the selection criterion for learners. However, I have been unable to discern a systematic policy in the GKPS description of English as to which properties should be mentioned in rules, and which should be freely instantiated but subject to constraints. I find it a little worrying to think that the GKPS policy might just have been to adopt whatever descriptive devices gave the most elegant and revealing account. Not only could this not readily be translated into practical maxims for learners, but also, since LPSG must differ from GPSG, it would imply that LPSG's descriptions must be LESS than optimally elegant or revealing. I think it may sometimes be necessary to sacrifice absolute grammar simplicity to achieve a system in which RELATIVE simplicity of alternative grammars correctly predicts learners' choices. However, an informal comparison between GPSG and LPSG as outlined below suggests that LPSG in fact sacrifices little if anything in the way of overall economy of description.

26 Also, Maxfield (1990) argues for revisions partly similar to those above as a means of streamlining the process of feature instantiation in GPSG, along the lines sketched by Shieber (1986).

27 Extraction from infinitive clauses is acceptable in Polish, and relativization shows extraction from tensed clauses and even WH-clauses; see references above. I will not attempt here to account for these interesting differences, but since they appear to represent universal trends they ought at some point to be integrated into the markedness theory established by the default feature specifications discussed below.

28 There are a couple of verbs in Polish which bridge extraction from a tensed clause, though the great majority do not. In this paper I will write as if none do. There are languages in which this is the case, e.g., American Sign Language (see Lillo-Martin, to appear).

29 There are other alternatives that might be considered, such as relaxation of

the doubly-filled Comp filter for languages permitting extraction from WH-clauses.

30 Again there are imaginable alternatives. For example, there might be three binary-valued parameters (or only two if NP is necessarily bounding) as shown in (i), with + as the initial value for each.

(i)

	Polish	English	Italian	Swedish
S' bounding	+	–	+	–
S bounding	+	+	–	–
NP bounding	+	+	+	+

31 I am setting aside here the idea that every possible language-specific constraint is innate and is deleted on the basis of positive data by learners of languages to which it is inapplicable. As noted in note 22 above, this approach does not escape the subset problem as long as simplicity is held to influence learners' choices. Though entertained briefly by Chomsky and Lasnik (1977), it became much more attractive when the constraints (filters) in question were regimented into principles and parameters in GB. The shift from one parameter value to the next often represents elimination of a constraint; but in a parameter theory framework there is no gain in grammar simplicity to encourage learners to make this shift prematurely. The approach I will develop below is similar to this idea that language-specific constraints are innate and eliminated when they conflict with positive data, but there is one important difference. This is that the innate constraints REMAIN in the grammar as default principles, and where they do not apply it is because they are overridden by rules (acquired on the basis of positive data). As will be explained, this avoids problems of grammar simplicity and overgeneration. See Fodor (to appear) for more specific discussion of the differences between these variants of the constraint-elimination approach to language-specific constraints.

32 FCR 20 expresses the WH-island constraint IF the WH feature is taken to be the feature that characterizes relative clauses, questions, and WH-complements to verbs like *wonder*. However, GKPS (p. 155) illustrate the need for this FCR not with a typical WH-island violation but with **Which books did you wonder whose reviews of had annoyed me?* Here the extraction is from a WH-phrase which is the subject and focus of the WH-complement to *wonder*. This extraction would also and independently be blocked by HFC. GKPS do not consistently distinguish between a WH-phrase in the sense of a question or relative focus, often "moved" (with or without pied piping) from its basic position, and a WH-phrase in the sense of a relative clause or a direct or indirect question. In fact there are two different patterns of WH feature percolation, suggesting that there are two distinct WH features. One feature can pass down inside a WH-focus phrase, for example from PP to NP to its determiner as in [*To whose aunt*] *do you think John was impolite?* but is blocked at certain nodes such as A' in **[Impolite to*

whose aunt] do you think John was?, and by S in *\[Of the fact that he had offended whom] was John unaware?* A different WH feature can pass down within the non-focus part of a WH-complement to license additional in situ WH-foci in multiple questions such as *Whose aunt did John say was impolite to whom?* and as this example shows, this percolation is not blocked at nodes such as A' or S. A more difficult issue is which of these two WH-features (if either!) is the one that characterizes questions and relatives. An intriguing possibility is that this can differ across languages, and that it underlies differences like those for which Lasnik and Saito (1984) proposed their parameterization of the WH-criterion; Chinese questions (with no WH-fronting) would have one WH feature, Italian (with no multiple-WH questions) would have the other, and English would have both. All of this needs to be looked into, but for present purposes I will simply assume that the WH in GKPS's FCR 20 is the WH that marks questions and relative clauses, whether or not it's the same as the WH that marks WH-focus phrases. (However, the WH in GKPS's FCRs 21 and 22, quoted in (26) below, MUST be the WH of a WH-focus phrase.)

33 FCR (3) itself wouldn't occur in the grammar of Polish if it were subsumed under some stronger constraint. This might be so, but I will assume here that it is not; see note 38 below.

34 For instance, FCR (6) cannot be corrected for Polish by adding [-ROOT] to the S in question; this would successfully differentiate between (4) and (7), but it would incorrectly exclude within-clause extractions in embedded questions in Polish. It might be possible to revise (6) so that it prohibits [SLASH] on S' rather than on S. (S and S' are distinguished in GPSG not by bar level but by the minor feature [COMP], whose values for English are *that, for, whether, if*, and NIL). This would be successful if the sister to a fronted WH-phrase were always S in Polish, while a non-WH clause argument to a verb were always S'. However it is not clear that this is so. See Cichocki (op. cit.).

35 The third major GPSG principle is the Head Feature Convention (HFC), but it is a default principle, not an absolute constraint. I will discuss it below.

36 Matters are a little more complicated than this because FFP applies only to instantiated features, not to features inherited from (specified by) a rule. By contrast, FCRs (hence LTRs on my assumptions here) apply to all features in trees. However, this limitation on FFP is an aspect of GPSG that I propose should be revised in LPSG for independent reasons; see below.

37 The learnability arguments also apply to language-specific default specifications; these are discussed in more detail in later sections (pp. 29-40). Note that default specifications can also in principle be within-category or cross-category, as well as language-specific or universal. GKPS refer to the within-category ones as Feature Specification Defaults (FSDs). The cross-

category ones (of which HFC is an example; see note 35 above) we may call Local Tree Defaults (LTDs).

38 Since by this argument neither Polish nor English is learnable, I don't need to rest any great weight here on the comparison between the two of them, that is, on the fact that (9) portrays Polish as having more constraints than English. This presupposes that the two Polish constraints don't fall together into something simpler than FCR 3 alone. But deciding this depends on establishing the exact details of the formulation of these two constraints, and that is not worthwhile here since both will be given up shortly.

39 The only assumption I am trading on in (10) is that the two rules for Swedish don't collapse together into something simpler than the one rule for English; if they did, English would still be unlearnable in this framework. But I will discuss such matters below.

40 I assume that even small differences of rule complexity (e.g., one feature specification more or less) can be significant, since they can influence learners' choices among alternative grammars when faced with a novel input. But this is not relevant to the difference between (10) and (9), which is a difference between different theories of grammars. If (10) is the right picture, the constraints in (9) will not even be an option that learners could contemplate.

41 The symbol H in rule (12) and other GPSG rules is a metavariable denoting the head daughter, most or all of whose features will be determined by general principles from the features of the mother. Also, the order in which daughter categories are specified in the rule is irrelevant. GPSG does not use traditional phrase structure rules but divides the information they contain between ID (Immediate Dominance) rules and LP (Linear Precedence) statements. Rule (12) is an ID rule. I will presuppose the necessary LP statements without stating them.

42 If feature instantiation relating ID rules to trees is dangerous, could GPSG use metarules instead? GPSG metarules are permitted to add feature specifications to underspecified ID rules. (See GKPS's STM1, whose only function is to add the feature [+NULL].) And though their application is restricted in later versions of the theory by the Lexical Head Constraint, that might perhaps be loosened. But metarules are no panacea because they too are unlearnable, for much the same sorts of reasons: the simpler they get, the more broadly they apply. See Fodor and Crain (in prep.) for discussion.

43 A context-sensitive default specification, such as HFC, can make a different value the default in a different context; see below.

44 I will show below that for learnability it doesn't matter which value is taken to be the default; all that matters is that the default be specific, not a disjunction. So in LPSG the default assignments can be decided on the basis of linguistic evidence.

45 It was noted in the first section that C2 is not easy to implement in all models. But it is achievable in LPSG; see pp. 49-52.

46 The argument relies not only on C2 but also on C4 above, that is, that the child will not alter (e.g., add to) his grammar more than his current input requires. For instance, learning would fail if a learner retained an incorrect rule he had hypothesized, as well as the correct rule he later discovered he needed. Note that ALL theories must assume that learners don't wantonly increase the generative power of their grammars (for example, in parameter theory by moving to a lower priority parameter value without justification in the input). C4 can be implemented by adherence to the simplicity metric. The argument above also requires that a rule licensing the marked value only is less complex than a rule licensing both the marked and the unmarked values; see discussion below. (An interesting consequence: exposure to a marked value will cause temporary loss of the unmarked value until it is relearned. This violates the strong form of C5 above; see note 9.)

47 To be more accurate: there is a cost associated with the addition of each clump of one or more constructions that necessarily co-exist due to universal principles; what costs is each move from one grammar to the next largest possible grammar that UG makes available. This must be the case if the Subset Principle is to be obeyed by a learner relying on simplicity as the selection criterion. I would concede, though, that there may be aspects of natural language for which this ranking seems wrong. For example, Zwicky (1986) suggests that both strict word order and completely free word order, which are succinctly characterizable, are unmarked, and that partially fixed order, whose details the grammar would have to specify, is the marked case. But this intuition of relative markedness does not comport with the markedness rankings needed to guide acquisition on the assumption of no negative data and a simplicity metric; rather, completely free order must be the most marked because it results in the largest language. It will be important for further research to determine whether it is possible to reconcile linguistic and learnability-based estimates of markedness in all cases.

48 Note that this does not commit LPSG to the claim that Swedish is a more difficult language to KNOW or USE once it has been learned. The differences in complexity between the grammars of different languages may be so small as to be trivial relative to the capacity of the language representation centers in the human brain. A difference of one feature specification would, I am assuming, influence a learner in selecting a grammar, but it would hardly affect the ability of an adult to use the grammar.

49 I am referring here to SYNTACTIC number. There are of course verbs like *disperse* that require semantically plural arguments.

50 Two points. (i) There could be gaps in a distribution, but I predict that they

would be morphological gaps at the lexical level, not syntactic gaps. The way to tell would be to see if that item appeared in some other context with the same syntactic features. If so, the gap could not be a morphological one. (ii) NP conjunction presents an interesting case in which the value of [PLU] on the mother is fully determined by UG, but assignment of a default to the feature facilitates statement of the determining principle. See Sag, Gazdar, Wasow, and Weisler (1985), who propose that plural is the default and that it then follows by unification that the mother is plural if any of the conjoined daughters is plural. (This may be more convincing in the case of other agreement features, such as syntactic gender, where semantic determinants of the mother's feature value are minimized.) Whether defaults that serve this purpose have exactly the same status as the defaults discussed above I don't know.

51 The Specific Defaults Principle is stated here from a learner's point of view. From an evolutionary point of view, this statement is upside down. The right picture is: regardless of what causal or chance events brought it about, human heads contain (a) FCRs for some features in some contexts, (b) FSDs for others, and (c) no constraints at all for still others. As a result, some features in some contexts [those falling under (a)] are universally fixed; others [those falling under (c)] are universally free; and still others [falling under (b)] are learnable on the basis of defaults. Rather than saying that learners don't need defaults to learn feature values that are universally free, the fact is that some feature values are universally free because they happen not to have innate defaults that would permit specific values to be learned.

52 Note that FSDs do not apply to FCRs. That is, non-specification of a feature value in an FCR should not invoke the default but should have the traditional disjunctive interpretation. Consider, for example, FCR 2: [VFORM] ⊃ [+V, -N]. This should not be construed as applying only to categories with the default value for SLASH (i.e., no SLASH); it should apply to all categories containing [VFORM], with or without SLASH. This is in accord with the claim of Fodor and Crain (in prep.) that FCRs and FSDs are both aspects of the universal (innate) metasemantics that determine the interpretation of language-specific rules.

53 I assume that the import of FSD 9 is in any case more properly captured by subcategorization of the complementizer *for* for an infinitival clause. GKPS do not treat complementizers like "normal" lexical items subcategorized for their sisters, but treat them as spelling out syntactic features.

54 In the discussion of the Standard Theory in the first section it was noted that context-sensitive rules cannot be learned without negative data. But the context sensitivity of these FSDs is not problematic since they must in any case be innate, not learned. Barton, Berwick, and Ristad (1987) have argued that context-sensitive defaults contribute to computational intrac-

tability in sentence processing. It may be, however, that this is one of those sources of intractability that is inherent in natural languages rather than being introduced by a certain type of grammar. On the other hand, it is also quite conceivable (however much we would wish otherwise) that aspects of grammar format which facilitate learning complicate processing, or vice versa.

55 It's not that GKPS intended there to be FSDs for SLASH and WH and just omitted to include them in the book. If they had, they would have had to write the marked values as options in their rules.

56 Though extremely general, this Elsewhere condition may not resolve all priorities. For instance, which should win if there were two conflicting default assignments, both context-sensitive and equally specific, but one with within-category context (an FSD) and the other with cross-category context (an LTD)? This sort of question can only be decided on the basis of more extensive language descriptions worked out in this framework. See Shieber (1986) for discussion of related issues in the earlier framework.

57 Two examples. (1) Preposition stranding in extraction constructions is rare across languages but is more natural in (colloquial) modern English than pied piping is. However, when one examines this "language-specific default" it disappears. What it actually amounts to is a preference for an NP antecedent over a PP antecedent when the NP is the focus of the sentence. And that it is in all likelihood a universal default. However it is a default that rarely gets a chance to show up. It can do so only in a language like English which has the marked property of permitting extraction of NP out of PP. Note that the first default (prefer an NP antecedent) concerns the top linking configuration for an extraction, while the second one (don't extract from PP) concerns the passing of SLASH through the middle of the construction; there is no direct conflict between them. (2) It is commonly claimed that masculine, say, is the default gender in some language, or plural is the default number, and it may be implied that a different value is the default in another language. It is important to consider what criterion for default (unmarked) status is being presupposed by such statements (see note 50 above). If the criterion is use in positions of SEMANTIC neutralization, then what is involved is a communicative rather than a syntactic default, and cross-language variation may be unproblematic. That is, it may be just that an item like *he* is lexically assigned both a specific masculine meaning and a gender-neutral meaning (with Gricean discourse principles favouring specificity where possible).

58 I won't trouble here with the difference between ~[NULL] and [-NULL]. It has to do with whether categories other than X[SLASH X] categories COULD be null in principle. And that has to do with whether GPSG ought to admit empty categories other than WH-trace (e.g., *pro*) with [+NULL] but no SLASH feature. I should note, however, that this whole treatment

of the A-over-A constraint presupposes that [+NULL] should be introduced by instantiation rather than by metarule (STM1) as GKPS propose.
This metarule is the only one they give whose sole function is to add a
feature specification. It would be undesirable in LPSG for learners to have
to choose between metarules and feature instantiation as mechanisms for
supplying features (see below). And since instantiation is the weaker of
the two mechanisms (it cannot add or delete whole categories), I assume it
is always adopted where either would do. (What GKPS gained by STM1
was that, since metarules are subject to the Lexical Head Constraint,
[+NULL] could only be introduced on categories with a lexical head sister.
This covers much the same ground as the lexical government condition of
the ECP. Most of it is ALSO covered by HFC, so there is some redundancy,
but HFC imposes weaker restrictions on parasitic gaps.)

59 This is oversimplified. See notes 50 and 57 above for other possible causes
of asymmetric distribution. Much more work is needed to sort out
whether there are different kinds of defaults.

60 To forestall a common confusion: though it is natural in a GPSG framework to think of a daughter node as INHERITING some of its feature values
from its mother, the term "inherited" is used by GKPS not in this sense but
in the sense of non-instantiated, that is, present in the local tree because
present in the licensing rule. I will keep to this use of the term in what
follows. (But Pollard & Sag appear to have switched to the other usage for
HPSG.)

61 For example, HFC need not (must not) apply to a top linking rule. (In
standard GPSG it would do so except that it is blocked because it conflicts
with FFP.) There are also other cases that run more smoothly if HFC does
NOT apply to daughters. For instance, in GPSG a head feature on a VP will
float up to S, and GPSG needs FCRs to block this where it is undesirable.
See, for instance, GKPS's FCR 5, which insists on [-SUBJ] in order to
prevent tense features from percolating up from VP to S; they must pass
down, of course, from VP to V' to V. In LPSG this restriction would be
unnecessary. There are some head features which do need to appear on S
as well as VP. For example, the various values of [VFORM] (for example,
FIN, BSE, PRP, etc.) are needed on S for purposes of matrix verb selection.
But a downward copying HFC could cope with this too. These features
would be INTRODUCED at the S level, rather than on VP, and then by HFC
they would trickle down to VP.

62 This need not be an absolute constraint; it would be sufficient if it were a
universal default. It would operate by the same sort of logic as for the
Specific Defaults Principle above. That is, as long as UG picks a PREFERRED
daughter to receive the SLASH, the outcomes of rules will be specific
enough to provide informative feedback, and so a learner will also be able

to learn constructions where the NON-preferred daughter receives SLASH. See Fodor (to appear) for discussion of this approach.

63 In fact there are arguably no lexical ID rules. Instead of (36a,b) there would be comparable subcategorization features in lexical entries; see Pollard and Sag (1987), Fodor (to appear). Then FFP/HFC would apply downward to rules and upward to subcategorization features.

64 Pollard and Sag don't give their reasons for parting company with the GPSG solution in which FFP applies only to inherited features. Note also that Pollard and Sag do NOT depart from GPSG with respect to the overgeneralizing tendencies of SLASH-passing rules: instantiation of SLASH is still free, so SLASH passing is permitted through any node, unless it is prevented by a language-specific constraint. For this reason, the HPSG approach to SLASH passing and linking could not be adopted without modification into LPSG.

65 A different top linking configuration is involved in *Tough* constructions. There the antecedent is a value of the SUBCAT feature on the lexical head sister to the SLASH category. But just as for the WH or topicalization constructions covered by (38), the default should be that the SLASH feature does not pass up to the mother.

66 Pollard and Sag themselves impose Strong Crossover by means of binding principle C, as has been proposed in GB. This locates the problem in the relationship between the intervening NP (= Y_i in (42) above) and the trace. (The HPSG binding principles are different from, but modelled on, the GB binding principles.) But the formulation of Crossover in (42) focuses on the relation between the intervening NP and the SLASH node path that goes past it. This is of interest because in GPSG not all extractions terminate in a trace; we have seen that there is no trace in the GKPS STM2 construction shown in (32a) above. The application of (42) is unaffected by whether the path ends in a trace or not. For both subject and object extractions, therefore, (42) will prevent crossover violations but will permit multiple gap constructions along the lines of (43), though unlike (43) these constitute normal parasitic gap constructions. For object extraction, an example would be *Who did you convince that you were related to?*; for subject extraction an example would be *Who did you convince was clever?*

67 Note that by revision (5) on p. 17, the acquisition of word order patterns must consist of adding LP rules to license word orders, not of adding or deleting LP constraints that restrict word orders. So there will be no ambiguity about descriptive devices here either.

68 Whether it's proper to use the single feature [VFORM] in this fashion to do the work of the two features [V] and [N], as GKPS allow, deserves discussion. But it's not of central concern here.

69 I have also not addressed questions concerning the complexity of the input necessary for acquisition, which are generally less theory-dependent.

Since root and non-root clauses can differ and the differences are not fully predictable, we must assume that learners take note of two-clause constructions (degree-1 input). I know of no reason for thinking that anything richer is needed. And Lightfoot (1989) may be right that something between degree 0 and degree 1 is sufficient. Both transformational and phrase structure theories these days have strong locality constraints so the problems of rule scope which Wexler and Culicover (1980) had to contend with don't arise.

REFERENCES

Atkinson, M. (1987). Mechanisms for language acquisition: learning, parameter-setting and triggering. *First Language* 7:3-30

Barton, G.E., Berwick, R.C., and Ristad, E.S. (1987). *Computational Complexity and Natural Language*. Cambridge, MA: Bradford Books, MIT Press

Berwick, R.C. (1985). *The Acquisition of Syntactic Knowledge*. Cambridge, MA: MIT Press

Chomsky, N. (1965). *Aspects of the Theory of Syntax*. Cambridge, MA: MIT Press

– (1970). Remarks on nominalization. In R.A. Jacobs and P.S. Rosenbaum (eds.), *Readings in English Transformational Grammar*. Waltham, MA: Ginn and Company

– and H. Lasnik (1977). Filters and control. *Linguistic Inquiry* 8:425-504

Cichocki, W. (1983). Multiple WH-questions in Polish: a two-comp analysis. In *Toronto Working Papers in Linguistics* 4:53-71

Clark, R. (1988). The problem of causality in models of language learnability. Paper presented at the Thirteenth Annual Boston University Conference on Language Development

– (1989). On the relationship between input data and parameter setting. In *Proceedings of NELS 19*. Ithaca, NY: Cornell University

Engdahl, E. (1982). Restrictions on unbounded dependencies in Swedish. In E. Engdahl and E. Ejerhed (eds.), *Readings on Unbounded Dependencies in Scandinavian Languages* (Umea Studies in the Humanities 43). Stockholm, Sweden: Almqvist & Wiksell International

Fodor, J.D. (1989a). Principle-based learning. In R. Rieber (ed.), *CUNYForum* 14:59-67

– (1989b). Learning the periphery. In R.J. Matthews and W. Demopoulos (eds.), *Learnability and Linguistic Theory*. Dordrecht: Kluwer

– (1989c). Empty categories in sentence processing. In G. Altmann (ed.), *Parsing and Interpretation* (Special Issue of *Language and Cognitive Processes*). Hove, Eng.: Lawrence Erlbaum Associates

– (1990). Sentence processing and the mental grammar. In T. Wasow, P. Sells, and S. Shieber (eds.), *Foundational Issues in Natural Language Processing*. Cambridge, MA: MIT Press

– (to appear). Islands, learnability and the lexicon. In H. Goodluck and M. Rochemont (eds.), *Island Constraints: Theory, Acquisition and Processing*. Dordrecht: Kluwer

– and Crain, S. (1987). Simplicity and generality of rules in language acquisition. In B. MacWhinney (ed.), *Mechanisms of Language Acquisition*. Hillsdale, NJ: Lawrence Erlbaum Associates

– (1990). Phrase structure parameters. *Linguistics and Philosophy* 13:591-633

– (in prep.) *On the Form of Innate Linguistic Knowledge*. To be published by Bradford Books

– and Smith, M.R. (1978). What kind of exception is *have got*? *Linguistic Inquiry* 9:45-66

Gair, J.W. (1987). Kinds of markedness in second language acquisition research. In S. Flynn and W. O'Neill (eds.), *Linguistic Theory and Second Language Acquisition*. Dordrecht: Reidel

Gazdar, G., Klein, E., Pullum, G.K., and Sag, I.A. (1985). *Generalized Phrase Structure Grammar*. Cambridge, MA: Harvard University Press

Grimshaw, J. and Pinker, S. (1989). Positive and negative evidence in language acquisition. *Behavioral and Brain Sciences* 12: 341-2

Keenan, E. (1974). The functional principle: generalizing the notion "subject of." In M. La Galy, R. Fox, and A. Bruck (eds.), *Papers from the 10th Regional Meeting of the Chicago Linguistics Society*. Chicago: Chicago Linguistics Society, 298-309

Klein, E. (1990). The Null-Prep Phenomenon in Second Language Acquisition. Unpublished Ph.D. dissertation, CUNY, New York

Kraskow, T. (ms.). Implications of Multiple WH-Movement for WH-Island Violation. Department of Linguistics, University of Pennsylvania

Lasnik, H. and Saito, M. (1984). On the nature of proper government. *Linguistic Inquiry* 15:235-89

Lightfoot, D. (1989). The child's trigger experience: "Degree-0" learnability. *Behavioral and Brain Sciences* 12: 321-75

Lillo-Martin, D. (to appear). Sentences as islands: on the boundedness of A'-movement in American sign language. In H. Goodluck and M. Rochemont (eds.), *On Island Constraints: Theory, Acquisition and Processing*. Dordrecht: Kluwer

Manzini, M.R. and Wexler, K. (1987). Parameters, binding theory, and learnability. *Linguistic Inquiry* 18:413-44

Maxfield, T.L. (1990). The Learnability of a Version of Generalized Phrase Structure Grammar. Unpublished Ph.D. dissertation, CUNY, New York

McCawley, J.D. (1974). Acquisition models as models of acquisition. In *Pro-*

ceedings of 1974 NWAVE Conference, Georgetown University, Washington, D.C.

Osherson, D.N., Stob, M., and Weinstein, S. (1984). Learning theory and natural language. *Cognition* 17: 1-28

Pinker, S. (1979). Formal models of language learning. *Cognition* 7: 217-83

– (1981). Comments on the paper by K. Wexler. In C.L. Baker and J.J. McCarthy (eds.), *The Logical Problem of Language Acquisition*. Cambridge, MA: MIT Press

– (1984). *Language Learnability and Language Development*. Cambridge, MA: MIT Press

Pollard, C. and Sag, I.A. (1987). *Information-Based Syntax and Semantics, Volume 1: Fundamentals* (CSLI Lecture Notes Number 13). Stanford: CSLI

– (to appear). *Information-Based Syntax and Semantics, Volume 2: Agreement, Binding and Control* (CSLI Lecture Notes Series). Stanford, CA: CSLI

– (ms.) Unbounded Dependency Constructions. Department of Linguistics, Stanford University

Rizzi, L. (1978). Violations of the Wh-island constraint in Italian and the subjacency condition. *Montreal Working Papers in Linguistics* 11

Sag, I., Gazdar, G., Wasow, T., and Weisler, S. (1985). Coordination and how to distinguish categories. *Natural Language and Linguistic Theory* 3: 117-72

Sells, P. (1985). *Lectures on Contemporary Syntactic Theories: An Introduction to Government-Binding Theory, Generalized Phrase Structure Grammar, and Lexical-Functional Grammar* (CSLI Lecture Notes Number 3). Stanford, CA: CSLI

Shieber, S. (1986). GPSG: A simple reconstruction. Technical Note 384. Menlo Park, CA: SRI International

Uszkoreit, H. (1986). Constraints on order. Report No. CSLI-86-46. Stanford, CA: Stanford University

Wexler, K. and Culicover, P.W. (1980). *Formal Principles of Language Acquisition*. Cambridge, MA: MIT Press

– and Manzini, M.R. (1987). Parameters and learnability in binding theory. In T. Roeper and E. Williams (eds.), *Parameter Setting*. Dordrecht: Reidel

Williams, E.S. (1981). Language acquisition, markedness and phrase structure. In S.L. Tavakolian (ed.), *Language Acquisition and Linguistic Theory*. Cambridge, MA: MIT Press

Zwicky, A.M. (1986). Free word order in GPSG. In *Interfaces* (Working Papers in Linguistics No. 32: Papers by Arnold Zwicky). Columbus, OH: Ohio State University

Comment

Jean Mark Gawron

Fodor's paper, "Learnability of Phrase Structure Grammars," has an important moral which agrees with intuitions that I think a number of GPSGers had in the early days, based on trying to do descriptively adequate work within the framework, rather than on a learnability argument: GPSG is in some sense an unfinished linguistic theory. It owes us at least a theory of markedness, and probably a theory of features. The interest in Fodor's paper lies not just in making an argument to this effect, but in making the argument directly from considerations of learnability.

In addition to arguing that the theory in its current form is inadequate, Fodor presents a revised version, Learnable Phrase Structure Grammar (LPSG): LPSG can be thought of as bearing the relationship to GPSG that REST bears to ST; that is, it is an evolutionary descendant of the original theory. One needs to show that one can do all the good work of the ancestor-theory in the descendant theory (and Fodor takes this assignment seriously); but one doesn't need to do point-by-point comparisons of analyses, as in considering rivals that differ substantially in their formal apparatus and mechanisms of explanation. LPSG is a close relative of GPSG. It is in fact only a slightly constrained version; certainly no new languages are describable in the successor theory; indeed, it may be that the theories are equivalent in both strong and weak capacity. I discuss here only the two sorts of revisions Fodor discusses in this paper: (1) ruling out certain sorts of generalization capturing statements, in particular Feature Co-occurrence Restrictions (FCRs) and language-particular defaults; (2) adding certain others, in particular universal defaults, if not for all features, then for all features whose instantiations are not determined by universal principle.

It may seem at first glance that ruling out FCRs changes the kinds of languages that can be generated, but in fact it only changes the grammars. Any FCR can be captured simply by stipulating all the allowed values in all the rules of the grammar. This may end up multiplying rules, and ultimately losing generalizations, but issues of generative capacity will remain untouched.

Fodor first argues that classical GPSG is unlearnable, specifically because of its treatments of defaults and FCRs. The burden Fodor undertakes in defending LPSG, then, is twofold: (1) she must show that her version of the theory evades the learnability objections she raises against classical GPSG; and (2) she must show that LPSG is still capable of meaningfully capturing linguistic generalizations.

I think that Fodor's argument against the learnability of GPSG is clear and stands on its own; I will have little to say about it. The revisions indicated for LPSG and the fact that they evade those problems follows almost as a corollary of the learnability argument. I will direct my comments here then to one area, examining the relationship of the Subset Principle that Fodor assumes to LPSG; I will argue that her approach raises some questions not just about the status of FCR's in GPSG, but about the status of negative syntactic constraints in general, even putatively universal constraints.

One point that follows directly from what we have said about LPSG thus far bears emphasizing. LPSG requires a theory of features, one that at the very least tells us how to determine from something about a feature what its universal default is, or whether it is universally free, or instantiated by some principle. This appears to presuppose a theory of possible features. But so far no one knows what a general theory of features looks like. There are reasons to grow anxious at the prospect. Languages differ so fantastically in what they morphologically encode, what with categories like evidentiality and noun-class. One might first want to make a distinction between morphological and syntactic features; GKPS motivates a feature VFORM with values like FINITE, but not a feature TENSE, with values like PAST and NON-PAST; though both are morphologically encoded in English, only VFORM directly affects syntactic distribution (one might quibble about sequence of tense phenomena, but one had better have a discourse-based account of that). So one could make a first cut at reducing the task for the feature theory of LPSG by saying that only syntactic features need apply. Even then, with agreement phenomena like Bantu word classes in the picture, there is reason to be sceptical about the prospects for a universal theory. Here is where some appeal to an auxiliary theory of agreement (such as may be in store in HPSG; see Pollard and Sag [forthcoming]) looks appealing.

NEGATIVE CONSTRAINTS

Fodor ultimately proposes five conditions on the selection criterion of a language learner, the first of which is the Subset Principle of Berwick (1985). That Condition differs slightly from the others in that it is stated directly as a condition on the selection of grammars compatible with the available evidence, whereas the others are stated as conditions on what I'll call LANGUAGE SEQUENCES, that is, on the sequences of languages the learner "knows" in the acquisition process.

Fodor's Subset Principle (fully formulated in the fourth section) requires that the selection criterion of a learner never chooses a grammar generating a language which is a proper superset of a language compatible with the available evidence. It is thus a Condition of Minimality: choose the possible grammar which generates the minimal language compatible with evidence. Before turning to Fodor's Condition, I want first to discuss a weaker condition on language sequences, which actually follows from Fodor's Subset Principle. I call this weaker condition the No-Negative-Data Principle: we rule out any language sequence $L_0,...,L_i$, in which L_0 is a superset of L_i. Being a condition on language sequences it is on equal footing with Fodor's C2 through C5, given in the fourth section. All that the No-Negative-Data Principle does is to literally implement the observation that learners have no access to negative evidence. It does not implement Fodor's Subset Principle because it is still possible for a learner to follow the No-Negative-Data Principle and overshoot a target grammar. All the No-Negative-Data Principle says is that once you overshoot there is no way of recovering; it says nothing about how to avoid overshooting. Fodor's Subset Principle is a prescription which, if followed, guarantees that the target grammar will never be overshot. If followed, it also guarantees the No-Negative Data Principle.

The No-Negative Data Principle is also distinct from but closely related to Fodor's C5: it follows from C5:

No-Negative Data: L_i may not be a proper superset of any succeeding L.

C5: L_i must be a subset of L_{i+1}

Now it seems to me that the absence of Negative Data gives us a very good reason to believe in the No-Negative-Data Principle; but whether or not we should believe in C5 is a completely different empirical question.[1] C5 is closely related to the idea that negative constraints aren't learnable, which is in turn related to the idea that there is no negative data (a negative constraint being something filter-like, which rules sentences out). The intuition behind C5 is that at no point in the ACQUISITION PROCESS do we ever twig to the fact that some of what we thought was ruled in is now ruled out. If there are any negative constraints, so this story goes, they must be universal, and what is ruled out by them is ruled out before the acquisition process even begins. All of which MIGHT seem to push us towards the following view, which is roughly the Subset Condition of Manzini and Wexler (1987): when a constraint appears not to be universal, like the injunction not to extract out of finite clauses, then what's really going on is that the constraint is universal but relaxable; and the right sort of positive data can overrule it (like a sentence which exhibits extraction from a finite clause).

But I want to draw a line here. When we adopt something like C5 or Manzini and Wexler's Subset Condition, we have moved from following the consequences of the absence of negative data into making speculative empirical claims. In fact a given constraint might be in force only in some languages without ever having to "relax" it. Here's a very simple example of how. Suppose what's universal is an Implicational Constraint. Suppose, for example, that when a language has limited free word order of the sort Polish does (roughly, you can't scramble outside of a maximal projection), then extraction out of finite clauses is not allowed. We might notate this:

$$\text{Constraint A: } FWO \subset \neg FCE$$

Then suppose there is a Stage A at which the learner hypothesizes some allowable set of word orders (e.g., SOV, VSO, SVO) which is, however, short of free. Then some later stage B, at which free word order is confirmed and adopted. Then there seems to be nothing wrong with hypothesizing a learner who assumes Unbounded (Swedish-type) extraction until she discovers she has a free word order language. On this scenario, the learner first knows Language A, which has free-extraction and almost free word order, and then Language B, which has free word order and extraction bounded in finite-clauses. Language A is NOT a superset of Language B, because it has a more constrained word order than Language B, so this is not a problem for Fodor's Subset Principle. But it IS a problem for C5. In fact, neither language is a subset of the other.[2]

What we have done is to exhibit a way of recovering from a LOCAL overgeneralization which involves no appeal to negative data. The overgeneralization involved one kind of phenomenon. If within the language there are OTHER phenomena that might trigger a conditioned constraint, then a learner can reasonably recover from such an overgeneralization.

This example shows that it is incorrect to argue from the impossibility of recovering from global overgeneralization, the acquisition of a real superset language, to the impossibility of recovering from local generalization. There are logically possible learning paths on which a learner acquires Swedish extraction facts first and Polish extraction facts later, and yet uses no negative data. Establishing such a conditioned constraint, then, would mean curtains for C5, and also, very likely, for the Subset Condition of Manzini and Wexler. Which is only to say that C5 and the Subset Condition of Manzini and Wexler make an empirical claim.

I now want to discuss the relationship of Constraint A to Fodor's Subset Principle. I want to argue that it, too, is incompatible with Constraint A, just as C5 was. But since the Subset Principle is not directly a condition on language sequences, the argument must be slightly different. In particular, I need to argue that the Subset Principle rules out the sort of learning path depicted for my fictional learner of Polish. Here is Fodor's Subset Principle as given in the fourth section:

$L(G_{i+1})$ is not a proper superset of $L(G_j)$ if G_j satisfies all other conditions that G_{i+1} is required to satisfy.

Informally, a learner hypothesizes the most restrictive humanly possible grammar compatible with the evidence.[3]

Let us review the steps. First a speaker learns some subset of the word orders of Polish. She also learns something about extraction, and hypothesizes that Polish has unbounded (Swedish) extraction. Then, on learning that Polish has other word orders, the learner appeals to Constraint A and retreats from the hypothesis of unbounded extraction to the correct hypothesis, no extraction from finite clauses. The problem point here is the point at which the learner hypothesizes unbounded extraction. Obviously, the data the learner has encountered to that point are compatible with finite clause extraction; what Fodor's Subset Principle then requires is that the learner ONLY hypothesize finite-clause extraction. The learner would not be entitled to try out unbounded extraction first because that is a less restrictive option. So if Fodor is right, there is no place in Universal Grammar for principles like A. More precisely, the Subset Principle doesn't rule them out. It just renders them useless. By the time Fodor's learner finds out Polish has free word order, she is in exactly the same state as my learner, and without the benefit of A.

Again, the fact that there is no negative data doesn't entail Fodor's Subset Principle. Whether or not there are principles like A above is an empirical question. If it turned out that at some point in learning Polish, children produced errors of overgenerous extraction, Fodor's Subset Principle would be in trouble.

Fodor's Subset Principle, along with C5, thus has a different character from Principles like C2, C3, and the No-Negative-data Principle. The latter Principles all seem fairly uncontroversial. The Subset Principle, on the other hand, makes a strong empirical claim. Moreover, Fodor proposes a theory, LPSG, which appears to be compatible with it. Support for the Subset Principle thus becomes support for LPSG.

I think the issue about Constraint A helps make clearer exactly what sort of enterprise Fodor is engaged in. Recall that LPSG dispenses with FCRs; note that Constraint A illustrates a way in which an FCR might be "acquired" in some sense, because we might implement no-finite-clause extraction in just the way GKPS would, with an FCR that outlaws nodes with all the offending features. It wouldn't be a language-particular FCR. It would be a universal FCR, only conditioned by an independent feature of the language. I take it that if the above conditioned constraint were universal, it would be pretty interesting, and we would want our theories to capture it somehow. But given the particular way I've cast the example, the theoretical revision is considerably greater than what Fodor proposes in LPSG; now GPSG would have to employ a very new kind of implicational constraint. If, in order to make FCRs learnable, we have to pay this price, we might as well adopt a different theory altogether. Part of the appeal of Fodor's proposal is that she proposes a revision which differs minimally from classical GPSG: eliminate FCRs. Some such revision is unquestionably due, because while one can IMAGINE ways to preserve both FCRs and learnability (through Constraints like A), some enhancement of the original theory seems to be required.

Although the particulars of Constraint A involve making reference to a global language property like free word order, the logic of the argument simply involves correlating a positive property with a negative property through an implicational constraint. I call free word order a positive property because it says something about what sorts of sentences are in, but nothing about what sorts are out. I call finite-clause extraction a negative property because it clearly rules certain sorts of sentences out. Let us call any constraint that connects a positive property with a negative property an Exclusionary Constraint. It appears as if Fodor's Subset Condition entails that no Exclusionary Constraints play a role in acquisition.

What about the trivial case of an Exclusionary Constraint? That is, what about a Universal Negative Constraint? There is, I think, no logical reason why Fodor needs to rule such things out. Suppose, for example, that Subjacency, in some form like that assumed in Chomsky (1981), were a universal. Then learners could employ Subjacency and obey the Subset Condition simply by never considering grammars that violated Subjacency among those compatible with available evidence.

But now a different question arises. If you believe in the Subset Principle, what's the use of Subjacency?[4] For the duration of the discussion, let's assume both the Subset Principle and the universality of Subjacency. In that case, Subjacency makes no predictions about the language sequences learners go through. With or without Subjacency being hard-wired into their heads, learners never hypothesize grammars that violate it, because they never encounter violations, and because they always postulate minimal grammars.

Can Subjacency do any work for our theory of acquisition, then? One possibility is that it may reduce the computational load of the learner who tries to APPLY the Subset Principle; there are fewer possible grammars to consider and so it ought to be easier to decide which is the minimal grammar compatible with the available evidence. This, however, seems elusive. It is far from obvious that reducing the set of grammars necessarily makes finding the smallest grammar computationally simpler. It does if one's only algorithm is searching down a list; but that had better not be the algorithm. For example, if one's phrase-structure formalism allows rules that give fully instantiated trees, then there is a fairly simple procedure for finding the minimal grammar for a given body of data, as Fodor points out in the fourth section. The procedure in LPSG appears to be only slightly more complicated. Adding or subtracting Subjacency to such a formalism does not make a bit of difference for computing minimality. Thus, specifically with regard to the theory which Fodor is urging on us here, it is not clear what work a principle like Subjacency could be doing.

The fact is that for Fodor's learner "ungrammatical" might just as well be synonymous with "I haven't heard it yet." Negative syntactic principles, universal or not, are for all practical purposes entirely dispensable. One might simply conclude that the status of Subjacency will be decided by cross-linguistic survey; if it turns out that all languages obey it, then it must be hard-wired in. But it seems to me that someone who believes in the Subset Principle need not be persuaded by this discovery. Sentences that violate Subjacency are hard to produce and hard to understand; the few odd instances that a learner might encounter might never reach the threshhold necessary for incorporation into the grammar. Subjacency might be a fact about all human languages – indeed a fact about the acquired grammars of all human languages – but still be entirely epiphenomenal!

The bite of the argument here rests on having available a linguistically interesting theory for which it can be demonstrated that a negative constraint makes absolutely no difference in acquisition, and thus that it need have no specific cognitive status (except perhaps as describing constructions hard to process). The question now becomes, what is the status of negative syntactic constraints in general? Typically, linguists have regarded negative constraints as interesting only to the extent that they predict a variety of interesting correlated phenomena. For instance, the C-command condition on pronoun Binding becomes more interesting when it can be related to Crossover violations, as illustrated by pairs of sentences like (1):

(1)   (a) He saw John's mother.
      (b) Whose mother did he see?

In (1a) the pronoun cannot be understood as referring to *John*; and in (1b) it cannot be understood as referring to the same person as *whose*, yielding the interpretation, for which x did x see x's mother? In contrast, the analogous co-indexings are possible in (2):

(2)   (a) John saw his mother.
      (b) Who saw his mother?

Such facts are striking and interesting and demand some explanation. It's also hard to see how they would be acquired. Nor, if they are indeed universal, is there any obvious reason to think that violations would be difficult to understand or process. Nor is it obvious how a theory which had a default of disjoint reference, analogous to Fodor's minus default for SLASH, could be made to work.

In sum, one can easily see how extraction constraints would fall out of a system that starts with the default: don't extract. But it is not easy to see how the method would carry over to anaphoric relations. So there may be an important difference between putative universal negative constraints like Subjacency and putative negative constraints like the C-command condition on anaphoric relations. It is tempting to try to capture the difference in terms of the apparatus of LPSG; perhaps there are no negative constraints statable in terms of the rule apparatus of LPSG, that is, in terms of tree descriptions consisting of dominance relations and syntactic feature-specifications. But perhaps there are other modules of a grammar where negative constraints do play a role. Perhaps the most interesting thing about this paper is that it raises unsettling questions about the status of negative constraints in general.

NOTES

1 The No-Negative-Data Principle is extremely weak, and is not intended to be interesting. To see how weak, note that it follows from Fodor's condition C3 and a slightly generalized form of C2. That is, it follows simply from excluding spurious grammar changes and requiring that all the data viewed thus far be incorporated into the current hypothesis. The argument is as follows. Let us consider the case of a learner with Grammar G_0 with language L_0. Let us assume that no revision of G_0 can be occasioned except by an input I_1 which is not in L_0 (this is just Fodor's Condition C3). We also assume that the revised Grammar G_1 has language L_1 which includes I. This is just Fodor's Condition C2.

But now we almost have the No-Negative-Data Principle. We have (i) I_1 is not in L_0 (C3) and (ii) I_1 is in L_1 (C2).

Therefore L_0 cannot be a superset of L_1. Now what is still in principle possible is that some later grammar change might lead us to throw out I_1. But remember I_1 is real input! That is, it wasn't a part of the language inferred by some overgeneralization. We assumed it was really encountered. It would be a strange learning theory indeed that allowed us to throw out actual sentences of the language in order to converge on the right Grammar. So we can derive the No-Negative-Data Principle with a generalization of Fodor's C2: (C2′) All grammar changing inputs $I_1,...,I_n$ are in L_n.

2 Constraint A appears to be an example of what Fodor and Crain (in press) call an Octopus Parameter.

3 There is another problem lurking here that may be of interest. The Subset Principle only definitively solves the problem of overgeneralization if in fact there is a unique minimal grammar compatible with the evidence. And that of course will be true if our grammar formalism allows us a way to generate EXACTLY the set of sentences thus far seen. But suppose our grammar formalism doesn't provide a way of generating EXACTLY the evidence thus far; suppose all available compatible grammars generate not just the data seen thus far, but also a little extra; then there remains the possibility that there are a number of minimal grammars, G. Each G would be minimal in the sense that there is no possible GRAMMAR G_i which generates a language L_i which both includes all the evidence and is a subset of $L(G)$. Each minimal G would generate all the evidence thus far seen plus a little "generalization" increment. Now of course the original problem has crept in through the back door again. Since if we just arbitrarily choose among these minimal grammars, we may choose incorrectly and let in something which should be kept out. My conjecture is that LPSG, because it comes so close to giving us fully instantiated trees, will not run into this problem, but it is something that remains to be shown.

4 The choice of Subjacency here is not entirely accidental. If we think of
   Subjacency as a principle which excludes single-movement extractions
   that cross two "bounding" nodes, then it is a principle which is extremely
   difficult, if not impossible, to state in GPSG (or LPSG). There are, however,
   various ways to get many of the effects of Subjacency, for example by
   making Relative Clause sentence nodes barriers to slash passing.

REFERENCES

Berwick, R.C. (1985). *The Acquisition of Syntactic Knowledge*. Cambridge, MA:
    MIT Press
Wexler, K. and Manzini, M. (1987). Parameters and learnability in binding
    theory. In T. Roeper and E. Williams (eds.), *Parameter Setting*. Dordrecht:
    Reidel

CHAPTER TWO

Dynamic Categorial Grammar

Richard T. Oehrle*

INTRODUCTION

From the point of view adopted here, categorial grammar is a general framework for linguistic analysis which is based on the idea that the properties of a complex linguistic expression can be represented as the application of a function to appropriate arguments – namely, the properties of the expression's component parts. Abstractly, then, categorial grammar has affinities with theories of functionality such as the λ-calculus, with universal algebra, and with logic. The linguistic interest of this point of view derives from the fact that it provides an elegant framework in which to investigate what might be called the problem of *generalized compositionality*: the relation between the properties of a complex expression in a number of dimensions – such as syntax, interpretation, phonology – to the corresponding properties of the expression's component parts and its mode of composition.

This paper begins with a brief review of some general properties of functions, emphasizing the existence of natural relations among functions which are of a very general character. It is possible to think of these relations as forming the basis of rules of "type-shifting" of various kinds, rules which allow "naturally-related" functions to be identified in ways of interest to grammatical analysis. We then introduce the notion of a categorial system and show how one system of this type – the Associative Syntactic Calculus **L** (Lambek 1958) – yields as theorems analogues of a number of the natural relations among functions already introduced. **L** has two features of special interest in grammatical applications.

First, **L** is decidable, which means that given an initial type-assignment which assigns a finite number of types to each element of the vocabulary *V* over which the language is characterized, it is possible to decide for any string s over V (that is to say, any element of V^+) and any type t, whether or not s is paired with t. For computational purposes, decidability is a very reassuring notion. Below I will sketch a proof (due to Lambek, who realized the affinity of this problem with problems in logic successfully resolved by Gentzen) of the decidability theorem of **L**.

The second attractive feature of **L**, originally observed by Buszkowski, is structural completeness, a strong form of associativity. Since **L** is associative, if there is a proof in **L** that a string s is assignable to a type t on a particular bracketing, then s is assignable to t on every well-formed bracketing. Structural completeness, the strengthened form of associativity, depends on the notion of an *f-structure*, namely, a well-formed bracketing in which each non-atomic constituent c contains a unique designated immediate constituent (called the *functor* of c). Structural completeness requires that if a string s is assignable to t, then it is assignable to t not just relative to any well-formed bracketing over s, but relative to any well-formed f-structure over s. Thus, structural completeness imposes a coherence condition that is not found in general in associative systems. A corollary, of relevance to linguistic questions involving constituency, is the fact that if s is assignable to a product-free type (a notion to be clarified below), then any connected non-empty substring of s is assignable to a product-free type. The consequences of structural completeness bear on a number of empirical linguistic issues. One of these involves the wide-ranging, almost cross-categorial, freedom of co-ordination in languages such as English. Moreover, the syntactic flexibility of **L** suggests that it provides a particularly useful framework in which to investigate natural language properties like the relation of intonational phrasing to other grammatical structures, relations which do not seem to respect the standard constituent structure of many alternative frameworks and thus are taken to be problematic. Finally, the property of structural completeness is one which can be beneficially exploited for parsing purposes. For example, if there is an analysis which assigns a string s to type t, then there are certain normal-form grammatical analyses particularly conducive to left-to-right incremental parsing.

In what follows, a review of type-shifting relations provides the setting for a description of the properties of **L**, leading up to a review of the proofs of **L**'s decidability and structural completeness and a discussion of some of the connections between **L** and other categorial systems. I then turn to some of the applications of these systems to the syntactic analysis of natural language. A sketch of some results of Michael Moortgat (1988, 1989), concerning natural language parsing within the general framework of L, vindicates to some small extent the occurrence of the word "dynamic" in the title. The last two sections address the integration of semantic and phonological information into the framework of categorial systems.

FUNCTIONS

A *function* $f : A \rightarrow B$ with *domain* A and *co-domain* B assigns to each element a in A a unique element $f(a)$ in B. To indicate the action of f on a single element in A, we write $f : a \mapsto f(a)$. If two functions $f : A \rightarrow B$ and $g : A \rightarrow B$ are such that $f(a) = g(a)$ for every a in A, we regard f and g as the same function. (Note that two distinct procedures can compute the same function, however, so the individuation of procedures is finer than the individuation of functions.) It is useful at times to represent functions using the notation of the lambda calculus: we write $(\lambda x.f(x))$ for f; the following terms represent the value assigned to a by $f : (\lambda x.f(x))(a) = [x/a]f(x) = f(a)$. Here, $[x/a]f(x)$ represents the result of replacing every free occurrence of x in $f(x)$ by a. For a less casual account, see Hindley & Seldin, 1986.

There are many natural relations among functions. For example, for any function $f : A \rightarrow B$, there is a corresponding function $f^* : Pow(A) \rightarrow Pow(B)$ mapping elements of the power set of A to elements of the power set of B in such a way that if M is any subset of A, then $f^*(M) = \{b : \text{for some element } m \in M , f(m) = b\}$. (The relation between f and f^* has a connection with the natural language contrast between singular and plural: if we regard the interpretation N' of a singular count noun N as a function from individuals to truth values – that is, as a function of type $< e,t >$ in Montague's type system – then N'^* is a function from sets of individuals to sets of truth values. Thus we might define the interpretation $(P(N))'$ of the plural $P(N)$ of N as mapping a set x of individuals to 1 if and only if both $N^*(x) = \{1\}$ and x is not a singleton.) A number of such natural relations among functions are relevant to what follows. Here are brief characterizations of some of them. (For terminology and discussion, see MacLane & Birkhoff 1967, especially Chapter 1, section 5.)

Functional composition

Two functions $g : A \rightarrow B$ and $f : B \rightarrow C$ uniquely determine the composite function $f \circ g : A \rightarrow C$, whose action is determined by the rule $(f \circ g)(a) = f(g(a))$ – apply f to the result of applying g. Note that we could represent the composition of g and f as $\lambda x.f(g(x))$.

Currying

Let B^A represent the set of all functions with domain A and co-domain B and let $S \times T$ represent the Cartesian product of S and T, the set of all ordered pairs $< s,t >$ whose first member s is an element of S and whose second element t is an element of T. Associated with any Cartesian product $S \times T$ there are projection functions $p_1 : < s,t > \mapsto s$ and $p_2 : < s,t > \mapsto t$. Now, there are bijections (one-to-one correspondences) between the three function sets

$$(B^S)^T \cong B^{S \times T} \cong (B^T)^S$$

based on the following identities:

$$\lambda x.(\lambda y.f(x)(y))(t)(s) = \lambda z.f(p_2(z))(p_1(z))(< s,t >) = \lambda y.(\lambda x.f(x)(y))(s)(t)$$

Note that the first case is related to the third by permuting the lambda-operators to the left of the function symbol as well as the arguments t and s. The content of these equivalences is that a function with two arguments (belonging, say, to the function set $B^{S \times T}$ may be identified with a function which acts on elements from either set underlying the Cartesian product and yields a function mapping elements from the other set underlying the Cartesian product to elements of B. Although we have stated these equivalences in terms which factor functions acting on pairs of arguments into functions which act on one argument at a time, an easy inductive argument demonstrates comparable equivalences involving k-fold Cartesian products (for $k \geq 2$).

Lifting

Let a be a member of A and let f be an arbitrarily-chosen member of the function set B^A. There is exactly one function $a^* : B^A \to B$ such that $a^*(f) = f(a)$, for all $f \in B^A$. Thus, we can embed (or "lift") A into the higher order type B^{B^A}. Lifting provides justification for allowing the functor-argument relation to be inverted. A simple counting argument shows that there is in general no inverse process of "lowering": since when A is non-empty and B has more than one member there are more functions $f : B^A \to B$ than there are elements in the set A, there can certainly be no unique element in A for each function $f : B^A \to B$.

Co-variant division

Given a function $t : S \to T$, any function $r : R \to S$, determines the composite function $t \circ r : R \to T$.

Contra-variant division

Given a function $t : S \to T$, any function $u : T \to U$ determines the composite function $u \circ t : S \to U$.

Remark

This discussion of such "natural" relations among functions has been based on semantical considerations related to the criteria by which functions are standardly individuated. The same set of relations may also be studied from a syntactical, or proof-theoretic, perspective – for example, from the general point of view of Cartesian closed categories (Lambek and Scott 1986).

CATEGORIAL SYSTEMS

Suppose we are given a vocabulary V consisting of a finite set of elements $v_1,\ldots,v_k$. We wish to assign each element v in V to a set of categories in a way that will determine its combinatorial properties. This requires a set of types and a set of rules stating how expressions assigned to various types may combine with one another.

Types

We begin with a set Cat of primitive types and a set $\{/,\backslash,\cdot\}$ containing three binary operation symbols. The set Cat^* consisting of the full set of types is defined recursively as the least set such that

(1) Cat is a subset of Cat^*;
(2) if x and y are members of Cat^*, so are (x/y), $(y\backslash x)$, and $(x\cdot y)$.

A set like Cat^* defined in this way relative to a set Ω of operation symbols (here $\{/,\backslash,\cdot\}$) and a basic set Σ (here Cat) is sometimes called the *free word-algebra* generated by Ω over Σ.

Initial type-assignment: lexical arrows

Let $\tau : V \to Pow(Cat^*)$ be a function which assigns to each $v \in V$ a

non-empty finite set of elements in *Cat**. We regard this function as
fixing the lexical types of V. If v is in V and x is in $\tau(v)$, we write $v \to x$.

Arrows

Our ultimate goal is to extend this initial type assignment over V to a
type assignment to all the members of the set V^+ of finite strings of
elements drawn from V, so that we can characterize the set of types
assigned to any such string. To do this, we establish a type calculus
which defines a relation of *assignability* between sequences of types
and individual types. If a sequence of types $t_1 \ldots t_k$ is assignable to t, we
write $t_1 \ldots t_k \to t$. We interpret this relation relative to V^+ as follows: if
$v_1 \ldots v_k$ is a sequence of words such that $v_i \to t_i$, $1 \le i \le k$, and $t_1 \ldots t_k \to t$
is valid in the type calculus, then $v_1 \ldots v_k \to t$. Somewhat more ab-
stractly, but perhaps more perspicuously, a lexical type assignment
function $\tau : V \to Pow(Cat^*)$, and a type calculus defining a relation on
$Cat^{*+} \times Cat^*$ together determine a unique relation on $V^+ \times Cat^*$. (It is
perhaps worth noting that this step does not depend at all on the
particular properties of the set of operation symbols $\{/, \backslash, \cdot\}$.)

L

Let X be any non-empty set of primitive types. The Associative
Lambek system **L** (perhaps, since our characterization depends on X,
we should say **L[X]**) has the following structure (Lambek 1958, 1988).
The set of types is the free word-algebra over X generated by the three
binary type-forming operators "$/$" and "$\backslash$" and "$\cdot$." The set of valid
arrows is defined by the following postulates:

$A1$ $\qquad\qquad\qquad\qquad\qquad x \to x$

$A2$ $\quad (x \cdot y) \cdot z \underset{c}{\to} x \cdot (y \cdot z)$ $\qquad\qquad A2'$ $\quad x \cdot (y \cdot z) \to (x \cdot y) \cdot z$

$R1 \qquad \dfrac{x \cdot y \to z}{x \to z/y}$ $\qquad\qquad R1' \qquad \dfrac{x \cdot y \to z}{y \to x \backslash z}$

$R2 \qquad \dfrac{x \to z/y}{x \cdot y \to z}$ $\qquad\qquad R2' \qquad \dfrac{y \to x \backslash z}{x \cdot y \to z}$

$R3 \qquad\qquad\qquad \dfrac{x \to y \qquad y \to z}{x \to z}$

Axiom $A1$ is the identity arrow. Axioms $A2$ and $A2'$ assert the associativity of the product operator $\cdot$. The inference rules $R1$, $R1'$, $R2$, and $R2'$ relate the product operator to the slash $/$ and the backslash $\backslash$ operators, in a way that implicitly defines the properties of the slash and backslash. $R3$ asserts the transitivity of $\rightarrow$.

The intuitive semantics for this system is that if expression $e_1 \rightarrow x$ and expression $e_2 \rightarrow y$, then the concatenation $e_1 \frown e_2 \rightarrow x{\cdot}y$; moreover, if e_1 is such that $e_1 \frown e_2 \rightarrow z$ for every expression e_2 of type y, then $e_1 \rightarrow z/y$; similarly for the backslash $\backslash$. On this interpretation (related to residuated algebraic systems (Lambek 1958; Buszkowski 1986; Došen 1985), it is easy to see that all of the above axioms and inference rules are true. For example, if $e_1 \rightarrow x$ and $xy \rightarrow z$, then for any e_2 such that $e_2 \rightarrow y$, we have (by the second premise) $e_1 \frown e_2 \rightarrow z$, and hence (by the interpretation of $/$), $e_1 \rightarrow z/y$.

Note that in the resulting grammatical logic, the arrows $(x/y){\cdot}y \rightarrow x$ and $y{\cdot}(y\backslash x) \rightarrow x$ are valid, and hence it makes sense to think of the type x/y as the type of a functor with domain y and co-domain x which combines with an expression of its domain-type y to its right to form an expression of its co-domain type x and similarly, to think of the type $y\backslash x$ as the type of a functor with domain y and co-domain x which combines with an expression of its domain-type y to its left to form an expression of its co-domain type x. On this interpretation, the slash and backslash operators encode information about the domain category and co-domain category of a functor, as well as information regarding how a functor combines with appropriate arguments. Since there are other possible relations between this information and the parts of the symbols x/y and $y\backslash x$, there are obviously other possible conventions for interpreting them. On one alternative convention (Steedman 1987, 1988), the left-most symbol denotes the co-domain of a functor, the slash or backslash denotes the direction in which the argument of the functor is to be found, and the last symbol denotes the domain. Thus, on this convention, the rules of functional application take the form $(x/y){\cdot}y \rightarrow_* x$ and $y{\cdot}(x\backslash y) \rightarrow_* x$, whose differences from the conventions codified in rules $R1$, $R1'$, $R2$, and $R2'$ are emphasized by using $\rightarrow_*$ in place of $\rightarrow$. There is another alternative convention (Moortgat 1988a) on which the first symbol represents the domain of a functor, the slash or backslash represents the direction in which the argument is to be found, and the last symbol represents the co-domain. On this convention, the rules of functional application take still a different form: $(x/y){\cdot}x \rightarrow^* y$ and $x{\cdot}(x\backslash y) \rightarrow^* y$. In addition, other authors, such as Richard Montague (1974), have used category symbols such as x/y in a way that requires an expression of this type to combine with an expression of type y to form an expression of type

x, but is nevertheless completely neutral about the form of the resulting expression. It is apparent, then, that the type-forming operators have no intrinsic content, but depend for their interpretation on a context in which the notion of valid arrow is defined. In what follows, we use the operators "/" and "\\" in a way that conforms to the properties of the above postulates.

Viewed as a deductive system, **L** yields a number of interesting theorems. We mention a few of these below, together with proofs in a few cases.

R-Splitting: $x \to (x \cdot y)/y$

$$\frac{x \cdot y \to x \cdot y \quad A1}{x \to (x \cdot y)/y \quad R1}$$

L-Splitting: $y \to x\backslash(x \cdot y)$

R-Application: $(z/y) \cdot y \to z$

$$\frac{z/y \to z/y \quad A1}{(z/y) \cdot y \to z \quad R2}$$

L-Application: $y \cdot (y\backslash z) \to z$

R-Lifting: $y \to (z/y)\backslash z$

$$\frac{(z/y) \cdot y \to z \quad \text{proof of R–Application}}{y \to (z/y)\backslash z \quad R1'}$$

L-Lifting: $y \to z/(y\backslash z)$

R-Composition: $(z/y) \cdot (y/x) \to z/x$

$$\frac{\dfrac{y/x \to y/x \quad \dfrac{z/y \to z/y \quad A1}{(z/y) \cdot y \to z} \, A1, R2}{\dfrac{(y/x) \cdot x \to y \quad y \to (z/y)\backslash z}{(y/x) \cdot x \to (z/y)\backslash z} \, R2, R1'}{\dfrac{\dfrac{((z/y) \cdot (y/x)) \cdot x \to (z/y) \cdot ((y/x) \cdot x) \quad (z/y) \cdot ((y/x) \cdot x) \to z}{((z/y) \cdot (y/x)) \cdot x \to z}}{(z/y) \cdot (y/x) \to z/x} \, R1}$$

Labels on the right: $R3$; $A2, R2'$

L-Composition: $(x\backslash y) \cdot (y\backslash z) \to x\backslash z$

R-Covariant Division: $z/y \to (z/x)/(y/x)$

L-Covariant Division: $y\backslash z \to (x\backslash y)\backslash(x\backslash z)$

Currying: $x\backslash(y/z) \leftrightarrow (x\backslash y)/z$

Slash-Dot Conversion: $(x/y)/z \leftrightarrow x/(z \cdot y)$; $z\backslash(y\backslash x) \leftrightarrow (y \cdot z)\backslash x$

R-Contravariant Division: $x/y \to (z/x)\backslash(z/y)$

L-Contravariant Division: $y\backslash x \to (y\backslash z)/(x\backslash z)$

There are also derived rules of inference. Here are two rules justifying forms of substitution.

$$R4 \quad \frac{x \to x' \qquad\qquad y \to y'}{x \cdot y \to x' \cdot y'} \qquad R5 \quad \frac{x \to x' \qquad\qquad y \to y'}{x/y' \to x'/y}$$

Remark. The names given to the above theorems provide mnemonic relations to the natural relations among functions discussed above in section 2. The valid arrows of **L** thus correspond to a type-shifting calculus: the language of the calculus is the free algebra generated by the operations $/$, $\backslash$, $\cdot$ over the set of primitive types; the calculus admits identity and associativity of the product operator (Axioms A1 and A2); and the calculus is closed under inference rules corresponding to (peripheral) abstraction (R1, R1$'$), functional application (R2, R2$'$), and composition (R3). The affinities of this system with variants of the λ-calculus have been exploited in studies of models of **L** and related systems (Buszkowski 1987; van Benthem 1988a). For connections with higher-order logic and category theory, see Lambek (1988, 1989), Lambek & Scott (1986), and van Benthem (1987).

L is decidable

A categorial system **C** is said to be *decidable* if it can be determined in an effective way whether relative to the axioms and inference rules of **C**, a finite string of elements is associated with any given type. Given the requirement that each element of the vocabulary is initially assigned a finite, non-empty set of types, and the fact that any finite sequence of vocabulary elements can be bracketed in only finitely many ways, then there are only finitely many bracketed type-structures which have to be examined. In categorial systems that only have rules (like Application) which have fewer operator symbols on the right of the arrow than they do on the left, decidability is easy to show: any application of a rule yields a simpler problem, hence it is only necessary to examine all the finitely-many possible applications of our rules and we'll find that either no rule is applicable or we will be given a set of simpler problems to solve – simpler in the sense that fewer type-forming connectives are involved. If we are able in this way to reduce our original problem to a set of problems in which we only have to prove axioms, we're done. If not, the arrow in question is invalid.

In the system **L**, however, this kind of reasoning is not enough, for **L** admits complexity-increasing rules (such as the various forms of Lifting and Division). Adapting proof-theoretic techniques of Gentzen, however, Lambek (1958) demonstrated the decidability of **L**. The proof goes in easy stages.

First, Lambek characterizes a calculus **LG** which is defined over the same language as **L**. As in Gentzen-style axiomatizations of logical calculi, for each binary operator, there are rules in **LG** governing the introduction of a single occurrence of the operator on the left of the arrow and on the right. It is obvious that **LG** is decidable: since the identity arrow is the only axiom and each rule of inference introduces exactly one operator, given any arrow, we may examine the results of applying each of the inference rules backwards to each of the possible bracketings on the left of the arrow, always attempting to remove the innermost operator. For each bracketing, this procedure either leads to a simpler problem (because the problem contains fewer connectives) or it halts: applying the procedure repeatedly either yields a set of problems in which only axioms occur (thus providing us with a proof of our original problem) or yields a set of problems in which no connective can be removed (either because there are none or because the innermost connective does not satisfy the criteria for removability). Thus, if there is a proof of a given arrow, we can find it. And by exhausting the (finitely many) possible proofs we can show that no proof exists. Thus, **LG** is decidable.

Second, it must be shown that the valid arrows of **L** and the valid arrows of **LG** coincide. This can be shown straightforwardly for a system which apparently extends **LG** by adding a new rule of inference (the *Cut* rule) corresponding to rule R3 (and yielding a system that we call **LG + Cut**). What remains to be shown, then, is the equivalence of **LG** and **LG + Cut**. The next section describes the different stages of this proof in more detail, closely following Lambek's original presentation.

LG

LG is a Gentzen-style formulation of **L**: for each type-forming operator, we have a pair of inference rules, one introducing the operator on the left of an arrow, and one introducing the operator on the right of an arrow. We begin with a definition:

Definition. The sequent $x_1, x_2, x_3, \ldots, x_n \to y$ stands for

$$(\ldots((x_1 x_2)x_3)\ldots x_n) \to y$$

Because of associativity in **L**, if **x** is any other bracketing of $x_1 x_2 x_3 \ldots x_n$, **x** $\to (\ldots((x_1 x_2)x_3)\ldots x_n)$. Hence the above sequent is equivalent to **x** $\to y$. In the rules below, capital letters P, Q, T, U, and V denote sequences of types. The letters U and V may denote the empty sequence, but P, Q, and T will always be taken to denote non-empty sequences of types. If U and V are both sequences of types, we use "U, V" to denote the sequence resulting by extending U by V (that is, if U is a k-place sequence and V is an m-place sequence, U, V is the $k + m$-place sequence defined in the obvious way: the k types of U occupy the first k places of U, V and the m types of U occupy the next m places).

G1 $\qquad\qquad\qquad\qquad x \to x$

G2 $\quad \dfrac{T, y \to x}{T \to x/y}$ $\qquad\qquad$ G2′ $\quad \dfrac{y, T \to x}{T \to y \setminus x}$

G3 $\quad \dfrac{T \to y \qquad U, x, V \to z}{U, x/y, T, V \to z}$ $\qquad$ G3′ $\quad \dfrac{T \to y \qquad U, x, V \to z}{U, T, y \setminus x, V \to z}$

G4 $\quad \dfrac{U, x, y, V \to z}{U, x \cdot y, V \to z}$

G5 $\quad \dfrac{P \to x \qquad Q \to y}{P, Q \to x \cdot y}$

LG ⊂ *L*

We want to show that any arrow valid in **LG** is valid in **L**. Four of the five cases to be checked are immediate:

- G1 is identical with A1.

- G2 corresponds to R1; G2′ corresponds to R1′.
- G4 is obvious from the meaning of "sequent."
- G5 corresponds to the derived inference rule R4.

To prove the remaining case – G3 (and its symmetric dual G3′) – consider first the case in which U and V are empty: if we replace T by some product t of its terms, then G3 takes the form: if $t \to y$ and $x \to z$, then $(x/y), t \to z$. Here is a proof of this fact in **L**:

$$\frac{\dfrac{x \to z \qquad\qquad t \to y}{x/y \to z/t} \quad R5}{(x/y) \cdot t \to z} \quad R2$$

If U is empty and V is not, replace V by a product v of its terms, in which case we can show:

$$\frac{\dfrac{xv \to z}{x \to z/v} \quad R2 \qquad\qquad\qquad\qquad t \to y}{\dfrac{(x/y) \cdot t \to z/v \quad \text{(as above)}}{((x/y) \cdot t) \cdot v \to z} \qquad R2}$$

The two remaining cases in which U is not empty can be treated similarly.

$$\mathbf{L} \subset \mathbf{LG} + Cut$$

Now we examine the equivalence of **L** and **LG** in the opposite direction. We first consider an apparently simpler problem, the equivalence of **L** and **LG + Cut**, where the latter is the system obtained from **LG** by adding the so-called **Cut** rule:

$$\frac{T \to x \quad U, x, V \to y}{U, T, V \to y}$$

Fact: any arrow valid in **L** is an arrow valid in **LG + Cut**.
- A1 is identical to G1.
- R3 is a special case of Cut, where U and V are empty.
- Here are proofs of A2, R1, and R2:

proof of A2:

$$\frac{\dfrac{y \to y}{x \to x \qquad \dfrac{}{y, z \to y \cdot z}} \qquad z \to z}{\begin{array}{l} x, y, z \to x \cdot (y \cdot z) \\ \hline x \cdot y, z \to x \cdot (y \cdot z) \\ \hline (x \cdot y) \cdot z \to x \cdot (y \cdot z) \end{array}} \begin{array}{l} G5 \\ G5 \\ G4 \\ G4 \end{array}$$

proof of R1:

$$\frac{\dfrac{x \to x \qquad y \to y}{x, y \to x \cdot y \ G5}}{x \to (x \cdot y)/y \ G2} \qquad \dfrac{y \to y \qquad x \cdot y \to z}{(x \cdot y)/y, y \to z \ G4}$$
$$\frac{x, y \to z \ \text{Cut}}{x \to z/y \ G2}$$

proof of R2:

$$\frac{x \to z/y \qquad \qquad \dfrac{y \to y \qquad \dfrac{\dfrac{y \to y}{z/y, y \to z \ G3} \quad z \to z}{(z/y) \cdot y \to z \ G4}}{}}{x, y \to (z/y) \cdot y \ G5}$$
$$\frac{x, y \to z \ \text{Cut}}{x \cdot y \to z \ G4}$$

The proofs of A2′, R1′, and R2′ are dual to these.

$$LG = LG + Cut$$

It remains to show that **LG** and **LG + Cut** are themselves equivalent. This is not at all obvious, but is nevertheless a consequence of the following theorem:

Cut-Elimination Theorem (Lambek-Gentzen): for any proof in **LG + Cut**, there is a (Cut-free) proof in **LG**.

The proof goes by reduction of the degree of the Cut. We begin by defining the *degree of a category* as the number of occurrences of the operators $\cdot, \backslash, /$ it contains. (For any category C, call this $deg(C)$.) The *degree of a sequence of categories* $T = t_1 \ldots t_k$ is $\sum_{i=1}^{k} deg(t_i)$, the sum of the degrees of the elements of the sequence. Now, the **Cut** rule has the form:

$$\frac{T \to x \qquad U, x, V \to y}{U; T, V \to y}$$

The *degree of any instantiation of Cut* is the sum:

$$\deg(T) + \deg(U) + \deg(V) + \deg(x) + \deg(y)$$

The basic strategy of the proof of the theorem is to show that any proof in **LG + Cut** which contains an application of Cut can be replaced by a proof which either eliminates the application of Cut in question or replaces it by an application of Cut with a lesser degree. If this degree is still positive, the proof shows that this new application can itself be either eliminated or replaced with an application of Cut of still lesser degree, and so on. At each step, we have the choice of elimination of the Cut or replacement of the Cut with a Cut inference of lesser degree. Since the degree of a Cut is always a finite, positive integer, it isn't possible to keep replacing a given Cut with Cuts of lesser degree forever. Thus, the given Cut and all its replacements must eventually be eliminated.

The actual proof examines a number of cases, not necessarily distinct, which collectively exhaust all the possible ways in which an application of Cut can be invoked.

Case 1: $T \rightarrow x$ is an instance of G1

Then $T = x$ and we have:

$$\frac{x \rightarrow x \qquad U, x, V \rightarrow y}{U, x, V \rightarrow y} \text{ Cut}$$

But the conclusion is already a premise, so such an application of Cut can be eliminated.

Case 2: $U, x, V \rightarrow y$ is an instance of G1

Then U and V are empty and $x = y$. Then the conclusion $U, T, V \rightarrow y$ is identical to the premise $T \rightarrow y$.

(Note that if neither of these first two cases is applicable to a given instance of Cut, then both premises must be derivable in **LG + Cut**.)

Case 3

The last step in the proof of $T \rightarrow x$ uses one of rules G2–G5, but does not introduce the main connective of x. Therefore, $T \rightarrow x$ is inferred by G3, G3', or G4 from one or two sequents, one of which has the form $T' \rightarrow x$, with degree(T') < degree(T). The Cut inference

$$\frac{T' \rightarrow x \qquad U, x, V \rightarrow y}{U, T', V \rightarrow y} \text{ Cut}$$

has smaller degree than the given Cut inference. And together with whichever rule was involved in inferring $T \to x$ from $T' \to x$ and possibly another premise can be invoked to derive $U, T, V \to x$ from $U, T', V \to x$.

Example

Suppose we have the following proof schema:

$$\frac{S \to w \qquad\qquad\qquad \dfrac{U', z, V' \to x}{}}{\dfrac{U', z/w, S, V' \to x \ \ G3 \qquad\qquad U, x, V \to y}{U, U', z/w, S, V', V \to y \ \text{Cut}}}$$

The degree of the Cut in this proof = degree($U',z/w,S,V'$) + degree(U) + degree(V) + degree(x) + degree(y). But we can derive the conclusion from the same premises using a proof in which the only Cut-inference has a smaller degree, as follows:

$$\frac{S \to w \qquad \dfrac{\dfrac{U', z, V' \to x \qquad U, x, V \to y}{U, U', z, V', V \to y \ \text{Cut}}}{}}{U, U', z/w, S, V', V \to y \ \text{G3}}$$

The degree of the Cut in this example = degree(U',z,V') + degree(U) + degree(V) + degree(x). This is less than the degree of the Cut in the previous proof.

Exercise

Show that reduction in degree holds when $T \to x$ is derived by G3' or G4.

Exercise: Case 4

The last step in the proof of $U,x,V \to y$ uses one of the rules G2–G5, but does not introduce the main connective of x.

Exercise: Case 5

The last steps in the proofs of both premises introduce the main connective of $x = x' \cdot x''$.

Exercise: Case 6

The last steps in the proofs of both premises introduce the main connective of $x = x'/x''$.

Exercise: Case 7

The last steps in the proofs of both premises introduce the main connective of $x = x' \backslash x''$.

L ⊂ LG

Having exhausted the possible cases, we see that every occurrence of a cut inference can be replaced by an inference of smaller degree, and hence that in this way every cut inference can be eliminated. Moreover, since **LG** is decidable, as shown above, we immediately have the following consequence of the Lambek-Gentzen theorem.

Corollary: **L** is decidable.

Flexibility and structural completeness

In addition to decidability, **L** has a second interesting property: *flexibility*. If there is a proof of the validity of the arrow $t_1,\ldots,t_k \to t_0$ relative to one bracketing of the sequence of types $t_1,\ldots,t_k$, then there is a proof of the validity of the arrow relative to any bracketing. In view of the associativity of the product operator, this is hardly surprising. But as noted by Buszkowski, the product-free variant of **L** is equally flexible. Thus, the flexibility of **L** does not depend solely on the associativity axiom.

In fact, Buszkowski proves a stronger result, whose intuitive content can be characterized in terms of the notion of a tree over a string. If the nodes of the tree are labeled in such a way that the immediate daughters of any given node are partitioned into a unique functor and a complement set of arguments, we call the tree an *f*-structure. Suppose a categorial system **C** counts the arrow $v_1 \ldots v_n \to x$ as valid relative to a particular *f*-structure over the string of *V*- elements $v_1 \ldots v_n$. Now, suppose that x is any primitive type. If **C** counts this arrow as valid relative to every *f*-structure over $v_1 \ldots v_n$, we say that **C** is structurally complete.

Theorem (Buszkowski). **L** is structurally complete.

A proof of this theorem may be found in Buszkowski (1988). Its import may be shown by considering a few examples. The simplest interesting case involves arrows with a two-element string on the left of the arrow, as shown below:

$$v_1 \cdot v_2 \to x$$

Then there are types t_1 and t_2 such that $v_1 \to t_1$ and $v_2 \to t_2$ and the arrow $t_1 \cdot t_2 \to x$ is valid. But then (by R1 and R1'), $t_1 \to x/t_2$ and $t_2 \to t_1 \backslash x$ are valid, and hence, $v_1 \to x/t_2$ and $v_2 \to t_1 \backslash x$. But then, since both $x/t_2 \cdot t_2 \to x$ and $t_1 \cdot t_1 \backslash x \to x$ are valid, $v_1 \cdot v_2 \to x$ is valid under all (=both) f-structures definable over $v_1 \cdot v_2$. This same technique extends easily to more complex cases. Suppose **L** is structurally complete for arrows of length $n - 1$ and consider the valid arrow $v_1 \ldots v_n \to x$. Choose any bracketing on $v_1 \ldots v_n$ which partitions it into connected sub-strings $a_1, \ldots, a_k$ and choose one of them, a_i, say, as functor. By the associativity rule and the transitivity of the $\to$-relation, $a_1, \ldots, a_k \to x$; repeated application of rules R2 and R2' yields the arrow $a_i \to a_{i-1} \backslash (\ldots \backslash (a_1 \backslash x/a_k)/ \ldots /a_{i+1}$ and it is easy to see that this yields a functional structure compatible with our chosen partition. By the same technique, we can analyze each member of the sequence into functional structures until we reach types which do not have the form of a product. Since every functional structure over $v_1 \ldots v_n$ can be characterized by appropriate choices in this way, we're done.

SOME SYSTEMS RELATED TO L

There are a number of categorial systems with affinities to **L**. We will only mention a few of them here.

Reducts of L

If we drop one or more of the type-forming operators of **L**, we obtain systems which are properly contained in **L**. This leads to the study of product-free variants of **L**, and product-free rightward or product-free leftward variants of **L**. Buszkowski (1988) surveys some of the formal properties of these systems.

Weakenings of L

Another way to find substructures of **L** is to drop one or more of the postulates. The most important example of this is the Ajdukiewicz-Bar-Hillel calculus **AB**, which drops the product operator (and is thus a reduct of **L**), but also drops the "abstraction" axioms $R1$ and $R1'$. **AB** represents the purely-applicative fragment of **L**. It is also important in view of Gaifman's Theorem (Bar-Hillel, Gaifman, & Shamir 1960): **AB**-grammars and context-free grammars are weakly equivalent.

There are categorial systems between **AB** and the product-free reduct of **L**: in **AB**, the composition arrows are not valid, but they can be added as axioms:

R-Composition: $x/y \cdot y/z \to x/z$ *L-Composition*: $z\backslash y \cdot y\backslash x \to z\backslash x$

The resulting system (found in Cohen 1967) is still not equivalent to **L** (Zielonka 1981), since it lacks a way of treating higher-order forms of composition. Second-order composition is illustrated by the following (right-directional) case:

$$x/y \cdot (y/z)/w \to (x/z)/w$$

It is a characteristic feature of **L** that all orders of composition are valid.

Another interesting subsystem of **L** can be defined by dropping axioms *A2* and *A2'*, which underly the associativity of the product operator. This system, the *non-associative* syntactic calculus **NL**, was introduced in Lambek (1961) and further studied by Kandulski (1988). Although it lacks Composition, Division, Currying, and other arrows which depend on the associativity of the product operator, the Lifting rules nevertheless hold. **NL** is a type calculus of bracketed sequences of categories, whereas (in view of product associativity) **L** is a calculus of unbracketed sequences. Linguistic facts seem to support bracketing in some cases, but not in others. This has suggested (at least to Oehrle & Zhang 1989) the investigation of partially-associative calculi with two kinds of product operators, one associative, the other non-associative.

Supersystems of L

In addition to subsystems, **L** stands in relation to various systems which properly contain it. For example, van Benthem (1988b) has explored a calculus **LP** which has the property that if the arrow $t_1,...,t_k \to t$ is valid, then so is the arrow $t_{\pi(1)},...,t_{\pi(k)} \to t$, where π is any permutation of $1,..., k$. In the presence of Lifting and Division, the resulting languages are permutation-closed. In fact, such systems generate exactly the permutation-closures of context-free languages. Investigations in this direction emphasize the affinity of the Lambek calculi with other sequent calculi, such as the intuitionistic propositional calculus (Gentzen's system **LJ**), formulations of relevance logic (Anderson & Belnap 1975), or linear logic (Girard 1987). From this point of view as well, the Associative Calculus **L** has a number of interesting characteristics. First, it lacks all three of Gentzen's "structural rules" of Interchange, Thinning, and Contraction:

$$\text{Interchange} \quad \frac{U, x, y, V \to z}{U, y, x, V \to z}$$

$$\text{Thinning} \quad \frac{U, V \to z}{U, x, V \to z}$$

$$\text{Contraction} \quad \frac{U, x, x, V \to z}{U, x, V \to z}$$

Essentially, then, **L** constitutes a logic of ordered occurrences of types: the antecedent of an arrow is a sequence, not a multiset (in which order is forgotten, but occurrence distinctions are not), nor simply a set (in which distinction of order and occurrence are both forgotten). For further discussion, see van Benthem (1988b), Lambek (1989), and Morrill (1989).

While there are many linguistic examples which conform to the occurrence-counting character of **L**, there are syntactic and semantic cases which seem to require different principles. Perhaps the most interesting syntactic case involves the study of parasitic gaps, as in **what she filed without . . . initializing . . . ,** where the initial wh-word **what** apparently binds both the argument positions indicated by ellipses. A comparable interpretive case can be found in Obligatory Control constructions like **try**, which can be associated with the syntactic type $(NP\backslash S)/INF$ with the corresponding semantical lambda recipe $\lambda v \lambda x.\mathbf{try}'(v(x))(x)$, which again has the property that the prefix λx binds in $\mathbf{try}'(v(x))(x)$ two occurrences of the free variable x. Steedman and Szabolcsi have observed the connection between such constructions and theories of functionality, and, in various writings (see especially, Steedman 1987, 1988; Szabolcsi 1987), have suggested analyses involving *functional substitution*, Curry's combinator **S**. (On combinators, see Curry & Feys 1958; Hindley & Seldin 1986; or Smullyan 1985.) Such analyses are beyond the power of **L** in its pure form.

Systems incomparable with L

Since there exist supersystems of **L** along a number of different dimensions, it is not surprising that there exist as well categorial systems which are not strictly comparable with **L**: such systems recognize arrows not valid in **L** while at the same time **L** recognizes arrows not valid in them.

One interesting example relevant to linguistic analysis involves the system (call it **NLP**) that results from adding the inference rule of bracket-preserving permutation to the system **NL**:

$$\text{Bracket-Preserving Permutation (R\pi)} \quad \frac{T \to x}{\pi(T) \to x}$$

(for π a permutation of T which preserves bracketing)

The cases of linguistic interest actually involve a partially-associative system, where bracketing is imposed only around members of specified categories. (The system in which every category is bracketed and composition is binary seems to be of no linguistic relevance.) Since all of the rules of **NL** respect bracketing, the addition of this rule leads to a system in which constituents are internally freely ordered, but constituents are *connected* in the sense that in any sequence of types $\ldots x \cdot y \cdot z \ldots$, if x and z are taken to belong to a single constituent C, then y also belongs to C. Many languages have been claimed to instantiate this requirement.

NLP and **L** are not ordered with respect to each other, since **NLP** lacks the axioms *A2* and *A2'*, yet recognizes as valid the *permutation arrow* $x/y \leftrightarrow y\backslash x$, which is not valid in **L**. Here is the proof in one direction:

$$\frac{\dfrac{\dfrac{\dfrac{x/y \to x/y}{(x/y \cdot y) \to x}}{(y \cdot x/y) \to x}}{x/y \to y \backslash x}}{} \quad \begin{matrix} A1 \\ R2 \\ R\pi \\ R3' \end{matrix}$$

The proof in the other direction is dual to this.

There are many other variants one might consider. For example, alongside the Division rules $x/y \to (x/z)/(y/z)$ and $y\backslash x \to (z\backslash y)\backslash(z\backslash x)$ we can consider the related arrows:

$$R\text{-}Zigzag: \quad x/y \to (z\backslash x)/(z\backslash y)$$
$$L\text{-}Zigzag: \quad y\backslash x \to (y/z)\backslash(x/y)$$

Not surprisingly, if we add these arrows as axioms to **L**, new forms of composition (of arbitrary finite order) are countenanced, of a kind advocated by Steedman (1987, 1990):

$$\text{Forward Crossed Composition:} \quad x/y \ z\backslash y \to z\backslash x$$
$$\text{Backward Crossed Composition:} \quad y/z \ y\backslash x \to x/z$$

These arrows are not valid in **L** and thus **L** is not a supersystem of any system in which they are valid. On the other hand, if we add the Division rules and the Zigzag rules to **AB**, we obtain a system which is incomparable to **L**, since it lacks the characteristic consequences of the abstraction rules *R1* and *R1'*, such as the Lifting arrows.

LINGUISTIC APPLICATIONS

Syntactically-minded grammarians have been attracted by the properties of **L** and its relatives for a number of reasons. Some of these reasons are discussed in the following paragraphs, but the few topics we shall touch on are only a small sample of representative work and many topics are ignored completely.

Combinatorial resources of categorial type systems

First of all, given an appropriate set of primitive types, the combinatorial properties of lexical elements can be directly encoded in the types they are associated with. (For example, **put**, as in **The postman put the mail on the step**, can be assigned to the type $((NP \backslash S)/PP)/NP$.) Syntactic composition of expressions depends on the logic of the categorial system in question, that is, the axioms and inference rules which characterize the set of valid arrows. As a result, no independent set of phrase structures is required to effect syntactic composition, although one of the functions that phrase structures serve – delimiting a class of allowable subcategorizations – can be replaced by a set of principles which characterize the notion "admissible type assignment" for a given language. It is of interest to note that just as classical transformational grammar offers in principle a variety of ways to characterize general linguistic properties and relations (via transformational rules, via closure conditions on the set of phrase structure rules as explored and exploited in interesting ways by work in GPSG [Gazdar et al. 1985], and via lexical rules), categorial systems offer a similar range of alternatives: general type-shifting rules, specific type-shifting rules, constraints on admissible type assignments, closure of the lexicon under some set of morphological rules. This range of alternatives is only beginning to be explored.

Conjunction

Second, the flexibility of constituency connected to structural completeness seems directly applicable to the complex syntax of conjunction. Structural completeness permits a multiplicity of analyses for any single complex expression. For example, given the set of types $\{S, N, NP\}$, we may assign the expressions **Kim**, **Whitney**, **Hilary** to the type NP, the expressions **documentary** and **cartoon** to N, the expressions **gave**, **offered**, and **showed** to $NP \backslash ((S/NP)/NP)$, and the expressions **a** and **the** to NP/N. We can then exhibit an analysis of **Kim showed Whitney a documentary** as follows:

Kim	showed	Whitney	a	documentary
NP	$NP\backslash((S/NP)/NP)$	NP	NP/N	N

$\underline{(S/NP)/NP)\ \text{LA}}\quad\underline{NP\ \text{RA}}$

$\underline{S/NP\ \text{RA}}$

$S\ \text{RA}$

The flexibility of **L** permits other analyses of this expression as well, based on the same initial type assignment. The following is a consequence of shifting $(S/NP)/NP$ to the type $S/(NP{\cdot}NP)$ (by Slash-Dot Conversion):

Kim	showed	Whitney	a	documentary
NP	$NP\backslash((S/NP)/NP)$	NP	NP/N	N

$\underline{(S/NP)/NP)\ \text{LA}}\quad\underline{NP\text{RA}}$

$\underline{S/(NP{\cdot}NP)\ (!)NP{\cdot}NP}$

S

In the following analysis, the verb **showed** is grouped first with the inner NP **Whitney**:

Kim	showed	Whitney	a	documentary
NP	$NP\backslash((S/NP)/NP)$	NP	NP/N	N

$\underline{(NP\backslash(S/NP))/NP\ \ \text{Curry}}\qquad\underline{}$

$\underline{NP\backslash(S/NP)\ \ \text{RA}}$

$\underline{S/NP\text{LA}}$

$S\ \text{RA}$

To see the relation of these analyses to co-ordination, note that, in simple cases, the syntactic generality in English of the Boolean operators **and** and **or** is widely recognized (Dougherty 1970; Keenan & Faltz 1985; Gazdar 1980; Partee & Rooth 1983; Steedman 1985; Dowty 1988). Thus, it is possible to co-ordinate a wide range of standard constituent types: NP (**Kim or Sandy**), AP (**honest and respected**), PP (**down the hall and into the room on the left**), and so on. Within the calculus **L**, this general character applies directly to a wider class of expressions, including compositions and products of classical constituents. Here are examples related to the analyses of the above paragraph, with the conjoined type specified on the left:

NP
Kim and Hilary showed Whitney a documentary.
Kim showed Whitney and Hilary a documentary.
Kim showed Whitney a documentary and a cartoon.

NP\ ((S/NP)/NP)
Kim gave or offered Whitney a documentary.

(S/NP)/NP
Kim gave and Hilary offered Whitney a documentary.

S/NP
Kim gave Hilary and Sal offered Whitney a documentary.

NP·NP
Kim gave Whitney a documentary and Hilary a cartoon.

[((NP\S)/NP)/NP)] \ [NP\S]
Kim gave Whitney a documentary and Hilary a cartoon.

NP\S/NP
Kim gave Whitney and offered Hilary a documentary.

NP\S
Kim gave Whitney a documentary and offered Hilary a cartoon.

In addition (Steedman 1985), functional composition allows an analysis of cases like the following automatically: **The lawyer will offer, and I am almost positive that the prosecutor is prepared to dispute, a motion of acquittal.** Here the crucial step is the assignment of the type *S/NP* to the expressions **The lawyer will offer and I am almost positive that the prosecutor is prepared to dispute.** In both cases, this is facilitated by functional composition, as in the following proof-tree:

the	lawyer	will	offer
NP/N	*N*	*NP\(S/VP)*	*VP/NP*
NP	RA		
		S/VP LA	
		S/NP RC	

The second case is longer, but based on the same principles.

Thus, the flexible constituency of **L** offers a way to accommodate a wide variety of conjunctions – including all forms of standard constituent conjunction, certain cases of "non-constituent" conjunction, and "right node raising" – as special cases of the single simple characterization of co-ordination of expressions of like category. Exactly how to treat in a general way the co-ordination of expressions of like category in **L** is not completely obvious, however, for there are alternative modes of analysis available.

For example, if we regard the Boolean operators **and** and **or** as typed expressions, they must be lexically associated with all types of the form $\chi \backslash \chi / \chi$, where χ is a variable ranging over a set of types, perhaps all the countably many types of Cat^*, perhaps a subset of "conjoinable types" (Partee & Rooth 1982, 1983). If this seems too extravagant, we could impose ad hoc restrictions on the set of types in questions, at the risk of begging the question of the generality of the Boolean operators. In any case, the introduction of polymorphic types such as $\chi \backslash \chi / \chi$ into the type system itself extends earlier assumptions about lexical type assignment, assumptions which bear on such issues as decidability.

An alternative is to extend **L** in another way, not by admitting polymorphic types, but by treating the Boolean connectives as syncategorematic operators. Three related steps are involved. First, the freely-generated type system must be extended to include two new unary operators, so that our set of operation symbols is extended from $\{/, \backslash, \cdot\}$ to $\{/, \backslash, \cdot, \textbf{and}, \textbf{or}\}$. Second, the recursive definition of Cat^* (compare section 2.1 above) is extended in the obvious way, to read:

Cat^* is the least set such that:
(1) Cat is a subset of Cat^*;
(2) if x and y are members of Cat^*, so are (x/y), $(y \backslash x)$, $(x \cdot y)$, $(x$ **and** $x)$, and $(x$ **or** $x)$.

Finally, we need inference rules governing the behaviour of the operators **and** and **or**. Here is one possibility:

G6[and]:
$$\frac{U, x, V \to y \quad U, z, V \to y}{U, x \textbf{ and } z, V \to y}$$

G6[or]:
$$\frac{U, x, V \to y \quad U, z, V \to y}{U, x \textbf{ or } z, V \to y}$$

Here is another:

G6[and]': $A \rightarrow x$ $\qquad\qquad$ $B \rightarrow x$ $\qquad$ $U, x, V \rightarrow y$
$$\overline{\qquad\qquad U, A \textbf{ and } B, V \rightarrow y \qquad\qquad}$$

G6[or]': $A \rightarrow x$ $\qquad\qquad$ $B \rightarrow x$ $\qquad$ $U, x, V \rightarrow y$
$$\overline{\qquad\qquad U, A \textbf{ or } B, V \rightarrow y \qquad\qquad}$$

These different proposals are not equivalent. For instance, the second of the two forms of inference rules discussed involves a form of cut-inference, while the first does not. In fact, the indeterminacy introduced by the cut-properties of this rule are the analogue of the indeterminacy introduced by the polymorphic type $\chi\backslash\chi/\chi$. While there are other technical points that differentiate these approaches from one another from the present perspective, they are also related in interesting ways to various proposals within the transformational literature. We will come back to how these proposals should be evaluated below.

Discontinuous dependencies

There are natural correspondences in **L** involving the symmetry of the slash operators. For example, there is an obvious bijection (that is, a 1-1 onto correspondence) between types of the form x/y and types of the form $y\backslash x$. We call this correspondence "permutation." (Caution: the "permutation arrow" $x/y \leftrightarrow y\backslash x$ is not valid in **L**, which instantiates a logic which respects order.) Note that an expression e_1 that belongs to both x/y and its Permutation $y\backslash x$ will combine with an expression e_2 of type y in two different ways: that is both $e_1 e_2$ and $e_2 e_1$ belong to category x. This suggests a technique for treating "movement alternations."

Consider two mutually exclusive structures X- $NP[+f]$-Z-W and X-Z-$NP[-f]$-W. A typical transformational account of such an alternation is to assume that one of these structures is basic and the other is derived from it by the obligatory application of a movement transformation. An interesting example of such a case is the system of clitic pronouns of French, where we have the following paradigm in a simple case exhibiting the positional possibilities of a third-person singular feminine noun phrase (**la réponse**) and the corresponding third-person singular feminine pronoun (**la**):

il sait la réponse "he knows the answer"

*il la réponse sait "he the answer knows"

*il sait la "he knows it"

il la sait "he knows it"

We might analyse the first example as follows (using *FVP* – "finite verb phrase" – to abbreviate $NP\backslash S$):

il	sait	la réponse
S/FVP	FVP/NP	NP

$$FVP \text{ RA}$$

$$S \text{ RA}$$

The distribution of the clitic pronoun **la** depends in some sense on the distribution of object *NP*s, but to assign them to the same category inevitably leads to further hypotheses, for they don't have the same distribution. An obvious categorial alternative is to assign **la** the type $FVP/(FVP/NP)$. This is the permutation of a type-lifted category for *NP* – namely, $(FVP/NP)\backslash FVP$. Thus, there is available a natural semantic interpretation (see below) as well, namely, the interpretation that one would assign to a third-singular feminine pronoun with the same distribution as non-pronominal object *NP*s such as **la réponse**. Writing the semantic interpretation of the expressions in questions in brackets and assuming (for the moment) that functional application in the syntax and functional application in the semantics go hand in hand, the resulting proof sub-tree is ("P_n" is a variable ranging over n-place predicates):

… **la** $[\lambda P_2 . (P_2(3sgfempro))]$	**sait** $[\lambda x\lambda y . sait'(x)(y)]$
… $FVP/(FVP/NP)$	FVP/NP

$$\text{FVP } [\lambda y . sait'(3sgfempro)(y)]$$

Thus, within the categorial framework, it is possible to assign a type to a clitic pronoun like **la** which characterizes its combinatorial possibilities directly, in a way that is semantically responsible. Nishida (1987) offers a detailed categorial analysis of Spanish cliticization along exactly these lines.

If we allow type-lifting and permutation to interact with functional composition, we have a way to model movement–alternations over a variable. Suppose that *NP*s may also be assigned the permutation $S/(S/NP)$ of the type-lifted category $(S/NP)\backslash S$. Now, consider the analysis of the following structures:

Beans,	**Kim**	**likes**	
$S/(S/NP)$	NP	$NP\backslash(S/NP)$	

$$\frac{\quad S/NP \quad}{S} \quad \begin{array}{l}\text{composition}\\\text{application}\end{array}$$

If the interpretation of **beans** is type-lifted in the obvious way (to $\lambda P_1(P_1(beans'))$, then under an appropriate model-theoretic interpretation, the interpretation of **Beans, Kim likes** will have the same truth value as **Kim likes beans**. This same technique extends directly to more complex structures (Ades & Steedman 1982; Steedman 1985):

Beans,	**Wim**	**claimed**	**that**	**Kim**	**likes**	
$S/(S/NP)$	NP	$NP\backslash(S/S')$	S'/S	NP	$NP\backslash(S/NP)$	

$$
\begin{array}{l}
\dfrac{\quad S/S' \quad}{} \qquad \dfrac{\quad S/NP \quad}{} \quad \text{application}\\[4pt]
\dfrac{\qquad\qquad S'/NP \qquad\qquad}{} \quad \text{composition}\\[4pt]
\dfrac{\qquad\qquad\qquad S/NP \qquad\qquad\qquad}{} \quad \text{composition}\\[4pt]
S
\end{array}
$$

Categorial systems allow other possibilities, of course. The Division rule $x/y \to (x/z)/(y/z)$, whose connections with functional composition are quite apparent in **L** (see particularly Zielonka 1981), may be construed as a rudimentary form of "Slash-Feature" propagation exploited beautifully in GPSG and related frameworks. This approach requires a rule which countenances arrows such as $NP \ S/NP \to S$, but in **L**, this arrow is equivalent to the arrow $NP \to S/(S/NP)$ (as well as equivalent to the "permutation arrow" $S/NP \to NP \backslash S$).

Non-peripheral extraction

As noted in Steedman (1985) and elsewhere, such systems need to be supplemented to handle cases of non-peripheral extraction, as in **The beer, we put in the refrigerator**. One possibility is to introduce a form of polymorphism into the type of shifting arrow just mentioned, yielding $NP \to (S/\chi)/((S/\chi)/NP)$. In the right-peripheral case, we allow S/χ to be matched simply by S. In a case of non-peripheral extraction such as **The beer, we put in the refrigerator**, however, we let S/χ be matched by S/PP.

Categorial systems are also compatible with other treatments of extraction phenomena – for example, axioms or inference rules of a form congenial to transformational analysis, such as the following:

A[np-fronting]: $x \cdot NP \cdot y \to NP \cdot x \cdot y$

R[wh-movement]: $\dfrac{x \cdot y[+wh] \cdot z \to s}{y[+wh] \cdot x \cdot z \to s'}$

Alternatively, it is possible to introduce new binary operators into **L** analogous to the "slash"-feature of GPSG: write $x \uparrow y$ to mean an expression of type x from which an expression of type y has been removed. The logic of this operator is assumed to respect the following rules:

$$A \uparrow: \qquad z/y \to z \uparrow y$$

$$R \uparrow \quad \frac{W, Y \to x \uparrow y \quad U, x, V \to z}{U, W, Y, V \to z \uparrow y}$$

In effect, the first of these rules allows a functor to combine with less than its full complement of arguments, and we may regard this step as the base case of a recursive characterization of the behavior of the $\uparrow$-operator whose recursive clause is given – somewhat too generously, on empirical grounds – by the second rule.

The interaction of conjunction and extraction

In isolation, the alternative accounts of conjunction and extraction discussed in the above paragraphs might seem to be notational variants of one another: the consequences of one version seem to be the same as the consequences of another. When we examine conjunction and extraction phenomena together, however, it doesn't take long to see that this apparent equivalence is an illusion. The cases to look at are those of the kind that motivated the Co-ordinate Structure Constraint of Ross (1967).

The empirical facts we need to refer to are simple enough: if a "filler" binds a "gap" in one conjunct of a co-ordinate structure, it binds a "gap" in every conjunct. Thus, we have the following contrast ('. . .' indicates a "gap"):

the book that Kim ordered . . . from Blackwell's and read . . . immediately

*the book that Kim ordered . . . from Blackwell's and read *War & Peace* **immediately**

*the book that Kim ordered Tolstoy's pamphlet from Blackwell's and read . . . immediately

Now, note first that in the presence of functional composition and Currying, assimilation of the Boolean connectives to the type system (regardless of whether they are assigned a single polymorphic type) cannot account for the above contrast. To see why, note first that if **and** (say) is typed, then since s **and** $s \to s$, we have **and** $\to s\backslash(s/s) \leftrightarrow (s\backslash s)/s$. But then if $A \to s$, then A **and** $\to s/s$, a category which may compose with an expression of type s/np to yield the type s/np. But such a derivation would result in an expression containing a gap in the right conjunct but no gap in the left conjunct, conflicting with empirical observation. So if we accept functional composition and Currying, we must reject assimilation of the Boolean operators to the type system.

A second moral to be drawn from the interaction of conjunction and extraction involves the categorial designation of an expression of type x from which an expression of type y has been removed. Suppose that we conjoin **ordered** ... **from Blackwell's** (which we may regard as of type $(((np\backslash s)/pp)/np)\cdot pp))$ and **read** ... **immediately** (which we may regard as of type $(((np\backslash s)/adv)/np\cdot adv)$. What type should be assigned to the conjunction? If we regard the type system as having the natural semantics in V^* – and in particular, if we require that any expression belonging to the product type $x \cdot y$ be factorable into a sequence of sub-expressions $a_1...a_j a_{j+1}...a_n$ such that $a_1...a_j \to x$ and $a_{j+1}...a_n \to y$, then clearly the conjunction of two product types cannot in general be a product type. Moreover, it is difficult to reconcile these two distinct categories with the elegant assumption that the category of a conjunction is the same as the category of its conjuncts.

Third, it is easy to see that treating extraction by a global inference rule offers no way of treating empirically-observed properties of gap-distribution in co-ordinate structures.

These considerations suggest that the Boolean connectives should be treated as the reflexes of categorial operators and that extraction should be dealt with in terms of a recursively defined abstraction operator. The resulting account has strong affinities with the GPSG account using the SLASH feature. (For further discussion, see Morill 1988; Moortgat 1989; Oehrle 1990.)

PARSING

Moortgat (1987, 1989) offers a penetrating study of natural language applications of the product-free reduct of **L**. The following brief remarks are based on his research. (Moortgat's work is not the only study of natural language parsing in a categorial framework: other important studies include Pareschi & Steedman 1987 and Wittenburg 1987.)

Parsing and decidability

If we consider the two systems **L** and **LG**, it is clear at once that the properties that make decidability so transparent in the case of **LG** fail to hold of **L**. The difficulty lies with the properties of R3, the transitivity arrow that allows us to infer $x \to z$ from the two premisses $x \to y$ and $y \to z$. If we wish to prove the validity of an arrow $x \to z$, we must consider the possibility that an inference of this form yields $x \to z$ from valid premisses $x \to y$ and $y \to z$. Which type y? There are countably many choices for y to choose from. No effective procedure can consider them all.

This problem is avoided in the system **LG**: in effect, the **Cut** rule is compiled into the rules $G3$ and $G3'$ in a harmless form. What makes the compiled form harmless is the fact that all the types of the premisses are preserved in the conclusion. As a consequence, unlike the **Cut** rule or $R3$ of **L**, there is no possibly missing type to be sought among the countably many types available: all the relevant types are sub-types of the conclusion. As noted earlier, then, there exists a decision procedure for **LG**: each inference rule introduces exactly one occurrence of a type-forming operator; we simply look at all the possible ways of removing such operators one at a time (by applying in each case an inference rule in reverse; if one of these ways results in a set of axioms of the form $x \to x$, we have in effect constructed a proof in reverse, starting with the arrow to be proved.

As an example, consider the sequent $np\ (np \setminus s)/vp\ vp/np\ np \to s$ (which we can think of as corresponding to a sentence such as **Kim may follow Sandy**). We can begin either by attempting to remove the slash operator in the type $(np \backslash s)/vp$ or by attempting to remove the slash operator in the type vp/np. Each of these can only be removed by a backward application of rule $G3$, as illustrated below:

$$\text{subproof 1:}\quad \frac{vp/np\ \ np \to vp \qquad np\ \ np \setminus s \to s}{np\ (np \setminus s)/vp\ vp/np\ np \to s}$$

$$\text{subproof 2:}\quad \frac{np \to np \qquad np\ (np \setminus s\ )/vp\ vp \to s}{np\ (np \setminus s)/vp\ vp/np\ np \to s}$$

To extend either of these subproofs to a valid proof, we need to show that the premisses of the valid subproof are themselves valid.

Thus, for each of the premisses we seek to remove a type-forming operator. This leads to the following:

subproof 1:

$$\frac{\dfrac{np \to np \quad vp \to vp}{vp/np \; np \to vp} \qquad \dfrac{np \to np \quad s \to s}{np \; np\backslash s \to s}}{np \; (np\backslash s)/vp \; vp/np \; np \to s}$$

subproof 2:

$$\frac{\qquad\qquad \dfrac{vp \to vp \quad np \; np\backslash s \to s}{np \; (np\backslash s)/vp \; vp \to s}}{np \; (np\backslash s)/vp \; vp/np \; np \to s} \; np \to np$$

Each of the branches of the proof-tree of subproof 1 is occupied by an instance of an axiom: thus subproof 1 is in fact a proof. We extend subproof 2 to a proof in one more step, by showing the validity of np $np\backslash s \to s$ (a proof of which is actually contained in the first step of the righthand branch of subproof 1). Obviously, if we reach a point in a subproof where we need to show the validity of a premiss which is not an axiom but which contains no occurrences of removable type-forming arrows, the subproof cannot be extended further in any valid way. If all possible subproofs built up from an arrow reach such a point, then no proof of the arrow in **LG** exists.

Moortgat shows how these ideas – found already in Lambek (1958) – can be realized in the form of a Prolog program: this provides an elegant realization of the slogan, "Grammar as logic, parsing as deduction." Thus, the decidability of **LG** can be converted into a parsing algorithm.

Parsing and structural flexibility

Recall that **L** possesses another property of linguistic interest: structural completeness. **LG** is structurally complete as well. Let X be any way in which the k types $x_1, \ldots, x_k$ can be bracketed in a binary fashion using the binary product-forming operator '·': successive applications (in reverse!) of rule G4 (which introduces the operator · on the left of the arrow of the conclusion) will remove each occurrence of the product operator, as well as its attendant bracketing. Thus, **L** and **LG** agree not only on the types assignable to sequences of types, they agree as well on the types assignable to bracketed sequences of types. But there is a difference: the types assignable to these bracketed sequences during the course of the proofs need not be the same.

For example, there is no cut-free proof of the arrow $np \; (np\backslash s)/vp$

$vp/np\ np \to s$ in which the (valid) arrow $np\ (np\backslash s)/vp \to s/vp$ plays a role. (To see why, just note that the types that appear in the premises of any inference rule of **LG** must appear as types or sub-types in the conclusion of the rule, but the type s/vp is not a sub-type in the arrow $np\ (np\backslash s)/vp\ vp/np\ np \to s$.)

This "intensional" property of the two extensionally-equivalent axiomatizations is relevant to the treatment of such problems as co-ordination. Pursuing the above example a bit further, suppose we wish to parse a sentence like **Kim may and Zim inevitably will follow Sandy**, which we will assume for expository purposes corresponds (apart from **and**) to checking the validity of the arrow:

$$np\ (np\backslash s)/vp \textbf{ and } np\ (np\backslash s)/(np\backslash s)\ (np\backslash s)/vp\ vp/np\ np \to s$$

All the accounts of **and** discussed above require that we find a type χ which meets the following criteria:

$$np\ (np\ \backslash s)/vp \to \chi$$

$$np\ (np\backslash s)/(np\backslash s)\ (np\backslash s)/vp \to \chi$$

$$\chi\ vp \to s$$

In this particular case, it is easy to see (by applying R1 to the last of these arrows) that χ must satisfy the arrow $\chi \to s/vp$. It is less easy to see how to give a completely general account which allows us to make, tractably, many guesses about the identity of χ.

Moortgat combines the parsing properties of **LG** with the necessity of cut-like inferences (in the style of **L**) in an interesting system **M**, which is derived from a third axiomatization **Z** of the product-free reduct of **L** based on work of Zielonka (1981). We cannot offer the details of this system here, but the interested reader can find these details and much more in Moortgat (1989).

MEANING AND PROOF

Given a sequence W of words $w_1 \ldots w_k$ such that $W \to q$, for some type q, how can we assign a model-theoretic interpretation to W? The general framework of categorial systems accommodates a range of solutions to this question, which we shall investigate briefly in this section.

Recall that if $W \to q$ in a categorial system **C**, then there are types $t_1, \ldots, t_k$ with $w_i \to t_i (1 \le i \le k)$ such that $t_1 \ldots t_k \to q$. The first question that arises is the relation of the interpretations of W and its components to the corresponding set of syntactic types. A second question of interest is the relation of semantic composition to the proof of $t_1 \ldots t_k \rightarrow q$.

While it is reasonable to suppose that there are aspects of interpretation which are in fact independent of the syntactic type system – the communicative effects associated with intonational range or voice quality are possible examples – these fall outside the range of standard model-theoretic scrutiny. At the same time, it is easy to think of cases in which syntactic categorization has a dramatic effect on interpretation. For example, **crate hammers** can be construed either as the plural of a compound noun or as an imperative, two categorizations with strikingly different interpretations, in spite of the identity of the lexical stems involved. Examples like this strongly support the assumption that the interpretation of an expression is constrained by its syntactic type. But by itself, this conclusion doesn't distinguish among the possible ways in which the constraints of syntactic typing make themselves felt on interpretation.

One possible view, found in Montague's work, is that each syntactic type determines a unique semantic type. In particular, in *PTQ* (Paper 8 in Montague 1974), the syntactic type system *Cat* is simply the free algebra generated by the operators / and // over the set $\{e,t\}$ and the system *Type* of Montague's intensional logic *IL* is the free algebra generated by the binary operator $<.,.>$ and the unary operator $< s,. >$ over the set $\{e,t\}$. The function f, which associates each syntactic type with a semantic type is the identity on $\{e,t\}$ and for syntactic types A and B associated with a semantic type $f(A)$ and $f(B)$, respectively, maps both A/B and $A//B$ to $<<s,f(B)>,f(A)>$. Since the set of possible denotations available to any semantic type in a given model is fixed by general principles, the mapping from syntactic types to semantic types imposes a constraint on the interpretation of an expression of a given syntactic type. In addition, the translation of a given expression into *IL* is supplemented by a set of meaning postulates, which impose equivalences in certain cases between expressions of one type and expressions of another. We can think of these equivalences as allowing a limited and highly constrained form of polymorphism, or multiple type assignment.

A more general form of polymorphism is this: with each syntactic type t, we associate a set $T(t)$ of semantic types; the semantic type of any interpretation of any expression of type t is required to belong to a type in $T(t)$. This general point of view admits a number of variations: each expression of type t may be associated with a single interpretation (of a single type belonging to $T(t)$), or each expression of type t may be associated systematically with interpretations of every type in $T(t)$, or we may have a mixed system in which some expressions have unique interpretations and others have families of interpretations. (For exemplification and discussion, see Partee & Rooth 1983; Rooth & Partee 1982; Klein & Sag 1985; Partee 1987; Hendriks 1987, 1989.) These issues are worth comparing to issues discussed in the syntactic and morphological literature concerning the distinction between lexicalizable and nonlexicalizable processes and its relation to productivity.

In any case, in the interests of generality, we may assume that each expression of type t is associated with a set of interpretations, each of a type contained in $T(t)$. This has the following consequence for our running example: if $W \rightarrow q$, then there must be semantic types $s_1,\ldots,s_k$ and a semantic type s_q, such that s_i is a member of $T(t_i)(1 \le i \le k)$ and s_q is a member of $T(q)$, together with a function which assigns k-tuples of interpretations of types $s_1,\ldots,s_k$, respectively, to an interpretation of type s_q. If $w'_1,\ldots,w'_k$ are interpretations of $w_1,\ldots,w_k$ (of semantic type $s_1,\ldots,s_k$ respectively), and q' is of semantic type s_q, we may denote the action of this function as follows:

$$w'_1,\ldots,w'_k \mapsto q'$$

Note that if $T(q)$ is not always a singleton set, there may be more than one such function which associates an interpretation with the arrow $W \rightarrow q$. But in any case, the question that arises most obviously is the exact relation between the syntactic arrow $W \mapsto q$ and the semantic arrow $w'_1,\ldots,w'_k \mapsto q'$. There are two extreme positions.

On one view, inspired by work on "type-driven semantics" of Klein and Sag (1985) and Hendriks (1987), we may regard the sequence of semantic arguments $w_1,\ldots,w_k$ as being determined by the string W, but the set of compositional functions represented by $w'_1,\ldots,w'_k \mapsto q'$ is determined by a categorial system (over the set of semantic types) which is independent of the syntactic calculus C in which $W \rightarrow q$ is evaluated, except that the function must respect constraints on admissible type-assignment.

On the other hand, it is possible that the interpretation of $W \rightarrow q$ depends not just on what types are admissible interpretations of the components of W and of q, but on the proof that $W \rightarrow q$. On this view, different proofs may give rise to different interpretations. A simple example (van Benthem 1986) involves the scope of modifiers: there are two non-equivalent ways of proving the arrow $s/s, s, s \backslash s \rightarrow s$, depending (in the Gentzen-style system) on which operator is removed first. We may regard these two proofs as introducing different

associated with different interpretations, one may equally well wonder whether different proofs always give rise to different interpretations. We can accommodate both these extremes within a single point
of view. For in general, we may partition the class of proofs of a given
arrow into equivalence classes in such a way that proofs belonging to
the same equivalence class are associated with the same interpretation. If different proofs have no bearing on the set of interpretations
associated with a given arrow, then there is only one equivalence
class. If distinct proofs are associated with distinct interpretations,
then the equivalence relation is virtually identical with the set of
proofs itself. Thus, this point of view accommodates the two extremes
just discussed and provides a framework for both empirical and theoretical investigation.

This general point of view is compatible with a variety of recent
work. In the category-theoretic account of Lambek (1988), for example, semantic interpretation is regarded as a functor Φ from a "syntactic" category to a "semantic" category, preserving the properties of
syntactic proofs. An alternative way to preserve the properties of
proofs is to provide an interpretation for each proof step. For example, following the lead of van Benthem, given types $\tau(x)$ for each basic
type in *Cat*, we extend the domain of τ to *Cat** by the inductive steps:

$$\tau(x \cdot y) = \tau(x) \times \tau(y)$$

$$\tau(x/y) = \tau(y \backslash x) = \lambda \upsilon_{\tau(y)} z_{\tau(x)}$$

In the following formulation of **LG**, roman variables ranging over
syntactic types are paired with Greek variables ranging over interpretations of the appropriate type, with paired elements joined by a
colon. (The interpretation of unpaired syntactic variables is invariant
in each rule.)

G1 $\qquad\qquad\qquad\qquad\qquad x : \alpha \to x : \alpha$

G2 $\quad \dfrac{T,y : \alpha \to x : \beta(\alpha)}{T \to x/y : \beta}$ $\qquad$ G2' $\quad \dfrac{y : \alpha, T \to x : \beta(\alpha)}{T \to y \backslash x : \beta}$

G3 $\dfrac{T \to y : \alpha\ U, x : \beta(\alpha), V \to z}{U, x/y : \beta, T, V \to z}$ G3' $\dfrac{T \to y : \alpha\ U, x : \beta(\alpha), V \to z}{U, T, y \backslash x : \beta, V \to z}$

G4 $\qquad\qquad \dfrac{U, x : \alpha, y : \beta, V \to z}{U, x \cdot y :< \alpha, \beta >, V \to z}$

G5
$$\frac{P \to x : \alpha \, , \, Q \to y : \beta}{P, \, Q \to x \cdot y :< \alpha,\beta >}$$

The above system of postulates effectively pairs two type-shifting calculi: the syntactic system **L** and a semantic system containing products, abstraction, and application. The proof of any **L**-valid arrow $W \to t$ will pair it with an interpretation, in such a way that the interpretation of t will depend on the interpretation of the elements of W. For example, here is an 'interpreted' proof of R-Lifting, with each line of the proof accompanied by a corresponding semantic arrow:

$$\frac{y : \eta \to y : \eta \quad z : \zeta(\eta) \to z : \zeta(\eta)}{\dfrac{z/y : \zeta, y \to z : \zeta(\eta)}{y \to (z/y)\backslash z : \lambda \xi_{\tau(z/y)}.\xi_{\tau(z/y)}(\eta)}} \quad \begin{array}{l} (G1,G1) \\[6pt] (G3) \\[6pt] (\,G2') \end{array}$$

Quantifiers and type-structures

A natural question to ask is how quantifiers are to be handled within such a type system. Before we consider various approaches, it is useful to consider Montague's solution to this problem in the extensional fragment of *PTQ*: he associated quantifiers with the syntactic type S/(S/NP) (where the slashes are independent of the direction of concatenation, which Montague specified independently); in the extensional fragment of *PTQ*, the corresponding semantic type is $<<e,t>,t>$; in combinations of subject and intransitive verb phrase, the subject is the functor; but in combinations of transitive verb and direct object, since the quantifier has a fixed type, the verb must thus be raised to a type which maps the quantifier type to the type of an intransitive verb phrase, and similarly for other NP-argument positions. In this way, we satisfy two interesting criteria: every syntactic type is associated with a single semantic type; and in such a way that there is a homomorphism from the syntactic type structure to the semantic type structure.

Of course, we don't want transitive verbs and other functors which act on quantifiers to act arbitrarily: to ensure that such functors act in a way that respects the properties of distinct quantifiers, Montague introduces appropriate meaning postulates. If we use an auxiliary language of semantic representation such as some version of the λ-calculus, we can compile the effects of the meaning postulates directly into the representation of transitive verb interpretations (Hendriks 1989): for example, the interpretation of a transitive verb like **catch** can be represented as $\lambda Q\lambda\chi Q\lambda y(\textbf{catch}'(y)(x))$, where x and y are individual variables and Q is a variable of type $<<e,t>,t>$.

A possible alternative is to assign multiple interpretations to quantifiers, in such a way that they map $n+1$-place predicates to n-place predicates, for $n \geq 0$, in a way that essentially is parasitic on the ordinary interpretation of quantifiers of type $<<e,t>,t>$ in a point-wise way. Representing such predicates as λ-terms, we can illustrate the semantic aspect of this approach as follows, where $\forall x_k$ maps a k-place predicate to a $k - 1$ -place predicate:

$$\forall^1 x : \lambda x\phi \rightarrow \forall x\phi$$

$$\forall^2 x : \lambda x\lambda y\phi \rightarrow \lambda y\forall x\phi$$

$$\vdots$$

$$\forall^{k+1} x : \lambda x\lambda y_k...\lambda y_1\phi \rightarrow \lambda y_k...\lambda y_1\forall x\phi$$

There are two ways to integrate this with syntactic considerations: one is to preserve a match between syntactic and semantic types on which each syntactic type is assigned a unique semantic type; the other relaxes this criterion and allows a different given syntactic type to be associated with a variety of semantic types.

Quantification within a rigid framework

Suppose each syntactically-typed expression is associated with a unique semantic type. The only way to introduce any kind of type-flexibility is to associate expressions with more than one syntactic type. Thus, **every student** might be assigned types and λ-terms as follows ($\sigma = \textbf{student}'$):

$S/(NP\backslash S)$	$\lambda x\phi \rightarrow \forall x(\sigma(x) \rightarrow \phi)$
$(S/NP)\backslash S$	$\lambda x\phi \rightarrow \forall x(\sigma(x) \rightarrow \phi)$
$(S/NP)/(NP\backslash(S/NP))$	$\lambda x\lambda y\phi \rightarrow \lambda y\forall x(\sigma(x) \rightarrow \phi)$
$((NP\backslash S)/NP)\backslash(NP\backslash S)$	$\lambda x\lambda y\phi \rightarrow \lambda y\forall x(\sigma(x) \rightarrow \phi)$

and so on. This rigid relation between syntactic and semantic types has a certain attractiveness: first, to each proof there corresponds a unique interpretation; moreover, the multiplicity of types assigned to quantifiers leads to a mild form of scope ambiguity. For instance, a simple transitive sentence such as **Some student telephoned every teacher** has two different analyses, correlated with different scope orders, based on the following arrows:

$$s/(np\backslash s) \cdot (np\backslash s)/np \cdot [(np\backslash s)/np]\backslash(np\backslash s) \rightarrow s$$

$$(s/np)/[(np\backslash s)/np] \cdot (np\backslash s)/np \cdot (s/np)\backslash s \rightarrow s$$

But although it is pleasant to find a system in which multiple scope orders for quantifiers arise as a side effect of polymorphic type assignment, the result is not entirely satisfactory. First, the possibility of different scope orders is an artefact of the medial occurrence of the verb: in a VSO language, there is no analog to the English example above – V cannot combine with O without combining with S first. Second, there is the slight suspicion that so many types is a bit excessive. Thus, we have some motivation for pursuing other avenues of attack on the problem.

Quantifiers and type-driven translation

In the above account, syntactic types are associated with unique semantic types and each proof of a syntactic arrow is associated with a unique interpretation. These properties are hardly necessary where two type systems are coupled. Here is an alternative conception, in the tradition of type polymorphism and type-driven translation (Klein & Sag 1985; Partee & Rooth 1982, 1983). It has two crucial features: first, a given syntactic category can be associated with a set of types, rather than a single type; second, the proof of a syntactic arrow can be associated with more than one interpretation. In particular, suppose that NP's are associated with either type e or type $<<e,t>,t>$, while intransitive verbs of syntactic type $NP \backslash S$ are always associated with type $<e,t>$. This gives us two semantic cases to consider with regard to the syntactic arrow $NP\ NP\backslash S \rightarrow S$:

$$N P : Q\ N P\backslash S : \lambda x f(x) \rightarrow S : Q\lambda x f(x)$$

$$N P : a\ N P\backslash S : \lambda x f(x) \rightarrow S : f(a)$$

The situation can be expressed formally as follows, writing $t : t'$ to indicate that syntactic type t is paired with semantic type t', and writing $\prod_1^k t_i$ to indicate a sequence of k types:

$$\textstyle\prod_1^k t_i \rightarrow t : \{t' \mid \forall i (1 \le i \le k) \exists t_i' t_i : t_i' \wedge \prod_1^k t_i' \rightarrow_\Sigma t'\}$$

Of course, the arrow $\rightarrow_\Sigma$ represents the assignability relation within the semantic calculus now. As Hendriks (1987) rightly observes, considerable care must be taken concerning how the two calculi are chosen. If the semantic calculus is too strong, unwanted readings may proliferate.

For example, if we have both $U,\alpha,<\alpha,\chi>,V \rightarrow_\Sigma U,\chi,V$ and $U,<\alpha,\chi>, a,U \rightarrow_\Sigma U,\chi,V$ – as in the permutation-closed calculus **LP**, then the proposal above leads (on standard assumptions) to assigning **Kim saw Sandy** and **Sandy saw Kim** the same set of interpretations.

But if we associate each quantifier with a set of higher order types (such as $\forall^1, \forall^2, \ldots$, as sketched above), and assume that the valid arrows of the semantic calculus are just those valid in **L**, we can account for the ambiguity of **Some student telephoned every teacher** as follows:

$$\frac{\quad np \rightarrow np : \exists^1 \qquad\qquad s \rightarrow s : \exists^1 \forall^2 \lambda x \lambda y f(x)(y) \quad}{\dfrac{np \rightarrow np : \forall^2 \qquad\quad np : \exists^1 \quad np\backslash s : \forall^2 \lambda x \lambda y f(x)(y) \rightarrow s}{np : \exists^1 \;\; (np\backslash s)/np : \lambda x \lambda y f(x)(y) \quad np : \forall^2 \rightarrow s : \exists^1 \forall^2 \lambda x \lambda y f(x)(y)}}$$

$$\frac{\quad np \rightarrow np : \forall^1 \qquad\qquad s \rightarrow s : \forall^1 \exists^2 \lambda y \lambda x f(x)(y) \quad}{\dfrac{np \rightarrow np : \exists^2 \qquad\quad s/np : \exists^2 \lambda y \lambda x f(x)(y) \quad np : \forall^1 \rightarrow s}{np : \exists^2 \;\; np\backslash(s/np) : \lambda y \lambda x f(x)(y) \quad np : \forall^1 \rightarrow s : \forall^1 \exists^2 \lambda y \lambda x f(x)(y)}}$$

An important role in this second proof is played by the tacit assumption that the arrow $(np\backslash s)/np : \lambda x \lambda y f(x)(y) \leftrightarrow np\backslash(s/np) : \lambda y \lambda x f(y)(x)$ is valid. The validity of this arrow is easily seen:

$$\frac{\quad np \rightarrow np : a \qquad\qquad s \rightarrow s : f(b)(a) \quad}{\dfrac{\dfrac{np \rightarrow np : b \qquad\quad np : a \quad np\backslash s \rightarrow s : f(b)(a)}{np : a \;\; (np\backslash s)/np \;\; np : b \rightarrow s : f(b)(a)}}{\dfrac{np : a \;\; (np\backslash s)/np \rightarrow s/np : \lambda x\, f(x)(a)}{(np\backslash s)/np : \lambda x \lambda y f(x)(y) \rightarrow np\backslash(s/np) : \lambda y \lambda x f(x)(y)}}}$$

This sub-proof, together with the **Cut** Rule, will yield the second proof on the basis of a single lexical assignment to the transitive verb. But this sub-proof is inaccessible in a purely cut-free system (since it requires a step in the proof which doesn't reduce the number of connectives).

This system, which relies on Currying and a polymorphic type system for quantifiers, allows a modest amount of scope ambiguity in certain restricted syntactic contexts. But although it manages to keep track of the relation between syntactic expressions and argument positions (unlike systems based on **LP** that are criticized by Hendriks 1987), it does not extend to cases in which adjacent quantifiers give rise to scope ambiguities, as in *SOV* or *VOS* or *V NP PP* structures. And at the same time, it offers only a weak perspective on the type-structures associated with natural language quantifiers. Nevertheless, it illustrates one way in which a non-rigid relation may hold between the arrows of a syntactic calculus and the associated arrows of a semantic calculus.

Syntactic-semantic calculi

We have looked thus far at two ways in which a syntactic calculus can be coupled with a semantic type calculus. In the first, each proof of a valid syntactic arrow is paired with a unique arrow of the semantic type calculus. In the second, a valid syntactic arrow can be paired with a set of semantic arrows. In both cases, the two calculi are co-ordinated only by rules which pair arrows in one with arrows in the other. It is of course possible to introduce inference rules which mediate the relation between the two, as Moortgat (1989) has shown, following Hendriks (1987, 1989). Apart from the intrinsic interest of this work, it also provides an interesting perspective on the relation of syntactic and semantic properties.

Suppose that we begin with the paired calculus of the type discussed just above, in which syntactic composition may give rise to a set of type-compatible interpretations. And suppose that we make the following assumptions about types, using the type system of the extensional fragment of *PTQ*.

standard name	*syntactic type*	*semantic type*
proper name	NP	e
quantifier	NP	$<< e,t >,t >$
intrans. verb phrase	NP\S	$< e,t >$
trans. verb	(NP\S)/NP	$< e,< e,t >>$

Notice that while NP's and the two kinds of verbs we have are syntactically compatible, yielding such valid arrows as

$$N P \, N P \backslash S \to S$$

and

$$N P \, (N P \backslash S)/N P \; N P \to S$$

there is a clash between the semantic type associated with quantifier NP's and the type associated with transitive verbs: in the direct object position, a transitive verb combines with the semantic type e, but the type associated with a quantifier NP does not match this type, nor does the transitive verb type match the argument type – $<e,t>$ – required by the quantifier NP type. We can resolve this standstill (locally) by countenancing the rule of Argument Raising (Hendriks 1987, 1989; Moortgat 1990):

$$\chi : \lambda y_{k+j}...\lambda y_k...\lambda y_1.\phi \Rightarrow \chi : \lambda y_{k+j}...\lambda y_{k+1}\lambda Q\lambda y_{k-1}...\lambda y_1 Q\lambda y_k.\phi$$

(We assume that ϕ is of type t.)

This rule associates a fixed syntactic category χ with a higher-order type. Applying this rule to a transitive verb interpretation of type $<e,<e,t>>$ such as $\lambda y_2\lambda y_1 f(y_2)(y_1)$, we may choose $k = 2$,yielding:

$$\lambda Q\lambda y_1 Q\lambda y_2 f(y_2)(y_1)$$

This formula corresponds to the reading on which a quantifier in object position has narrow scope relative to the interpretation of the subject position. On the other hand, applying the rule twice, first with $k = 1$ and then with $k = 2$, yields a formula compatible with wide scope for a quantifier in object position:

$$\lambda Q_2 Q_2 \lambda y_2 Q_1 Q_1 \lambda y_1 f(y_2)(y_1)$$

The semantic transition involved in Argument Raising is not valid in **L**, but it is valid in **LP**, and is related to the algebraic notion of currying discussed earlier in the section on Currying. As Moortgat shows, Argument Raising can be factored into three more primitive operations: a permutation (invalid in **L**, but valid in **LP**), an application of Lifting (valid in **L** as well as in **LP**), and a second permutation which reverses the effects of the first. In effect, then, this combination of type transitions allows a set of higher-order interpretations (including interpretations which account for local scope ambiguities) to be associated with a given expression, in a way that does not affect its syntactic characteristics. And it does so in a way compatible with a single type, $<< e,t>,t>$ for the quantifiers discussed here.

PHONOLOGICAL INTERPRETATION

The formulation of L above contains a single phonological operation: concatenation. This is not a matter of principle – merely a matter of convenience. There are categorial systems with richer type structures in the phonological domain, structures which more accurately reflect the phonological properties of natural language expressions. (See Wheeler 1981, 1988; Schmerling 1981, 1982, 1989; Bach & Wheeler 1981; Oehrle 1988a, 1988b; Moortgat 1989; Steedman 1989.)

It is easy to see the difficulties that face a system which regards complex phonological expressions as arising purely by concatenation of phonological atoms (regardless of the phonological sophistication of the atoms). Most importantly, viewing the phonological structure of a complex expression as the concatenation of phonological atoms offers no way to treat global phonological properties such as prosody and intonation. By the same token, the striking word-internal effects of these global phenomena have no obvious analysis. Moreover, concatenation systems are unable to differentiate different modes of juncture between phonological units; as a result, even local problems involving sandhi rules seem to be beyond the scope of purely concatenative systems.

This brief section will discuss a variety of ways in which the phonological effects associated with syntactic and semantic composition can be more adequately treated within the general categorial perspective, with particular emphasis on the Lambek calculi. Because of the property of structural completeness, the calculus L provides an interesting framework in which to investigate the flexibility of phonological phrasing.

In considering how a categorial grammar can be coupled with phonological operations which are not purely concatenative, it is clear in advance that in some respects, the alternatives available are very similar to the alternatives available in characterizing the relation of syntax and semantics: in particular, we can ask how and to what extent the phonological properties of an utterance depend on its proof – that is, on its syntactic analysis – and we can imagine systems in which phonological properties are proof-independent (so that different proofs are phonologically undetectible) and systems in which phonological properties are proof-dependent (so that, in the extreme, distinct proofs correspond to phonologically-distinguishable utterances). Additionally, there is a question concerning the properties available to particular elements, and the properties that are predictable consequences of phonological composition. In the discussion to follow, we shall touch on some of these issues.

Bracketing and phrasing

A traditional approach to the interaction of syntactic composition and phonological properties is to assume that the phonological structure of a complex utterance consists of a bracketed sequence of words, the bracketing being inherited from a phrase-structure system relative to which syntactic composition is defined. To overcome the fact that a single syntactic bracketing may apparently support a variety of phonological interpretations – most obviously, a variety of phrasings – a relation is introduced between syntactic bracketings and phonological bracketings to constrain the class of phonological phrasings compatible with a given syntactic bracketing, on the assumption that the relation between a phonological bracketing and a particular phrasing of an utterance is simple. In principle, then, different syntactic structures may correspond to different prosodic structures. But in the absence of further details, this general view is not inherently strong.

When we consider these problems from the point of view of the Lambek calculi, two things are obvious: first, given the property of structural completeness, we cannot use the bracketing properties of particular proofs to constrain phonological phrasing; second, it is possible to impose phonological properties which constrain the analyses compatible with a given expression. The following sections touch on a few ways in which this can be done.

The prosodic hierarchy

The phonological structure of speech may be regarded as hierarchical, in the sense that it can be partitioned in several distinct, but compatible, ways: we may partition the speech stream into features, into segments (each consisting of a set of features), into syllables (each consisting of a sequence of segments), into feet (each consisting of a sequence of syllables), into phonological phrases (each consisting of a sequence of feet), and into intonational phrases. (This casual characterization of course leaves open such questions as whether every segment of an utterance belongs to a syllable, what the relation of sonority to syllabicity is, and so on. I hope that this will not be construed as indicating that I regard such questions as either unimportant or uninteresting.)

Now, one obvious way in which we can make the phonological effects of syntactic composition sensitive to this "prosodic hierarchy" (to use a term found in the work of Selkirk & Hayes) is to recognize several kinds of phonological operation, initially of two basic kinds. First, we need operations which construct elements of one level from appropriate elements of a lower level. Second, we need operations which will concatenate elements of a given level, yielding sequences of syllables, sequences of feet, and so on. If the units of composition are always of like rank, such a system has an appealing simplicity: to construct complex phonological expressions, first concatenate, then add appropriate higher-order structure. But what if the units of concatenation we wish to concatenate belong to different levels? What if we want to concatenate a syllable with a foot or a sequence of feet? The obvious thing to do is to appeal to general principles which resolve how this is to be done.

Generalized concatenation

In the simplest cases, there are two obvious approaches. Both approaches agree that if two expressions are of the same rank, then their "generalized concatenation" is the same as their ordinary concatenation within this rank. If they are of different ranks, then one of them is of a higher rank. This is where two cases arise, for we can either preserve the structure of the higher rank by adjoining the lower-ranking element to it (by concatenation at the lower level) or we can preserve the lower-level structure, by adding additional structure to the lower-ranking expression until the two expressions are of equal rank, and concatenation then reverts to its ordinary meaning at this level.

The first of these methods offers a way to deal with such problems as the rank of the marker of possession in such English expressions as **the queen of England's**. Although such examples are often regarded as bracketing mismatches, we may account for them straightforwardly: we assign to **'s** the syntactic category $NP \backslash (NP/N)$, but give it the phonological structure of a segment. Automatically, it will adjoin to the final syllable of its argument. And we may regard the dissimilation that occurs in such examples as **the girl from Kansas's** as a phonological property of syllable construction, related to the Obligatory Contour Principle of autosegmental phonology.

Non-associativity of phonological bracketing

Generalized concatenation, however it is to be defined, is only a first step in a more thoroughgoing account of sandhi phenomena. A useful second step is to notice that while concatenation is an associative operation, phonological variants of concatenation in general fail to be, often because the different bracketings $(ab)c$ and $a(bc)$ can easily trigger automatic, higher-level effects, as in the phonological structures associated with the expressions **lark spur**, **lark's purr**, and **lark's burr**, where the bracketing of segments interacts with phonological effects of syllabification in well-known ways. Similarly, we find temporal asymmetries depending on bracketing in the distinctiveness of such pairs as **Borda racer**, **board a racer**, and **board eraser**. Thus, there is reason to think that at least in certain cases, phonological composition is non-associative. One way in which this can arise is to assume that syntactic composition is non-associative, in which case phonological bracketing can be taken to be imposed by syntactic bracketing. (Even here, there are a range of cases to consider: at one extreme, bracketing is completely rigid; at the other extreme – that is, in the associative system – bracketing is completely dispensible; in between lie systems of partial associativity (Lambek 1961; Kandulski 1988; Oehrle & Zhang 1989.) Alternatively, we may assume that the syntactic algebra is associative, but that it is the phonological algebra which is inherently non-associative and imposes bracketing conditions (Moortgat 1989).

Bracketing and phonological phrasing

A related issue is the question of temporal and intonational phrasing. Here are some examples based on Bing (1979):

(1) NP: **These are the famous ducks Huey, Dewey, and Louie.**
(2) app: **These are the famous ducks – Huey, Dewey, and Louie.**
(3) voc: **These are the famous ducks, my friend.**

The intended interpretation of these cases is that in (1), **the famous ducks Huey, Dewey, and Louie** forms a single intonational phrase, in (2), **the famous ducks** and **Huey, Dewey, and Louie** form two intonational phrases, with the latter phrase understood as an appositive with respect to the first, and in (3), **my friend** is to be understood as a vocative. In fact, as Bing points out, we can find the same range of interpretations with a single sequence of words, such as **This is my sister Eunice**.

The correlation that we observe in these cases between phonological interpretation and syntactic/semantic function goes deeper. It is natural to pronounce the examples above with falling intonation: in (1), the intonation goes across the entire sentence and culminates with the nuclear accent on the first syllable of **Louie**; in (2), since we have two intonational phrases, we have two nuclear accents in two contours, both falling; in (3), we have a single nuclear accent, on **ducks**, with the vocative pronounced with a low pitch, perhaps accompanied by a rising boundary tone. But it is also possible to pronounce them with other intonational contours. In the first case, of course, since the phrase **the famous ducks Huey, Dewey, and Louie** contains the nuclear accent of the entire sentence, the contour associated with the phrase depends (in particular) on how the contour in question is to be associated with metrically-structured segmental texts (see Liberman 1975; Pierrehumbert 1979). What is perhaps surprising is the fact that in the second case (the appositive reading), the intonational contour is the same on both intonational phrases. In the third case, the pitch of the vocative is determined by the post-tonic properties of the intonation contour: it is low at the end of a falling contour and high at the end of a rising contour. How are such prosodic dependencies to be grammatically expressed?

I cannot offer an answer to this question here, but it is perhaps appropriate to consider what kinds of answers are possible relative to particular grammatical architectures. One possibility is to assume that grammatical composition is essentially intonation-free, and that intonational properties depend completely on the choice of an intonation contour and a syntactically structured expression. This is the standard approach within the generative tradition. In the categorial framework, there are some interesting alternatives available, primarily because syntactic, semantic, and phonological composition is possible in parallel. For this reason, a review of the rapidly growing literature on the relation of phonological properties to syntax and interpretation from a categorial perspective could be very worthwhile.

SUMMARY

In this paper, I have sketched some of the properties and prospects of one strand of categorial grammar – the strand that has grown from the logical and algebraic roots of Lambek's work. The sketch is incomplete in many respects. It does full justice to neither the mathematical foundations nor the linguistic foundations of the subject. Moreover, it neglects both the many other strands of categorial grammar currently under vigorous development and the relationship of this work to the many other interesting currents of contemporary linguistic research. The systematic exploration of the linguistic space that these theories have opened up and the interaction of this work with the empirical research that these theories feed on and spawn will lead, I hope, to a much deeper insight into the basis of the human language faculty.

NOTE

* Portions of this paper were presented at a Linguistics Department colloquium at the University of Arizona and at a Computer Science Department colloquium at the University of Chicago. In addition to the members of these audiences and the audience at the 1989 Simon Fraser Cognitive Science conference, I would like to thank Susan Steele, Ed Keenan, Polly Jacobson, Mark Steedman, Merrill Garrett, and, especially, Wojciech Buszkowski and Michael Moortgat, for discussion and support. Finally, I would like to express my appreciation of the hospitality of the University of Pennsylvania departments of Linguistics and Computer and Information Science: the final draft of this paper was written during the course of a sabbatical year at Penn in the happy atmosphere these departments provide.

REFERENCES

Anderson, A. and Belnap, N. (1975). *Entailment*. Princeton: Princeton University Press

Bach, E. and Wheeler, D. (1981). Montague phonology: a preliminary account. In W. Chao and D. Wheeler (eds.), *University of Massachusetts Occasional Papers in Linguistics*, VII:27-45

Bar-Hillel, Y., Gaifman, C., and Shamir, E. (1960). On categorial and phrase-structure grammars. *Bull. Res. Council Israel* F9:1-16. Reprinted in Y. Bar-Hillel (1964), *Language and Information*, Reading, MA.: Addison-Wesley

Benthem, J. van (1986). *Essays in Logical Semantics*. Dordrecht: Reidel

– (1988a). The semantics of variety in categorial grammar. In Buszkowski, Marciszewski, and van Benthem, 37-55

– (1988b). The Lambek calculus. In Oehrle, Bach, and Wheeler, 35-68

Bing, J. (1979). Aspects of English Prosody. Ph.D. dissertation, University of Massachusetts at Amherst

Buszkowski, W. (1986). Algebraic models of categorial grammars. In G. Dorn and P. Weingartner (eds.), *Foundation of Logic and Linguistics: Problems and Their Solutions*. New York: Plenum

– (1987). The logic of types. In J. Srzednicki (ed.), *Initiatives in Logic*, 180-206. Dordrecht: Nijhoff

– (1988). Generative power of categorial grammars. In Oehrle, Bach, and Wheeler, 69-94

– (1989). Principles of categorical grammar in the light of current formalisms. In K. Szaniawski (ed.), *The Vienna Circle and the Lvov-Warsaw School*. Dordrecht: Kluwer, 113-37

– , Marciszewski, W., and van Benthem, J. (eds.) (1988). *Categorial Grammar*. Amsterdam: J. Benjamins

Cohen, J. (1967). The equivalence of two concepts of categorial grammar. *Information and Control* 10:475-84

Curry, H. and Feys, R. (1958). *Combinatory Logic*. Volume I. Amsterdam: North-Holland

Došen, K. (1985). A completeness theorem for the Lambek calculus of syntactic categories. *Zeitschr. f. math. Logik und Grundlagen d. Math.* 31:235-41

Dougherty, R. (1970). A grammar of coordinate conjoined structures I. *Language* 46:850-98

– (1970). A grammar of coordinate conjoined structures II. *Language* 47:298-339

Dowty, D. (1988). Type-raising, functional composition, and non-constituent conjunction. In Oehrle, Bach, and Wheeler, 153-98

Gazdar, G. (1980). A cross-categorial semantics for conjunction. *Linguistics and Philosophy* 3:407-9

– , Klein, E., Pullum, G., and Sag, I. (1985). *Generalized Phrase Structure Grammar*. Cambridge, MA: Harvard University Press

Girard, J.-Y. (1987). Linear logic. *Theoretical Computer Science* 50:1-102

Hendriks, H. (1987). Type change in semantics: the scope of quantification and coordination. In Klein and van Benthem, 95-119

– (1989). Flexible Montague Grammar. Paper prepared for the Groningen summer school

Hindley, J.R. and Seldin, J.P. (1986). *Introduction to Combinators and λ-Calculus*. Cambridge, Eng.: Cambridge University Press

Kandulski, M. (1988). The nonassociative Lambek calculus. In Buzskowski et al., 141-51

Keenan, E. and Faltz, L. (1985). *Boolean Semantics for Natural Language*. Dordrecht: Reidel

Klein, E. and van Benthem, J. (eds.) (1988). *Categories, Polymorphism, and Unification*. Centre for Cognitive Science, University of Edinburgh / Institute for Language, Logic, and Information, University of Amsterdam

– and Sag, I. (1985). Type-driven translation. *Linguistics and Philosophy* 8:163-202

Lambek, J. (1958). The mathematics of sentence structure. *American Mathematical Monthly* 65:154-70. Reprinted in Buszkowski et al. (1988), 153-72

– (1961). On the calculus of syntactic types. In R. Jakobson (ed.), *Amer. Math. Soc. Proc. Symposia Appl. Math. 12:Structure of Language and its Mathematical Aspect*. Providence: American Mathematical Society, 166-78

– (1988). Categorial and categorical grammar. In Oehrle, Bach, and Wheeler, 297-317

– (1989). On a connection between algebra, logic, and linguistics. *Les Actes des*

Journées d'Études "Esquisses, Logique, Informatique Théorique," Université Paris, 7 juin 1989 (to appear)

– and Scott, P. (1986). *Introduction to Higher Order Categorial Logic.* Cambridge, Eng.: Cambridge University Press

Liberman, M. (1975). The Intonational System of English. Ph.D. dissertation, MIT

MacLane, S. and Birkhoff, G. (1967). *Algebra.* New York: Macmillan

Montague, R. (1974). *Formal Philosophy: Selected Writings of Richard Montague,* edited and with an introduction by R. Thomason. New Haven: Yale University Press

Moortgat, M. (1988). Lambek theorem proving. In Klein and van Benthem, 169-200

– (1989). *Categorial Investigations: Logical and Linguistic Aspects of the Lambek Calculus.* Dordrecht: Foris

– (1990). The quantification calculus. DYANA project report

Morrill, G. (1988). Extraction and Coordination in Phrase Structure Grammar and Categorial Grammar. Ph.D. dissertation, University of Edinburgh

– (1989). *Intensionality, Boundedness, and Modal Logic.* Centre for Cognitive Science, Edinburgh

Nishida, C. (1987). Interplay between Morphology and Syntax in Spanish. Ph.D. dissertation, University of Arizona

Oehrle, R.T. (1988a). Multi-dimensional compositional functions as a basis for grammatical analysis. In Oehrle, Bach, and Wheeler, 349-89

(1988b). Multidimensional categorial grammars and linguistic analysis. In Klein and van Benthem, 231-60

– (1990). Categorial frameworks, co-ordination, and extraction. *WCCFL* 9, to appear

– Bach, E., and Wheeler, D. (1988). *Categorial Grammars and Natural Language Structures.* Dordrecht: Reidel

– and Zhang, S. (1989). Lambek calculus and extraction from embedded subjects. *CLS* 25 (to appear)

Pareschi, R. and Steedman, M. (1987). A lazy way to chart-part with categorial grammars. *Proceedings of the 25th Annual Meeting of the Association for Computational Linguistics,* 81-8

Partee, B. (1987). Noun phrase interpretation and type-shifting principles. In J. Groenendijk, D. de Jongh, and M. Stokhof (eds.), *Studies in Discourse Representation Theory and the Theory of Generalized Quantifiers,* 115-43. Dordrecht: Foris

– and Rooth, M. (1983). Generalized conjunction and type ambiguity. In R. Bauerle, C. Schwarze, and A. von Stechow (eds.), *Meaning, Use, and Interpretation of Language,* 361-83. Berlin: Walter de Gruyter

Pierrehumbert, J. (1979). The Phonology and Phonetics of English Intonation. Ph.D. dissertation, MIT

Rooth, M. and Partee, B. (1982). Conjunction, type ambiguity, and wide scope "or." *WCCFL* 1:353-62

Ross, J.R. (1967). Constraints on Variables in Syntax. Ph.D. dissertation, MIT

Schmerling, S. (1982). The proper treatment of the relationship between syntax and phonology. *Texas Linguistic Forum* 19:151-66

– (1983). Montague morphophonemics. *Papers from the Parasession on the Interplay of Phonology, Morphology, and Syntax*, 222-37. Chicago: Chicago Linguistic Society

– (1989). Eliminating "agreement" in phonologically based categorial grammar: a new perspective on person, number, and gender. Paper presented at the Conference on Advances in Categorial Grammar, Tucson, July 1989

Smullyan, R. (1985). *To Mock a Mocking-bird*. New York: Knopf

Steedman, M. (1985). Dependency and coordination in the grammar of Dutch and English. *Language* 61:523-68

– (1987). Combinatory grammars and parasitic gaps. *NLLT* 5:403-40

– (1988). Combinators and grammars. In Oehrle, Bach, and Wheeler, 417-42

– (1989). Structure and intonation. Paper presented at the conference "Advances in Categorial Grammar," Tucson, 17 July 1989

– (1990). Gapping as constituent coordination. *Linguistics and Philosophy*, to appear

Szabolcsi, A. (1987). Bound variables in syntax (are there any?). Paper presented at the 6th Amsterdam Colloquium. To appear in R. Bartsch et al. (eds.), *Semantics and Contextual Expressions*. Dordrecht: Foris

Wheeler, D. (1988). Phonological consequences of some categorially-motivated assumptions. In Oehrle, Bach, and Wheeler, 467-88

Wittenburg, K. (1987). Predictive combinators: a method for efficient processing of combinatory categorial grammars. *Proceedings of the 25th Annual Meeting of the Association for Computational Linguistics*, 73-80

Zielonka, W. (1981). Axiomatizability of Ajdukiewicz-Lambek calculus by means of cancellation schemes. *Zeitschr. f. math. Logik und Grundlagen d. Math.* 27:215-24

Comment
Flexible Categorial Grammars: Questions and Prospects*

Pauline Jacobson

In "Dynamic Categorial Grammar" Oehrle examines the Associative Lambek Calculus, which is a version of Categorial Grammar (hereafter, CG) with at least two appealing properties. The first is that it is decidable. The second, and somewhat more interesting property, is structural completeness: if there is a proof of the well-formedness of a string under some bracketing then the same string has well-formedness proofs under all possible bracketings. To phrase this in the more usual terminology of syntactic theory: any well-formed sentence has as many structures as there are possible ways to bracket the string and this, as Oehrle points out, has two very nice consequences.

The first is that this provides an elegant account of the fact that virtually any sequence of words in a sentence – including sequences not standardly analysed as forming a single constituent – behaves like a constituent under conjunction. (This property of certain kinds of CGs is studied in detail in Dowty [1987].) Examples of this kind of "non-constituent" conjunction are shown in (1), where those in (c)-(e) are especially surprising:

(1) (a)   I gave a book to Mary and a record to Sue.
    (b)   John hoed and Mary weeded the garden.
    (c)   I put a book on and a record under the table.
    (d)   I carefully placed and Sam carelessly laid napkins on
          and rugs under the square tables.
    (e)   I cooked several and Bill ate a few tasty pigeons.

With structural completeness these reduce to cases of constituent conjunct – a sentence like *I put the book on the table* has one anaylsis in which *a book on* is a constituent and so this may conjoin with another constituent of the same category such as *a record under*.

A second potential advantage of structural completeness centres on parsing considerations. It is reasonably well accepted that people parse sentences on-line in some kind of left-to-right fashion; they do not wait until the end before beginning to compute the meaning. Consider a theory with structural completeness coupled with the view (taken in almost all of the CG literature) that the semantic composition of an expression is built "in tandem" with the syntactic composition. If a sentence can be analysed under all possible bracketings, then one of these is a completely left-branching structure. It thus follows that in parsing, the meaning of each incoming word can be combined with a meaning already computed for the previous words. Of course there is no reason to think that parsing must proceed in such a strict incremental left-to-right way; the literature on parsing has generally assumed that some portion of the sentence can be temporarily held in memory before being interpreted and combined with the previously interpreted material. One might, then, object that completely left-branching structures for every sentence is not, in fact, required for a theory of parsing. Nonetheless, structural completeness obviously provides at least one fairly straightforward view of the fact that parsing proceeds in a roughly incremental left-to-right way.

The version (actually, family of versions) of CG examined by Oehrle is part of a larger family of CG systems, systems which are sometimes referred to as "flexible Categorial Grammars." What distinguishes these from some other versions of CG (such as those with only functional application) is the fact that a given sentence generally has a number of different bracketings (where these different bracketings need not correspond to any semantic ambiguity). While not all such systems need have structural completeness, they all have in common the property that they do allow for multiple analyses of a single sentence and, concomitantly, they allow for at least a certain amount of left-branching. Moreover, because of the flexibility in how the words may be combined, they also all account for the type of conjunction facts noted earlier. (Of course different types of flexible CGs will make different predictions as to just how much freedom of conjunction there is; without structural completeness there will be some limits on what can conjoin. There will nonetheless be far more possibilities than in theories which do not contain this kind of multiple bracketing).[1]

This possibility of multiple bracketings is a consequence of the fact that such CGs contain other operations besides just functional application. In particular, they generally contain at least type-lifting and composition and/or division, and the combination of these operations allows material to be combined in a variety of ways. A thorough discussion of these operations and their consequences is provided by Oehrle; two that will play a central role in my remarks below are type-lifting and function composition. Type lifting takes some a in a set A and yields a function f whose domain is the set of functions in $A \times B$ and whose range is B, where for any function c in $A \times B$, $f(c) = c(a)$. The composition of two functions f from A to B and g from B to C is that function (notated $g \circ f$) from A to C which, for any a in A yields as value $g(f(a))$. Other possible operations are discussed in Oehrle, and it is worth noting that some of these are interdefinable (for instance, Oehrle discusses the division operation, where composition can be derived from division plus application).

"Flexible CG" thus refers to a family of systems, but those which have been extensively studied in the literature have two properties in common which distinguish them from some of the other work within CG such as, for example, Bach (1979, 1980), Dowty (1982a, 1982b), Chierchia (1984), and many others. First (as discussed in detail in Szabolcsi, to appear), very little if anything is stated in the syntax beyond just a statement that operations like application, type-lifting, etc. may apply. Instead, much of what has traditionally been seen as part of the syntax is encoded into the initial lexical types; the reason for this will be clarified below.

Second, work within flexible CG has generally contained no notion of a "discontinuous constituent" as in, for example, Bach (1979). Thus, working within a somewhat different version of CG, Bach proposed that when two expressions combine in the syntax they need not combine only by concatenation. In addition to concatenation, a functor expression may be split apart and "wrapped" around its argument (hence the term wrap for this operation). As will be discussed below, flexible CGs have generally not made use of a wrap operation, for it is unclear how to incorporate this into a theory with operations like composition and lifting. Even more puzzling is the question of what, if anything, would be meant by structural completeness in a theory with wrap, for the notion of a possible bracketing generally assumes that only contiguous material may be bracketed together. Thus many researchers working within a version of flexible CG have tried to account for the evidence for Wrap by allowing some kind of simulation of wrap (Szabolcsi 1987; Kang 1988; Evans 1989; Hepple 1990); I return to this later.

These observations form the point of departure for my remarks below – remarks which should be taken in the spirit of comment and speculation rather than as an attempt to present a fully articulated version of CG. The main thrust of these remarks is to suggest on the one hand that some kind of flexible CG is correct, but to provide evidence on the other hand that wrap needs to be incorporated into this system. I will, moreover, sketch one way that this can be done, where my proposal is based on that of Pollard (1984). The remainder of my remarks, then, will be structured as follows. In the first part of the Background section I review some of the initial motivation for a categorial syntax primarily to (very briefly) familiarize readers who are not so familiar with CG with some of the basic phenomena that it handles elegantly. The second part of the Background section turns to the implications of these phenomena for a flexible CG; in particular I discuss the reason that flexible CG encodes a number of generalizations into lexical entries. The next section turns to the status of wrap. I first review some of the past motivation for this, and then show how such an operation might be incorporated into a flexible CG. The third section turns to linguistic questions. Here I focus on Antecedent Contained VP Deletion, and show that some rather intricate facts are handled quite elegantly in a flexible CG. Moreover, Antecedent Contained Deletion provides some new evidence for wrap. The fourth section contains some concluding remarks.

BACKGROUND

Some initial motivation for a categorial syntax

To begin, let us consider some of the initial motivation for a categorial syntax. First, and perhaps foremost, a categorial syntax is arguably nothing more than an explicit statement of apparatus which is implicit in most other theories. Consider, for example, subcategorization. It is quite uncontroversial that part of the syntactic information associated with the lexical entry for a verb is a statement of what kind of complement it selects: *hope* subcategorizes for an S, *devour* for an NP, while *die* takes no complements within a VP. All theories, then, will contain the information that, for example, *hope* is a verb which wants an S complement. But this information can also be stated by saying that *hope* is a function which maps expressions of the category S into expressions of the category VP – in categorial notation, a VP/S. It is easy to generalize from this and note that "VP" itself can be defined as something which maps an expression of category NP (or perhaps of some other category) into S, and so *hope* is an (S/NP)/S. (Note that I am at the moment not using directional slashes – under the notation here, the category A/B does not specify whether it wants its arguments to the left or to the right. I return to word order below.) While these remarks are perhaps elementary, it is worth pointing out that a categorial syntax is thus one way to implement a proposal which has become quite generally accepted in most theories: at least part of the information required by the combinatory syntactic rules can be "projected" from the lexical entries, and so phrase structure rules need not be listed separately in the grammar. In other words, continuing to ignore word order for the moment, it follows from the categorial specification of *hope* that it can take an S complement and then an NP to give an S, and so no phrase structure rules are needed to spell this out.

A second attraction of this view of syntactic categories is that it fits well with an explicit theory of the semantic composition of an expression. Indeed, one of the most important points stressed in the work of Montague is that the syntactic composition should be taken quite seriously as an indicator of the semantic composition, and much of the work inspired by Montague's program has shown that positing functions and arguments in the syntax leads to a very clean view of the semantics where meanings are also built up by applying functions to arguments. (This view has been extended straightforwardly in flexible CGs. If, for example, two expressions combine in the syntax by function composition then their meanings also combine by function composition.) In fact, while Montague's work assumed that with each syntactic rule is listed a corresponding semantic rule, it has often been noted that this is not necessary. Given a direct correspondence between syntactic and semantic types (such that, for example, an expression of category A/B denotes a function from the semantic type of category B to the type of category A) and given a direct correspondence between the syntactic and the semantic composition, the semantic operation can be predicted from the syntactic mode of combination.

But there are also more subtle ways in which building the notion of a function/argument structure into the syntax allows for a statement of various generalizations. Take, for example, what has become known as "Keenan's generalization" (Keenan 1974), which is that agreement is always between a functor and its arguments and, more specifically, the functor agrees with the argument. To give some empirical content to this claim: we find verbs agreeing with their subjects; there are languages in which a verb agrees with an object; and there are languages in which determiners agree with nouns. But we would not expect to find a language in which, for example, a verb taking an S complement agreed with the subject of that complement.[2] The interest in Keenan's generalization is not simply that the domain of agreement can be described in terms of functions and arguments, but more importantly that this follows immediately under a categorial syntax and so need not be stipulated. This is because agreement can be seen simply as a special case of subcategorization. For example, take the two forms *kill* and *kills*. These have two slightly different categories, where *kill* (ignoring person agreement) is of category

S/NP [PLUR] and *kills* of category S/NP [SING]. To say that a functor "agrees" with the argument is merely to say that the functor selects the category of the argument, which is, of course, true by definition.[3]

Moreover, almost all theories recognize that given a verb and its arguments, there is some kind of asymmetry between these arguments; subjects, for example, are in some sense more prominent than objects. Different theories have different mechanisms for conveying these asymmetries: in Relational Grammar (which was, perhaps, the first theory to study these asymmetries in depth) grammatical relations like "subject" and "object" are primitive notions which are ordered on a hierarchy. In GB these notions are configurationally defined, but the asymmetry between arguments is taken to be a consequence of the tree structure, where relative prominence is usually defined in terms of c-command. In CG, this asymmetry can be stated in terms of the order in which a verb combines with its arguments: a later argument can be said to "arg-command" an earlier argument (see Dowty [1982a] for detailed discussion of this).

It is extremely difficult to distinguish between these different views on the asymmetry between arguments (and even harder to find evidence in support of one or the other). But where the CG view does appear to have an advantage is that – given the usual assumption in CG that the syntactic composition is a direct reflection of the semantic composition – this syntactic asymmetry also correlates directly with an asymmetry in the semantic composition. Hence, just as the subject is a later argument in the syntactic composition, so also is it a later argument in the semantic composition. The interest in this is that we would therefore expect this kind of asymmetry to play a role in certain semantic processes.

Take, for example, the case of reflexives, where the asymmetry is manifested in the familiar facts in (2):

(2) (a) He loves himself.
     (b) *Himself loves him.

Consider the basic account of reflexive in Szabolcsi (1987) (I adopt this for expository convenience; the same basic remarks also hold for the account in Bach & Partee 1980, as well as for most other accounts which have been developed within the CG and related literature). Oversimplifying somewhat, a reflexive on this analysis is an "argument reducer:" it is of syntactic category (X/NP) / ((X/NP) / NP) and its meaning is $\lambda f[\lambda x[f(x)(x)]]$.[4] To illustrate with the case of an ordinary transitive verb V, reflexive applies to the two-place relation V' and returns a function which characterizes the set of all x such that

x stands in the V' relation to x. The asymmetry between subject and object positions is thus an automatic consequence of the meaning of the reflexive.

The above remarks are phrased under a version of CG with a clear distinction between functions and arguments, and where arguments are always introduced in the "expected" order. Consider, however, a flexible CG. In particular, let us consider one which includes type lifting and composition. With type lifting, the function/argument structure can "flip-flop." Suppose, for example, that the lexical type of an intransitive verb is S/NP and so it takes a subject NP as argument. But the subject NP can raise to an S/(S/NP) where this is accompanied by a corresponding semantic operation. If the meaning of the input NP is NP', then the meaning of the output S/(S/NP) is $\lambda P[P(NP')]$ (for P a variable over VP-type meanings). (Following Partee & Rooth 1983 I assume here and throughout this discussion that an NP like *John* denotes an individual and hence the lexical meaning of an intransitive verb is a function of type $< e, t >$. I will be ignoring quantified NPs and their consequences for type raising until the next section.) This means that a simple case like *John walks* has two analyses. In one, *walks* is a function taking *John* as argument (and the semantics is parallel – walk' applies to j). In the other analysis (familiar from Montague, 1974) *John* is the function taking *walks* as argument where the semantic composition is $\lambda P[P(j)](walks')$. When function composition is added, even more possibilities result in a sentence with three or more words. Consider, for example, *John sees Mary*. Among the possible analyses is one where *John* type lifts and composes with *see* to give an S/NP *John sees*, whose meaning is $\lambda P[P(j)]^{\circ}see' = \lambda x[\lambda P[P(j)] (see'(x))] = \lambda x[see'(x)(j)]$. This can then take *Mary* as argument (alternatively, *Mary* can lift to take *John sees* as argument).

The question immediately arises, then, as to whether or not the generalizations concerning function/argument asymmetries and the generalizations regarding different argument positions are captured in a flexible CG. The answer is that these are – provided that the relevant generalizations are initially encoded into the lexical entries. By way of illustration, consider again Keenan's generalization. Suppose, contrary to what was proposed above, that this were a generalization about the syntactic combinatory rules. In other words, suppose that the correct principle underlying Keenan's generalization were a principle like the following:

(3) Whenever a function A/B combines with an argument B, some feature of B may be copied onto the expression of category A/B, and this is the only way in which feature copying is allowed.

In this view, type-lifting would wreak havoc with Keenan's generalization, for a subject can type-lift and take a verb as argument; we would thus expect to find cases where a feature of the verb is copied onto the subject. Even more seriously, simple subject-verb agreement will not always occur, for when the subject is the functor its agreement features will not be copied on to the verb.

But, as noted above, Keenan's generalization need not be stipulated in this way. Agreement is, rather, a property of lexical items and reduces to a kind of subcategorization. Hence a verb like *kill* is listed in the lexicon as S/NP[PLUR] while *John* is listed as NP[SING]. By definition, type-lifting raises an expression of category A to one of category B/(B/A), and so *John* can lift to (among others) S/(S/NP[SING]). But it cannot lift to become an S/(S/NP[PLUR]). In this way the correct agreement pattern is preserved, regardless of which is the functor and which is the argument.

Similar remarks hold for word order. There are two different ways to handle word order which have been explored within the categorial literature. In one, word order generalizations are stated in this syntax; this can be accomplished by adopting something akin to the LP principles of GPSG. While the exact LP rules of Gazdar, Klein, Pullum and Sag (1985) cannot be immediately imported into CG, rules within much the same spirit can. To make this more concrete, we can consider one such system which is briefly explored in Jacobson (1990) where LP principles are stated in terms of functions, arguments, and result categories. Thus, for example, one generalization about English word order is that subjects (regardless of their category) precede VPs, while in most other cases functors precede arguments. (I am for the moment ignoring those cases which have been analysed as involving a wrap operation; this is a topic to which I return below.) One might, then, adopt the following two word order statements: (1) when two expressions combine to form an S the argument goes to the left, (2) in all other cases the argument goes to the right. (These statements would undoubtedly need considerable refinement and are offered here primarily for illustration.) It is obvious that statements like these cannot be maintained in a CG with type-lifting. If, for example, *John* lifts to take *walks* as argument then the resulting order would be *walks John*. Nor could one hope to refine these statements by making use of the syntactic categories of the combining expressions, since these categories can of course change dramatically under type-lifting.

Thus the alternative view, which is generally adopted within a flexible CG, builds word order into the lexical entries by means of "directional slashes" in such a way that operations like type-lifting and composition will not damage the word order possibilities. Thus a lexical expression which is a function specifies where it wants its arguments. I should at this point note that there are two different notational systems for this within the CG literature. Some authors (e.g., Lambek 1958, Oehrle [this volume], and others working within the Lambek calculus) have used the notation $B\backslash A$ to denote a function from domain B to range A. Hence $B\backslash A$ is a function wanting a B to its left, while A/B is a function wanting an A to its right. Other authors (e.g., Dowty 1988; Steedman 1987, 1988) have used $B\backslash A$ in exactly the opposite way: this is a function from domain A to range B. (For a spirited debate on the relative merits of each notation, the interested reader might consult the first two issues of the *Categorial Grammar Newsletter*.) To avoid notational confusion I will adopt a third notation which uses subscripts: $A/_L B$ is a function wanting a B to its left to give A, while $A/_R B$ wants a B to its right. (I will, moreover, omit the subscripts when this is not relevant to the immediate point at hand.)

Before continuing, we can note two important points about the claim that word order is encoded in the lexical entries. First, the notion that word order is encoded in lexical entries does not mean that no generalizations can be stated about word order for one can, of course, have rules governing possible lexical items. In English, for example, one such rule would be that any lexical item of category $((S/\alpha)/X)$ is actually of category $((S/_L\alpha)/X)$ (for α a variable over categories, and X a variable over any sequence of categories and slashes); this ensures that subjects always go on the left.

The second point is one which is heavily exploited in the remarks below. Under the view that lexical items specify the direction in which they combine with their arguments, a lexical item like *walks* can be viewed quite literally as a function from fully ordered strings to fully ordered strings. (More accurately, a lexical item and in fact any linguistic expression is an ordered triple of some (phonological) string, a syntactic category which, if it is a functor category, corresponds to some function from strings to strings, and a meaning.) Thus the function corresponding to the category of *walks* maps the NP *John* into the string *John walks* and for each NP it yields a unique fully ordered string. Under a system without directional slashes in the lexicon, the lexical category of *walks* does not correspond to a function from ordered strings to ordered strings. Rather, it corresponds to a function to some more abstract object (what Dowty [1982a], following Curry [1963], has called the tectogrammatical structure). Here, then, the item *walks* is a lexical item which maps *John* into some more abstract tecto-grammatical object, and the syntax specifies the actual surface string.

Given the view that word order is encoded into the lexical entries, there is no difficulty in preserving the correct word order under operations like lifting and composition. Lifting, for example, can be defined so that an expression of category A lifts to become a $B/_R(B/_LA)$ or a $B_L/(B/_RA)$. In the derivation of *John walks*, the lexical category of *John* is NP and that of *walks* is $S/_LNP$. *John* can lift to become $S_R/(S/_LNP)$ but not, for example, $S_L/(S/_LNP)$, and so *walks John* is not possible. Similarly for function composition. Let us suppose that only two kinds of composition are allowed. An expression of category $A/_RB$ may combine with a $B/_RC$ to its right to yield an expression of category $A/_RC$, or an $A/_LB$ may combine with a $B/_LC$ to its left to yield an $A/_LC$. Take, then, the analysis discussed earlier for *John sees Mary*. *John* lifts to $S/_R(S/_LNP)$ and so may compose with *sees* to give $S/_RNP$, which then combines with *Mary*. Note that there is no derivation which would yield, for example, *sees John Mary*.

At first glance, this might appear like a rather stipulative way to preserve word order. Why, for example, can an A lift to a $B/_R(B/_LA)$ but not to a $B_L/(B/_LA)$? But under the view that functor categories specify functions from fully ordered strings to fully ordered strings the allowable lifting operations in fact need not be stipulated; these follow from the definition of lifting. (I am grateful to Dick Oehrle for pointing this out to me, especially since this observation plays a central role in the wrap proposal to be developed below.) Recall that by definition lifting takes an item a and yields a function f in $((A \times B) \times B)$ such that for any function c in $A \times B$, $f(c) = c(a)$. Consequently, *John* can lift to a function f such that $f(walks) = walks(John)$. But *walks* is a function which maps *John* into the string *John walks*, and so the lifted category of *John* must, by definition of lifting, map *walks* into this same string. The same point holds for function composition; it follows directly from the definition of function composition that $A/_RB$ composes with a $B/_RC$ to its right, and that the result is $A/_RC$ and not $A/_LC$.

The status of mixed composition

In addition to the two cases of composition described above, Steedman (1987) proposes that natural language also, in certain circumstances, uses "mixed composition" as shown in (4):

(4)   (i) $A/_R B + B/_L C = A/_L C$
       (ii) $B/_R C + A/_L B = A/_R C$

Note that in both cases the slash direction on the composed category is inherited from the secondary function (where f is the secondary function in $g \circ f$), while the position of the secondary function vis-a-vis the primary function is determined by the slash direction of the latter. (Kang [1988] argues for additional types of mixed composition for Korean.)

While I will momentarily discuss some evidence for something like the operations in (4), note that under the view that syntatic functions map ordered strings into ordered strings, these operations are not actually function composition. To illustrate, take a verb like *said* of category $(S/_L NP)/_R S$ and a verb like *left* of category $S/_L NP$. If these combine by the operation in (4i) then the result is *said left* of category $(S/_L NP)/_L NP$ and this would ultimately give a sentence like **John Tom said left*. (It should be noted that Steedman's particular proposal does not allow mixing composition in all cases and so his proposal does not allow this sentence.) What has gone wrong here is that *said* and *left* have not actually combined by function composition. Since *said* maps *John left* into *said John left* and *left* maps *John* into *John left*, then *said o left* by definition is that function which maps *John* into *said John left*. But using only directional slashes, there is no way to specify this resulting function.

To put this in somewhat different terms, the grammar contains a set of syntactic categories as follows: there is some set of basic categories, and a recursive specification of additional categories as follows: if α and β are categories, then $\alpha/_R \beta$ is a category, $\alpha/_L \beta$ is a category, and nothing else is. Each linguistic string has a syntactic category, and each such functor category has a corresponding function. If x is of category $\alpha/_R \beta$ then the corresponding function is a mapping from a string y of category β to the string xy of category α. Let F be the set of functions corresponding to the set of syntactic functor categories. Then F is not closed under function composition. As illustrated above, for example, the composition of the function corresponding to $A/_R B$ and the function corresponding to $B/_L C$ yields a function with no corresponding category. We would thus not expect to find that such categories can compose.

Indeed, I will present some evidence in the third section that in general they cannot, and this fact provides interesting support for this view of syntactic categories. However, it should be noted that there also appear to be limited cases in which something akin to the operations in (4) do apply. (Steedman also proposes that these operations

do not apply freely and are only allowed with particular categories.)
In addition to those cases discussed in Steedman, consider the Raising
to Object construction exemplified in (5):

(5) John expects Mary to win.

In Jacobson (1990, to appear) I argue that this is derived by the composition of *expect* (of category VP/S[INF]) with the S[INF]/NP *to win*;
this yields the VP/NP *expect to win* which then combines with *Mary*
by wrap. Space precludes a discussion of the motivation for this analysis here; several arguments are provided in Jacobson (1990).

My analysis there was cast within a system without directional
slashes, and I also claimed that a Raising verb like *expect* is marked in
a special way in the lexicon to indicate that it can and must undergo
function composition. But it may be possible to slightly recast this
basic idea into a system with directional slashes. First, let us continue
to assume that mixed composition does not exist, for the reasons
discusssed above. Second, *expect* is of category $VP/_RS$. However, its
unusual property (and that of other Raising to Object verbs) is that it
is marked in the lexicon as being required to combine with an $S/_LX$ to
yield a VP/X – that is, it combines by something like mixed composition. (The semantics associated with this operation is ordinary function composition.) Similar remarks hold for Raising to Subject verbs
like *seem*. In my analysis, *John seems to be tall* is derived by composing
seem (of category S/S[INF]) with the S[INF]/NP *to be tall* to give the
S[INF]/NP *seems to be tall*. But again only certain verbs allow this kind
of "composition," and so *seem* (and other Raising to Subject verbs)
must also have some unusual lexical property. If these are listed in the
lexicon as being of category $S/_RS$ (rather than $S/_LS$) then these too can
be analysed as having the special property of undergoing mixed
"composition."

Note further that (unlike the proposal of Steedman) I assume that
the directional feature on the result of this operation is not inherited
from the secondary functor (for discussion, see Jacobson 1990).
Whether this is also specified as part of the category of *expect* or is
specified in some other way is a matter I will leave open here. I will
also leave open exactly how to specify in the lexical entry for Raising
verbs so that these combine by mixed "composition;" nor is it clear
just how this operation can be incorproated into the general framework under discussion here. But for the present purposes, the important point is that while there do appear to be instances of (something
like) the kinds of operations shown in (4), these cannot generally

apply, which follows from the view of syntactic functions as mappings from strings to strings.

WRAP

Initial motivation for wrap

We turn now to the major focus of these remarks: the status of a wrap operation as proposed in, for example, Bach (1979, 1980), Dowty (1982a), Jacobson (1983, 1987), Hoeksema (1984), Pollard (1984), and others. These works have all argued that a function can combine with an argument not only by an operation which concatenates the two expressions, but also by a wrap operation which allows a functor expression to be split apart and the argument to be inserted inside the functor. One explicit formalization whose properties are well understood is developed in Pollard (1984); this relies on the view that the syntactic operations take as input *headed* strings and combine them to give new headed strings. One possible operation, then, is that an argument is placed before (or after) the head of the functor string. I will return to Pollard's proposal in more detail below, as I will suggest that his analysis can be adapted and incorporated into a flexible CG with some rather interesting results.

The claim that natural language syntax includes a wrap operation has most often been motivated by a consideration of English VPs. Take, for instance, *give the book to Mary*. Beginning with Chomsky (1957), a number of researchers have argued that *give to Mary* is in some sense a constituent – Chomsky's particular implementation of this relied of course on a transformation, and so he analysed this VP as having the underlying structure *give to Mary the book*. This basic idea has been fleshed out slightly differently within the CG literature. Bach (1979, 1980), Dowty (1982a) and others have proposed that *give* first combines with *to Mary* to give the expression *give to Mary* of category (S/NP)/NP and this in turn combines with the object *the book*, where the object is "wrapped in" and placed after the verb. (Wrap presumably also applies in the case of an (S/NP)/NP consisting of a single word like *kill*, where here again the object is placed to the right of the verb but the wrap effect is vacuous.) A few points of terminology: I will henceforth refer to an expression of category (S/NP)/NP as a TVP (transitive verb phrase) and I will refer to the NP which is wrapped into such an expression as the DO.

There are various considerations in support of this analysis. Note first that in addition to VPs like *give the book to Mary* there are also VPs like *give to Mary the book I wrote*. Under the Bach/Dowty analysis such cases need not be derived by "Heavy NP Shift." Rather, we can assume that the object of a transitive verb may either be introduced by wrap or may also just concatenate with the TVP to give the Heavy NP Shift construction.[5] Second, consider the subject/object asymmetry discussed earlier with respect to reflexive. As is well-known reflexive (and many other phenomena) also exhibits an asymmetry between the direct and indirect objects as is shown below:

(6) (a) I introduced him to himself.
     (b) *I introduced himself to him.

This is not surprising under the Wrap analysis. *introduce* in (6a) first combines with *to himself*; using the basic idea discussed above, *to himself* is the function taking the verb as argument. The meaning of the resulting expression *introduce to himself* is $\lambda x[\text{introduce}'(x)(x)]$ and so the correct meaning will result when the object is introduced. (6b) is impossible because here the reflexive is introduced later than the indirect object *to him*; a reflexive in this position could only be "bound" by the subject. Other sorts of asymmetries along these lines have been extensively discussed in the Relational Grammar literature (see also Dowty 1982a), and additional arguments for wrap are provided in Jacobson (1987, 1990) as well as in the third section below.

Wrap has been studied in the most detail with respect to English VPs, but this operation has also been suggested for VSO languages, where there is a good deal of evidence for the claim that the verb and the object form some kind of constituent (see, for example, Anderson and Chung 1977; Emonds 1980; McCloskey 1983; among many others). Similarly, this operation has sometimes been suggested for the case of subject-aux inversion in English. It is also worth noting that this general kind of proposal is explored in much of the recent GB literature; see especially Larson (1988).

Wrap in a flexible CG

Despite the kinds of evidence discussed briefly above, most versions of flexible CG have assumed, either implicitly or explicitly, that the only way two expressions may combine in the syntax is by concatenation, and so such theories do not contain a wrap operation. Indeed, as noted in the introduction, certain flexible CGs have the interesting property of structural completeness, and it is not at all clear that this would be preserved (or even be meaningful) with the incoproration of wrap. Even in flexible CGs without structural completeness, wrap appears problematic, for it is not immediately obvious how to fold such an operation into a grammar with type-lifting, composition (and/or division), etc.

Consequently, beginning with Szabolcsi (1987), various researchers within flexible CG have accounted for the kinds of facts discussed above by some kind of wrap simulation (see, e.g., Szabolcsi 1987; Kang 1988; Evans 1989; Hepple 1990). The basic idea is that the lexical type of, for example, *give* (in *give the book to Mary*) is the Bach/Dowty type: it is an ((S/NP)/NP)/PP. The Heavy NP Shift facts can be accounted for in roughly the way suggested above – one option is for *give* to simply concatenate with its arguments to give a VP like *give to Mary the book that I wrote*. An ordinary VP like *give the book to Mary* is derived in most of these analyses by fixing the types in such a way that *the book* and *to Mary* can first compose, and the expression *the book to Mary* then takes *give* as argument. These proposals are also designed to account for the asymmetry with respect to reflexive shown in (6), but as these accounts are somewhat intricate I will not discuss them here. Suffice it to say that it is not obvious that these wrap simulations can account for the full range of data motivating wrap. In particular, I do not see how to extend these to the interaction of Raising and wrap discussed in Jacobson (1990, to appear) nor to the evidence for wrap which will be adduced in the third section.

Thus, rather than simulating wrap, I would like to suggest that a true wrap operation can and should be incorporated into a flexible CG. In the remainder of this section I will sketch a way to do this. My proposal is quite directly based on that of Pollard (1984), with various adaptions to fit the basic framework of flexible CG. In the next section I will turn in detail to one fairly complex area, namely, the interaction of Antecedent Contained VP Deletion and quantifiers – and will show how this provides additional evidence both for a wrap operation and for some of the other apparatus of a flexible CG.

As mentioned above, the most explicit formalization of wrap is in Pollard (1984). Adapting his proposal to fit the general framework here, the key idea is that a linguistic expression is not simply a string, but a headed string. Thus each string contains one distinguished element which is the head, and which we will notate by underlining. Embedding this into a CG, this means that a syntactic function is a mapping from headed strings to headed strings, which in turn means that the category of the functor must include information pertaining not only to the linear order of the new string, but must also specify the head of the new string. We can assume that there are two possibilities: either the head of the functor becomes the head of the resulting string, or the head of the argument does. I will notate this as follows: A^F/B

indicates that the result head is that of the functor, while A^A/B indicates that the result head is that of the argument.

Consider, for example, a verb like *say* which takes a sentential complement to give a VP. Each lexical item is its own head, and so the actual lexical item is the string *say*. When it combines with its complement, its head (in this case, itself) becomes the head of the VP. Hence *say* is of category $(S^F/_LNP)^F/_RS$. (I assume here that the verb is also the head of the S, but nothing hinges on this.) This means that when it takes as argument an S like *Bill left* the result is the headed string *say Bill left* of category $S^F/_LNP$.

Notice that by specifying head inheritance in this way we can again preserve the correct head relations under type-lifting and composition. By the definition of lifting, there are two possibilities (I am ignoring here the directional features on the slashes):

(7) $A \rightarrow B^F/(B^A/A)$
     $A \rightarrow B^A/(B^F/A)$

By definition, the lifted expression must, when applied to an argument y, give as value that headed string which would be obtained by applying y to the input of the lifting rule, and so the liftings shown in (7) are the only possibilities. For example, A cannot lift to $B^F/(B^F/A)$. Suppose, then, that a headed S like *Bill left* type-lifts to take *say* as argument. Its lifted category will be $(S^F/_LNP)^A/_L((S^F/_LNP)^F/_RS)$. Accordingly, it will take *say* to its left, and yield a structure such that the head of the argument is the head of the result, and so the result will again be *say Bill left*.

Composition is similar. There are four possible inputs to composition, as shown in (8):

(8) (i) $A^F/B \circ B^F/C$
     (ii) $A^F/B \circ B^A/C$
     (iii) $A^A/B \circ B^F/C$
     (iv) $A^A/B \circ B^A/C$

By the definition of composition, two things are required regarding the output expression and its category. First, if the primary function is A^F/B then its head is the head of the resulting expression; if the primary function is A^A/B then the head of the secondary function is the head of the result. Second, whichever function contributes the head also contributes the superscript on the new slash; thus the resulting categories are shown in (9):

(9) (i) $A^F/B \circ B^F/C = A^F/C$
   (ii) $A^F/B \circ B^A/C = A^F/C$
   (iii) $A^A/B \circ B^F/C = A^F/C$
   (iv) $A^A/B \circ B^A/C = A^A/C$

Strictly speaking, in case (iv), where A^A/B composes with B^A/C, the definition of function composition itself does not determine what is the head of the new expression, as the interested reader may verify. In the final result, the head will be supplied by the head of C, and so it does not matter what is the head of the string resulting from (iv). I assume for simplicity that it is the head of the secondary functor, as in the case in (iii).

With this foundation, we can now turn to wrap. Following Bach (1979), Pollard proposes that there are actually two wrap operations: right wrap places the argument to the right of the head of the functor, and correspondingly for left wrap.[6] Since we have now incorporated the notion that a linguistic expression is a headed string, Pollard's proposal can be adapted in a reasonably straightforward manner. The key is to allow two new types of syntactic functions. One says that it wants to wrap around its argument, and the other is an infix; it wants to go inside its argument. (For a similar proposal, see Hoeksema & Janda 1988.)

Thus let us introduce four new kinds of "directional" slashes on lexical items. An expression x of category $A/_{RW}B$ is a function which maps a headed string y of category B into a headed string of category A, where the resulting string is formed by placing y to the right of x's head. (The new head will, of course, be supplied in accordance with the superscript feature which is supressed here.) An expression x of category $A/_{RI}B$ is what we can think of as an infix. It maps a headed string y of category B into a headed string of category A where the result is obtained by placing x to the right of the head of y. $A/_{LW}B$ and $A/_{LI}B$ are the corresponding left wrap and left infix categories.

Once again, the correct word order possibilities are preserved under lifting. By definition, only the following four lifting operations with wrap/infix slashes are possible:

(10) $A \rightarrow B/_{RI}(B/_{RW}A)$
     $A \rightarrow B/_{RW}(B/_{RI}A)$
     $A \rightarrow B/_{LI}(B/_{LW}A)$
     $A \rightarrow B/_{LW}(B/_{LI}A)$

We illustrate this system with two derivations of the VP *give the book to Mary*.

(11) (a)

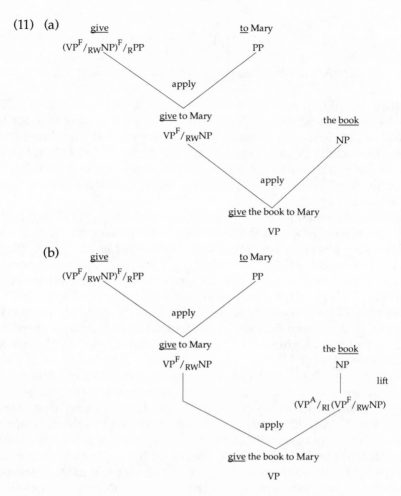

(b)

Finally, one might wonder what happens to the wrap/infix slashes under composition. To go through each possible case would be rather tedious, but it can be noted that in some cases a category with a wrap or infix slash cannot compose for the same reason that there is (in general) no mixed composition: the output category required by the definition of function composition is not within the set of categories allowed in this system. As one example, consider a string with three expressions: v of category $A^F/_RB$, wxy of category $B^F/_{RW}C$, and z of category C. In the straightforward application derivation, wxy applies to z to give the headed string $wxzy$ of category B, and this in turn occurs as the argument of v to give the headed string $vwxzy$. Now suppose v were to first compose with wxy. By the definition of function composition, the resulting expression should be one which will then place z after x. Yet also by definition the head of the composed string must be v and not x, since the head of the final result must be v. We would thus need functions containing information beyond that which is allowed by the conventions here, and so there is no way to compose these functions. As will be shown in the next section, this turns out to be a very welcome result.

There are two final comments before turning to the evidence for this kind of system. First, as regards the Heavy NP Shift cases I assume that the basic line discussed above is correct. In other words, TVPs in English can either wrap around their arguments or simply take their arguments to the right. This means that there is a redundancy rule to the effect that any expression of category $((S/NP)/_{RW}NP)/X$ is also of category $((S/NP)/_R NP)/X$. In the next section I will be discussing a case where a VP like *said Mary read the book* can be obtained by composing *said* with *Mary read*. As the interested reader can verify, this should be impossibe when *read* is of category $(S/_LNP)^F/_{RW}NP$, as this turns out to be exactly an instance of the case described above. However, *read* also has the ordinary category $(S/NP)^F/_RNP$ and so this composition is possible.[7] (Under the non-wrap version of *read*, when *say* composes with *Mary read* the head of the new string will be *say*, and so the head of the resulting VP will be the same as in the application-only derivation. Note that the category which results from this composition does not need to specify that the NP is wrapped in after *read*; here the output category simply specifies that the NP is placed to the right. It is for this reason that function composition in this case yields a category which is within the set of syntactic categories, while in the case where *read* has the wrap category the requisite output category cannot be stated.)

Second, given the adoption of wrap slashes, one might wonder whether the remarks in the first section regarding mixed composition still hold. In other words, I claimed that mixed composition is not a free option (although a related operation appears to apply in special cases) precisely because it is not an actual function composition. Moreover, I noted that while there is some function from $A/_RB$ to $B/_LC$, which is the composite of these two functions, such a function is not one within the set of functions that constitute syntactic categories. However, it might now appear that with the expansion of the set of syntactic functions to include wrappers and infixes it should be possible to give an appropriate output of mixed composition, where this output would be $A/_{RW}C$. To illustrate, *say* should be able to compose with *left* to give the headed string *say left* of category $VP/_{RW}NP$; this would then wrap around *Mary* to give the VP *say*

Mary left. However, it is only an accident that in this case this kind of mixed composition gives the right result; whenever the primary function in the input to function composition does not have its head on the extreme right then the wrong result will occur. In general, then, $A/_{RW}C$ is not the actual function which is the composite of $A/_RB$ and $B/_LC$, and so it remains the case that the result of composing these two functions is a function not specificable by any category within the set of syntactic categories.

ANTECEDENT CONTAINED VP DELETION

In the remainder of these remarks, I will turn in some detail to one interesting and quite intricate phenomenon: Antecedent Contained VP Deletion and its interactions with quantifier scopes. This phenomenon provides some rather nice evidence for a number of the points touched on above. First, it provides evidence for some kind of flexible CG and shows how under this theory some phenomena which have previously been taken to necessitate a level of logical form can be handled without such a level. In fact, there is at least one case for which the approach here fares better than the traditional LF approach; I turn to this at the end. Second, the account here provides new evidence for a wrap operation. Third, I suggested above that mixed composition is not (in general) allowed, nor are certain kinds of compositions involving wrap slashes. These restrictions themselves follow from more general considerations: if the set of syntactic functions are only those which can be specified by the devices discussed above (directional slashes including wrap and infix slashes and features which specify head inheritance), and if by a syntactic function we actually mean a mapping from headed, ordered strings to headed, ordered strings, then these kinds of function compositions are impossible, as they require output categories which cannot be specified. The interest in Antecedent Contained Deletion is that it provides evidence that those restrictions which follow from this more general view are correct.

Background

Before turning to the analysis of the relevant phenomena, some background remarks are in order concerning the broader theoretical implications surrounding phenomena like quantifier scopes and VP Deletion. Perhaps the single most vigorously debated issue regarding the syntax/semantics interface has been the question of whether a surface sentence directly receives a model-theoretic interpretation, or whether it instead corresponds to one (or more) abstract level(s) of representation from which are read off certain aspects of its meaning. The first approach, which I will refer to as the *direct interpretation approach*, has been pursued in much of the work within Categorial Grammar and related theories like GPSG. The second approach, which I will refer to as the *abstract level(s) approach*, is taken in GB, the Generative Semantics work of the late 1960s and early 1970s, and also much of the earlier work within "classical" transformational grammar.

The abstract level(s) vs. direct interpretation debate has been carried out in greatest detail with respect to the treatment of quantifier scope ambiguities as in (12) and de re/de dicto ambiguities as in (13):

(12) Every student read some book.
(13) John said that Mary should read every book.

The abstract level solution to this ambiguity is well-known: in general, a quantified NP "pulled out" at Logical Form (LF) in such a way as to mark its scope, while its surface position is marked with a variable. Thus in (13), for example, the de re (or, wide scope) reading is obtained by pulling *every book* out at LF and having it attached in such a way that it c-commands everything else; as such it has scope over both clauses. On the de dicto (or, narrow scope) reading it c-commands only the embedded sentence, and hence the description *every book* is within the scope of *say*. This kind of account of these ambiguities was first investigated in the linguistics literature in works such as Bach (1968), McCawley (1970), and Lakoff (1971), and was later adopted by May (1977) and many subsequent researchers.

There are, however, alternative accounts to the ambiguities in (12) and (13). Within the direct interpetation approach, the best known is the storage analysis of Cooper (1983). But one of the most intriguing aspects of flexible CGs is that these contain mechanisms for accounting for these ambiguities under direct interpretation, without invoking the (arguably) rather complex semantic apparatus involved in Cooper stores. Thus such ambiguities can account for using a certain amount of flexibility in the combinatorics and/or unary type-shifting operations which allow a linguistic expression to have more than one syntactic category and, correspondingly, to have more than one meaning.

One account of these ambiguities is developed in detail in Hendriks (1987) (and see also Oehrle's discussion in this volume) and relies only on unary type-shifting rules which take a functor expression and allow any of its argument positions to shift such that it takes a type-raised argument. The general idea is familiar from Montague's (lexical) type-raising on the object position of an ordinary transitive verb like *read*. Thus, following the basic idea put forth in Partee and Rooth (1983), the lexical meaning of an ordinary transitive verb like *read* is a function of type $< e, < e, t>>$. However, Hendriks proposes that either or both argument positions can raise such that the function is waiting for an argument of type $<<e,t>, t>$ and can thus take a quantified NP. We will assume that this is accompanied by a corresponding syntactic lift. Thus, for example, the verb *read* of category (S/NP)/NP can lift to (S/NP)/(S/(S/NP)). The meaning of the lifted expression is $\lambda\wp[\lambda x[\wp (\lambda y[\text{read}'(y)(x)])]]$. Hendriks generalizes this in such a way that the subject position can also lift, but if both positions lift then the order in which the liftings occur yields different results. If the object position lifts first the subject has wide scope; if the order is reversed then the object has wide scope. The de re/de dicto ambiguity in (13) is similarly accounted for by a series of lift operations.

Hendriks' particular proposal makes no essential use of function composition to get the appropriate readings, and hence if this system is correct then these ambiguities provide no direct evidence for a grammar with composition. But as noted in the introduction, function composition (or possibly division) allows for the kind of multiple bracketings which in turn explain a good deal of the "non-constituent conjunction" cases. Steedman (1987, 1988) has also exploited function composition quite successfully in his account of extraction.

Let us assume, then, that function composition is independently motivated, and turn again to the de re/de dicto ambiguity in (13). Each reading has several possible derivations; the most straightforward derivation of the de dicto reading is one in which *read* first argument lifts on its object position, then takes the object NP as argument, and the rest of derivation is the run-of-the-mill derivation with application only. As to the de re reading, there is one derivation of this which involves "holding off" on the introduction of the object NP and letting the rest of the matrix VP first compose. (Recall that read has one category without a wrap slash, and so can participate in function composition.) At this point the expression *said that Mary should read* can argument lift on the object position and apply to the object NP so as to give wide scope on the object. This is illustrated in (14); note that (14) uses the non-wrap version of *read* where it is $(S/_LNP)/_RNP$. (Since the notion head is not crucially involved in the discussion, I suppress here those features pertaining to head inheritance, and I do not indicate the head of each string.)

(14)

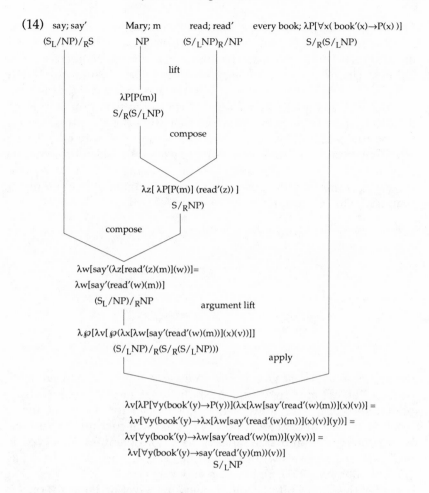

Note that under this approach there is another possibility, which is that *read* first argument lifts on its object position, and then the rest of the derivation proceeds as in (14). This will give the de dicto rather than the de re reading on the object position, even though here – as in (14) – the object is brought in after the rest composes to give the expression *say Mary read*. However, notice that in this case the expression *say Mary read* is of category (S/NP)/(S/(S/NP)) and not of the ordinary transitive verb category (S/NP)/NP. This fact will be important below.

We will now leave quantification for the moment, and turn to the phenomenon of VP Deletion, as exemplified in (15):

(15) John saw Mary and Bill will too.

The abstract level(s) and the direct interpretation approaches have also led to rather different views on this phenomenon; oversimplifying somewhat, the two main positions here can be characterized as follows. Under the abstract level approach, the meaning of (15) is assigned in a two-stage process. First, the antecedent VP (in this case *saw Mary*) is mapped into a Logical From representation. Although the usual assumption is that this representation is a λ-expression, this will be irrelevant for our purposes, and so let us simply take the LF representation of the antecedent VP to be *love(m)*. This representation is then copied in to the position of the "missing VP" in the second conjunct; in this way the second conjunct ultimately has an LF representation which is roughly along the lines of (16):

(16)

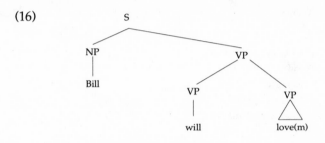

(In some theories, *will* would be treated as a sentential and not a VP operator at LF, and so would be pulled out in (16) so as to have sentential scope. This, however, is not crucial for the point under discussion here, and so for expository ease I will continue to treat *will* both syntactically and semantically as a VP operator.) This type of proposal, or proposals within this same general spirit, is made in Sag (1976), Williams (1977), and Larson and May (1990).

Under the direct interpretation view, no level of Logical Form is necessary. Rather, the meaning of *will* is a function from properties to properties; for our purposes assume that a "property" is a function which characterizes a set of individuals. (Crucially, then, a "property" is not an expression of LF but is an actual model-theoretic object, although we might choose to represent this object using the same kind of logical formula used above.) Hence when an auxiliary like *will* is "missing" its VP argument, as in (15), its meaning will directly apply to some property which is the meaning of some other actual VP in the discourse. One important point concerning VP Deletion is that, as discussed in Hankamer and Sag (1976), the property that it picks up must be the meaning of some actual overt VP in the discourse. (Just why this is so, and how to account for the differences between this kind of so-called "surface" anaphora and "deep" anaphora in which there need not be an overt antecedent, is a matter which I will not consider here.) This view has been explored in, among others, Ladusaw (1979) and Partee and Bach (1981). Under a Categorial syntax without empty categories there are some open questions concerning the syntax; I will assume that an (S/NP)/(S/NP) like *will* can category change into an S/NP, with the accompanying semantics that will' applies to a property supplied by some other VP.

Now consider the phenomenon of "Antecedent Contained Deletion" (hereafter, ACD), as exemplified in (17):

(17) John read every book that Mary will.

The existence of sentences like (17) is often used to motivate the abstract level solution to both VP Deletion and to quantified NPs. Thus the conventional wisdom is as follows. Under the direct interpretation approach it would appear that the meaning of *will* is looking for the meaning of some other VP in the discourse and it applies to this property. The problem, however, is that there is no actual VP whose meaning can be the appropriate one. Surely the meaning of the "missing VP" is not the property denoted by the matrix VP: since the former is contained within the latter this would lead to an infinite regress. The direct interpretation approach therefore appears at first blush to have no account of (17). Under the abstract level approach, on the other hand, (17) is straightforward. That is, suppose that quantified NPs are pulled out at LF, and then an LF representation is copied in to the position of the "missing" VP. Then before the copying takes place, we have roughly the following representation for (17) (the exact details of the representation vary from account to account and depend on the precise treatment of the LF representation for quantified NPs, but these details need not concern us here):

(18)

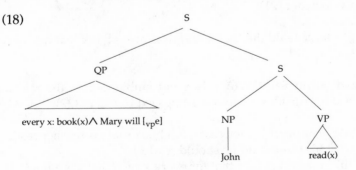

The LF representation *read (x)* can now be copied into the empty VP position. The key point is that by pulling out the quantified NP and leaving a variable in its surface position, there is a VP formula which is appropriate to be copied in to the position of the missing VP. There is, then, no infinite regress because at the level of LF the position of the missing VP is not contained within its antecedent, as the antecedent VP is one which just contains a variable in object position.

The abstract level approach to Antecedent Contained Deletion combined with this approach to quantifier scopes appears to receive some striking confirmation from the interaction of de re/de dicto ambiguities and Antecedent Contained Deletion. The crucial case showing this is one which has been discussed in Sag (1976) and (using a slightly different kind of sentence) by Williams (1977). Thus consider first a sentence like (19):

> (19) His father said that he should read every book that his teacher said he should read.

Like (13) this is ambiguous between a de re and a de dicto interpretation for the object; thus the phrase *every book that his teacher said he should read* can have wide scope with respect to *say* (the de re reading) or narrow scope (the de dicto reading). Similar remarks hold for (20) in which there is a "missing" VP following *should*:

> (20) His father said he should read every book that his teacher said he should.

Again this is ambiguous between the de re and the de dicto reading of the object NP.

But now consider (21):

> (21) His father said that he should read every book that his teacher did.

As pointed out in Sag (1976), this is not ambiguous in the relevant way. To clarify, consider the four readings expressed in (22):

> (22) (a) For every x such that x is a book that his teacher read, his father said he should read x.
>
>   (b) His father said that for every x such that x is a book that his teacher read, he should read x.
>
>   (c) For every x such that x is a book that his teacher said that he should read, his father said that he should read x.

(d)   His father said that for every x such that x is a book
      that his teacher said he should read, he should read x.

What we are interested in here is the readings in (22c) and (22d); both
of which are possible paraphrases for (19) and (20). However, only
(22c) – the de re reading – is a possible paraphrase for (21). (It of
course also has the readings paraphrased in (22a) and (22b), but it
does not have a de dicto reading where the "missing" VP is understood as *said he should read*.)

Sag and Williams demonstrate that the difference between (20) and
(21) follows immediately under the abstract level approach to quantifiers and to Antecedent Contained Deletion. Under the de re reading
paraphrased in (22c), the LF before the copying takes place will be
roughly as follows:

(23)

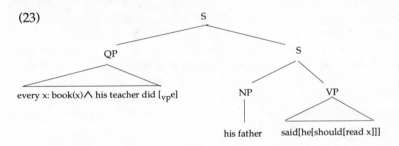

Thus the LF *said[he[should[read x]]]* can be copied into the position of
the empty VP; the resulting LF will have a meaning paraphrasable as
(22c). Consider, however, the representation of (21) before copying
under the de dicto reading for the object:

(24)

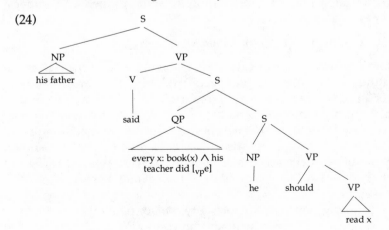

The only VP representation which could be copied in to the position of the empty VP is the LF *read x*, and this will give the meaning which is paraphrased in (22b), not the meaning paraphrased in (22d). (There is, of course, another VP here, *should read x*; presumably this is blocked as a possible antecedent due to some conflict with *did*.) That there is no de dicto reading here follows from the fact that if the object NP is scoped out only to be underneath *say*, then there is no single VP which can be copied in without leading to the sort of infinite regress discussed above. Thus the LF representation for the upper VP cannot be copied into the empty position since it contains this position, and no full LF would be supplied this way.

Antecedent Contained Deletion in a flexible CG

What I would like to show here is that, using a flexible Categorial Grammar, exactly the same predictions are made by the direct interpretation approach (and in an analogous way); my remarks here extend some of the basic observations of Evans (1988). Hence the existence of Antecedent Contained Deletion and its interaction with de re and de dicto readings is not in fact evidence against the direct interpretation approach, for all of these phenomena are handled equally naturally under this approach. We begin by considering first the simple antecedent contained deletion (17):

(17) John read every book which Mary will.

As mentioned above, an infinite regress results under direct interpretation given the assumption that <u>will'</u> must apply to some property which is the meaning of some surface VP. The fallacy, however, lies in the assumption that <u>will'</u> must apply to some property. Consider a fuller case like (25):

(25) John read every book which Mary will read.

Under the kind of view of extraction taken in much of the Categorial literature (see, for example, Steedman 1987, 1988) the phrase *Mary will read* is an S/NP and denotes a property. While there are open questions concerning the exact structure of noun phrases containing relative clauses; assume for the present purposes that a relative pronoun like *which* takes such a constituent as argument to give a common noun modifier; hence *which* is of category $(N/_LN)/_R(S/_RNP)$. The key point, then, is that *Mary will read* in (25) is not an S but an $S/_RNP$; *will read* itself is an $(S/_LNP)/_RNP$ which can compose with (type-lifted) Mary. Similarly, <u>will-read'</u> denotes a two-place relation between individuals, and it composes with the function $\lambda P[P(m)]$. Evans (1988) points out that by the same token the material following Mary in (17) should also denote a two-place relation between individuals. The upshot, then, is that if a missing property is supplied as argument of will' then the material following <u>which</u> will have the wrong kind of meaning. Rather, the meaning of (17) can be derived if <u>will'</u> actually function composes with some two-place relation – that is, with the meaning of an ordinary transitive verb (or, transitive verb phrase). As in the case of a "missing" VP, we can assume that what is supplied here is the meaning of some actual TVP in the discourse. Hence the missing material can be understood simply as <u>read'</u>, and this composes with <u>will'</u>. Again there are some open questions regarding the syntax, but I will assume a category changing rule by which an (S/NP)/(S/NP) can become an (S/NP)/NP, where its meaning composes with some two place relations. The main steps are shown below, where the material in braces is the relation supplied by some other overt TVP in the discourse:

(26)

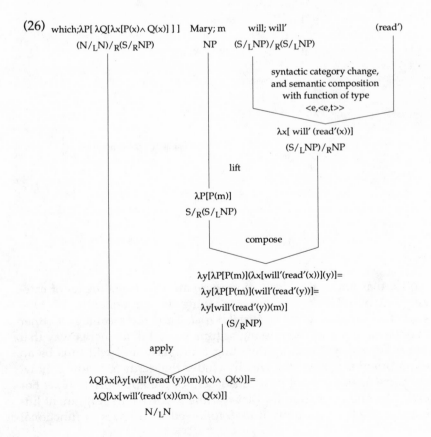

which;λP[λQ[λx[P(x)∧ Q(x)]]]   Mary; m   will; will'   (read')

$(N/_L N)/_R (S/_R NP)$ NP $(S/_L NP)/_R (S/_L NP)$

syntactic category change,
and semantic composition
with function of type
<e,<e,t>>

λx[will' (read'(x))]
$(S/_L NP)/_R NP$

lift

λP[P(m)]
$S/_R (S/_L NP)$

compose

λy[λP[P(m)](λx[will'(read'(x))](y)]=
λy[λP[P(m)](will'(read'(y))]=
λy[will'(read'(y))(m)]
$(S/_R NP)$

apply

λQ[λx[λy[will'(read'(y))(m)](x)∧ Q(x)]]=
λQ[λx[will'(read'(x))(m)∧ Q(x)]]
$N/_L N$

The basic analysis of Antecedent Contained Deletion is thus straight-forward. What is especially interesting is that exactly the right predictions are made with respect to the ambiguities in (20) and (21). Consider first (20). Here the "missing" material can be understood as the meaning of the transitive verb *read*, and this analysis correctly predicts that in this case the object NP can still be understood de re or de dicto as the reader can verify. But now consider (21). As discussed earlier, the de re reading on the object can be derived as follows (we will not show out the full semantics here as this is given in (14)):

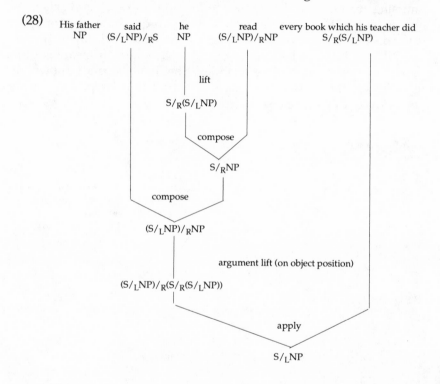

Notice that under this derivation there are two constituents of category (S/NP)/NP and whose meaning is consequently of type <e,<e,t>> – *read* and *said he (should) read*. Thus the meaning of either may be supplied as the missing argument of did' in such a way that *his teacher did* will end up denoting a property and will thus be an appropriate argument for which'. Under the de dicto reading, however, *said he read* cannot be a constituent of the appropriate type. For example, one derivation for that reading involves first argument lifting on the object position of *read*, followed by a series of functional applications. This is sketched schematically in (28) (the reader can verify that this gives the de dicto reading):

(27)

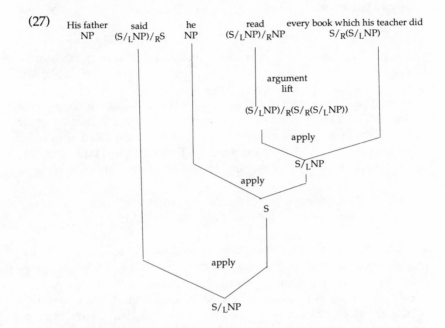

Here the only (S/NP)/NP is *read*; its meaning is, of course, appropriate to compose with <u>did'</u>, but this gives (22b) and not (22d). Alternatively, *read* can first argument lift on the object position, compose with (type-lifted) *he* and then *he read* composes with *say*. This does in fact give the de dicto reading for the object, and it does yield a constituent *say he read*. But, as noted earlier, here *say he read* is not an ordinary transitive verb phrase and does not denote a relation of the appropriate type; rather it is an (S/NP)/(S/(S/NP)) whose meaning is of type <<<e,t>,t><e,t>>. Thus if this meaning were picked up and composed with <u>did'</u> the entire phrase *his teacher did* would not have a denotation of type <e,t> and thus would not be an appropriate argument for the meaning of <u>which'</u>. In a nutshell, then, *said John read* can be a transitive verb phrase (and denote a function of type <e,<e,t>>) only if the object has wide scope, and so (22d) is not a possible reading here. (I should also point out that although this looks rather different from the level(s) of representation solution sketched in (23)-(24), I believe it is actually quite similar. This becomes clearer if one strips away the variables from the LF representation in (23) and (24) and if one thinks of "variables" as simply missing arguments.)

Antecedent Contained Deletion and wrap

The basic idea in the analysis above is that when *did* is within a relative clause and is missing its complement, its meaning does not apply to some VP-type meaning. Rather, this function must function-compose with some TVP-type meaning; this is the only way that the entire relative clause will have the appropriate meaning. With function composition in the syntax, we can derive complex TVPs like *said he should read* and the meaning of this expression can therefore supply the "missing" two-place relation. Recall, though, that in the case of ordinary VP Deletion the missing property must be supplied by some overt expression of the category VP; it cannot be supplied simply by some property arrived at by inferencing. For example, Hankamer and Sag (1976) note that even cases like the following are impossible:

(29) The oats were taken down to the bin by Sue. John did too.
      (≠ John also took the oats down to the bin.)

There is no reason to believe that Antecedent Contained Deletion is any different in this regard, and so presumably the "missing" two-place relation must be the meaning of an actual TVP.

But now consider Antecedent Contained Deletion cases like (30) which are at worst somewhat awkward. (Baltin 1987 claims that examples of this general form are bad, but I have checked these with at least seven speakers, all of whom confirm my judgment that the examples in (30) are only slightly awkward. Larson & May 1990 also claim that these sorts of examples are good, and note that the particular examples constructed by Baltin may have independent problems.)

(30) (a) John put all of the furniture that Mary had asked him to
           into the living room.
      (b) John gave every present that Mary wanted him to to
           Sammy.

In (30a), for example, the missing relation can easily be understood as *put into the living room*. I see no way to account for this unless *put into the living room* forms an actual TVP. This, of course, is exactly the claim under the wrap analysis and so these sentences provide quite striking evidence for wrap.

Moreover, Antecedent Contained Deletion provides interesting confirmation for some of the other remarks in the second section. As discussed there, while "mixed composition" is not an operation freely available in the grammar, it appears that an operation with this effect does apply just in case particular lexical items are appropriately marked (just how and why this is so is an open question). In particular, this is what happens in the Raising to Object construction, where in (31) *consider* composes with *to be foolish* to give a new TVP:

(31) John considers Mary to be foolish.

We would thus expect *consider to be foolish* to be a TVP whose meaning is accessible in Antecedent Contained Deletion, and this prediction is borne out:

(32) ?John considers everyone that Bill also does to be foolish.

However, it follows from the general view adopted here that "mixed composition" is not generally available, for the requisite output category is not among the set of syntactic functions. Consider, then, a sentence like (33):

(33) John said (that) Mary would leave.

We do not want to allow a "Raising" type derivation for this where *said (that) would leave* composes and takes *Mary* as argument. (Among other pieces of evidence that this is not analogous to a Raising case is the fact that there is no Heavy NP Shift here; see Postal 1974.) In other words, there is no analysis of this sentence whereby *said (that) would leave* is a TVP, and so this material should not be available in Antecedent Contained Deletion. Again this prediction is correct; Larson and May (1990) observe that sentences like (34) are impossible, and they point out the particularly robust contrast in (35):

(34) *John said (that) everyone who Bill also did would leave.
      (≠ John said that everyone who Bill also said would leave would leave.)

(35) (a) John expects everyone that Mary also does to win.
      (b) *John expects (that) everyone that Mary also does will win.

(Larson and May's explanation for these contrasts is rather different than the one proposed here, and relies on ECP effects.)

Finally, I also suggested earlier that function composition is disallowed with wrap/infix categories in cases where here, too, the output expression would have to be a function which is not specifiable by the set of syntactic functions. Such a case is exemplified in (36):

(36) John said that Mary put the book on the shelf.

This is exactly a case of the type developed schematically in the second section. To clarify, suppose that *Mary* and *put on the shelf* could compose to give the headed string *Mary put on the shelf* of category $S/_{RW}NP$. Were this to then compose with *said*, the resulting expression must contain the information that the NP object will be placed after *put*, but it must also contain the information that *say* is the new head. Since a syntactic category cannot say both of these, function composition is impossible. The prediction, then, is that Antecedent Contained Deletion cannot pick up the meaning of *said Mary put on the shelf* but only the meaning *put on the shelf*. (37) confirms this prediction:

(37) John said that Mary put every book that Bill also did on the shelf.
(= John said that Mary put every book that Bill also put on the shelf on the shelf.)
(≠ John said that Mary put every book that Bill also said she put on the shelf on the shelf.)

Quite strikingly, this meaning does emerge in the corresponding Heavy NP Shift case:

(38) John said that Mary put on the shelf every book that Bill also did.

This is as expected, for here *put* is of the non-wrap category $((S/_LNP)/_RNP)/_RPP$ and so function composition can apply to give the TVP *said that Mary put on the shelf*.

One final note: these facts also provide support for the type of analysis developed here over the standard analysis of Antecedent Contained Deletion within the abstract levels approach. Given the assumption that Antecedent Contained Deletion involves Quantifier Raising, there is no obvious reason why *every book that Bill also did* in (37) cannot raise, yielding the LF VP *said Mary put x on the shelf*. This LF VP should then be accessible to fill in the missing complement of *did*.

CONCLUSION

In these remarks I have tried to present evidence on the one hand that some kind of flexible CG is correct, but on the other hand that such a CG should incorporate a wrap operation. Using the basic ideas of Pollard (1984), it appears that such an operation can be incorporated into a flexible CG and that it is, moreover, compatible with the view of syntactic functions whereby these map fully ordered (and, under the proposals here, headed) strings into fully ordered (headed) strings. A number of open questions of course remain; for example I have suggested that an operation akin to mixed composition applies in limited cases, but it is not clear just how to fold this in to the basic system under discussion here.

But the claim that there are wrap operations raises interesting questions for CGs of the type discussed in Oehrle's paper. Most significantly, the notion of structural completeness must be re-examined, and it is certainly not at all clear that a flexible CG with wrap will have this property (or that this property is even meaningful). It reamins to be seen, then, whether a flexible CG with wrap has the same advantages as the kinds of CGs discussed by Oehrle. Nonetheless, there seems to be sufficient evidence for wrap as to warrant further investigation of these questions.

NOTES

* For extremely helpful and clarifying discussion of many of the issues here, I am grateful to David Dowty and Dick Oehrle. This research was partially supported by NSF grant #BNS-9014676.

1 The question of whether or not conjunction is entirely free in the way predicted under a theory with structural completeness seems to me to be an open one. A number of cases where conjunction is impossible have been discussed in the literature, but the literature also contains disagreements as to the actual facts and some of the bad cases improve with the substitution of different lexical items.

2 One must be careful in sorting out exactly what is the empirical claim here. Were one to find such a situation, this could actually be described. Let the appropriate feature on the subject category be encoded into the S category by some feature [f]; a verb which "agrees" with the embedded subject is thus one which selects for an S[f]. The point, though, is that this is somewhat complex, as it requires additional categories. Thus "Keenan's generalization" should be seen as a markedness claim rather than as an absolute

prediction – such situations are less likely to occur than direct agreement between a functor and its argument.

3   I do not mean to suggest here that agreement must be accounted for in the syntax; Dowty and Jacobson (1988) (among many others) actually argue for a fully semantic account of agreement. But the same basic remarks will hold under the semantic account. Under one possible implementation of semantic agreement, the meaning of *kill* is, roughly, a function defined only for plural objects, and the meaning of *kills* is defined only for singular objects. It still follows that the effects of "agreement" hold only when the functor expression agrees with the argument, since the meaning of the functor expression can only apply to an argument with the appropriate meaning.

4   As stated here, this does not account for the cases in which a subject reflexive "binds" an indirect object. For discussion, see Bach and Partee (1980), Szabolcsi (1987), and Kang (1988).

5   It is unclear how to block a case where a non-heavy NP is on the right, as in:

   (i) ? I gave to John the book.

   However, it has often been noted that even cases like this are possible with stress on *the book*. I assume, then, that the syntax freely allows NPs to concatenate with TVPs, where prosodic and/or discourse considerations come into play to predict the strangeness of this in certain cases. This is, of course, rather vague and promissory, but it would seem that this kind of solution will have to be adopted in any theory, since no theory provides mechanisms in the syntax to ensure that only heavy or stressed NPs occur in the rightmost position.

6   Hoeksema and Janda (1988) provide very interesting arguments that the appropriate notion for wrap is not head but rather some item on the margin of the wrapped expression. What counts as an "item" depends on the level involved; syntactic wrap operations would generally look to the first (or last) word while other operations could look to, for example, syllables. Whether the basic idea of the proposal here extends to the data discussed by Hoeksema and Janda is a question I leave open.

7   Similarly, if extraction is handled using function composition as proposed in Steedman (1987, 1988), then a sentence like (i) cannot be derived using the wrap category for *read*:

   (i) Which book did John say that Bill gave to Mary?

   It can, however, be derived using *read* of category $(S/_L NP)/_R NP$.

REFERENCES

Anderson, S. and Chung, S. (1977). On grammatical relations and clause structure in verb-initial languages. In P. Cole and J. M. Sadock (eds.), *Syntax and Semantics 8: Grammatical Relations*. New York: Academic Press, 1-26

Bach, E. (1968) Nouns and noun phrases. In E. Bach and R. Harms (eds.), *Universals in Linguistic Theory*. New York: Holt, Rinehart, and Winston, 91-122

– (1979). Control in Montague Grammar. *Linguistic Inquiry* 10:515-31

– (1980). In defense of passive. *Linguistics and Philosophy* 3:297-341

– and Partee, B. (1980). Anaphora and semantic structure. In J. Kreiman and A. Ojeda (eds.), *CSL Parasession on Anaphora*. Chicago: Chicago Linguistic Society, 29-40

Baltin, M. (1987). Do antecedent-contained deletions exist? *Linguistic Inquiry* 18:579-95

Categorial Grammar Newsletter 1 and 2

Chierchia, G. (1984). Topics in the Syntax and Semantics of Infinitives and Gerunds. Ph. D. dissertation, GLSA. Amherst: University of Massachussetts

Chomsky, N. (1957). *Syntactic Structures*. The Hague: Mouton

Cooper, R. (1983). *Quantification and Syntactic Theory*. Dordrecht: Reidel

Curry, H. (1963). Some logical aspects of grammatical structure. In R. Jakobson (ed.), *Structure of Language and its Mathematical Aspects: Proceedings of the Twelfth Symposium in Applied Mathematics*. Providence: American Mathematical Society, 56-68

Dowty, D. (1982a). Grammatical relations and Montague Grammar. In P. Jacobson and G.K. Pullum (eds.), *The Nature of Syntactic Representation*. Dordrecht: Reidel, 79-130

– (1982b). More on the categorial theory of grammatical relations. In A. Zaenen (ed.), *Subjects and Other Subjects: Proceedings of the Harvard Conference on Grammatical Relations*. Bloomington: Indiana University Linguistics Club

– (1988). Type raising, functional composition, and non-constituent conjunction. In R. Oehrle, E. Bach, and D. Wheeler (eds.), *Categorial Grammars and Natural Language Structures*. Dordrecht: Reidel, 153-97

– and Jacobson, P. (1988). Agreement as a semantic phenomenon. In J. Powers and K. de Jong (eds.), *Proceedings of the 5th Annual Eastern States Conference on Linguistics*. Columbus: Ohio State University, 95-108

Emonds, J. (1980). Word order in generative grammar. *Journal of Linguistic Research* 1

Evans, F. (1988). Binding into anaphoric verb phrases. In J. Powers and K. de

Jong (eds.), *Proceedings of the 5th Annual Eastern States Conference on Linguistics*. Columbus: Ohio State University, 122-9

– (1989). Combinatory grammars and wrap. Pesented at the Conference on Categorial Grammar, LSA Summer Institute, Tucson

Gazdar, G., Klein, E., Pullum, G., and Sag, I. (1985). *Generalized Phrase Structure Grammar*. Cambridge, MA: Harvard University Press

Hankamer, J. and Sag, I. (1976). Deep and surface anaphora. *Linguistic Inquiry* 7:391-428

Hendriks, H. (1987). Type change in semantics: the scope of quantification and coordination. In E. Klein and J. van Benthem (eds.), *Categories, Polymorphism, and Unification*. Centre for Cognitive Science, University of Edinburgh/Institute for Language, Logic, and Information, University of Amsterdam

Hepple, M. (1990). Grammatical relations and the Lambek calculus. Presented at the Conference on Discontinuous Constituents, Amsterdam

Hoeksema, J. (1984) Categorial Morphology. Ph.D. dissertation, Rijkuniversiteit, Groningen. New York: Garland, Inc. (Outstanding Dissertations in Linguistics Series), 1985

– and Janda, R. (1988). Implications of process-morphology. In R. Oehrle, E. Bach, and D. Wheeler (eds.), *Categorial Grammars and Natural Language Structures*. Dordrecht: Reidel, 199-248

Jacobson, P. (1983). Phrase structure and grammatical relations. Colloquium talk, LSA Annual Meeting, Minneapolis

– (1987). Phrase structure, grammatical relations, and discontinuous constituents. In G. Huck and A. Ojeda (eds.), *Syntax and Semantics 20: Discontinuous Constituence*. New York: Academic Press, 27-69

– (1990). Raising as function composition. *Linguistics and Philosophy* 13

– (to appear). Raising without movement. In R. Larson et al. (eds.), *Control and Grammatical Theory*.

Kang, B. (1988). Functional Inheritance, Anaphora, and Semantic Interpretation in a Generalized Categorial Grammar. Ph.D. dissertation, Brown University, Providence, RI

Keenan, E. (1974). The functional principle: generalizing the notion of "subject of." In M. La Galy, R. Fox, and A. Bruck (eds.), *Papers from the 10th Regional Meeting of the Chicago Linguistics Society*. Chicago: Chicago Linguistics Society, 298-309

Ladusaw, W. (1979). Polarity Sensitivity as Inherent Scope Relations. Ph.D. Dissertation, University of Texas, Austin. New York: Garland, Inc. (Outstanding Dissertations in Linguistics Series)

Lakoff, G. (1971). On generative semantics. In D. Steinberg and L. Jakobovits (eds.), *Semantics*. Cambridge, Eng.: Cambridge University Press, 232-96

Lambek, J. (1958). The mathematics of sentence structure. *American Mathematical Monthly* 65:154-70

Larson, R. (1988). On the double object construction. *Linguistic Inquiry* 19:335-91

– and May, R. (1990). Antecedent containment or vacuous movement: reply to Baltin. *Linguistic Inquiry* 21:103-22

May, R. (1977). The Grammar of Quantification. Ph.D. Dissertation, MIT

McCawley, J. (1970). Where do noun phrases come from? In R. Jacobs and P. Rosenbaum (eds.), *Readings in English Transformational Grammar*. Waltham, MA: Ginn and Co., 166-83

McCloskey, J. (1983). A VP in a VSO language? In G. Gazdar, E. Klein, and G.K. Pullum (eds.), *Order, Concord and Constituency*. Dordrecht: Foris, 9-55

Montague, R. (1974) The proper treatment of quantification in ordinary English. In R. Thomason (ed.), *Formal Philosophy*. New Haven: Yale University Press, 247-270

Partee, B. and Bach, E. (1981). Quantification, pronouns, and VP anaphora. In J. Groenendijk, T. Janssen, and M. Stokhof (eds.), *Formal Methods in the Study of Language: Proceedings of the Third Amsterdam Colloquium*. Amsterdam: Mathematisch Centrum, 445-82

– and Mats Rooth (1983). Generalized conjunction and type ambiguity. In R. Bauerle, C. Schwarze, and A. von Stechow (eds.), *Meaning, Use and Interpretation of Language*. Berlin: de Gruyter, 361-83

Pollard, C. (1984). Generalized Phrase Structure Grammars, Head Grammars and Natural Languages. Ph.D. dissertation, Stanford University

Postal, P. (1974). *On Raising*. Cambridge, MA: MIT Press

Sag, I. (1976). Deletion and Logical Form. Ph.D. dissertation, MIT. Distributed by the Indiana University Linguistics Club, Bloomington

Steedman, M. (1987). Combinatory grammars and parasitic gaps. *Natural Language and Linguistic Theory* 5:403-40

– (1988). Combinators and grammars. In R. Oehrle, E. Bach, and D. Wheeler (eds.), *Categorial Grammar and Natural Language Structures*. Dordrecht: Reidel, 417-42

Szabolcsi, A. (1987). Bound variables in syntax: are there any? In J. Groenendijk et al. (eds.), *Proceedings of the 6th Amsterdam Colloquium*, ITLI

– (to appear). Combinatory categorial grammar and projection from the lexicon. In I. Sag and A. Szabolcsi (eds.), *Lexical Matters*. Stanford: CSLI

Williams, E. (1977). Discourse and logical form. *Linguistic Inquiry* 8:101-39

CHAPTER THREE

Categorial Grammars, Lexical Rules, and the English Predicative

Bob Carpenter

INTRODUCTION

When applying categorial grammars to the study of natural languages, it is traditional to assume a *universal* collection of phrase-structure schemes. Not only are these phrase-structure schemes applied cross-linguistically, but a compositional type-driven functional semantics is usually assumed to be determined by syntactic structure. It follows from these strong semantic and syntactic restrictions that all language-specific generalizations must be lexically determined in a categorial grammar; once the lexicon is established for a language, universal rules of syntactic and semantic combination take over to completely determine the set of grammatical expressions and their meanings. With such a large responsibility being assigned to the lexicon, it is not surprising that a simple list is not a sufficiently structured way of organizing lexical information. To achieve any degree of empirical coverage, lexical mechanisms must be provided to account for natural generalizations that exist within the lexicon of a single language.

In this paper, we will study the possibilities for applying *lexical rules* to the analysis of English syntax, and in particular the structure of the verb phrase. We will develop a lexicon whose empirical coverage extends to the full range of verb subcategories, complex adverbial phrases, auxiliaries, the passive construction, yes/no questions and the particularly troublesome case of predicatives. The effect of a lexical rule, in our system, will be to produce new lexical entries from old lexical entries. The similarity between our system and the metarule system of generalized phrase-structure grammar (GPSG, as presented in Gazdar et al. 1985) is not coincidental. Our lexical rules serve much the same purpose as metarules in GPSG, which were restricted to lexical phrase structure rules. The similarity is in a large part due to the fact that with the universal phrase-structure schemes being fixed, the role of a lexical category assignment in effect determines phrase-structure in much the same way as a lexical category entry and lexical phrase-structure rule determines lexical phrase-structure in GPSG. Our lexical rules will also bear a relationship to the lexical rules found in lexical-functional grammar (LFG, see Bresnan 1982a), as LFG rules are driven by the grammatical role assigned to arguments. Many of our analyses were first applied to either LFG or GPSG, as these were the first serious linguistic theories based on a notion of unification. In the process of explaining the basic principles behind categorial grammar and developing our lexical rule system, we will establish a categorial grammar lexicon with coverage of English syntactic constructions comparable to that achieved within published accounts of the GPSG or LFG frameworks.

Language, at its most abstract level, is simply a relation between expressions and meanings. Syntacticians are primarily interested in the structure of the set of grammatical or well-formed expressions, while semanticists concentrate on the range of possible meanings that can be expressed by a language and the relation of these meanings to the world, to cognitive agents, or to both. In categorial grammars, lexical assignments to basic expressions and potential syntactic constructions are restricted in such a way that only semantically meaningful combinations of syntactic categories are allowed. The combinatorial semantics can, in a strong sense, be read directly from the syntactic categories involved and their analysis, much as in the type-driven translation scheme of Klein and Sag (1985). We will not be interested in particular semantic claims, either to do with the nature of meaning or the particular meanings associated with individual lexical items, but will instead be concerned with the purely compositional aspects of semantic interpretation having to do with the way complex phrase meanings are built up from meanings and categories assigned to lexical entries.

The paper is organized roughly as follows. We start by presenting the basics of categorial grammar, including the directional functional category system, the nature of the lexicon, the semantic domain structure and the basic applicative universal phrase-structure schemes. We then turn to English and develop the simple noun phrase and verb phrase syntax, with a brief diversion to discuss the nature of modification in categorial grammar. Next, we develop a detailed account of the core verbal lexicon, concentrating especially on the auxiliary system, control verbs, and complex adverbials. Next, we turn our attention to the development of a lexical rule system and apply it to the core lexicon that we have created, concentrating on verbal lexical rules and the predicative constructions in particular.

We will not be concerned, in this paper, with how unbounded dependency and co-ordinate constructions can be treated within categorial grammars. Our attention in the base lexicon is focused on basic complement selection and in the lexical rules on bounded phenomena. The addition of type-raising and composition rule schemes, abstraction metarules and other devices allow unbounded dependency and co-ordination constructions to be handled in a semantically appropriate fashion. In particular, the approaches of Steedman (1985, 1987, 1988), Morrill (1987b, 1988), and Moortgat (1987c, 1988a, 1988b) to unbounded dependency and co-ordination constructions extend and are compatible with the applicative phrase structure schemes presented in this paper.

APPLICATIVE CATEGORIAL GRAMMAR

The study of categorial grammars originated with Ajdukiewicz (1935), who developed a logical language in which the combinatory properties of expressions could be expressed functionally. As in most linguistic analyses, every basic or lexical expression is assigned to one or more categories in categorial grammar. These lexical category assignments fully determine the combinatorial properties of expressions, because the set of phrase structure rules is assumed to be universal. Thus, any language specific details and generalizations must be expressed in the lexicon. Before introducing our system of lexical rules, we will pause to lay out the basics of Bar-Hillel's (1953) pure directed categorial grammar system, which will serve as the basis for our analysis of the English core lexicon.

Category system

The basic assumption of categorial grammar is that there is some fixed finite set BasCat of *basic categories* from which other categories are constructed. For our purposes here, it will be sufficient to assume that BasCat contains the following basic categories:

(1)   Category   Description
       np (P, N, C) *noun phrase*
       $n(N)$ *noun*
       $s(V)$ *sentence*

where *P, N, C*, and *V* range over *features* drawn from the following *finite* lists:[1]

(2) | Variable | Feature | Values |
     |----------|---------|--------|
     | *P* | person | 1,2,3 |
     | *N* | number | *sing, plu* |
     | *C* | case | *subj, obj* |
     | *V* | verb form | *bse, fin, perf, pred, inf* |

We thus have 12 *np* possibilities, 2 *n* possibilities and 5 possibilities for *s*, depending on the values assigned to features. We can simply assume that we have 19 basic categories and not worry about the structure of these categories in terms of features.[2] The finite set of basic categories is used to generate an infinite set of functional categories, each of which specifies a (possibly complex) argument and result category. The fundamental operation is that of concatenating an expression assigned to a functional category to an expression of its argument category to form an expression of its result category, with the order of the concatenation being determined by the functional category. For example, a determiner will be specified as a functional category that takes a noun complement to its right to form a noun phrase result, with agreement being handled by identity of simple features. More formally, we take the complete set CAT(BASCAT) of *categories* generated from the basic categories BASCAT to be the least such that:

(3) • $\alpha \in$ CAT(BASCAT) if $\alpha \in$ BASCAT
     • $\alpha/\beta, \alpha\backslash\beta \in$ CAT(BASCAT) if $\alpha, \beta \in$ CAT(BASCAT)

A category $\alpha \backslash \beta$ or α / β is said to be a *functor* category and to have a *domain* or *argument* category of β and a *range* or *result* category of α. A functional category of the form α / β is said to be a *forward functor* and looks for its β argument to the right, while the *backward functor* $\alpha \backslash \beta$ looks for its argument to the left. With our choice BASCAT of basic categories, the following would all be categories in CAT(BASCAT):

(4) *n(sing), n(plu)* \ *n(plu))* / *np(2, plu, obj)*,
     (s(fin) \ *np(3, sing, subj))* / *(s(fin)* \ *np(3, sing, subj))*,
     ((s(fin) / *np(3, sing, subj))* / *np(2, plu, obj))* / *np2, sing, obj)*

From now on, we will omit disambiguating parentheses within categories, taking the slashes to be left-associative operators, so that, for instance:

(5) $\alpha \setminus \beta / \beta = (\alpha \setminus \beta) / \beta$
        $\alpha \setminus \beta / \beta \setminus \alpha = ((\alpha \setminus \beta) / \beta) \setminus \alpha$
        $\alpha \setminus \beta / (\alpha \setminus \beta) / \gamma = ((\alpha \setminus \beta) / (\alpha \setminus \beta)) / \gamma$

Semantic domains

One basic tenet of categorial grammar is that the category assigned to an expression should express its semantic functionality directly (this idea can be traced back at least to Montague 1970). The semantics of an expression is usually encoded using Church's (1940) simple theory of functional types, where arbitrary semantic domains are assigned to basic categories and simple functional domains are assigned to functor categories. For the sake of simplicity, we assume such a simply typed semantics, though other semantics for the λ-calculus could be adapted just as easily (for instance, see Chierchia & Turner, forthcoming, who use an untyped [or mono-typed] λ-calculus semantics for a categorial grammar analysis of properties and nominalization). The set of types TYP is defined following Church (1940) by taking the minimal set such that:

(6)   • $\alpha \in$ TYP if $\alpha \in$ BASCAT
        • $\langle t_1, t_2 \rangle \in$ TYP if $t_1, t_2 \in$ TYP

A type $\langle \alpha, \beta \rangle$ is intuitively meant to denote the type of functions from objects of type α to objects of type β. We can define a simple typing function $\tau :$ CAT(BASCAT) $\rightarrow$ TYP that assigns a type to every category by setting:

(7)   • $\tau(\alpha) = \alpha$ if $\alpha \in$ BASCAT
        • $\tau(\alpha / \beta) = \tau(\alpha \setminus \beta) = \langle \beta, \alpha \rangle$

Finally, we will define a *semantic domain* D_t for every type $t \in$ TYP in the same way as Church, by assuming that every basic type $\alpha \in$ TYP is assigned to some set D_α and that every complex type $\langle t_1, t_2 \rangle$ is assigned a type according to the scheme:

(8) $D_{\langle t1, t2 \rangle} = D_{t_2}^{D_{t_1}}$

where we take A^B to be the set of total functions from the set B to the set A. The result is that every category is assigned to exactly one semantic domain. It is important to note that there is no requirement that the domains assigned to different basic categories be disjoint, so that for instance, the domains $D_{np(3,sing,subj)}$ and $D_{np(2,sing,obj)}$ could be identical. Similarly, there is no restriction preventing the domains assigned to basic categories from being equivalent to other functional domains that do not involve them; in Montague's (1970) analysis, the semantic domain assigned to the complex verb phrase category was the same as that assigned to the basic noun category. We will write α : f for the pair consisting of the syntactic category α and a semantic object f drawn from the domain $D_{\tau(\alpha)}$.[3]

We will not be interested in the fine-grained analysis of any particular semantic domain D_t, since it will not be relevant to the task at hand. A number of categorial semantics have been worked out which are more or less compatible with the categorial grammar presented here (see Montague 1970; Dowty 1979; Carpenter 1989; Chierchia & Turner forthcoming).

Lexical assignments

As is usual in formal grammars, we will suppose that we have some finite set BASEXP of *basic expressions*. For our purposes, BASEXP can be taken to be a finite subset of English words.[4] A *lexicon* is then simply taken to be a relation between basic expressions and pairs consisting of syntactic categories and semantic objects of the appropriate types. For instance, we could have a lexical entry $np(3,sing,subj)$: **opus** for the word *opus* if the constant **opus** were an element of the domain $D_{np(3,sing,subj)}$. More formally, a *lexicon* is a relation:

(9)   LEX $\subseteq$ BASEXP $\times$ (CAT(BASCAT) $\times$ D)

subject to the semantic well-typing constraint that:

(10) if $\langle e, \ldots\alpha, f\rangle \in$ LEX is a lexical entry then f is an element of the domain $D_{\tau(\alpha)}$.

Note that nothing in this definition rules out lexical syntactic or semantic ambiguity, which would correspond to lexical entries of the form $\langle e, \ldots\alpha, f\rangle$ and $\langle e, \langle\alpha', f'\rangle\rangle$ where $\alpha \neq \alpha'$ and/or $f \neq f'$.

Most of the work in this paper will be directed toward the construction of a suitably rich lexicon for dealing with the basic syntactic constructions of English.

Application schemes

Categorial grammar is essentially a phrase-structure formalism. What we mean by this is that there are lexical assignments to basic expressions and a set of phrase-structure rules that combine expressions to produce phrases purely on the basis of syntactic categorization. Categorial grammars are unique among linguistic theories in postulating an *infinite* set of categories and phrase structure rules rather than the finite set found in context-free phrase structure grammars. Luckily, the set of rules used in categorial grammar is quite well-behaved, and in the case of the pure applicative categorial grammar, can be derived as instances of two schemes. The reliance on phrase-structure rules guarantees a resulting theory that is purely concatenative in that grammar rules have locally determined behavior.[5]

Following our intuitive explanation of $\alpha \, / \, \beta$ as a forward-looking functor and $\alpha \setminus \beta$ as a backward-looking functor, we postulate the following two application schemes:

(11)   • $\alpha \, / \, \beta : f \quad \beta : g \qquad \rightarrow \qquad \alpha : f(g) \qquad$ *(forward application)*
       • $\beta : g \quad \alpha \setminus \beta : f \qquad \rightarrow \qquad \alpha : f(g) \qquad$ *(backward application)*

where $\alpha, \beta \in$ Cat(BasCat) range over all syntactic categories and where $f \in D_{\tau(\alpha \, / \, \beta)} = D_{\tau(\alpha \setminus \beta)}$ and $g \in D_{\tau(\beta)}$. We have written our phrase-structure schemes with a bottom-up orientation, as is common in categorial grammars. Note that because we have $f \in D_{...\tau(\beta),\tau(\alpha)>}$ and $g \in D_{\tau(\beta)}$ we will have $f(g) \in D_{\tau(\alpha)}$, thus ensuring that the semantic type of the result is appropriate for the resulting syntactic category α.

It should be obvious that with a finite lexicon only a finite number of instances of the application phrase structure schemes will ever be necessary. Instances with more slashes than lexical categories will never be invoked, since the rules strictly reduce the number of slashes in categories. This means that any finite categorial lexicon, together with the application schemes, will determine a grammar structurally equivalent to a context-free grammar. Somewhat surprisingly, the converse to this result also holds in the weak generative case, as was proved by Gaifman (Bar-Hillel, Gaifman, & Shamir 1960). That is, every context-free language (set of expressions generated by a finite context-free grammar) can be generated by a categorial grammar applying the application schemes to a finite lexicon. Consequently, evidence beyond simple acceptability of sentences must be employed to distinguish between categorial and context-free grammars. The strongest motiviation for using categorial grammars is the ease with which they can be extended to provide adequate semantic analyses of unbounded dependency and co-ordination constructions.

BASIC ENGLISH LEXICON

In this section, we will provide a lexical characterization of the core syntactic constructions available in English. We begin with the simple noun and verb phrases, then consider the nature of modifiers, and finally conclude with a more detailed analysis of the verb phrase. The point here is to create a sufficiently rich base lexicon from which to begin to study lexical rules and other extensions to the basic categorial framework.

Simple noun phrases

We begin our study of English with the simplest kinds of noun phrases, including proper names, pronouns, and simple determiner-noun constructions. We will use the determiner-noun analysis to illustrate the way in which agreement can be handled in a simple way through schematic lexical entries expressed in terms of features.

Proper names and pronouns

Proper names are the simplest kind of noun phrase, taking third person singular agreement and occurring in either subject or object position. We will use the following notation to express lexical category assignments:

(12) $np(3,sing,C)$ $\rightarrow$ *opus, bill, milo*

We follow the convention of assuming that the variables can take on any of the possible values of the feature over which they range. Thus, the above lexical entry is really schematically representing two lexical entries, one where $C = subj$ and another where $C = obj$. We will also assume that there is a constant of the appropriate sort attached to each lexical entry for each word. Thus the complete lexical entries for *Opus* would be $np(3,sing,subj)$: **opus** and $np(3,sing,obj)$: **opus**. Even though we will only provide a single lexical entry for many categories, the reader is urged to use his or her imagination to fill in the lexical categories of related expressions.

The next simplest category is that of pronouns, which evidence a large degree of variation in feature assignment. Pronoun distribution can be accounted for with the following lexical entries:

(13) $np(1,sing,subj)$, $\rightarrow$ *i*
       $np(1,sing,obj)$, $\rightarrow$ *me*
       $np(1,plu,subj)$, $\rightarrow$ *we*

$$np(1,plu,obj), \quad \rightarrow \quad us$$
$$np(2,N,C), \quad \rightarrow \quad you$$
$$np(3,sing,subj), \quad \rightarrow \quad he, she$$
$$np(3,sing,C), \quad \rightarrow \quad it$$
$$np(3,sing,obj), \quad \rightarrow \quad him, her$$
$$np(3,plu,subj), \quad \rightarrow \quad they$$
$$np(3,plu,obj), \quad \rightarrow \quad them$$

It can be seen from this list that pronouns, unlike proper names, can take a wide variety of person, number, and case agreement features. This will allow us to account for their pattern of distribution in verb phrases and modifiers when we come to discuss the uses of noun phrases as complements.

Nouns and determiners

Besides being composed of a basic expression, a noun phrase can consist of a determiner followed by a noun that agrees with the determiner in number. The result will be a third person noun phrase which can show up in subject or object position. For nouns, we take the following lexical entries:

(14) $\quad n(sing) \rightarrow kid, man, penguin$
$\quad\quad\; n(plu) \rightarrow kids, men, penguins$
$\quad\quad\; n(N) \rightarrow sheep, fish$

Thus we can see that there are nouns which are singular, those which are plural, and those which can be both. Notice that since the category $n(N)$ really has two possible instantiations, we are not committed to providing the same semantic constant for both the $n(sing)$ and $n(plu)$ entries of a noun like *sheep*.

Determiners are our first example of a functional category. We classify determiners as functors which take a noun argument to their right to produce a noun phrase. This gives us the following lexical entries:

(15) $\quad np(3,sing,C) / n(sing) \rightarrow every, a$
$\quad\quad\; np(3,plu,C) / n(plu) \rightarrow most, three$
$\quad\quad\; np(3,N,C) / n(N) \rightarrow the$

In the entry for *the* we must pick one value for the number feature N and use it in both places, thus getting an entry for *the* which is of the same syntactic category as *most* and another which is of the same category as *every*.

We are now in a position to provide some phrase structure analyses. We make the standard assumptions about admissible trees under a given lexicon and set of phrase-structure rules. We have the following analysis of the noun phrase *every kid*:

(16)

every	kid

$$\frac{np(3,sing,C) \ / \ n(sing) : \textbf{every} \quad n(sing) : \textbf{kid}}{np(3,sing,C) : \textbf{every(kid)}}$$

We have used a categorial grammar notation for phrase-structure trees due to Steedman, with the root of the tree at the bottom and the leaves along the top, with lines spanning the branches. We will include feature variables in trees if the tree is admissible for *any* possible substitution of features.[6] Using the grammar as it stands, it is not possible to derive a category for strings such as * *three kid* or * *every men* (we employ the standard notation of marking ungrammatical strings with an asterisk). Similarly, *the kid* could only be analysed as belonging to the category $np(3,sing,C) : \textbf{the(kid)}$, and not to the category $np(3,plu,C) : \textbf{the(kid)}$, since the determiner *the* can not be instantiated to the category $np(3,plu,C) \ / \ n(sing)$ because the same variable occurs in the noun phrase and noun in the lexical entry for *the*.

It is interesting to note that this is not the only possible categorial analysis of noun phrase structure. Another possibility which immediately presents itself is illustrated by the following two potential lexical entries:

(17) $det(sing)$ $\qquad\qquad \rightarrow \quad$ *every*
$\qquad np(3,N,C) \setminus det(N) \quad \rightarrow \quad$ *sheep*

Note that (17) assumes that determiners are assigned to a basic category and that nouns are analysed functionally. This assumption will lead to unsightly categories both syntactically and semantically even in the simple cases of nominal modifiers such as prepositional phrases and adjectives. While (17) would provide the same distributional analysis as the one presented so far, it turns out to be much simpler from the semantic point of view to interpret nouns as basic categories and treat determiners functionally. In extended categorial grammars, type-lifted analyses are often automatically generated for nouns such as *kid*, in which they are assigned the category:

(18) $np(P,N,C) \setminus (np(P,N,C) \ / \ n(N)) : \lambda D^{(n,np)}.D(\textbf{kid})$.

In λ-abstracts such as this, we will write the type of a variable as a superscript in the abstraction, usually omitting the features for the sake of readability.

Simple verb phrases

We will classify verb phrases functionally as categories which form sentences when they are combined with a noun phrase to their left. Note that the verbal agreement properties of a verb phrase are marked on its sentential result and its nominal agreement properties are marked on its noun phrase argument. Typically, unification categorial grammars based on feature structures allow features to be marked directly on a functional category and do not require them to be reduced to a pattern of markings on basic categories (Karttunen 1986; Uszkoreit 1986; Zeevat, Klein, & Calder 1987). This liberal distribution of features on functional categories is also found in the head-driven phrases structure grammars (HPSG) of Pollard and Sag (1987). We take the more conservative approach in this paper of only allowing features to be marked on basic categories, assuming that the more general approach could be adopted later if it were found to be necessary to express certain types of syntactic distinctions. Explicit conventions such as the head feature principles of GPSG and HPSG will be implicitly modelled by the distribution of features in functional categories such as transitive verbs, relative pronouns, and modifiers.

Intransitive verbs

The simplest kind of verb phrase consists of a single intransitive verb. The categorization for a simple base form intransitive verb is as follows:

(19) $s(bse) \setminus np(P,N,subj)$ $\rightarrow$ *sneeze, run, sing*

Finite form verb phrases show the following agreement classes:

(20) $s(fin) \setminus np(3,sing,subj)$ $\rightarrow$ *sneezes, runs, sings*
         $s(fin) \setminus np(2,N,subj)$ $\rightarrow$ *sneeze, run, sing*
         $s(fin) \setminus np(1,N,subj)$ $\rightarrow$ *sneeze, run, sing*
         $s(fin) \setminus np(P,plu,subj)$ $\rightarrow$ *sneeze, run, sing*

Finally, there are predicative and perfective entries for simple verbs:

(21) $s(pred) \setminus np(P,N,subj)$ $\rightarrow$ *sneezing, running, singing*
         $s(perf) \setminus np(P,N,subj)$ $\rightarrow$ *sneezed, run, sung*

There are no basic lexical entries with the verb form *inf*; we make the assumption common in unification grammars that *to* is to be categorized as an auxiliary that takes a *bse* form verb phrase argument to produce an *inf* form result. Note that three separate listings are necessary for the non-third-singular finite verbs. Grammars that actually allow features to be manipulated in a sensible way, such as HPSG, will not have this problem, which really only arises due to our simplified treatment of categories as atomic objects. A common way to express the lexical entry for *sneeze* would be using logical descriptions, as in:

(22) $s(V) \setminus np(P,N,subj) \rightarrow$ *sneeze*
        where
        $V = bse$ or
        $V = fin$ and $(P = 1$ or $P = 2$ or $N = plu)$

For instance, see Pollard and Sag (1987) for this kind of logical treatment of lexical entries in HPSG. In any case, as far as the lexicon is concerned, there are really just 13 fully specified lexical entries for *sneeze*, corresponding to the assignments of values to variables in the lexical entry that satisfy the logical description.

We can now analyse simple finite sentences as follows:

(23)

opus	*sneezed*
$np(3,sing,subj)$: **opus**	$s(fin) \setminus np(3,sing,subj)$: **sneezed**

$$s(fin) : \textbf{sneezed(opus)}$$

Note that we will also be able to analyse non-finite sentences such as *Opus running* (which are sometimes referred to as *small clauses*) as being of category *s(pred)* using our lexical entries. We make the contentious, but non-problematic, assumption that all verbs mark their subjects for case. This means that we will be able to analyse the string *he running*, but not the string * *him running* as being of category *s(pred)*. Particular claims about these so-called *small clause* analyses may differ with respect to the case assigned to the complement noun phrases in predicative verbal lexical entries. The reason that we will not suffer any problems on account of this decision is that we assume that control verbs such as *persuade* independently take arguments corresponding to the object noun phrase and infinitive verb phrase in verb phrases such as *believe him to be running*. Thus, the main verb will be assigning case to the *him* which semantically plays the role of the subject of the running.

Basic modifiers

In categorial grammars, a modifier will be any category which eventually combines with arguments to produce a category of the form α / α or $\alpha \setminus \alpha$, which are called *saturated modifier* categories. We can formalize the notion of eventually producing a saturated modifier in terms of categories that have applicative results which are saturated modifiers. We define the notion of *applicative result* by the following clauses:

(24) • α is (trivially) an *applicative result* of α
 • γ is an *applicative result* of α / β or $\alpha \setminus \beta$ if γ is an *applicative result* of α

A *modifier* will then be any category with an applicative result of the form α / α or $\alpha \setminus \alpha$.

An important fact to keep in mind concerning the behaviour of modifiers is that they iterate. The iteration occurs in the following two schemes instantiating the application schemes:

(25) • $\alpha / \alpha : f \quad \alpha : g \quad \rightarrow \quad \alpha : f(g)$
 • $\alpha : g \quad \alpha / \alpha : f \quad \rightarrow \quad \alpha : f(g)$

Thus any number of expressions of category α / α may precede an expression of category α, and similarly any number of expressions of category $\alpha \setminus \alpha$ may follow an expression of category α.

Basic adjectives and intensifiers

The simplest kind of modifier is the basic adjective. In English, adjectives combine with nouns to their right to produce a noun result. We thus have the following categorization:

(26) $n(N) / n(N) \qquad \rightarrow \qquad red, tall, fake$

This gives us the following analysis of a simple adjective-noun construction:

(27)

red	herring
$n(sing) / n(sing)$: **red**	$n(sing)$: **herring**
$n(sing)$: **red(herring)**	

Note that the number feature on both the argument and result categories in the adjectives is identical. This will ensure that an adjective-noun construction will be given the same number feature as its noun. In other languages where adjectives are marked for agreement, an adjective might have restrictions placed on its number value. But it is important to note that there is no separate marking for number on adjectives other than those that occur in its argument and result categories.

Intensifiers can be thought of as modifiers of adjectives, so that they take adjectives as arguments to produce adjectives as results. This gives us the lexical entries:

(28) $n(N) / n(N) / (n(N) / n(N))$ →   *very, quite*

We can use this lexical assignment to provide the following analysis of nominal intensifiers:

(29)

very	*red*	*herring*
$n(sing) / n(sing)$: **very** $/ (n(sing) / n(sing))$	$n(sing) / n(sing)$: **red**	$n(sing)$: **herring**

$n(sing) / n(sing)$: **very(red)**

$n(sing)$: **very(red)(herring)**

In this example, we have stacked complements to conserve space. We will not otherwise change our bracketing conventions.

Basic adverbs

Adverbs are only slightly more complicated than adjectives in that they modify verb phrase categories matching the scheme $s(V) \setminus np(P, N, C)$. Adverbs also show up in both the pre-verbal and post-verbal positions, with some restrictions on their distributions. We can account for these facts with the following lexical entries:

(30) $s(V) \setminus np(P, N, C) / (s(V) \setminus np (P, N, C))$ → *probably, willingly, slowly*
      $s(V) \setminus np(P, N, C) \setminus (s(V) \setminus np (P, N, C))$ → *yesterday, willingly, slowly*

These entries will ensure that modal adverbs like *probably* only occur before verb phrases, temporal adverbials like *yesterday* show up only after verb phrases, and that manner adverbs such as *slowly* and *willingly* can show up in either position. Again, rather than stating two entries for *willingly* and *slowly*, logical unification mechanisms can be employed to capture the generalization of directedness by employing a feature for the direction of the complement (this approach is taken in Zeevat, Klein, & Calder 1987). The following is an instance of the way in which adverbs function:

(31)

probably	cheating
$s(pred) \setminus np(P,N,C) / (s(pred) \setminus np(P,N,C))$	$s(pred) \setminus np(P,N,C)$
probably	**cheating**

$$s(pred) \setminus np(P,N,C) : \textbf{probably(cheating)}$$

Remember that the variables occurring in the trees are interpreted in such a way that any substitution will yield an admissible tree. Just as with the adjectives, the features on the verb phrase are percolated up to the result due to the identity between the features in the argument and result categories of adverbials. Backward looking adverbs will behave in the same way.

Intensifiers for adverbs work the same way as intensifiers for adjectives, but we will refrain from listing their category as it is of the form:

(32) $s \setminus np / (s \setminus np) / (s \setminus np / (s \setminus np))$

with the additional complications of feature equivalences and the fact that verbal intensifiers can also modify post-verbal adverbs.

Prepositional phrases

Prepositional phrases provide our first example of modifiers which take arguments. We will first consider prepositional phrases in their nominal modifier capacity and then look at their similar role in the verb phrase. To allow prepositional phrases to act as post-nominal modifiers of nouns, we give them the following lexical entry:

(33) $n(N) \setminus n(N) / np(P, N2, obj) \rightarrow in, with, beside$

Thus, an expression categorized as an object position noun phrase following a preposition will create a nominal modifier. A simple prepositional phrase will be analysed as in:

(34)

beside	opus
$n(N) \setminus n(N) / np(3,sing,obj) : \textbf{beside}$	$np(3,sing,obj) : \textbf{opus}$

$$n(N) \setminus n(N) : \textbf{beside(opus)}$$

There are convincing semantic arguments for treating prepositional phrases as attaching to nouns rather than to noun phrases (which would also be a possible categorization), since they fall within the scope of quantificational determiners in examples such as:[7]

(35)   Every [student in the class] is bored.

In this case, the universal quantification introduced by *every* is restricted to students in the class.

Since prepositional phrases occur after nouns, they will create well-known structural ambiguities when used in conjunction with adjectives. This is evidenced by the following parse trees:

(36) $\dfrac{tall}{n(sing)/n(sing) : \textbf{tall}}$ $\dfrac{penguin}{n(sing) : \textbf{penguin}}$ $\dfrac{beside\ opus}{n(sing)\backslash n(sing) : \textbf{beside(opus)}}$

$\dfrac{n(sing) : \textbf{tall(penguin)}}{n(sing) : \textbf{beside(opus)(tall(penguin))}}$

(37) $\dfrac{tall}{n(sing)/n(sing) : \textbf{tall}}$ $\dfrac{penguin}{n(sing) : \textbf{penguin}}$ $\dfrac{beside\ opus}{n(sing)\backslash n(sing) : \textbf{beside(opus)}}$

$\dfrac{n(sing) : \textbf{beside(opus)(penguin)}}{n(sing) : \textbf{tall(beside(opus)(penguin))}}$

The structural ambiguity is reflected in the semantics at the root of the trees. In these cases of structural ambiguity, the lexical semantics assigned to the modifiers might be such that there is no resulting semantic ambiguity.

Prepositions are unlike simple adverbs and adjectives in that they apply to both nouns and verb phrases. Since we have categorized nouns as category n and assigned verb phrases to the major category $s \backslash np$, we will have to assign prepositional phrases to two distinct categories, one of which is the noun modifying category which we have already seen, and the second of which is the following verb modifying categorization:[8]

(38) $s(V)\backslash np(P,N,C)\backslash(s(V)\backslash np(P,N,C))/np(P2,N2,obj) \rightarrow in,with,beside$

This lexical entry will allow prepositions to occur as post-verbal modifiers, thus allowing a prepositional phrase such as *in Chicago* to show up in all of the places that any other post-verbal modifier such as *yesterday* would. Note that there is a different person and number assigned to the object of the prepositional phrase than the subject of the sentence through the modifying category. This does not require the person and number of the prepositional object and modified verb phrase to be different, but simply states that they do not have to be identical.

It is also possible to have prepositional phrases that do not take noun phrase complements. These prepositions have the following simplified lexical entries:

(39) $s(V) \setminus np(P,N,C) \setminus (s(V) \setminus np(P,N,C))$ →   *inside, outside*
      $n(N) \setminus n(N)$ →   *inside, outside*

Note that again we must provide two lexical schemes for these prepositions, one for their role as nominal modifiers and one for their role as verbal modifiers.[9]

There has been some discussion regarding the actual category that is being modified by verbal prepositional phrases. While there is strong semantic evidence that the prepositional phrase is a noun modifier in the nominal case, there is really nothing semantically that points toward verb phrase as opposed to sentential modification. Thus, a possible lexical entry for the verbal prepositional phrase would be:

(40) $s(V) \setminus s(V) / np(P,N,obj)$ →   *in, with, beside*

One difficulty in settling this issue is the fact that in extended categorial grammars, the verb phrase modifier categorization follows from the sentential modifier categorization. Rather than assuming that the matter is settled, we simply assume the now more or less standard verb phrase modifier category for prepositional phrases at the lexical level.

Auxiliaries

In this section we present a categorial treatment of auxiliaries in English along the lines of Gazdar et al. (1982) and Bach (1983b). The sequencing and sub-categorization requirements of auxiliaries are directly represented in our lexical entries. It is assumed that an auxiliary category will take a verb phrase argument of one verb form and produce a result of a possibly different verb form and a possibly more restricted assignment of feature values. The semantic behavior of auxiliaries can also be captured naturally within this system (see Carpenter 1989).

Modal and temporal

The simplest auxiliaries are the *temporal* auxiliaries *do*, *does*, and *did* and the *modal* auxiliaries such as *will, might, should*, and *could*. These auxiliaries always produce a finite verb phrase as a result and take as arguments base form verb phrases such as *eat* or *eat yesterday in the park*.

The forms of *do* all act as temporal adverbs and can be captured by the lexical entries:

(41) $s(fin) \setminus np(P,N,subj) / (s(bse) \setminus np(P,N,subj))$ $\rightarrow$ *did*
$s(fin) \setminus np(3, sing, subj) / (s(bse) \setminus np(3, sing,subj))$ $\rightarrow$ *does*
$s(fin) \setminus np(P,N,subj) / (s(bse) \setminus np(P,N,subj))$ $\rightarrow$ *do*
       where ($P \neq 3$ or $N \neq sing$)

In the last lexical entry we have restricted the values of the person and number feature so that they can be anything but the combination of third person and singular. Notice that the argument verb phrase and result verb phrase categories share their person and number features. This will be true of all auxiliary entries, some of which may in addition restrict the person and number features, as is found with *does* and *do*.

The modal adverbs are syntactically distributed in exactly the same way as the temporal adverbs in terms of verb form, but they are not marked for any nominal agreement. We thus provide the following lexical entries:

(42) $s(fin) \setminus np(P,N,subj) / (s(bse) \setminus np(P,N,subj)) \rightarrow$ *will, should, might*

Using these auxiliary categories we get the following tree:

(43)
do		*swim*
$s(fin) \setminus np(3,plu,subj)$ $/ (s(bse) \setminus np(3,plu,subj))$	: **do**	$s(bse) \setminus np(3,plu,subj)$: **swim**
	$s(fin) \setminus np(3,plu,subj)$: **do(swim)**	

The verb phrase *do run* could then combine with a third person plural subject such as *the penguins* to form a finite sentence.

Predicative

The various forms of *be*, often referred to as the *copula*, can be used before predicative verb phrases such as *eating the herring* to produce verb phrases displaying the entire range of verb forms. We will take the following lexical entry for the base form of the copula:

(44) $s(bse) \setminus np(P,N,subj) / (s(pred) \setminus np(P,N,subj)) \rightarrow be$

The predicative auxiliary displays the full range of nominal agreement, as can be seen from the following finite lexical entries:

(45) $s(fin) \setminus np(3, sing,subj) / (s(pred) \setminus np(3,sing,subj)) \rightarrow is$
      $s(fin) \setminus np(1,sing,subj) / (s(pred) \setminus np(1,sing,subj)) \rightarrow am$
      $s(fin) \setminus np(P,N,subj) / (s(pred) \setminus np(P,N,subj)) \rightarrow are$
      where $N = plu$ or $P = 2$
      $s(fin) \setminus np(P,sing,subj) / (s(pred) \setminus np(P, sing,subj)) \rightarrow was$
      where $P = 1$ or $P = 3$
      $s(fin) \setminus np(P,N,subj) / (s(pred) \setminus np(P,N,subj)) \rightarrow were$
      where $N = plu$ or $P = 2$

The auxiliary verbs are unusual in that they have irregular inflectional patterns, as is displayed by *am*, *are*, *was*, and *were*.

Finally, we have predicative and perfective forms of *be*, which display the following categories:

(46) $s(pred) \setminus np(P,N,subj) / (s(pred) \setminus np(P,N,subj)) \rightarrow being$
      $s(perf) \setminus np(P,N,subj) / (s(pred) \setminus np(P,N,subj)) \rightarrow been$

Consider the example parse trees:

(47)

$$\frac{am}{s(fin)\setminus np(1,sing,subj)/(s(pred)\setminus np(1,sing,subj))} \quad \frac{eating}{s(pred)\setminus np(1,sing,subj)}$$
$$s(fin) \setminus np(1,sing,subj)$$

(48)

$$\frac{I}{np(1,sing,subj)} \quad \frac{am\ eating}{s(fin) \setminus np(1,sing,subj)}$$
$$s(fin)$$

From now on we will suppress the semantic constants as we did in this example, since they are fully determined by the phrase-structure schemes and lexical constants.

We will see more of the predicative auxiliary when we consider lexical rules and give an account of the range of possible predicative complements. One benefit of our analysis is that we will not have to provide further lexical entries for the copula. GPSG and LFG treat the copula as a degenerate auxiliary which is not marked for any feature in its complement other than *PRED* : + to explicitly mark the predicative aspect and *BAR* : 2 to restrict attention to saturated phrases (corresponding to maximal projections). These are features that show up on adjectives, progressive verb phrases, noun phrases, and prepositional phrases, among others. This option of only restricting the complement by a few features is not open to us in a strict categorial grammar framework; the adjectives, verb phrases, and adverbial phrases simply do not share a single category and could thus not be provided with a single syntactic lexical entry (although a single semantic constant might be provided for all of the different lexical entries in a mono-typed semantics such as that provided by Chierchia & Turner, forthcoming).

Perfective

The various forms of *have* take perfective verb phrase arguments and produce a range of results, much like the predicative auxiliary forms. The base form perfective auxiliary entry is:

(49) $s(bse) \setminus np(P,N,subj) / (s(perf) \setminus np(P,N,subj)) \rightarrow$ *have*

Notice that like the other auxiliaries, the only function of the base form *have* is to carry along the nominal features and shift the verb form of its argument. The inflected forms will all be restrictions of this category and include the following:[10]

(50) $s(fin) \setminus np(P,N,subj) / (s(perf) \setminus np(P,N,subj))$ $\rightarrow$ *had*
     $s(fin) \setminus np(3,sing,subj) / (s(perf) \setminus np(3,sing,subj))$ $\rightarrow$ *has*
     $s(fin) \setminus np(P,N,subj) / (s(perf) \setminus np(P,N,subj))$ $\rightarrow$ *have*

These lexical entries will allow the following phrase-structure tree:

(51)   *have*   *eaten*
   ‾‾‾   ‾‾‾‾‾‾‾‾‾‾‾‾‾‾‾‾‾‾‾‾‾‾‾‾‾‾‾
   $s(fin) \setminus np(P,N,subj) / (s(perf) \setminus np(P,N,subj))$ $s(bse) \setminus np(P,N,subj)$
   ‾‾
                          $s(bse) \setminus np(P,N,subj)$

Note that we can analyse even longer sequences of auxiliaries such as *will have been eating* without overgenerating parse trees for syntactically ill-formed sequences.

Infinitive

Following Gazdar et al. (1982), we will categorize *to* as a special kind of auxiliary without finite forms. The category we assign to *to* will produce infinitive form verb phrases from base form verb phrases, thus requiring the lexical entry:

(52) $s(inf) \setminus np(P,N,subj) / (s(bse) \setminus np(P,N,subj)) \rightarrow to$

This entry will result in expressions such as *to eat* being categorized as infinitive verb phrases without person or number restrictions. Note that the categorization that we provide will allow us to wantonly generate split infinitives.

We will only consider the role of infinitives as providing clausal complements to control verbs such as *promise* and *believe*. We do not disucss the use of infinitives in sentential subject constructions such as:

(53)   (a)   [to run] is fun.
       (b)   [(for us) to vote] would be useless.

We will also not discuss the role of *for* in optionally providing subjects to infinitive clauses. *To* also occurs with base form verbs in purpose clauses and infinitival relatives as described in Gazdar et al. (1985):

(54)   (a)   The man [(for us) to meet with] is here.
       (b)   They are too crazy [(for us) to meet with].

In all of these cases, there is an unbounded dependency construction where a noun phrase is missing from the infinitival verb phrase.

Negative

For lack of a better section in which to include the negative modifier, we include it under our treatment of auxiliaries. We take lexical entries for *not* according to the following scheme:

(55) $s(V) \setminus np(P,N,C) / (s(V) \setminus np(P,N,C)) \rightarrow not$
       where $V \neq fin$

This accounts for the fact that negation can be applied to any form of verb phrase other than finite. Consider the following analysis:

(56)
$$\frac{\dfrac{not}{s(bse) \setminus np(P,N,subj) / (s(bse) \setminus np(P,N,subj)} \quad \dfrac{sing}{s(bse) \setminus np(P,N,subj)}}{s(bse) \setminus np(P,N,subj)}$$

(57)
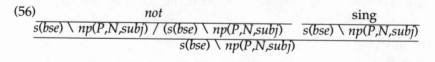
$$\frac{\dfrac{does}{s(fin) \setminus np(3,sing,subj) / (s(bse) \setminus np(3,sing,subj))} \quad \dfrac{not\ sing}{s(bse) \setminus np(3,sing,subj)}}{s(fin) \setminus np(3,sing,subj)}$$

It should be noted that the category for the negative is actually a modifier and takes the verb form of its argument as the resulting verb form and carries along person and number features. This will allow us to correctly categorize expressions involving nested auxiliaries and negations such as:

(58)   Opus would not have been not eating herring.

Complemented categories

In this section we will consider a number of additional lexical entries which produce categories that we have already discussed as applicative results.

Simple polytransitive verbs

A verb may take noun phrase arguments in addition to the subject, as is evidenced by transitive and ditransitive verbs such as *hit* and *give*. These verbs have the following lexical entries:

(59) $s(bse) \setminus np(P,N,subj) / np(P2,N2,obj)$ $\rightarrow$ *hit*
     $s(bse) \setminus np(P,N,subj) / np(P2,N2,obj) / np(P3,N3,obj)$ $\rightarrow$ *give*

From now on, we will only present verbs in their base form; the inflected categories of these verbs is wholly determined by their base forms, as only the verb form of the final sentential result changes. Notice that the complements other than the subject have to be noun phrases with object case marking. We thus capture the following simple contrast:

(60)   (a) Opus gave him the herring.
     (b) * Opus gave he herring.
     (c) He hit Opus.
     (d) * Him hit Opus.

In keeping with our methodology of distinguishing category assignments by means of surface distribution, we will distinguish between different verbs in terms of their lexical entries. In government-binding theory, on the other hand, all verbs are assigned the same basic lexical category *V* according to *X*-theory and analysed with identical phrase-structure rule instances. A verb phrase such as *sneezed* might be analysed as:

(61) $[[[run]_V]_{V'}]_{V''}$

and a verb-phrase such as *hit Opus* might be analysed as:

(62) $[[[hit]_V[opus]_{N''}]_{V'}]_{V''}$

Proponents of government-binding theory are led to this kind of analysis because they adhere to a convention of assigning verbs such as *sneeze* and *hit*, that require different numbers of arguments, to the same lexical category assigned to all verbs.[11] The number of arguments that a particular verb requires is also marked in government-binding theory, but this information is not dealt with in terms of differing phrase structure rules, but by an independent module called the θ-criterion, whose job it is to filter out analyses in which a lexical head is assigned to an inappropriate number of complements or complements go unassigned.[12] The fact that we allow different verbs to be assigned to different categories in which complements are determined directly greatly reduces the depth and complexity of the resulting phrase-structure trees. Of course, we must assume that there is some principled method of assigning lexical categories to basic expressions in the same way that government-binding theory must assume that there is some method of determining the θ-roles appropriate for each each basic expression. One step in the direction of determing θ-roles in a principled way has been taken within the LFG framework (see Bresnan 1982c; Levin 1987).

Sentential complement verbs

Besides taking noun phrase objects, a verb may take sentential complements. Consider the following lexical entries:

(63) $s(bse) \setminus np(P,N,subj) / s(fin) \rightarrow$ *know, believe*

With this lexical scheme we produce analyses such as:

(64)

$$\frac{\dfrac{knew}{s(bse) \setminus np(P,N,subj) / s(fin)} \quad \dfrac{opus\ ran}{s(fin)}}{s(fin) \setminus np(P,N,subj)}$$

Notice that the only verbs of this sort take finite sentences as complements. The subject case marking on the subject of the complement is enforced by the verb phrase within the complement sentence. For instance, we capture the following distinction:

(65)   (a)   Opus believed he ate.
        (b)   * Opus believed him ate.

This is because the sentence must be analysed with *he ate* forming a subtree, and ate requires its subject argument to be marked with subject case.

There are sound lexical motivations for analysing sentential complement verbs with the lexical entry in (63) rather than with the alternative given in (66):

(66) $s(bse) \backslash np(P,N,subj) / (s(fin) \backslash np(P2,N2,subj)) / np(P2,N2,subj) \rightarrow know$

The primary lexical evidence comes from rules which apply to verb complements, such as passivization and detranstivization; these rules do not apply to the subject within a sentential complement verb phrase such as *believe Opus ate*. For instance, we have:

(67)   (a)   Opus [[knew him] [to eat herring]].
        (b)   He was known to eat herring by Opus.
        (c)   Opus [saw [he [ate herring]]].
        (d)   * He was seen ate herring by Opus.

These examples also provide evidence for our analysis of control verbs below, which does allow lexical rules to act on their objects.

Complementized sentential complement verbs

In this section we will consider complementized sentences and their role as complements, such as those bracketed in:

(68)   (a)   I believe [that Opus ate].
        (b)   I wonder [whether Opus ate].
        (c)   I persuaded Binkley [that Opus ate].
        (d)   I bet Binkley five dollars [that Opus ate].
        (e)   I prefer [that Opus eat].

Our account will follow that presented for GPSG in Gazdar et al. (1985). We will simply include some additional verb forms, which in this case are limited to *whether*, *that*, and *thatb*. We assume the following lexical entries for the complementizers themselves:

(69) $s(that) / s(fin)$ $\rightarrow$ *that*
      $s(thatb) / s(bse)$ $\rightarrow$ *that*
      $s(whether) / s(fin)$ $\rightarrow$ *whether*

Note that the second entry for *that* takes sentential complements which are in base form. (69) allows us to produce analyses such as:

(70)

whether	*Opus*	*ate*
s(whether) / s(fin)	np(3,sing,subj)	s(fin) \ np(3,sing,subj)

$$\text{s(fin)}$$

$$\text{s(whether)}$$

We could then provide the main verbs in (68) with the following lexical entries:

(71) s(bse) \ np(P,N,subj) / s(that)   → *believe, know*
  s(bse) \ np(P,N,subj) / s(that) / np(P2,N2,obj)   → *persuade*
  s(bse) \ np(P,N,subj) / s(that) / np(P2,N2,obj) / np(P3,N3,obj) → *bet*
  s(bse) \ np(P,N,subj) / s(whether)   → *wonder*
  s(bse) \ np(P,N,subj) / s(thatb)   → *prefer*

These entries provide the means to analyse all of the sentences in (68) with complementized sentential complements with different features. Complementized sentences display different behaviour from sentences found without complementizers, as can be seen in the case of unbounded dependency constructions in relative clauses, such as:

(72) (a) * who I believe that ran
   (b) who I believe ran

Transformational theories have gone to great length to differentiate the two cases, beginning with Chomsky and Lasnik's (1977) *that*-trace filter, which still surfaces in a more generalized form in current analyses employing Chomsky's government-binding framework.

Prepositional complement verbs

In this section we study the role of prepositions as case-markers in sentences such as:

(73) (a) Opus approved [of the herring].
   (b) Bill gave the herring [to Opus].
   (c) Bill bought the herring [for Opus].
   (d) Opus talked [to Bill] [about the herring].
   (e) Opus conceded [to Binkley] that Bill stank.
   (f) Binkley required [of Opus] that he eat.

Following the GPSG analysis (Gazdar et al. 1985), we will assume that the bracketed prepositions in (73) are simply marking the thematic participant roles of the verbs' arguments. Note that the traditional analysis of (73b) takes the *to* to be a dative case marker.

Under this analysis, we will simply have prepositions take noun phrase arguments and return specially case marked noun phrases such as *np(3,sing,to)* or *np(2,plu,for)*. We use the following lexical entries:

(74) $np(P,N,for) \, / \, np(P,N,obj) \rightarrow$ *for*
       $np(P,N,to) \, / \, np(P,N,obj) \rightarrow$ *to*

We must include parallel entries for the prepositional complementizers such as about, of, and with. This will allow us to produce parse trees for prepositional complements such as:

(75)

for	*you*
$np(2,plu,for) \, / \, np(2,plu,obj)$	$np(2,plu,obj)$
$np(2,plu,for)$	

We can now simply sub-categorize our prepositional complement verbs for the types of prepositional arguments that they take, as in the following:

(76) $s(bse) \setminus np(P,N,subj) \, / \, np(P2,N2,of)$ $\rightarrow$ *approve*
       $s(bse) \setminus np(P,N,subj) \, / \, np(P2,N2,to) \, / \, np(P3,N3,obj)$ $\rightarrow$ *give*
       $s(bse) \setminus np(P,N,subj) \, / \, np(P2,N2,for) \, / \, np(P3,N3,obj)$ $\rightarrow$ *buy*
       $s(bse) \setminus np(P,N,subj) \, / \, np(P2,N2,about) \, / \, np(P3,N3,to)$ $\rightarrow$ *talk*
       $s(bse) \setminus np(P,N,subj) \, / \, s(that) \, / \, np(P2,N2,to)$ $\rightarrow$ *conceded*
       $s(bse) \setminus np(P,N,subj) \, / \, s(thatb) \, / \, np(P2,N2,of)$ $\rightarrow$ *required*

It is important to keep in mind the order in which objects are sequenced. In pure categorial grammars, a functor consumes arguments which are closest to it first. Taking the lexical entries in (76) would then allow the following analysis of a ditransitive dative verb like give:

(77)

give the herring	*to opus*
$s(fin) \setminus np(P,N,subj) \, / \, np(P,N,to)$	$np(3,sing,to)$
$s(fin) \setminus np(P,N,subj)$	

Note that we will need two distinct lexical entries to get the different orderings displayed in:

(78)   (a)   Opus talked to Binkley about herring.
        (b)   Opus talked about herring to Binkley.

Another alternative would be to treat one of the orderings as basic and assume that the other orderings are derived with some sort of heavy constituent shifting rule.

It is important to keep in mind the distinction between prepositional complements, preposition-like expressions occurring in idiomatic verbs such as *hang up*, and freely occurring modifiers such as *walk under*. Consider the following examples:

(79)   (a)   I hung up the phone.
        (b)   I hung the phone up.
        (c)   The phone was hung up.

(80)   (a)   I gave the herring to Opus.
        (b)   * Opus was given the herring to.
        (c)   * Opus was given to the herring.

(81)   (a)   I walked under the bridge.
        (b)   The bridge was walked under.

Bresnan (1972, 1982c) argued that particles such as *up* and even free modifiers such as *under* could, in some situations, form lexical compounds with closely related verbs like *hang* and *walk*, thus allowing lexical rules like passive to operate over the results. One possibility in this case would be to follow GPSG (Gazdar et al. 1985) and use categories such as the following:

(82) $s(bse) \setminus np(P,N,subj) / np(P2,N2,obj) / part(up)$ →   *hang*
        $part(up)$ →   *up*

So-called "particle movement" as displayed in (79b) could then be treated in exactly the same manner as other instances of heavy noun phrase shift (see Morrill 1988). The proper treatment of phrasal verbs and verbs with particles, as found in (79) and (81), is far from settled, so we have simply demonstrated how prepositional phrases can be analysed as case-marked noun phrases.

Expletive subject verbs

Some verbs do not take normal subject noun phrases, and, instead, require that their subjects be the expletive *it*. For instance, consider the case of:

(83)   (a) It is raining.
        (b) * Opus is raining.

We will introduce a special case marking *it* to indicate the expletive subject in the lexical entry:

(84) $np(3,sing,it)$ $\rightarrow$ *it*

We then assume that an expletive subject verb like *raining* will be subcategorized for just this kind of subject, which leads to the lexical entry:

(85) $s(bse) \setminus np(3,sing,it)$ $\rightarrow$ *rain*

We give these verbs third singular marking simply because that is their agreement pattern and will allow us to make other lexical entries more uniform, but not because we believe that they are in some sense assigned a person or number. With these lexical entries we will get the following analysis tree:

(86)
$$\frac{\dfrac{it}{np(3,sing,it)} \qquad \dfrac{rained}{s(fin) \setminus np(3,sing,it)}}{s(fin)}$$

Of course, this will lead to a slight problem in that the meaning assigned will be **rained(it)**, whereas the **it** subject is really serving only as a dummy. This could be captured by assigning a constant function (with, for instance, a vacuous abstraction in the λ-term) as the semantics of rain and some arbitrary interpretation to the constant **it**.

To allow analyses of sentences involving both auxiliaries and expletive subjects, it is actually necessary to slightly generalize the lexical entries for the auxiliaries. Thus, where we previously allowed third person singular auxiliaries to have only subject case marking, we will also allow them to have expletive *it* case marking. Thus, for instance, we will need the additional entry:

(87) $s(bse) \setminus np(P,N,it) / (s(pred) \setminus np(P,N,it)) \rightarrow be$

Of course, this could be marked on the original entry using a straightforward feature logic.

Control verbs

We will take the class of *control* verbs to loosely include all verbs which take a verb phrase complement and determine the semantics of the complement verb phrase's subject, possibly in conjunction with other complements.[13] We will not be concerned with the semantics of control verbs or how they supply subjects for their complements. It is quite easy to do so in unification grammars (see Bresnan 1982b) or with the kind of higher-order typed semantics employed here (see Klein & Sag 1985). Control verbs are traditionally classified along two dimensions. The first of these is the subject/object dimension, which determines whether the subject or direct object of the main verb controls the complement subject. The second distinction is between the so-called *raising* and *equi* verbs, the raising verbs being those which do not provide the controlling complement a thematic role, while the equi verbs do provide such a role. Examples of the various possibilities are as follows:

(88)	(Subject-Equi)	Opus wants to eat.
		* It wants to rain.
	(Subject-Equi)	Opus promised Binkley to eat.
		* It promised Opus to rain.
	(Object-Equi)	Binkley persuaded Opus to eat.
		* Binkley persuaded it to rain.
	(Object-Equi)	Binkley appealed to Opus to eat.
		* Binkley appealed to it to rain.
	(Subject-Raising)	Opus tends to eat.
		It tends to rain.
	(Subject-Raising)	Opus seems to Binkley to eat.
		It seems to Opus to rain.
	(Object-Raising)	Binkley believed Opus to eat.
		Binkley believed it to rain.

This distribution can be accounted for with the following lexical entries:[14]

(89) $s(bse) \setminus np(P,N,subj) / s(inf) / np(P,N,subj) / np(P2,N2,obj)$ $\rightarrow$ *promise, want*

$s(bse) \setminus np(P,N,subj) / s(inf) / np(P2,N2,subj) / np(P2,N2,obj)$ $\rightarrow$ *persuade*

$s(bse) \setminus np(P,N,subj) / s(inf) / np(P2,N2,subj) / np(P2,N2,to)$ $\rightarrow$ *appeal*

$s(bse) \setminus np(P,N,C) / s(inf) \setminus np(P,N,C))$ $\rightarrow$ *tend*
   where $C = subj$ or $C = it$
$s(bse) \setminus np(P,N,C) / (s(inf) \setminus np(P,N,C)) / np(P2,N2,to)$ $\rightarrow$ *seem*
   where $C = subj$ or $C = it$
$s(bse) \setminus np(P,N,subj) / (s(inf) \setminus np(P2,N2,C1)) / np(P2,N2,C2)$ $\rightarrow$ *believe, want*
   where $(C1 = it$ and $C2 = it)$ or $(C1 = subj$ and $C2 = obj)$

The contrast between subject and object control is expressed in terms
of the agreement features of the noun phrase complement within the
infinitive complement. The contrast between raising and equi control
is captured by the distribution of the case marking. Presumably, these
syntactic distinctions will be reflected in the meanings assigned to the
control verbs. Using our lexical entries, we produce the following
parse trees:

(90)

persuading	*opus*
$s(pred) \setminus np(P,N,subj)$	$np(3,sing,obj)$
$/ (s(inf) \setminus np(3,sing,subj))$	
$/ np(3,sing,obj)$	

$s(pred) \setminus np(P,N,subj) / (s(inf) \setminus np(3,sing,subj))$

(91)   *persuading opus*   *to run*

$s(pred) \setminus np(P,N,subj)$ $s(inf) \setminus np(3,sing,subj)$
$/(s(inf) \setminus np(3,sing,subj))$

$s(pred) \setminus np(P,N,subj)$

Notice the contrast between the agreement between features found in
the previous analysis of the object control verb *persuade* and the subject control verb *promise* in the following parse trees:

(92)   *promised*   *them*

$s(pred)\setminus np(P,N,subj)\setminus(s(inf)\setminus np(P,N,subj))/np(2,plu,obj)$ $np(2,plu,obj)$

$s(pred) \setminus np(P,N,subj) \setminus (s(inf) \setminus np(P,N,subj))$

(93)   *promised them*   *to run*

$s(pred) \setminus np(P,N,subj) \setminus (s(inf) \setminus np(P,N,subj))$ $s(inf) \setminus np(P,N,subj)$

$s(pred) \setminus np(P,N,subj)$

We can analyse the raising verb *seem* with an expletive complement as
follows:

(94)

seemed	*to rain*
s(fin) \ np(3,sing,it) / (s(inf) \ np (3,sing,it))	s(inf) \ np(3,sing,it)
s(fin) \ np(3,sing,it)	

These lexical categorizations will in fact respect the grammaticality judgments expressed in (88).

We will analyse perception verbs such as *see* and *watch* in the same manner as other object raising verbs. We thus assume the following lexical entries:

(95) s(bse) \ np(P,N,subj) / (s(pred) \ np(P2,N2,C1)) / np(P2,N2,C2) → *see, notice*
        where (C1 = it and C2 = it) or (C1 = subj and C2 = obj)
      s(bse) \ np(P,N,subj) / (s(bse) \ np(P2,N2,C1)) / np(P2,N2,C2) → *hear, watch*
        where (C1 = it and C2 = it) or (C1 = subj and C2 = obj)

The only difference between these and the other raising verbs is the verb form of the complement clause. This will allow us to provide the correct analysis of the following sentences:

(96)   (a) I saw Opus eating.
        (b) I saw it raining.
        (c) I probably did watch Opus eat.
        (d) I will see it rain.

An interesting class of verbs that seem to share many properties of the control verbs are those that take adjectival complements such as *appear* and *look*. These can be captured by the lexical entries:

(97) s(bse) \ np(P,N,subj) / (n(N) / n(N)) → *appear, look*

These lexical entries are necessary to produce readings for sentences such as:

(98) The herring will look red.

The more complicated entry:

(99) s(bse) \ np(P,N,subj) / np(P2,N2,to) / (n(N) / n(N)) → *appear, look*

could be employed to handle sentences such as:

(100) The herring appeared red to Opus.

Lexical predicatives

There is an entire class of verb-like basic expressions which show up primarily as complements to the copula and as adverbial and adnominal expressions. Consider the following:[15]

(101) (a) angry [about the weather]
      (b) afraid [that Opus sneezed]
      (c) insistent [that Opus run]
      (d) eager [to run]

These expressions will all be lexically categorized as having applicative results which are predicative verb phrases. They will not be inflected for other verb forms. Our lexical rules will then map the predicative entry into the other functions that these phrases can perform. We need the following lexical entries:

(102) $s(pred) \setminus np(P,N,subj) / np(P2,N2,about)$ $\rightarrow$ *angry*
       $s(pred) \setminus np(P,N,subj) / s(that)$ $\rightarrow$ *afraid*
       $s(pred) \setminus np(P,N,subj) / s(thatb)$ $\rightarrow$ *insistent*
       $s(pred) \setminus np(P,N,subj) / (s(inf) \setminus np(P,N,subj))$ $\rightarrow$ *eager*

These lexical categorizations will ensure that all of the examples in (101) will be able to serve as predicative verb phrases and thus act as complements to the various forms of *be*.

Sentential adverbials

There are adverbs such as *because* and *while* which take finite sentential arguments and produce post-verbal modifiers as a result. This leads to the following lexical entries:

(103) $s(V) \setminus np(P,N,subj) \setminus (s(V) \setminus np(P,N,subj)) / s(fin)$ $\rightarrow$ *because, while, after, if*

These entries allow us to provide expressions such as *because Opus ate the herring* with the same category as a simple post-verbal adverb such as *yesterday*.

Control adverbials

Adverbs also parallel complex verbs in taking either verb phrases or a combination of a verb phrase and an object noun phrase complement. For instance, we have the following acceptable sentences:

(104) (a) Opus swam after eating.

    (b) Opus probably swam to be moving.
    (c) Opus swam with Binkley cheering.

For these adverbs, we assume the following lexical entries:

(105) $s(V) \setminus np(P,N,subj) \setminus (s(V) \setminus np(P,N,subj)) \;\rightarrow\;$ *while, before*
        / $(s(pred) \setminus np(P,N,subj))$
      $s(V) \setminus np(P,N,subj) \setminus (s(V) \setminus np(P,N,subj)) \;\rightarrow\;$ *to*
        / $(s(bse) \setminus np(P,N,subj))$
      $s(V) \setminus np(P,N,subj) \setminus (s(V) \setminus np(P,N,subj)) \;\rightarrow\;$ *with*
        / $(s(pred) \setminus np(P2,N2,subj))$
        / $np(P2,N2,obj)$

Notice that the first two entries are subject control adverbs in that the subject of the main clause is forced to agree with the subject of the clause embedded in the adverb, while in the last entry, the embedded verb phrase agrees with the embedded object. Of course, these facts have more effect on the semantics than the syntax, since non-finite clauses in English are not marked for agreement.

Complementized nouns

Since we are concentrating primarily on details of the verb phrase, we will not present an extended analysis of nouns which are sub-categorized for complements. Consider the following examples of complementized nouns drawn from the GPSG grammar in Gazdar et al. (1985):

(106) (a) love [of herring]
      (b) argument [with Opus] [about the herring]
      (c) gift [of herring] [to Opus]
      (d) belief [that it will rain]
      (e) request [that Opus eat]
      (f) plan [to eat]

It is possible to account for the complement behaviour of all of these nouns, by simply adding the lexical entries:

(107) $n(sing) / np(P,N,of)$ $\rightarrow$ *love*
      $n(sing) / np(P,N,about) / np(P2,N2,with)$ $\rightarrow$ *argument*
      $n(sing) / np(P,N,to) / np(P2,N2,of)$ $\rightarrow$ *gift*
      $n(sing) / s(that)$ $\rightarrow$ *belief*
      $n(sing) / s(thatb)$ $\rightarrow$ *request*
      $n(sing) / (s(inf) \setminus np(P,sing,subj))$ $\rightarrow$ *plan*

We will not consider the interesting phenomena of nominalization, as seen in such cases as:

(108) (a) Binkley's running
      (b) The running of Binkley
      (c) The giving of the herring to Opus by Binkley

It is not clear whether the genitive in (108a) or the prepositions in (108b) or (108c) are to be analysed as modifiers or as complements. Either analysis would be possible within the framework we are developing here.

Another matter that is not handled by our lexical entries is the fact that prepositionally marked complements can often occur in any order. For instance, in (106b) and (106c), we could also have:

(109) (a) argument about herring with the silly penguin
      (b) gift to Opus of the funny little fish

It is not clear from these examples whether there is a true free word order or something like heavy noun phrase shift being employed. If it is some kind of noun phrase shift, then these examples would naturally be handled with the same syntactic mechanisms as are involved in unbounded dependency constructions (see Morrill 1987b, 1988; Gazdar et al. 1985). If the alternation between the examples in (106) and (109) is not an example of heavy shift, then an alternative explanation is required. One possibility would be to simply list multiple lexical entries with the different orders indicated. A similar problem is encountered in an attempt to apply the simple directed categorial grammar we employ here to free word order languages such as German (see Reape 1989 and Steedman 1985 for treatments of free word order in a categorial framework).

Possessives

We can analyse the simple possessive construction with the following lexical entry:

(110) $np(3,N,C) / n(N) \setminus np(P2,N2,obj) \rightarrow \text{'s}$

This will allow us to produce the following noun phrase analysis.

(111)

Opus	's	herring
$np(3,sing,C2))$	$np(3,sing,C) / n(sing) \setminus np(3,sing,C2)$	$n(sing)$

$$\frac{np(3,sing,C) / n(sing)}{np(3,sing,C)}$$

We have made sure that the possessive marking combines with a noun phrase to produce a determiner category which then applies to a noun to produce a noun phrase. Stricly speaking, the possessor argument can not be a pronoun, as there are special lexical entries for possessive pronouns. We will also not consider the use of genitive noun phrases such as *Opus's* where they are obviously playing some sort of complement role, in cases such as:

(112)   (a)   The herring of Opus's is red.
        (b)   Opus's giving of the herring to Bill was unwise.

We could, on the other hand, simply add another entry for the possessive marker to produce genitive noun phrase results, as in:

(113) $np(3,N,gen) \setminus np(3,N,C) \rightarrow$'s

which would allow *Opus's* to be categorized as $np(3,sing,gen)$. The possessive *of* could then be lexically marked to take a genitive noun phrase object. Evidence for the fact that more than one entry is necessary for *'s* is given by the following two noun phrases:

(114)   (a)   my herring
        (b)   Opus's herring
        (c)   the herring of mine
        (d)   the herring of Binkley's.

Then we could classify *my* as a determiner, while *mine* would be classified as $np(3,sing,gen)$.

LEXICAL RULES

What we have presented up to this point forms the core lexicon of our grammar and consists of assignments of categories to basic expressions. We have also seen examples of how the application rules recursively determine the compositional assignment of syntactic and semantic categorizations to complex expressions in terms of the assignments to their constituent expressions. But the lexical entries that we have provided are not sufficient to account for many patterns of distribution displayed by the expressions that we have introduced. For instance, predicative verb phrases can occur as post-nominal modifiers and plural nouns can serve as noun phrases without the aid of a determiner. To account for additional categorizations which are predictable on the basis of core lexical assignments, we introduce a system of lexical rules.

Lexical rules serve the purpose of expressing lexical regularities. Functionally, they create new lexical entries which are predictable from existing lexical entries. By continuing to apply lexical rules until no more entries can be found, we generate a closed lexicon. Nothing in the lexical rule affects the application schemes, so distributional regularities must be accounted for solely in terms of additional lexical category assignments. Viewed in this way, our lexical rules serve much the same purpose as the lexical metarules of GPSG (Gazdar et al. 1985) and the lexical rules of LFG (Bresnan 1982a). In GPSG, meta-rules produced new phrase structure schemes from existing ones. Our lexical categorizations, when coupled with the universal application schemes, correspond quite closely to phrase structure rules. Producing new lexical entries in a categorial grammar serves the same purpose as producing new basic categories and lexical phrase structure rules in a context-free grammar.

In categorial grammar contexts, it is common to follow Dowty's (1982) proposal to encode grammatical role information, such as the object and subject distinction, directly in the category by means of argument order. Under this positional encoding of the obliqueness hierarchy, the arguments consumed earliest by a category are considered most oblique.[16] For instance, in the case of the ditransitive verb category $s \setminus np_1 / np_2 / np_3$, we would have np_1 as the subject argument, np_2 as the object, and np_3 as the indirect object. A transitive verb category such as $s \setminus np_1 / np_2$ would not have an indirect object, and other categories, such as those assigned to control verbs, would have phrasal or sentential complements. These assumptions concerning grammatical functions are directly incorporated into the semantic portion of GPSG (Gazdar et al. 1985) and into the lexical hierarchy of HPSG (Pollard & Sag 1987). The way our lexical rules are defined, they will have access to arguments of verbs in certain positions determined by obliqueness, thus giving them the power to perform operations which apply to subjects, the most oblique argument, and so on. Passive is a prime example of where this sort of re-encoding of complement order is carried out, and, functionally, our lexical rules share a striking resemblance to those defined over grammatical roles such as subject and object in Lexical Functional Grammar (Bresnan 1982c). In addition, LFG lexical rules can delete noun phrase complements from lexical entries for verbs (where verbs are the heads of sentences, and thus have sentences as their applicative results, in our terminology), change the case marking of complements, alter the final result category, and so on. In this section, we will see examples of lexical rules with all of these functions.

It is significant that we have assumed a set of lexical rules rather than a set of unary rules that might apply at any stage in a derivation. By forcing our rules to apply before syntactic applications and, more specifically, before any other kind of unbounded dependency construction, their effects will be strictly localized or *bounded*. That is, our rules operate solely over a lexical category and its complements. This property is also shared by the LFG lexical rules and GPSG metarules.[17]

We should make clear from the start that we will not be concerned with any form of inflectional or derivational morphology. We have avoided inflectional morphology by choosing an inflectionally impoverished language, namely English, for which it is possible to simply list all of the available lexical forms (sometimes using schematic entries employing variables over features). In particular, both singular and plural forms of nouns and various verb forms must be explicitly listed for each word in our core lexicon. We will similarly ignore derivational morphology such as prefixation and suffixation. Of course, it would be nice to have a characterization of inflectional and derivational morphology compatible with the lexicon presented here, but none has been worked out in detail. Nothing in the present system places any restrictions on the way that morphological or inflectional morphology might be realized. Both the approaches of Moortgat (1987c, 1988b) and Dowty (1979) to morphology in categorial grammar are compatible with the lexicon presented here. In fact, it has been argued that a categorial system is actually useful in describing derivational morphological operations (Hoeksema & Janda 1988; Keenan & Timberlake 1988; Moortgat 1987c, 1988b). To carry out a thorough morphological analysis, operations will be needed of similar functionality to those developed below for handling lexical redundancy rules. Conceptually, inflectional and derivational operations would apply before the types of lexical rules that we consider here. We simply assume a fully generated base lexicon consisting of the results of the inflectional and derivational systems. Our lexical rules are meant to account for distributional regularities of a fixed morphological form rather than generating more lexical entries by applying derivational or inflectional operations. Before going into the technical details of the lexical rule system, we will present simple rules for bare plurals and for so-called subject-auxiliary inversion.

Bare plurals

We will consider the case of bare plurals first, where the basic pattern to be accounted for is as follows:

(115) (a) (Some) Penguins ate herring.
      (b) (Some) Tall penguins ran quickly.
      (c) (Some) Penguins in the band played yesterday.

The parenthetical determiners are optional for plural nouns. The sentences in (115) are all perfectly grammatical without the determiners. We will account for this fact with the simplest of our lexical rules:

(116) $n(plu)$ \$ $\Rightarrow$ $np(3,plu,C)$ \$
      $\lambda\phi.\lambda x_1....\lambda x_n.\mathbf{indef}(\phi(x_1)...(x_n))$

There are a number of components of this rule which require individual explanation. The syntactic operation performed by a lexical rule is expressed by a category rewriting rule with the possible occurrence of the string variable \$. We use the \$ in the same way as Ades and Steedman (1982), to range over strings of alternating slashes and categories beginning with a slash and ending with a category, such as / np, / np / np, and \ np \ (s \ np) / np. The intuition here is that any lexical entry whose syntactic category matches the pattern $n(plu)$ \$ will be an acceptable input to the bare pluralization rule. A category that matches this pattern will have a final applicative result of $n(plu)$ with an arbitrary string of complements coming in either direction. The \$ will always be used in this way to allow rules to operate over applicative results and simply pass the complementation of the input category to the output category. The same information could be expressed recursively rather than via string pattern matching, but the recursive presentation is quite messy.[18] It should be noted that the unification categorial grammar system of Zeevat et al. (1987) treats complementation with a data structure consisting of a string of categories marked for directionality; in a system such as theirs, it is quite natural to express lexical rules such as the ones presented here by employing an operation of string unification, although this is not something that is actually done in their system.[19] The syntactic ouput of the bare pluralization rule will then consist of the output pattern with the same instantiation of the \$ variable. Examples of the syntactic effects of this rule are given in the following table, where the input category, output category, and string of slashes and categories that match the \$ string variable are given:

(117) | Word | INPUT | OUTPUT | $ |
|---|---|---|---|
| kids | n(plu) | np(3,plu,C) | ε |
| tall | n(plu) / n(plu) | np(3,plu,C) / n(plu) | / n(plu) |
| in | n(plu) \ n(plu) | np(3,plu,C) \ n(plu) | \ n(plu) / np(P2,N2,obj) |
| | / np(P2,N2,obj) | / np(P2,N2,obj) | |

We have used the symbol ε to stand for the null string. The overall syntactic effect is to take a lexical entry whose syntactic category matches the input to the rule and produce a lexical categorization whose syntax is given by the output of the rule. Ignoring the semantics for the time being, the bare pluralization rule will take the lexical entries:

(118) $n(plu)$ $\rightarrow$ penguins
$n(plu) / n(plu)$ $\rightarrow$ tall
$n(plu) \setminus n(plu) / np(P2,N2,obj)$ $\rightarrow$ in

and produce the following lexical entries:

(119) $np(3,plu,C)$ $\rightarrow$ penguins
$np(3,plu,C) / n(plu)$ $\rightarrow$ tall
$np(3,plu,C) \setminus n(plu) / np(P2,N2,obj)$ $\rightarrow$ in

The new noun phrase lexical entry for the plural *penguins* has the obvious utility of allowing us to parse sentences such as penguins waddle. For the functor categories, consider the following parse trees:

(120)

tall	kids
np(3,plu,C) / n(plu)	n(plu)

np(3,plu,C)

(121)

kids	in	Pittsburgh
n(plu)	np(3,plu,C) \ n(plu) / np(3,sing,obj)	np(3,sing,obj)

np(3,plu,C) \ n(plu)

np(3,plu,C)

The significant thing to note here is that the lexical rules do not operate on the traditional *head* of a phrase, but on the category that produces the final applicative result. Thus, since the root of the tree in (120) is determined by the applicative result of the adjective, the lexical rule must be applied to the adjective. Similarly, in (121), the rule must be applied to the preposition, as it will provide the final applicative result. The lexical rules, by means of the $ variable, can access the eventual applicative result of a category and modify it. Thus, by applying the lexical rule to every category which can eventually produce an $n(plu)$ result, we are guaranteed that any tree which is rooted at an $n(plu)$ has a corresponding tree rooted at $np(3,plu,C)$, since the lexical rule could have been applied to the functor that produced the $n(plu)$ result. Thus, we have really achieved the result of adding a unary syntactic rule of the form:

(122) $n(plu)$ → $np(3,plu,C)$

With this rule operating in the syntax, we would get parse trees such as:

(123)

tall	*kids*
$n(plu) \,/\, n(plu)$	$n(plu)$

$$n(plu)$$
$$np(3,plu,C)$$

In the case of bare pluralization, exactly the same set of strings will be accepted with the lexicon after applying the bare pluralization rule as would be accepted by adding a syntactic unary rule such as (122) to account for bare plurals.[20]

We turn now to the semantic effects of lexical rules. The semantic component of a lexical rule is expressed as a polyadic λ-term which, when applied to the semantics of the input category, produces the semantics of the output category. The first argument, φ, will be the semantics of the input. Complications arise from the fact that lexical rules operate over varying syntactic types, so a single semantic operation will not suffice. For the bare pluralization rule in (116), and in subsequent rules, the semantic function will contain a string of abstracted variables $x_1,\cdots,x_n$ whose types will not be known until the types of the category matching the $ symbol are known. It is assumed that if we take the $ variable to match a string of categories and slashes $|_n \alpha_n |_{n-1} \alpha_{n-1} \cdots |_1 \alpha_1$ (where $|_i$ is either a forward or backward leaning slash), then the type of the variable x_i is taken to be the type of α_i (the orders are reversed because of the conventions for arguments being reversed in λ-abstractions and categorial grammar complements). Thus, in the case of the bare pluralization rule, the semantic effect is given as follows:

(124) Category   Semantic Rule
      n $\lambda\phi^n.\mathbf{indef}(\phi)$
      $n \,/\, n$ $\lambda\phi^{\langle n,n\rangle}.\lambda x_1^n.\mathbf{indef}(\phi(x_1))$
      $n \setminus n \,/\, np$ $\lambda\phi^{\langle np,\langle n,n\rangle\rangle}.\lambda x_1^{np}.\lambda x_2^n.\mathbf{indef}(\phi(x_1)(x_2))$

It is also worth noticing that the semantic constant **indef** must be of the type $\langle n,np\rangle$ to ensure that the resulting term is well defined. Any constants introduced by lexical rules will be of a single fixed type. The polymorphic behaviour of the semantic operation comes from not knowing in advance how many complements are going to be taken to match the \$. In all of our lexical rules, these unknown arguments are simply fed back into the semantics of the input so that the semantics of the lexical rule can have a uniform effect. In the case of our bare plural rule, we will get the following lexical entries as a result (again suppressing the features on types for readability):

(125) $np(3,plu,C) : \mathbf{indef}(\mathbf{kids})$ $\rightarrow$ *kids*
      $np(3,plu,C) \,/\, n(plu) : \lambda x_1^n.\mathbf{indef}(\mathbf{tall}(x_1))$ $\rightarrow$ *tall*
      $np(3,plu,C) \setminus n(plu) \,/\, np(P2,N2,obj) : \lambda x_1^{np}.\lambda x_2^n.\mathbf{indef}(\mathbf{in}(x_1)(x_2))$ $\rightarrow$ *in*

The bare pluralization rule will also apply to other categories with plural nominal results, such as intensifiers and complementized nouns.

Yes/no questions

Before going on to handle the general case of predicatives, we will consider another simple lexical rule which can be used to account for yes/no questions such as the following:

(126) (a) Did Opus eat?
      (b) Is Opus eating?
      (c) Has Opus eaten?

Assuming that we include an additional verb form *ynq* for yes/no questions, we can use the following lexical rule to capture the use of auxiliaries to form questions:

(127) $s(fin) \setminus np(P,N,C)$ $\Rightarrow$ $s(ynq)$
        $/\,(s(V) \setminus np(P,N,C))$ $/\,(s(V) \setminus np(P,N,C))$
                                         $/\,np(P,N,C)$

      $\lambda\phi.\lambda x^{np}.\lambda x^{\langle np,s\rangle}.\mathbf{ques}(v(x))$
      where $V \neq fin$ and $V \neq inf$

This rule will apply to an auxiliary category and output a category which takes a noun phrase and verb phrase argument to produce a yes/no question as a result. This rule will result in the following basic and derived lexical entries:

(128) $s(fin) \setminus np(2,plu,subj) / (s(bse) \setminus np(2,plu,subj)) \rightarrow do$
 do

   $s(ynq) \ (s(bse) \setminus np(2,plu,subj) \setminus np(2,plu,subj) \rightarrow do$
   $\lambda x^{np}.\lambda v^{\langle np,s \rangle}.\textbf{ques}(\textbf{do}(v)(x))$

(129) $s(fin) \setminus np(1,sing,subj) / (s(pred) \setminus np(3,plu,subj)) \rightarrow am$
 am

   $s(ynq) \ (s(spred) \setminus np(1,sing,subj) \setminus np(1,sing,subj) \rightarrow am$
   $\lambda x^{np}.\lambda v^{\langle np,s \rangle}.\textbf{ques}(\textbf{am}(v)(x))$

(130) $s(fin) \setminus np(3,sing,subj) / (s(perf) \setminus np(3,sing,subj)) \rightarrow has$
 has

   $s(ynq) \ (s(perf) \setminus np(3,sing,subj)) / np(3,sing,subj) \rightarrow has$
   $\lambda x^{np}.\lambda v^{\langle np,s \rangle}.\textbf{ques}(\textbf{has}(v)(x))$

These new lexical entries can be used in analyses such as the following:

(131)

am	*I*	*running*
$s(ynq)$	$np(1,sing,subj)$	$s(pred)$
$/ (s(pred) \setminus np(1,sing,subj))$ **i**		$\setminus np(1,sing,subj)$
$/ np(1,sing,subj)$		**running**
$\lambda x^{\langle np \rangle}.\lambda v^{\langle np, s \rangle}.\textbf{ques}(\textbf{am}(v)(x))$		

$s(ynq)$
$/ (s(pred) \setminus np(1,sing,subj))$
$\lambda v^{\langle np, s \rangle}.\textbf{ques}(\textbf{am}(v)(\textbf{i}))$

$s(ynq) : \textbf{ques}(\textbf{am}(\textbf{running})(\textbf{i}))$

PREDICATIVES

In this section, we will present a detailed analysis of the distribution of predicatives in English and, in so doing, demonstrate the utility of schematic lexical rules with complement string variables.

Passivization

While passivization might be more fairly characterized as a morpho-logical operation, we will discuss its effects on syntactic and semantic categorizations and ignore its phonological and orthographic effects. The passive rule provides an excellent example of the full power of schematic lexical rules. The passive operation applies to a verbal cate-gory that produces a sentential result and takes at least one object-marked nominal complement to its right. The syntactic result is a new category whose most oblique *obj* marked noun phrase complement is replaced with an optional *by* marked noun phrase. Semantically, the subject and most oblique complement switch thematic roles. For in-stance, consider who is doing what to whom in the following active and passive constructions:

(132) (a) Opus loved Bill.
       (b) Bill was loved by Opus.
       (c) Bill was loved.
       (d) Bill was loved by something.

In both (132a) and (132b), Opus is the "lover" and Bill the "lovee." In the case of (132c) Bill still plays the role of "lovee," but there is now an existential quantification of some variety filling in the missing role so that (132c) is roughly equivalent in meaning to (132d).[21]

Our primary consideration in treating the passive in this section is that it produces a predicative verb phrase result (note the necessary copula in the passives in (132)). Our claim is that in any context where a predicative verb phrase such as *hitting Opus* is licensed, it is also possible to have a passive verb phrase such as *hit by Opus* (of course, the thematic roles are reversed in the passive version). Consider the following examples:

(133) (a) Binkley saw Bill hitting Opus.
       (b) Binkley saw Opus hit by Bill.
       (c) Opus danced when watching Bill.
       (d) Opus danced when watched by Bill.
       (e) Opus ate herring with Bill offending him.
       (f) Opus ate herring with Bill offended by him.
       (g) Was Opus hit by Bill?

It should be kept in mind while reading this section that anything that gets classified as a predicative verb phrase will be able to occur in any location in which a lexical predicative verb phrase may be found. This is due to the fact that there is nothing in a categorial analysis that is sensitive to derivational histories; every analysis involving a complex expression is determined solely on the basis of the category assigned to the root of its parse tree. In government-binding theory, on the other hand, the number of traces and indices within a phrase-marker is quite significant as it interacts with modules such as the binding, subjacency, and empty category principles.

In our official notation, the passive rule is as follows:

(134) $s(bse) \setminus np(P1,N1,subj) \$ \Rightarrow s(pred) \setminus np(P2,N2,subj) \$$
        $/ np(P2,N2,obj)$ $/ np(P1,N1,by)$
        $\lambda\phi.\lambda x_1.\cdots\lambda x_n.\lambda y_2.\lambda y_1.\phi(y_1)(x_1)\cdots(x_n)(y_2)$

Note that the *by* marked noun phrase occurs inside of the $ in the result, thus forcing it to occur after the other complements in the verb phrase.

As we have allowed ourselves no direct representation of optional complementation, we will need the following additional rule to deal with the situation where the *by*-phrase is omitted:

(135) $s(bse)\setminus np(P1,N1,subj)\$/np(P2,N2,obj) \Rightarrow s(pred)\setminus np(P2,N2,subj) \$$
        $\lambda\phi.\lambda x_1.\cdots\lambda x_n.\lambda y_1.\phi(y_1)(x_1)\cdots(x_n)(\textbf{something})$

We will consider how these rules apply to the different categorizations that we have given to transitive and poly-transitive verbs in the rest of this section.

Simple transitive passives

Consider the distribution of the passives in the following simple transitive and bitransitive verbs:

(136)   (a) Opus hit Binkley.
        (b) Binkley was hit (by Opus).

(137)   (a) Bill gave Opus herring.
        (b) Opus was given the herring (by Bill).
        (c) The herring was given (by Bill).

To derive this example by application of the passive rule, it is first necessary to be able to derive the detransitivized active version: *Bill gave the herring*.

(138) (a) Bill gave herring to Opus.
       (b) Herring was given to Opus (by Bill).

In the case of (136), we have the following basic lexical entries and entries derived by applying the passivization rules:[22]

(139) $s(bse) \setminus np(subj) / np(obj) : hit$ $\rightarrow$ *hit*
       $s(pred) \setminus np(subj) / np(by) : \lambda x.\lambda y.\mathbf{hit}(y)(x)$ $\rightarrow$ *hit*
       $s(pred) \setminus np(subj) : \lambda y.\mathbf{hit}(y)(\mathbf{something})$ $\rightarrow$ *hit*

This will give us the following analysis for the passive in (136b):

(140)

Binkley	*was*	*hit*	*by Opus*
np	$s(fin) \setminus np)$	$s(pred) \setminus np / np(by)$	$np(by)$
binkley	$/ (s(pred) \setminus np)$	$\lambda x.\lambda y.\mathbf{hit}(y)(x)$	**opus**
	was		

$$s(pred) \setminus np$$
$$\lambda y.(\mathbf{hit}(y)(\mathbf{opus}))$$

$$s(fin) \setminus np$$
$$\mathbf{was}(\lambda y.(\mathbf{hit}(y)(\mathbf{opus})))$$

$$s(fin) \setminus np$$
$$\mathbf{was}(\lambda y.(\mathbf{hit}(y)(\mathbf{opus})))(\mathbf{binkley})$$

Now suppose that we fix a simple control-based semantics for **was**, such as:

(141) $\mathbf{was} =_{def} \lambda P^{\langle np,s \rangle}.\lambda x^{np}.\mathbf{past}(P(x))$

In the case of the passive analysis, we would then have:

(142) $\mathbf{was}(\lambda y.\mathbf{hit}(y)(\mathbf{opus}))(\mathbf{binkley}) = \mathbf{past}(\mathbf{hit}(\mathbf{binkley})(\mathbf{opus}))$

This semantic treatment of passivization is for illustrative purposes only and should not be taken as a serious proposal. But it does illustrate how the thematic roles are preserved from the usual derivation of the active version in (136a):

(143)

Opus	*hit*	*Binkley*
np	$s \setminus np / np$	np
opus	**hit**	**binkley**

$$s \setminus np$$
$$\mathbf{hit}(\mathbf{binkley})$$

$$s(fin)$$
$$\mathbf{hit}(\mathbf{binkley})(\mathbf{opus})$$

In the situation where the by-phrase is omitted, the second lexical rule for passivization in (135) will apply, effectively filling the semantic position that would have been contributed by the subject with **something**. For instance, this would give us the following semantics for (136b) without the *by Opus* complement:

(144) (a) Binkley was hit.
       (b) **past((hit)(binkley)(something))**

Next consider what happens to the semantics of a bitransitive verb such as *give* when it undergoes passivization:

(145) $s \setminus np(subj) / np(obj) / np(obj)$: **give**   → *give*
       $s \setminus np(subj) / np(by) / np(obj)$: $\lambda x.\lambda y.\lambda z.$**give**$(z)(x)(y)$ → *given*

This will result in the following semantic analyses:

(146) (a) Bill gave Opus the herring.
       (b) **give(opus)(the(herring))(bill)**

(147) (a) Opus was given the herring by Bill.
       (b) **past(give(opus)(the(herring))(bill))**

In the case of the *to* marked bitransitive we would have the basic and derived lexical entries:

(148) $s \setminus np(subj) / np(to) / np(obj)$: **giveto**   → *give*
       $s \setminus np(subj) / np(by) / np(to)$: $\lambda x.\lambda y.\lambda z.$**giveto**$(z)(x)(y)$ → *given*

The result is the following semantic assignments:

(149) (a) Bill gave the herring to Opus.
       (b) **giveto(the(herring))(opus)(bill)**

(150) (a) The herring was given to Opus by Bill.
       (b) **past(giveto(the(herring))(opus)(bill))**

Ordinarily, a lexical rule of some sort would be employed to produce a bitransitive entry for (145) from the *to* marked version for (148) (see Bresnan 1982c, for example). This operation is usually referred to as *dative shift*, to indicate that the preposition *to* marks what is classically the dative case. This is the type of rule which we will not consider, because it is not fully productive (that is, not all dative or *to* marked arguments can be shifted to an indirect object position). But the effects of such a shift could be described as follows in the cases where *to* marked arguments become indirect objects:

(151) $s \setminus np(subj) / np(to) / np(obj) \Rightarrow s \setminus np(subj) / np(obj) / np(obj)$
        $\lambda\phi.\lambda x.\lambda y.\lambda z.\phi(y)(x)(z)$

If we assumed that the *to* marked version resulted from this rule, we would have:

(152)   **giveto** = $\lambda x.\lambda y.\lambda z.\textbf{give}(y)(x)(z)$

Consequently, (149a) and (146a) would be assigned the same semantics. There are a number of subtle thematic effects that must be accounted for at the level of the base lexicon which we will not consider (but see Dowty 1979).

The following transitive sentential complement verbs will undergo passivization in exactly the same way as bitransitive verbs such as *give*:

(153)   (a)   I convinced Bill that Opus ate.
        (b)   Bill was convinced that Opus ate (by me).

The syntactic category $s \setminus np / s$ assigned to *know* is not of the correct category to undergo passivization, so that we get the correct prediction:

(154)   (a)   I know Opus ate.
        (b)   * Opus was known ate (by me).

Passive and control

Consider the following cases of passivization with control verbs:

(155)   (a)   Opus persuaded Bill to eat the herring.
        (b)   Bill was persuaded to eat the herring.

(156)   (a)   Opus promised Bill to eat the herring.
        (b)   * Bill was promised to eat the herring.

(157)   (a)   Bill saw Opus eating.
        (b)   Opus was seen eating.

In all of the situations where the passive is acceptable, the following syntactic conversion is carried out:

(158) $s \setminus np(subj) / (s \setminus np) / np(obj) \Rightarrow s \setminus np(subj) / np(by) / (s \setminus np)$

Just as in the previous cases, the semantics will be unaffected. What remains to be explained is *Visser's generalization* that only object-control verbs may undergo passivization. The distinction is explained in terms of the completeness and coherence conditions which require specified thematic roles to be filled (Bresnan 1982c). We must rely on general semantic selectional restrictions, which will be necessary in any case to handle morphological operations, which are known to be particularly selective about the lexical semantics of their inputs (see Dowty 1979:Ch. 6, for similar arguments concerning such lexical operations as the causative).

An interesting case arises for raising verbs such as *believe*, since passivization will have to account for the possibility of expletive objects moving into subject position. Consider the pair:

(159)   (a)   Milo believed it to be raining.
        (b)   It was believed to be raining (by Milo).

Our lexical rule will need to be generalized to apply to oblique complements marked with *it* and carry this marking into their new surface role as subjects. For instance, we would warrant the following syntactic operation on the expletive version of *believe*:

(160) $s \setminus np(subj) / (s \setminus np(it)) / np(it) \Rightarrow s \setminus np(it) / np(by) / (s \setminus np(it))$

Sentential subjects and passivization

Not only can expletives be made into subjects by passivization, but complementized sentences can also be promoted to subjecthood, as seen in:

(161)   (a)   Bill knew that Opus ate.
        (b)   That opus ate was known (by Bill).
        (c)   Bill wondered whether Opus ate.
        (d)   * Whether Opus ate was wondered (by Bill).

These examples will not be handled by the current passivization rule. One solution to this would be to abandon our treatment of complementizers as marking verb forms, and instead consider them to be a special kind of case marked determiner of the category

$np(3,sing,that)$ / $s(fin)$. This is very similar to the proposal of Sag et al. (1985), based on Weisler (1982), which admits $NP[NFORM : S]$ as a categorization of complementized sentences. We would then need to assume that complementized sentential complement verbs like *knew* were syntactically categorized as $s \setminus np(subj)$ / $np(that)$. In this case, we could treat *that* in the same way as the expletive marked *it* subjects in (160) using the generalized passive rule to deal with normal, expletive, and sentential subjects. The details of this proposal remain to be worked out, and consideration should also be given to infinitival sentential subjects such as in:

(162)   ((For Opus) to eat herring) is annoying.

In this case, there is an additional complication stemming from the optionality of the *for* noun phrase, which plays the role of the subject of the infinitival subject.

Overgeneration, selection, and phrasal passives

The way in which our lexical rules are defined, passivization will also apply to verbal adjuncts that take object nominal arguments. For instance, consider the category assigned to prepositions and the resulting output of applying the passivization rule to it:

(163) $s(bse)\setminus np(P,N,C)\setminus(s(bse)\setminus np(P,N,C))/np(P2,N2,obj)$
$\Rightarrow s(pred)\setminus np(P2,N2,subj)\setminus(s(pred)\setminus np(P2,N2,subj))/np(P,N,by)$

This would allow us to generate the unacceptable example in (164b), but not the acceptable example in (164c):

(164)   (a)   Opus was walking under the bridge.
         (b)   * The bridge was walking under by Opus.
         (c)   The bridge was walked under by Opus.

Obviously, some restrictions must apply to the application of passivization. The simplest thing to do would be to mark the sentential applicative result of actual verbs with some binary feature that marked whether or not it was a verb. This is the usual strategy employed in unification grammar theories such as GPSG or HPSG to account for this kind of selectional restriction. An alternative would be to block the analysis morphologically by not allowing anything other than verbs to be marked as passive.

To account for the grammatical instance of passivization in (164b), it is necessary to treat *walk under* as a unit which is categorized as a transitive verb (Bresnan 1982c).

Adnominal predicatives

One of the major types of predicative is the adnominal, in either its adjectival or post-nominal forms. Consider the following examples of the predicative functions of adnominals:

(165) (a) The herring was [red] yesterday.
      (b) The herring was probably [extremely red].
      (c) The herring was believed to be [with Opus].
      (d) A herring is usually eaten when [red].
      (e) Was the herring [with Opus] yesterday?
      (f) Is the herring not [very tasty] in Pittsburgh?

In all of these examples, a nominal modifier is used in the same manner as a predicative verb phrase. For instance, the nominal modifiers are modified by pre and post-verbal adverbials, and may show up in yes/no questions. Our account of this distribution is different from other accounts, such as those found in GPSG (Sag et al. 1985), in that we assume a lexical rule that provides an entry with the applicative result $s(pred) \setminus np$ when applied to adnominals. To achieve this, we assume the following two lexical rules for the pre-nominal and post-nominal modifiers:

(166) $n(N) / n(N)$ \$ $\Rightarrow$ $s(pred) \setminus np(P,N,subj)$ \$
      $\lambda\phi.\lambda x_1 \cdots x_n.\lambda y.\textbf{pred}(\phi(x_1)\cdots(x_n))(y)$

(167) $n(N) \setminus n(N)$ \$ $\Rightarrow$ $s(pred) \setminus np(P,N,subj)$ \$
      $\lambda\phi.\lambda x_1 \cdots x_n.\lambda y.\textbf{pred}(\phi(x_1)\cdots(X_n))(y)$

In these lexical rules, **pred** must be of the type $\langle\langle n(N),n(N)\rangle,\langle np(P,N,subj),s(pred)\rangle\rangle$, thus taking an adnominal and noun phrase argument to produce a predicative sentential category. We will not be concerned about the denotation of **pred**, but we have supplied it with all of the arguments that it could possibly require.

Consider the first of these rules, which applies to pre-nominal adnominals, with the following results:

(168) $n(N) / n(N)$: **red** $\rightarrow$ *red*
      $s(pred) \setminus np(P,N,subj)$: **pred(red)** $\rightarrow$ *red*

(169) $n(N)/n(N)/(n(N)/n(N))$: **very** $\rightarrow$ *very*

   $s(pred)\backslash np(P,N,subj)/(n(N)/n(N)) : \lambda x^{\langle n,n \rangle}.\mathbf{pred}(\mathbf{very}(x))$ $\rightarrow$ *very*

The second rule will apply to prepositions as follows:

(170) $n(N)\backslash n(N)/np(P2,N2,obj)$: **with** $\rightarrow$ *with*

   $s(pred)\backslash np(P,N,subj)/np(P2,N2,obj) : \lambda x^{np}.\lambda y^{np}.\mathbf{pred}(\mathbf{with}(x))(y)$ $\rightarrow$ *with*

A similar category will result when the lexical rule is applied to prepositions which do not take complements, such as *inside*. These new categories will allow the following syntactic derivations:

(171)

with	*Opus*
$s(pred) \backslash np(P,N,subj) / np(3,sing,obj)$	$np(3,sing,obj)$

$$s(pred) \backslash np(P,N,subj)$$

(172)

probably	*very*	*tall*
$s(pred) \backslash np(P,N,subj)$	$s(pred) \backslash np(P,N,subj)$	$n(N) / n(N)$
$/ s(pred) \backslash np(P,N,subj))$	$/ (n(N) / n(N))$	

$$s(pred) \backslash np(P,N,subj)$$

$$s(pred) \backslash np(P,N,subj)$$

Again, it is important to note that this lexical rule will allow adnominals (those with result category $n \backslash n$ or n / n) to occur in any location that a predicative verb phrase might occur.

While we have not dealt with relative clauses, since their proper treatment depends on an analysis of unbounded dependency constructions, we present a simplified account of subject relative clauses for the sake of illustrating the way in which agreement is handled by lexical rules. The following pair consists of the basic entry for the subject relative *who* along with the result of applying the adnominal predication lexical rule:[23]

(173) $n(N) \backslash n(N) / (s(fin) \backslash np(P,N,subj))$ $\rightarrow$ *who*

   $s(pred) \backslash np(P2,N,subj) / (s(fin) \backslash np(P,N,subj))$ $\rightarrow$ *who*

These entries will account for the following contrast:

(174) (a) The penguin who sings
       (b) * The penguin who sing
       (c) Opus is who sings.
       (d) * Opus is who sing.

The reason that the second example cannot be analysed is that the number of the verb phrase argument to the relative clause will be the same as the number of the resulting adnominal, which, in turn, will be the number of the predicative result. This can be seen in:

(175)

$$\frac{\dfrac{who}{n(sing) \setminus (sing)}\ /\ s(fin) \setminus np(P2,sing,subj)) \qquad \dfrac{sings}{s(fin) \setminus np(P2,sing,subj)}}{n(sing) \setminus (sing)}$$

(176)

$$\frac{\dfrac{who}{s(pred) \setminus np(P,sing,subj)}\ /\ s(fin) \setminus np(P2,sing,subj)) \qquad \dfrac{sings}{s(fin) \setminus np(P2,sing,subj)}}{s(pred) \setminus np(P,sing,subj)}$$

The auxiliary *be* will then pass along the number agreement information from the predicative *who sings*, requiring the subject of the main clause to be singular.

Nominal predicatives

Full noun phrases can also be used as predicatives, as long as they do not have quantificational force. This can be seen in the examples:

(177) (a) Opus is [a hero].
       (b) * The penguins is a hero.
       (c) The penguins were known to be [the real heros].
       (d) Opus celebrated while still [a hero] in Bloom County.
       (e) Was Opus really [a penguin]?

Note that there has to be agreement between the number of the predicative noun phrase and the number of the subject, as evidenced by (177a) and (177b).[24] We can account for the distribution of nominal predicatives with the following lexical rule:

(178) $np(P,N,obj)\ \$ \Rightarrow s(pred) \setminus np(P2,N,subj)\ \$$
       $\lambda\phi.\lambda x_1 \cdots x_n.\lambda y^{np}.\mathbf{npred}(\phi(x_1)\cdots(x_n))(y)$

Again, we will not be concerned with the actual content of the **npred** constant, other than the fact that it takes two noun phrase arguments and produces a predicative sentential result. The requirement that the noun phrase undergoing the lexical rule be in object case is so that we capture the contrast in:

(179)   (a)   Opus is him.
        (b) * Opus is he.

Some examples of the application of this rule are as follows:

(180) $np(3,sing,obj)$: **opus** $\rightarrow$ *Opus*
        $s(pred) \setminus np(P,sing,subj)$: **npred(opus)** $\rightarrow$ *Opus*

(181) $np(3,N,obj) / n(N)$: **the** $\rightarrow$ *the*
        $s(pred) \setminus np(P,N,subj) / n(N)$: λx^n.**npred((the)(x))** $\rightarrow$ *the*

This rule will provide our first example of nested lexical rule application. By applying the bare pluralization rule, it was possible to convert any category that produced a result of category $n(plu)$ into one with the same complements that produced an applicative result of the category $np(3,plu,C)$. All of these plural nominals, such as *penguins*, *tall*, and *with* will also serve as input to the predication rule. For instance, we have:

(182) $np(plu) \setminus n(plu) / np(P,N,obj)$ $\rightarrow$ *with*
        $s(pred) \setminus np(P2,plu,subj) \setminus n(plu) / np(P,N,obj)$ $\rightarrow$ *with*

This entry will allow the following analysis:

(183)
penguins	*with*	*Opus*
$n(plu)$	$s(pred) \setminus np(P,plu,subj) \setminus n(plu)$ $/ np(3,sing,obj)$	$np(3,sing,obj)$

$$s(pred) \setminus np(P,plu,subj) \setminus n(plu)$$
$$s(pred) \setminus np(P,plu,subj)$$

Sentential co-ordination and predicatives

The standard co-ordination scheme used in phrase structure grammars to account for sentential co-ordination allows two identical verbal categories to be conjoined to form a result of the same category. This is usually captured by means of a phrase structure scheme of the form:

(184) $\alpha : \phi(f_1)(f_2)$ $\rightarrow$ $\alpha : f_1$ $co : \phi$ $\alpha : f_2$

where α is taken to be an arbitrary category that produces a sentential applicative result of any verb form and where *co* is the syntactic category assigned to co-ordinators such as *and* and *or*.[25] As it stands, this co-ordination scheme is not sufficient to deal with noun phrase co-ordinations, which raise a number of syntactic and semantic difficulties (see Hoeksema 1987; Carpenter 1989).

For instance, we want to be able to produce analyses such as:

(185)

Opus ate	*and*	*Opus drank*
$s(\mathit{fin})$: **ate(opus)**	*co* : **and**	$s(\mathit{fin})$: **ate(opus)**
	$s(\mathit{fin})$: **and(ate(opus))(drank(opus))**	

As usual, we will not be concerned with the value of **and**, but the situation is slightly different here in that **and** must be polymorphic and apply to an arbitrary pair of verbal categories (see Gazdar 1980). A verbal category is defined as any category with an applicative result of *s*. For the sake of illustration, we make the following semantic assumption:

(186) $\phi(\mathbf{f})(\mathbf{g}) = \lambda x_1 \cdots x_n . \phi(\mathbf{f}(x_1) \cdots (x_n))(\mathbf{g}(x_1) \cdots (x_n))$

where ϕ is the semantics of the co-ordinator and where $\mathbf{f}(x_1) \cdots (x_n)$ is of type s.[26] Thus, we would have the following semantic assignment:

(187)

loves	*and*	*hates*
$s \backslash np \mathbin{/} np$: **love**	*co* : **and**	$s \backslash np \mathbin{/} np$: **hate**
	$s \backslash np \mathbin{/} np$: $\lambda x_1 . \lambda x_2 .\mathbf{and}(\mathbf{love}(x_1)(x_2))(\mathbf{hate}(x_1)(x_2))$	

The problem that is usually encountered with the co-ordination of predicatives is that they are not assigned to the same categories, so that they cannot be co-ordinated according to this co-ordination scheme. This has led those working within unification grammar formalisms to extend the operations and allow an operation of generalization, since predicatives are usually assumed to share a feature $PRED : +$ (see Karttunen 1984). Having ensured by means of lexical rules that the predicatives are uniformly assigned to the category $s(\mathit{pred}) \backslash np$, there is no difficulty encountered with the co-ordination of "unlike" categories. For instance, we would have the analysis:

(188)

short	*and*	*a penguin*
$s(\mathit{pred})\backslash np$: **pred(short)**	*co* : **and**	$s(\mathit{pred})\backslash np$: **npred(a(penguin))**
	$s(\mathit{pred})\backslash np$: $\lambda x.\mathbf{and}(\mathbf{pred}(\mathbf{short})(x))(\mathbf{npred}(\mathbf{a}(\mathbf{penguin}))(x))$	

Using this verb phrase analysis and our simple control semantics for *was* would produce the following semantic analysis:

(189) (a) Opus was [[short] and [a penguin]].
      (b) **past(and(pred(short)(opus))(npred(a(penguin))(opus)))**

In a similar fashion, we could analyse all of the sentences in:

(190) (a) Opus is [short] and [a penguin].
      (b) Opus is [in the kitchen] and [eating].
      (c) Opus ate herring with Binkley [sick] and [watching the whole affair].
      (d) Opus is [tired], but [eager to eat].
      (e) Milo is [the editor of the paper] and [afraid that Opus will leave].

Of course, extending the binary co-ordination scheme to an *n*-ary version would allow multiple predicatives to be co-ordinated.

Predicatives as adjuncts

Besides occurring as complements to the copula *be*, another major function of predicatives is to act as adjuncts. In this capacity, predicatives can modify either nouns or verb phrases. We will consider these uses in turn.

Predicatives as adnominals

When used as adnominals, predicatives show up post-nominally. This distribution can be accounted for with the following lexical rule:

(191) $s(pred) \setminus np(P,N,C)$ \$ $\Rightarrow$ $n(N) \setminus n(N)$ \$
        $\lambda \phi. \lambda x_1 \cdots x_n. \lambda y^n.\mathbf{adn}(\phi(x_{1)} \cdots (x_n))(y)$

In this case, **adn** is of the semantic type $\langle \langle np,s \rangle, \langle n,n \rangle \rangle$ so that it takes a predicative verb phrase as input and produces an adnominal. We will not be concerned with the actual content of **adn**.

This rule of predicative adnominalization will simply allow predicatives to occur as post-nominal modifiers. When applied to derived verbal predicatives, this will result in the grammaticality of the following noun phrases:

(192) (a) the kid [**talking**]
       (b) $s(pred) \setminus np \Rightarrow n \setminus n$

(193) (a) the cat [**hitting** Opus]
       (b) $s(pred) \setminus np / np \Rightarrow n \setminus n / np$

(194) (a) the kid [[**persuading** Opus] [to eat the herring]]
       (b) $s(pred) \setminus np / (s(inf) \setminus np) / np \Rightarrow n \setminus n / (s(inf) \setminus np) / np$

(195) (a) the herring [**being** eaten]
       (b) the herring [**not** [seen by opus]]
       (c) $s(pred) \setminus np / (s(pred) \setminus np) \Rightarrow n \setminus n / (s(pred) \setminus np)$

In these examples, the verb that undergoes the lexical shift has been put in boldface, with the resulting categorial transformation listed below. Notice that in the last example, the negative *not* and auxiliary *being* are assigned to identical syntactic categories, and thus undergo exactly the same lexical rules. Also note that with respect to co-ordination, an adnominalized predicative such as *admiring* is assigned to the same category as a nominal preposition, so that the following sentence would be allowed:

(196) The kid [with and admiring] the short penguin eating herring.

Predicative adnominalization will also apply to verbal modifers, with the following effects:

(197) (a) the herring [**probably** [being eaten]]
       (b) $s(pred) \setminus np / (s(pred) \setminus np) \Rightarrow n \setminus n / (s(pred) \setminus np)$

(198) (a) the herring [eaten **yesterday**]
       (b) $s(pred) \setminus np \setminus (s(pred) \setminus np) \Rightarrow n \setminus n \setminus (s(pred) \setminus np)$

It is important to note that the adverbials will still be required to modify a predicative verb phrase, since that is their only categorization that can serve as input to the rule. This will rule out potential noun phrases such as:

(199) * the herring eat yesterday

Adjunct attachment ambiguities will be preserved by the adnominalization rules, and hence the following noun phrase has two analyses, depending on which adverb is being operated on by the lexical rule:

(200) (a) the herring [**probably** [being eaten today]]
       (b) the herring [[probably being eaten] **today**]

Besides the simple adverbs, predicative adnominalization will also apply to prepositional phrases and other complementized adjuncts. For instance, we will have the following:

(201) (a) the herring [swimming [**beside** Opus]]
     (b) $s(pred) \backslash np \backslash (s(pred) \backslash np) / np \Rightarrow n \backslash n \backslash (s(pred) \backslash np) / np$

(202) (a) the penguin [[eating herring] [**while** swimming]]
     (b) $s(pred) \backslash np \backslash (s(pred) \backslash np) / (s(pred) \backslash np)$
        $\Rightarrow n \backslash n / (s(pred) \backslash np) / (s(pred) \backslash np)$

(203) (a) the penguin [swimming [**with** [the water] [nearly freezing]]]
     (b) $s(pred) \backslash np \backslash (s(pred) \backslash np) / (s(pred) \backslash np) / np$
        $\Rightarrow n \backslash n \backslash (s(pred) \backslash np) / (s(pred) \backslash np) / np$

The predicative adnominalization rule produces output with a final applicative result of n, with the possibility that it will be $n(plu)$. Thus the output of any application of the adnominalization rule will serve as valid input to the bare pluralization rule. Consequently, all of the examples given above with a final applicative result of $n(plu)$ will also have a categorization with a final applicative result of $np(3,plu,C)$. Thus, we could derive all of the previous examples without determiners if plural nouns were substituted for the singular ones. For instance, all of the following can be analysed as plural noun phrases after the boldfaced predicative adnominals undergo bare pluralization:

(204) (a) cats **hitting** opus
      (b) penguins **being** hit by cats
      (c) penguins **probably** hitting cats
      (d) penguins swimming **beside** the herring
      (e) penguins eating herring **while** swimming

In conjunction with the adnominal predication rule (50), the predicative adnominalization rule (74) will lead to circularity in the lexicon. This can easily be seen from the categorial effects of the rules:

(205) $s(pred) \setminus np(P,N,C)$ \$
   $\Rightarrow n(N) \setminus n(N)$ \$
   $\Rightarrow s(pred) \setminus np(P,N,subj)$ \$

This leads to circular derivations such as the following in the case of nominal prepositions:

(206) $n(sing) \setminus n(sing) / np$
   $\Rightarrow s(pred) \setminus np / np$
   $\Rightarrow n(sing) \setminus n(sing) / np$

While this does not lead to any additional strings being accepted, it will cause problems for implementations if there is not some test for redundancy. For instance, every time a new lexical entry is created, a test could be performed to determine whether or not it has already been generated. This is a typical step in any kind of straightforward closure algorithm. The real problem, though, will be semantic, if there is no way to make sure that the semantic value of the circular derivations turn out to be the same.

Another interesting thing to recognize about the interaction of the predication and adnominalization rules is that they will generate post-nominal adnominal categories for every pre-nominal adjective (but not conversely), according to the following derivation chain:

(207) $n(N) / n(N)$ \$ $\Rightarrow$ $s(pred) \setminus np(P,N,subj)$ \$ $\Rightarrow$ $n(N) \setminus n(N)$ \$

The resulting categorizations will allow us to derive the following "poetic" uses of adjectives such as:

(208) (a) the ocean **blue**
   (b) the trees [**tall** and **broad**]
   (c) the herring [**red** and **delicious**]

The only explanation for why these adjectives do not show up in this location more often seems to be that they already have a perfectly good home before the nominals that they modify. Presumably, there is some pragmatic rule operating which requires more simple forms to be used in the case where there are two possible locations. Such rules can, and will, be overridden where other pragmatic considerations are more significant.

Predicatives as adverbials

It is possible for predicatives to function as adverbials in the same manner that they function as adnominals. Their standard position is post-verbal in these cases, but they will often be found in a fronted position. We will only be concerned with their standard post-verbal position and assume that the fronted versions are analysed by some kind of topicalization rule. The lexical rule we propose is as follows:

(209) $s(pred) \setminus np(P,N,C)$ \$ $\Rightarrow$ $s(V) \setminus np(P,N,C) \setminus (s(V) \setminus np(P,N,C))$ \$
        $\lambda\phi.\lambda x_1 \cdots x_n.\lambda y^{\langle np,s\rangle}.\mathbf{predadv}(\phi(x_1)\cdots(x_n))(y)$

In this case, the constant **predadv** must be of the type $\langle\langle np,s(pred)\rangle,\langle\langle np,s(V)\rangle,\langle np,s(V)\rangle\rangle\rangle$, so that it takes a predicative verb phrase and returns a modifier of an arbitrary verb.

The application of this rule can be seen in the following examples of well formed sentences, using the same notational conventions as previously, where we have included the topicalized versions in some cases for comparison:[27]

(210) (a) Opus ate herring **swimming**.
       (b) Swimming, Opus ate herring.
       (c) $s(pred) \setminus np \Rightarrow s(V) \setminus np \setminus (s(V) \setminus np)$

(211) (a) Opus swam upstream [**singing** [a little song]].
       (b) Singing a little song, Opus swam upstream.
       (c) $s(pred) \setminus np / np \Rightarrow s(V) \setminus np \setminus (s(V) \setminus np) / np$

(212) (a) The band performed [**wanting** Opus [to sing]].
       (b) $s(pred)\setminus np/np/s(inf)\setminus np \Rightarrow s(V)\setminus np\setminus(s(V)\setminus np)/np/s(inf)\setminus np$

(213) (a) Opus performed [**looking** awfully red]
       (b) $s(pred) \setminus np / (n / n) \Rightarrow s(V) \setminus np \setminus (s(V) \setminus np) / (n / n)$

Just as in the adnominal case, the adverbialization rule will apply to adjuncts, thus allowing modified predicative verb phrases to act as adverbials. Consider the following examples:

(214) (a) Opus was probably bored [[singing in the shower]
            yesterday].
       (b) $s(pred)\setminus np\setminus(s(pred)\setminus np) \Rightarrow s(V)\setminus np\setminus(s(V)\setminus np)\setminus(s(pred)\setminus np)$

(215) (a) Opus showed his skill yesterday [swimming [**in** [the
            ocean]].

(b) $s(pred) \setminus np \setminus (s(pred) \setminus np) / np \Rightarrow$
$s(V) \setminus np \setminus (s(V) \setminus np) \setminus (s(pred) \setminus np) / np$

(216) (a) Opus [set a new record] [swimming [**after** [Binkley danced]]].
      (b) $s(pred) \setminus np \setminus (s(pred) \setminus np) / s(fin)$
          $\Rightarrow s(V) \setminus np \setminus (s(V) \setminus np) \setminus (s(pred) \setminus np) / s(fin)$

(217) (a) Opus [was happy] [swimming [**while** [watched by Binkley]]].
      (b) $s(pred) \setminus np \setminus (s(pred) \setminus np) / (s(pred) \setminus np)$
          $\Rightarrow s(V) \setminus np \setminus (s(V) \setminus np) \setminus (s(pred) \setminus np) / (s(pred) \setminus np)$

Not counting the circular derivations derived from the interaction between predicative adnominalization and adnominal predication, the lexicon generated from a finite base lexicon would always be finite. But with the inclusion of the predicative adverbialization rule, a lexicon with an infinite number of distinct categories will be generated, since the rule will apply to its own output to form a larger category in terms of the number of complements that it takes. Simply consider the following initial segment of an infinite derivation chain:

(218) $s(pred) \setminus np$
      $\Rightarrow s(pred) \setminus np \setminus (s(pred) \setminus np)$
      $\Rightarrow s(pred) \setminus np \setminus (s(pred) \setminus np) \setminus (s(pred) \setminus np)$
      $\Rightarrow s(pred) \setminus np \setminus (s(pred) \setminus np) \setminus (s(pred) \setminus np) \setminus (s(pred) \setminus np)$
      $\Rightarrow \cdots$

Examples employing the first few elements of this sequence are as follows:

(219) (a) Opus performed the piece **shaking**.
      (b) Opus performed the piece [[singing the words] **shaking**].
      (c) Opus performed the piece ⋯

As with most constructions that can be nested, the acceptability of the sentences drops off quickly above a few levels of embedding. The usual argument is that the constructions are grammatical, but simply difficult to process.

CONCLUSION

The grammar that finally results from the application of all of our rules will be equivalent to a fairly straightforward context-free grammar, and is thus decidable. But the use of rules that produce infinite sequences of unique categorizations will not allow the entire lexicon to be pre-compiled in an implementation. Some sort of top-down information will be necessary to ensure that useless categories are not generated. Unfortunately, as we prove in the appendix, arbitrary lexical rules operating over a finite lexicon can generate undecidable languages.

The benefit of the system presented here is that it is possible to retain a universal set of phrase-structure schemata, preserving the radical lexicalist hypothesis that all language-specific structure is encoded in the lexicon. The lexicon presented here should be of use to anyone working on topics such as unbounded dependency and co-ordination phenomena in extended categorial grammars, as it provides evidence that the basic phrase-structure of a language can be captured naturally in terms of categorial lexical entries. Viewed from the most abstract level, a categorial lexicon is simply a method for encoding information about the complements an expression can take; the lexicon presented here shows how many constructions can be captured when this information is employed with only simple applicative categorial phrase-structure rules.

APPENDIX: GENERATIVE POWER OF CATEGORIAL GRAMMARS WITH LEXICAL RULES

In this section, our main result will be the fact that string recognition in our language is R.E.-complete. What this means is that an arbitrary recursively enumerable language can be generated by a finite lexicon closed under a finite set of lexical rules. Furthermore, every language generated by a finite lexicon closed under a finite set of lexical rules will in fact be recursively enumerable. Of course, this means that in general, string recognition with respect to a specified grammar and lexical rule system will be undecidable in the worst case. Besides this result, we will also present a characterization of the possible parse trees that limits the categories that can arise as a linear function of the number of basic expressions in a string. Before going on to our system, we will briefly review similar results that have been found to hold for formal grammars such as GPSG, which employ context-free rules and metarules.

Generative power of context-free grammars with metarules

The main result in this direction is a theorem of Uszkoreit and Peters

(1985) which shows that context-free grammars augmented with metarules of one essential variable are R.E.-complete in the sense that they generate all and only the set of recursively enumerable languages.

A meta context-free grammar (MCFG) is a quintuple $G = \langle C,s,E,R,M\rangle$ where:

(220) • C is a finite set of *category symbols*
  • s is the *start symbol*
  • E is a finite set of *basic expressions*
  • R is a finite set of *context-free rules* of one of the two following forms:
    – (Lexical Entry)
      $c \rightarrow e$ where $c \in C$ and $e \in E$
    – (Phrase Structure Rule)
      $c_0 \rightarrow c_1 c_2 \cdots c_n$ where $c_i \in C$ and $n \geq 1$
  • M is a finite set of *metarules* of the form:
    $(c_0 \rightarrow c_1 c_2 \cdots c_n \ X \ c_{n+1} c_{n+2} \cdots c_k)$
    $\Rightarrow (d_0 \rightarrow d_1 d_2 \cdots d_m \ X \ d_{m+1} \ d_{m+2} \cdots d_j)$

where X is a special symbol which will be interpreted to range over arbitrary strings of categories and $c_i, d_e \in C$.

We think of an MCFG $G = \langle C,s,E,R,M\rangle$ as generating a possibly infinite set of phrase structure rules $M(R)$ defined to be the minimal set such that:

(221) • $R \subseteq M(R)$
  • if $(c_0 \rightarrow c_1 \cdots c_n b_1 \cdots b_i c_{n+1} \cdots c_k) \in M(R)$
    and $((c_0 \rightarrow c_1 c_2 \ldots c_n X c_{n+1} c_{n+2} \cdots c_k) \in M$
    $\Rightarrow (d_0 \rightarrow d_1 d_2 \cdots d_m X d_{m+1} d_{m+2} \cdots d_j))$
    then $(d_0 \rightarrow d_1 d_2 \cdots d_m b_1 b_2 \cdots b_i d_{m+1} \cdots d_j) \in M(R)$

We are thus thinking of the X as a variable ranging over arbitrary strings on the right-hand sides of rules. Acceptability of a string with respect to an MCFG G is then determined by acceptability with respect to the possibly infinite phrase structure grammar $M(R)$ in the usual way, starting from the start symbol s. Various tricks were employed in GPSG, which used this sort of metarule system, to ensure that the set of rules generated remained finite, and thus generated a purely context-free grammar. The primary restriction which ensured the finiteness of the result was not to use the fully closed set $M(R)$, but rather to generate a finite set of rules by applying the metarules to the basic set, making sure to never apply a rule to its own output, even indirectly (Thompson 1982). Uszkoreit's and Peter's theorem tells us that things can be much worse in the general case.

Theorem 1 (Uszkoreit and Peters): *If L is a recursively enumerable language then there is a meta-context-free grammar $G = \langle C,s,E,R,M \rangle$ such that the language generated by the phrase-structure grammar $M(R)$ is exactly L.*

The proof of this theorem employs an effective reduction of an arbitrary generalized rewriting system to a context-free grammar and set of metarules that generates exactly the same language. That is, for every generalized rewriting system, an MCFG could be found that generates exactly the same set of strings, and conversely.

In the proofs presented below, we use a direct reduction from generalized rewriting systems, so we pause to define them now. A *generalized rewriting grammar* $G = \langle V,s,T,R \rangle$ is a quadruple such that V is a finite set of non-terminal category symbols, $s \in V$ is the start symbol, T is a set of terminal expression symbols, and $R \subseteq (V^* \times V^*) \cup (V \times T)$ is a finite set of rewriting rules and lexical rules, which are usually written in the forms:

(222)   • $v_1 \cdots v_n \to v_1' \cdots v_m'$ where $v_i, v_j' \in V$
        • $v \to t$ where $v \in V$ and $t \in T$

String rewriting is defined so that:

(223) $x_1 \cdots x_n \sigma x_{n+1} \cdots x_{n+m} \to x_1 \cdots x_n \tau x_{n+1} \cdots x_{n+m}$

if $\sigma \to \tau \in R$ is a rule, where σ and τ are strings in V^*. The language $L(G)$ generated by a general rewriting system G is defined to be

(224) $L(G) = \{\sigma \in T^* \mid s \overset{*}{\to} \sigma \}$

where s is the start symbol and $\overset{*}{\to}$ is the transitive closure of the $\to$ relation. It is well known that:

Theorem 2: *A language L is recursively enumerable if and only if there is a generalized rewriting grammar $G = \langle V,s,T,R \rangle$ such that $L = L(G)$.*

Thus, the problem of generalized rewriting system recognition is R.E.-complete. MCFG recognition is just as hard as recognizing arbitrary recursively enumerable languages, since every recursively enumerable language can be expressed as an MCFG. Of course, MCFG recognition is no harder, since all possible derivations can be easily enumerated by considering derivations in order of complexity.

Categorial grammars with lexical rules

To formally define our system, we will say that a *categorial grammar with lexical rules (CG+L)* is a tuple $G = \langle \text{Exp}, s, \text{BasCat}, \Lambda, L \rangle$ with a finite set Exp of basic expressions, finite set BasCat of basic categories, a start symbol $s \in$ BasCat, a finite lexicon Λ where $\Lambda \subseteq$ Exp $\times$ Cat(BasCat), and set of lexical rules Λ of the form:

$$(225) \quad a_0 \mid_1^a a_1 \cdots \mid_i^a a_i \$ \mid_1^b b_1 \cdots \mid_j^b b_j \;\Rightarrow\; c_0 \mid_1^c c_1 \cdots \mid_k^c c_k \$ \mid_1^d d_1 \cdots \mid_m^d d_m$$

where $\mid_j^i$ is a forward or backward slash. In this section, we will only be concerned with the syntactic portion of our categorial grammars and lexical rule systems.[28] We will assume that a CG+L grammar $G = \langle \text{Exp}, \text{BasCat}, s, \Lambda, L \rangle$ generates a possibly empty set of lexical entries closed under the lexical rules by taking the least set $L(\Lambda)$ such that:

(226) • $\Lambda \subseteq L(\Lambda)$
 • if $(a_0 \mid_1^a a_1 \cdots \mid_i^a a_i \mid_1^e e_1 \cdots \mid_n^e e_n \mid_1^b b_1 \cdots \mid_j^b b_j \;\rightarrow\; \omega) \in L(\Lambda)$
   and $(a_0 \mid_1^a a_1 \cdots \mid_i^a a_i \$ \mid_1^b b_1 \cdots \mid_j^b b_j$
   $\Rightarrow c_0 \mid_1^c c_1 \cdots \mid_k^c c_k \$ \mid_1^d d_1 \cdots \mid_m^d d_m) \quad \in L$
   then $(c_0 \mid_1^c c_1 \cdots \mid_k^c c_k \mid_1^e e_1 \cdots \mid_n^e e_n \mid_1^d d_1 \cdots \mid_m^d d_m \;\rightarrow\; \omega) \in L(\Lambda$
(Λ)

We assume exactly the same application phrase structure schemata:

(227) • $\alpha \rightarrow \alpha / \beta \; \beta$ (forward application)
 • $\alpha \rightarrow \beta \; \alpha \setminus \beta$ (backward application)

where $\alpha, \beta \in$ Cat(BasCat), and generate analyses in the usual way according to our now possibly infinite set of rules and lexical entries. Note that we can now no longer infer that the set of rule instances necessary will be finite, because the lexical rules can generate an infinite number of unique categories, as could be seen with the predicative adverbialization rule.

We present two theorems, the first of which characterizes the complexity of the output of lexical rules and the second of which characterizes the weak generative power of the CG+L grammar formalism.

Argument complexity bounds

The complexity of a category is measured in terms of the number of complements it takes to result in a basic category. The complexity of a category is given as follows:

(228)   • $C(\alpha) = 0$ if $\alpha \in \textsc{BasCat}$
        • $C(\alpha \,/\, \beta) = C(\alpha \setminus \beta) = 1 + C(\alpha)$

Thus the complexity of $\alpha_0 \mid_1 \alpha_1 \cdots \mid_n \alpha_n$ is n if α_0 is a basic category. In the following theorem, we show that there is a finite bound to the complexity of arguments, but no upper bound to the complexity of the overall category resulting from closing a finite lexicon under a finite set of lexical rules.

Theorem 3: *Given a finite categorial grammar with lexical rules $G = \langle \textsc{Exp}, s, \textsc{BasCat}, \Lambda, L \rangle$ there is a bound k such that the result $L(\Lambda)$ of closing the categorial grammar under the lexical rules contains only lexical entries with arguments of complexity less than k.*

Proof: Since there are only a finite number of lexical entries in Λ, there will be a bound on the maximal complexity of arguments in the core lexicon. Since there are only a finite number of lexical rules in L, there will be a finite bound on the maximal complexity of arguments in the output to lexical rules. Since lexical rules can only produce outputs whose arguments were in the input or in the lexical rule, there will be a finite bound for the resulting grammar.   □

Note that while it is possible to derive categories of unbounded complexity, as seen with (218), it is not possible to derive categories with *arguments* of unbounded complexity.

It should be noted that every derivation tree rooted at the start symbol s for a string $e_1 e_2 \cdots e_n \in \textsc{Exp}^*$ of length n cannot involve a main functor category of complexity greater than n, since the complexity of the mother is only going to be one less than the complexity of the functional daughter. Together with the previous theorem, this gives us an upper bound on the number of parse trees that need to be considered for any given input string. Alas, the problem is still undecidable, as the previous theorem shows. Of course, this situation will change when extended categorial grammar systems are considered, although many of these systems provide normal form derivation results that allow every derivation to be carried out within some complexity bound on the size of the categories based on the size of the input string.

Decidability

In this section, we show how to effectively reduce an arbitrary generalized rewriting grammar to a categorial grammar with lexical rules. Since it should be obvious that categorial grammar recognition with lexical rules is a recursively enumerable problem, we get the following:

Theorem 4: *A language S is recursively enumerable if and only if there is a CG+L grammar $G = \langle \text{Exp}, s, \text{BasCat}, \Lambda, L \rangle$ such that $\{start \cdot \sigma \mid \sigma \in S\}$ is the set of strings generated from s with the lexicon $L(\Lambda)$.*

Proof: We proceed by a reduction of generalized rewriting grammars. Suppose that we have a generalized rewriting system $G = \langle V, s, T, R \rangle$. We will show how to construct a weakly equivalent categorial grammar $G'' = \langle \text{Exp}, s', \text{BasCat}, \Lambda, L \rangle$. We begin by assuming that:

(229) $\text{BasCat} = V \cup \{t' \mid t \in T\} \cup \{\#\}$.

We have just added a basic category t' for every terminal symbol t in the rewriting system.

We will represent an arbitrary string $v_1 v_2 \cdots v_n \in V^*$ by means of the categorial grammar category $\#/v_n \cdots / v_1$, where the # symbol is just an arbitrary end marker.

We will then need a pair of special lexical rules of the form:

(230) • $v_1 \$ / v_2 \;\Rightarrow\; v_2 / v_1 \$$
      • $v_2 / v_1 \$ \;\Rightarrow\; v_1 \$ / v_2$

for each $v_1, v_2 \in V \cup \{\#\}$. These will mean that we will also get a lexical entry of the form:

(231) $v_{m+1} / v_{m+2} \cdots / v_n / \# / v_1 / v_2 \cdots / v_m \;\rightarrow\; e$

for every lexical entry we have of the form:

(232) $\# / v_1 \cdots / v_n \;\rightarrow\; e$

where $0 \le m \le n$. Furthermore, for every rule in the rewriting system R of the form:

(233) $v_1 \cdots v_n \rightarrow v'_1 \cdots v'_m$

we will take a lexical rule of the form:

(234) $\$/v_n \,/\, v_{n-1} \cdots /\, v_1 \Rightarrow \$/v'_m \,/v'_{m-1} \cdots /v'_1 \in L$

Given our previous observation, this means that if we have:

(235) $x_1 \cdots x_i v_1 \cdots v_n y_1 \rightarrow \cdots y_j \rightarrow x_1 \cdots x_i v'_1 \cdots v'_m y_1 \cdots y_j$

then we will have:

(236) $\#/y_j \cdots /\, y_1/v_n \cdots /\, v_1/x_i \cdots /\, x_1$
  $\quad \Rightarrow x_i \cdots /\, x_1/\#/y_j \cdots /\, y_1/v_n \cdots /\, v_1$
  $\quad \Rightarrow x_i \cdots /x_1/\#/y_j \cdots /y_1/v'_m \cdots /v'_1$
  $\quad \Rightarrow \#/y_j \cdots /y_1/v'_m \cdots /v'_1/x_i \cdots /x_1$

A simple induction then gives us the fact that:

(237) $x_1 \cdots x_i \overset{*}{\Rightarrow} y_1 \cdots y_j$ if and only if $\#/x_i \cdots /\, x_1 \overset{*}{\Rightarrow} \#/y_j \cdots /\, y_1$

where $\overset{*}{\Rightarrow}$ simply the transitive closure of the lexical rule derivation relation.

Finally, we assume that we have a lexical entry of the form:

(238) $\#/s \rightarrow start \in \Lambda$

to account for the initialization and lexical entries of the form:

(239) $t' \rightarrow t \in \Lambda$

This means that we have:

(240) $s \overset{*}{\Rightarrow} v_1 \cdots v_n$

if and only if

(241) $\#/v_1 \cdots /\, v_n \rightarrow start$

With the lexical entries that we have, we only need the lexical rule:

(242) $\#\$ \Rightarrow s'\$$

where s' is the start symbol of the categorial grammar G'', which will ensure that the categorial grammar $L(\Lambda)$ generates exactly the set $\{start \cdot t_1 \cdots t_n \mid t_1 \cdots t_n \in \mathbf{L}(G)\}$ of strings. $\square$

NOTES

The primary motivation for this paper was the long hours spent working out categorial grammar fragments for English with Glyn Morrill. Roughly similar though less extensive lexicons can be found in both of our doctoral dissertations, both of which were concerned with other matters (Glyn's with unbounded dependencies and co-ordination, and mine with event-based semantics and quantification). Our goal was to develop and implement categorial grammars with broader coverage than other formal grammars. Our primary methodology was a minimalist approach that only invoked those mechanisms which were absolutely necessary. The resulting grammar was obviously greatly influenced by LFG, GPSG, and HPSG and other categorial and unification grammar analyses.

The fragment presented in this paper has evolved over a number of years and presentations. Comments were kindly received at the University of Edinburgh, University of Pennsylvania, University of Pittsburgh, University of California – Los Angeles, The Ohio State Universiy, Xerox Palo Alto Research Center, and the Center for the Study of Language and Information at Stanford University. Mark Steedman and Ewan Klein deserve special thanks in this regard for sitting through more than one presentation of this material. Mark also deserves extra credit for inventing the best notation in which to display categorial grammar categories and trees. I should also thank Stu Shieber for suggesting that the lexical rule system was undecidable, but the primary thanks along formal lines go to Kevin Kelly, who provided a fundamental insight which led to the discovery of the reduction of rewriting systems to categorial grammars presented here. I would also like to thank Alex Franz and Mitzi Morris for reading the final draft and providing a number of useful suggestions. Finally, I would like to thank Bob Levine for both editorial and contentful suggestions, as well as enormous patience waiting for the paper to be written.

1 We will later extend the possible verb forms and cases to account for complementized sentences, expletives, and prepositional arguments. More fine-grained linguistic analyses would presumably assume a finite number of additional features and corresponding values.

2 Our notation is intentionally suggestive of logic grammars, which are a particular kind of unification grammar employing first-order terms for data structures. The entire system presented here, including the lexical

rules, has been implemented straightforwardly in Prolog by simply using first-order terms for basic categories and taking the slashes to be infix binary functions. More sophisticated categorial logic grammars have been investigated for syntactic analysis by Moortgat (1987a) and Morrill (1988) and for semantic analysis by Carpenter (1989).

3 To be more precise, we follow Montague (1970) in using a λ-calculus expression as a stand-in for a semantic object.

4 We will not consider phrasal lexical entries, though the formalism can be easily extended to handle them by simply assuming that the lexicon can assign categories to arbitrary expressions. We will also not consider building words out of morphemes categorially, though see Dowty (1979), Keenan and Timberlake (1988), and Moortgat (1987c).

5 Gazdar (1981a) contains an interesting and relevant discussion of the role of syntactic categories in phrase-structure grammars as fully determining distributional behaviour locally. Gazdar contrasts the strict phrase-structure approach with transformational analyses, and the paper contains a reply from Chomsky.

6 Logically, this means that we give the variables universal readings.

7 See Partee (1975) for an argument in favour of the analysis presented here. Bach and Cooper (1978) later showed how the underlying semantic scoping could be recovered with an *np*-modifier categorization of prepositional phrases.

8 The use of distinct variables P and $P2$ indicates possibly different values of the person feature. But keep in mind that all occurrences of the same variable must be identical.

9 A uniform treatment of prepositional phrase semantics under these syntactic assignments is provided in Carpenter (1989) with an event-based sentential semantics.

10 The auxiliary forms of *have* should not be confused with the homonymous transitive verb *have* as in *having fun*.

11 The problem is compounded in most recent versions of government-binding theory, which require maximal projections for agreement, inflection, and sometimes even for tense and aspect.

12 A similar factoring of labour between thematic role and phrase structure information is found in LFG (Kaplan & Bresnan 1982).

13 These verbs have typically been referred to as *obligatory control* verbs, to distinguish them from verbs which can display control-like behaviour that is not determined purely syntactically.

14 We will simply assume a basic entry for the version of *want* that does not take a direct object and for the version of *seem* that does not take a prepositionally marked noun phrase. The reason we do not try to account for detransitivization is that the rule is very selective and does not apply productively. We assume its operation is closely linked with an analysis of

lexical semantics. See Bresnan (1982d) for an analysis of detransitivization and the interaction between the grammatical and thematic aspects of control.

15 Note that the analysis of *easy*, which is usually contrasted with that of *eager* and other tough-class adnominals involves an analysis of unbounded dependency constructions and will thus fall outside the scope of this paper. See Morrill (1988) for a compatible analysis of tough-class adnominals.

16 Our notion of obliqueness is different from that of Pollard and Sag (1987), where a distinction is made between obliqueness and order of argument combination.

17 Unbounded dependencies were treated in GPSG (Gazdar et al. 1985) by the passing of features, some of which are *introduced* by lexical metarules. The *slash* features bear a striking similarity to the slashes in categorial grammar, and the way in which they are propagated is reminiscent of the abstraction rules applied in extended categorial grammars (Morrill 1988).

18 One possibility is to build bindings for the $ variable recursively, generating an infinite set of lexical rule instances without string variables, with the ground case being where the $ is instantiated to the empty string.

19 See Siekmann (1989) for a discussion of universal unification, which concerns building equational theories into the unification algorithm. The unification of strings built up by concatenation is captured by an equational theory with an associative binary operator representing concatenation and an identity element representing the null string.

20 In general, lexical rules will not be equivalent to the corresponding unary rules. For instance, adnominal predication, which applies to lexical categories of the form $n\ /\ n$ to account for verb phrases such as *is tall* will not apply to expressions such as *tall fat* which can be syntactically analysed as category $n\ /\ n$ by means of extended composition rules necessary for unbounded dependency and co-ordination constructions. Similarly, there is no way to express a unary rule for a lexical operation like passivization without resorting to some sort of wrapping operation or $ string variable convention (see Bach 1980, 1984; Dowty ,1978), since the most oblique argument and subject must be simultaneously affected.

21 In the case of quantified subjects, as in the sentence *Every cat was loved*, the existentially quantified position for the 'lover' would have to take narrow scope to account for the fact that a different individual may love each cat.

22 We will not consider how the phonological or orthographic representation is affected in the move from the base form to the passive form, such as in the derivation of the passive forms *eaten*, *hit*, and *loved* from the stem forms *eat*, *hit*, and *love*.

23 Object relative pronouns could be assigned to the category

$$n\ \backslash\ n\ /\ (s\ /\ np(obj)),$$

with sentences lacking object noun phrases such as *Bill hit* and *Opus believed he hit* analysed as being of the category *s / np* using extended categorial operations (see Morrill 1987b, 1988; Steedman 1987, 1988). Of course, it would also be possible to treat slashes denoting gaps or traces as occurring in a different feature than those for normal complements (see Pollard & Sag forthcoming or Zeevat, Klein, & Calder 1987).

24 Robert Levine has pointed out (personal communication) that subtle problems with agreement arise in cases with plural subjects and singular predicatives in examples such as:

> Booze and cars are a bad combination.
> and
> The Johnsons are a formidable team.

In both cases, a plural auxiliary is needed and there is an understanding of the subject as a group-like entity.

25 This scheme is usually extended to deal with constructions consisting of multiple co-ordinators such as *either-or* constructions, as well as constructions consisting of more than two conjuncts (see Gazdar 1981b). Binary co-ordination will serve to illustrate our major points.

26 A non-distributive semantics will actually be necessary to avoid the usual problems surrounding the interaction between quantification and co-ordination in sentences such as *every penguin waddles or swims*, which does not necessarily mean that every penguin waddles or that every penguin swims (see Carpenter 1989).

27 If in fact, the fronted versions of these adjuncts are not topicalized, then they could be accounted for by another lexical rule of the syntactic form:

$$s(V) \setminus np \setminus (s(V) \setminus np) \$ \Rightarrow s(V) / s(V) \$.$$

This rule would allow for arbitrary post-verbal adverbs to be fronted, but not create unbounded dependencies where they could modify embedded clauses.

28 The semantic function attached to this rule would have to be of the form:
$$\lambda\varphi^{\langle\tau(b_j),\ldots,\tau(b_1),\tau(y_n),\ldots,\tau(y_1),\tau(a_j),\ldots,\tau(a_1)\rangle}.x_m^{\tau(d_m)} \ldots x_1^{\tau(d_1)}.y_n\ldots y_1.z_k^{\tau(c_k)} \ldots z_1^{\tau(c_1)}.$$
$$R\,(\lambda w_j^{\tau(b_j)} \ldots w_1^{\tau(b_1)}.\varphi(w_j) \cdots (w_1)(y_n) \cdots (y_1))(x_m) \cdots (x_1)(z_k) \cdots (z_1).$$
where **R** is a semantic constant of the appropriate type.

REFERENCES

Ades, A.E. and Steedman, M.J. (1982). On the order of words. *Linguistics and Philosophy* 4:517-58

Aho, A.V. and Ullman, J.D. (1972). *The Theory of Parsing, Translation and Compiling*. Englewood Cliffs, NJ: Prentice Hall

Aho, A.V. and Ullman, J.D. (1972). *The Theory of Parsing, Translation and Compiling*. Englewood Cliffs, NJ: Prentice Hall

Ajdukiewicz, K. (1935). Die syntaktische Konnexität. *Studia Philosophica* 1:1-27

Bach, E. (1980). In defense of passive. *Linguistics and Philosophy* 3:297-341

– (1983a). On the relationship between word-grammar and phrase-grammar. *Natural Language and Linguistic Theory* 1:65-89

– (1983b). Generalized categorial grammars and the English auxiliary. In F. Heny and B. Richards (eds.), *Linguistic Categories, Auxiliaries, and Related Puzzles – II*. Dordrecht: D. Reidel

– (1984). Some generalizations of categorial grammars. In F. Landman and F. Veltman (eds.), *Varieties of Formal Semantics: Proceedings of the Fourth Amsterdam Colloquium*. Dordrecht: Foris

– and Cooper, R. (1978). The NP-S analysis of relative clauses and compositional semantics. *Linguistics and Philosophy* 2:265-99

Bar-Hillel, Y. (1953). A quasi-arithmetical notation for syntatic description. *Language* 25

–, Gaifman, C., and Shamir, E. (1960). On categorial and phrase structure grammars. *Bulletin of the Research Council of Israel* 9F:1-16

Benthem, J. van (1986a). Categorial grammar. In J. van Benthem, *Essays in Logical Semantics*. Dordrecht: D. Reidel

– (1986b). Categorial grammar and lambda calculus. In V. Skordev (ed.), *Druzhba Summer School in Applied Logic*. New York: Plenum Press

– (1987). Semantic type change and syntactic recognition. In G. Chierchia, B. Partee, and R. Turner (eds.), *Categories, Types and Semantics*. Dordrecht: D. Reidel

Bresnan J.W. (1972). Theory of Complementation in English Syntax. Ph.D. dissertation. Cambridge, MA: Massachusetts Institute of Technology. Also New York: Garland Press (1979)

– (ed.) (1982a). *The Mental Representation of Grammatical Relations*. Cambridge, MA: MIT Press

– (1982b). Control and complementation. *Linguistic Inquiry* 13:343-434

– (1982c). The passive in lexical theory. In Bresnan (1982a), 3-86

– (1982d). Polyadicity. In Bresnan (1982a), 149-72

Carpenter, B. (1989). Phrase Meaning and Categorial Grammar. Ph.D. dissertation. Edinburgh: University of Edinburgh

Chierchia, G. and Turner, R. (forthcoming). Semantics and property theory. *Linguistics and Philosophy*

Chomsky, N. and Lasnik, H. (1977). Filters and control. *Linguistic Inquiry* 8:425-504

Church, A. (1940). A formulation of a simple theory of types. *Journal of Symbolic Logic* 5:56-68

Dowty, D.R. (1978). Lexically governed transformations as lexical rules in a Montague grammar. *Linguistic Inquiry* 9:393-426

– (1979). *Word Meaning and Montague Grammar*. Synthese Language Library, Vol. 7. Dordrecht: D. Reidel

– (1982). Grammatical relations and Montague Grammar. In P. Jacobson and G.K. Pullum (eds.), *The Nature of Syntactic Representation* 79-130. Dordrecht: D. Reidel

– (1988). Type-raising, functional composition and non-constituent coordination. In Oehrle et al. (1988)

Gazdar, G. (1980). A cross-categorial semantics for coordination. *Linguistics and Philosophy* 3:407-9

– (1981a). On syntactic categories. *Philosophical Transactions of the Royal Society (Series B)* 295:267-83

– (1981b). Unbounded dependencies and coordinate structure. *Linguistic Inquiry* 12:155-84

– (1982). Phrase structure grammar. In P. Jacobson and G.K. Pullum (eds.), *The Nature of Syntactic Representation*. Dordrecht: D. Reidel

–, Klein, E., Pullum, G., and Sag, I. (1985). *Generalized Phrase Structure Grammar*. Oxford: Basil Blackwell

– and Pullum, G. (1981). Subcategorization, constituent order and the notion of 'Head.' In M. Moortgat, H. van der Hulst, and T. Hoekstra (eds.), *The Scope of Lexical Rules*, 107-23. Dordrecht: Foris

–, Pullum, G.K., and Sag, I.A. (1982). Auxiliaries and related phenomena in a restrictive theory of grammar. *Language* 58:591-638

Geach, P.T. (1972). A program for syntax. *Synthèse* 22:3-17

Haddock, N.J. (1987). Incremental interpretation and combinatory categorial grammar. In *Proceedings of the Tenth International Joint Conference on Artificial Intelligence* 661-3. Milan

Hendriks, H. (1987). Type change in semantics: the scope of quantification and coordination. In Klein and van Benthem (eds.) (1987), 95-120

Hoeksema, J. (1987). Semantics of non-boolean "and." *Journal of Semantics* 6:19-40

– and Janda, R.D. (1988). Implications of process morphology. In Oehrle et al. (1988)

Hopcroft, J. and Ullman, J. (1979). *Introduction to Automata Theory, Languages and Computation*. Reading, MA: Addison-Wesley

Kaplan, R. and Bresnan, J. (1982). Lexical-functional grammar: a formal system for grammatical representation. In Bresnan (1982a), 173-281

Karttunen, L. (1984). Features and values. In *Proceedings of Coling 1984*, 28-33

– (1986). *Radical Lexicalism*. Report CSLI-86-68. Stanford: Center for the Study of Language and Information, Stanford University

Keenan, E.L. and Timberlake, A. (1988). Natural language motivations for extending categorial grammar. In Oehrle et al. (1988)

Klein, E. and Sag, I.A. (1985). Type-driven translation. *Linguistics and Philosophy* 8:163-201

– and van Benthem, J. (1987). (eds.) *Categories, Polymorphism and Unification.* Edinburgh: Centre for Cognitive Science

Lambek, J. (1958). The mathematics of sentence structure. *American Mathematical Monthly* 65:154-69

– (1961). On the calculus of syntactic types. In R. Jakobson (ed.), *Structure of Language and its Mathematical Aspects, Proceedings of Symposia in Applied Mathematics* 166-78. Providence, RI: American Mathematical Society

Levin, L. (1987). *Toward a Linking Theory of Relation Changing Rules in LFG.* Report CSLI-87-115. Stanford: Center for the Study of Language and Information, Stanford University

Montague, R. (1974). Universal grammar. In R. Thomason (ed.), *Formal Philosophy* 222-46. New Haven: Yale University Press

Moortgat, M. (1984). A Fregean restriction on metarules. *Proceedings of NELS* 14

– (1987a). *Parsing Lambek Categorial Grammars.* Report INL WP 87-05. Leiden: Instituut voor Nederlandse Lexicologie

– (1987b). Lambek theorem proving. In Klein and van Benthem (eds.), (1987), 169-200

– (1987c). Compositionality and the syntax of words. In J. Groenendijk, D. de Jongh, and M. Stokhof (eds.), *Foundations of Pragmatics and Lexical Semantics.* Dordrecht: Foris

– (1988a). Mixed composition and discontinuous dependencies. In Oehrle et al. (1988)

– (1988b). Categorial Investigations: Logical and Linguistic Aspects of the Lambek Calculus. Academisch Proefschrift (dissertation), University of Amsterdam

Morrill, G. (1987a). Meta-categorial grammar. In Morrill et al. (1987)

– (1987b). Phrase structure grammar and categorial grammar. In Klein and van Benthem (eds.) (1987), 201-77

– (1988). Extraction and Coordination in Phrase Structure Grammar and Categorial Grammar. Ph.D. dissertation. Edinburgh: University of Edinburgh

– and Carpenter, B. (in press). Compositionality, implicational logics and theories of grammar. *Linguistics and Philosophy.*

–, Haddock, N.J., and Klein, E. (eds.) (1987). *Categorial Grammar, Unification Grammar and Parsing.* Edinburgh: Centre for Cognitive Science

Oehrle, R., Bach, E., and Wheeler, D. (eds.) (1988). *Categorial Grammars and Natural Language Structures.* Dordrecht: D. Reidel

Partee, B. (1975). Montague grammar and transformational grammar. *Linguistic Inquiry* 6:203-300

Pereira, F.C.N. and Warren, D.H.D. (1980). Definite clause grammars for language analysis–a survey of the formalism and a comparison with augmented transition networks. *Artificial Intelligence* 13:231-78

Pollard, C.J. (1988). Phrase-structure grammars and categorial grammars: an excursion on the syntax-semantics frontier. In Oehrle et al. (1988)

– and Sag, I.A. (1987). *Information-Based Syntax and Semantics: Volume I: Fundamentals*. CSLI Lecture Notes. Chicago: University of Chicago Press

– and Sag, I.A. (forthcoming). *Information-Based Syntax and Semantics: Volume II*. CSLI Lecture Notes. Chicago: University of Chicago Press

Reape, M. (1989). A logical treatment of semi-free word order and bounded discontinous constituency. *European ACL Proceedings*

Sag, I., Gazdar, G., Wasow, T., and Wexler, S. (1985). Coordination and how to distinguish categories. *Natural Language and Linguistic Theory* 3:117-71

Schönfinkel, M. (1924). Über die Baustein der mathematischen Logik. *Mathematische Annalen* 92:305-16

Siekmann, J.H. (1989). Unification theory. *Journal of Symbolic Computation* 7:207-74

Steedman, M. (1985). Dependency and coordination in the grammar of Dutch and English. *Language* 61:523-68

– (1987). Combinatory grammars and parasitic gaps. In Morrill et al. (1987)

– (1988). Combinators and grammars. In Oehrle et al. (1988)

– (1989). Prosody and Combinatory Grammars. University of Pennsylvania, manuscript

Thompson, H. (1984). Handling metarules in a parser for GPSG. In *Proceedings of the 21st Meeting of the ACL*, 26-37

Uszkoreit, H. (1986). Categorial unification grammars. In *Proceedings of Coling*. Bonn

– and Peters, P.S. (1986). *On some Formal Properties of Metarules*. Report CSLI-85-43. Stanford: Center for the Study of Language and Information, Stanford University

Weisler, S. (1982). Coordination and the syntax of that-clauses. In A. Prince and S. Weisler (eds.), *University of Massachusetts: Amherst Occasional Working Papers in Cognitive Science*, 112-34. Amherst: University of Massachusetts

Wittenberg, K.B. (1986). Natural Language Parsing with Combinatory Categorial Grammar in a Graph-Unification Based Formalism. Ph.D. dissertation. Austin: University of Texas

Zeevat, H., Klein, E., and Calder, J. (1987). Unification categorial grammar. In Morrill et al. (1987)

CHAPTER FOUR

Implementing Government Binding Theories

Edward P. Stabler, Jr.*

INTRODUCTION

In *Knowledge of Language* Chomsky describes two major developments in the tradition of Government and Binding theories. The first is an emphasis on human knowledge of language, that is, on grammars and the structures they define, rather than on the set of grammatical sentences defined by the grammars. This emphasis brings the acquisition problem to a central position, since our hypotheses about human knowledge of language must be such as to allow for the acquisition of this knowledge. This view also brings out the relevance of accounting for contrasts among ungrammatical sentences. For example, although neither of the following two sentences is fully grammatical, it is clear that the second is much worse than the first:[1]

* *What$_i$[$_{ip}$do you wonder [$_{cp}$how [$_{ip}$John [$_{vp}$ fixed t_i]]]]?*
* *Who$_i$ do you wonder how [$_{ip}$ t_i fixed the car]?*

Speakers of English notice the difference between these two sentences, and recent GB theories provide an account of this perceived difference in terms of differences among the violations of different grammatical principles. In fact, Chomsky has proposed that some principles may have a graded effect on acceptability. For example, violations of "*n*-subjacency" may produce more or less unacceptable sentences depending on the lowest *n* for which the principle is violated.

The second major development in recent Government Binding theories is the shift away from construction-specific rules in the phrase structure and transformational components to sets of general and rather simple principles, some of which are parameterized for language-specific variation. Rather than proposing grammars involving phrase structure rules, together with construction-specific transformational rules ("SD-SC" rules), with rule-specific conditions of application, order and cyclicity constraints, and constraints on certain movements, we have a very general movement rule which interacts with other quite general principles to define the appropriate structures and properties. This development, though it is still at an early stage, makes the acquisition problem appear more tractable by allowing the precise definition of parameters of language-specific variation. It also makes the determination of the central, "core" properties of structures more complex, since they will now derive entirely from the interaction of general principles and the specific properties projected from lexical constituents. Chomsky says: "Unless some phenomenon is consigned to the periphery, we must account for it by a computational (essentially deductive) process, which may be complex…from invariant principles with parameters fixed" (Chomsky 1986a).

These developments in GB theories imply corresponding changes in what it could mean to "implement" a GB theory. Three computational traditions can be distinguished by their different goals. One has emphasized getting systems that feasibly compute some roughly GB-like structures for at least a small fragment of the fully grammatical sentences of English. A second tradition has goals that are much more in harmony with those of GB theory. It attempts to define systems that compute all and only the properties and relations on structures that the grammar defines, including properties of ungrammatical structures, using the principles of the grammar directly. A third tradition aims to formulate psychological models of human language use, models in which GB principles are realized just insofar as they are realized in the mechanisms of human linguistic performance. This third tradition is certainly the most difficult, but psychological studies of language use have at least made the valuable contribution of teaching us not to underestimate the complexity of human performance even on seemingly simple tasks like word identification. For some reason, almost all the work in GB-based computational linguistics has been in the first tradition or the last, but I want to suggest that the second of the traditions mentioned is feasible and can lead to valuable applications. That is, we can proceed at roughly the same level of idealization as does the linguistic theory, using *transparent* representations of GB principles to compute all and only the properties and relations on structures that the grammar defines, whenever these properties and relations are computable. In *this* tradition, more than either of the others, changes in GB theory will have an impact. I will show that computing systems that implement GB theories in this way can be useful for the development and assessment of linguistic theories, and perhaps in other applications as well. Furthermore, I think that this is one of the most fruitful ways to approach the more difficult goal of the third tradition: the problem of providing a model of human performance. Performance models with relatively opaque and ad hoc relations to the grammar have very little plausibility, though I will not argue this point here.

FORMALIZING A GB THEORY

Here is one possible strategy for formalizing GB theory. Find some computationally tractable formalism, and use it to formalize as many GB or GB-like principles as possible. This is not the strategy I will pursue. It contrasts sharply with GB methodology, which has been to state the significant linguistic generalizations as simply and succinctly as possible, without any limitation to a particular restrictive formal-ism. We can adopt a similar goal in our formalization effort: to formalize GB theories in a system that is powerful enough to allow linguistic principles to have a simple and succinct expression, close to the linguists' own statements of them. It turns out that a standard and very well-known system suffices for this purpose: first order logic. There are, of course, some things that first order logic cannot represent at all. For example, first order logic does not allow one to represent the proposition that some (unspecified) relation is symmetric, or that there are only finitely many things. But GB theory does not call for the representation of such things. There are also some things that first order logic can represent, but only awkwardly, such as the fact that there are exactly 100 things. But it turns out that GB principles never need to "count" anything in this way. Finally, there are some things that can be represented in first order logic, but which pose particularly severe computational problems. One relation of this sort deserves careful attention: namely, equality, but as I will show in a moment, we can get transparent representations of GB principles with a relatively tractable equality theory.

First order logic appears to be powerful enough to allow a quite transparent representation of GB principles. In this respect, it differs from the standard notations of formal language theory, and also from weaker logics such as the subset of logic used by prolog. Applications of GB theory should have abandoned the language processing techniques of formal language theories long ago: so much of GB theory involves relations which cannot be naturally handled with phrase structure parsing techniques. We will show that there are specialized, sound, and complete automatic theorem provers which can use the first order theory directly. This capability is already useful for students and researchers who want to explore the consequences of their theories or check their hand-calculated derivations, with the option of easily changing any part of the theory. With a little more effort, more efficient "transformations" of GB theories can also be formulated and used in more traditional natural language processing applications. I will briefly discuss these two sorts of applications.

SYNTACTIC EQUALITY

Let's briefly consider the equality problem, because it will have an influence on our formalization of linguistic claims, and because it is a problem that does not arise in more familiar approaches to parsing with grammars that are expressively rather weak.[2] It is very hard to formalize much of interest without any equality. Consider, for example, expressing the fact that the only things that have property p are a and b. With equality, this has a very simple representation: $p(X) \leftrightarrow X = a \lor X = b$. GB theory does require that such things be expressed. For example, we might want to say that n, v, p, and a are the only *lexical* categories, or that *singular* and *plural* are the only possible values of the *number* feature. The problem with these claims is that the presence of equations can make it extremely difficult to find proofs with any automatic method. Whenever trying to prove any proposition, like $p(c)$, one must consider the possibility that c is equal to one of the things known to have property p under some other name. Particularly when the term in question is not a constant like a, b, or c but a function expression with positive arity, these searches for alternative names at every step in the proof can be an absolutely unmanageable computational burden. Thus we face a dilemma: equality is needed but will make our theory even less tractable than it might otherwise have been.

Fortunately, many theorem-proving projects have faced this problem, and a variety of techniques have been found for getting out of the dilemma. In the first place, notice that there is one particular kind of equality theory that avoids most of the computational burden: this is the "syntactic equality" theory, the theory that says that every pair of distinct variable-free terms has distinct denotations. In other words, there is at most one name for any thing in the domain of the theory. In this case, when we are trying to prove a proposition like $p(c)$, no other names for c need to be considered; there is no need to be constructing transitive chains of equations or substitutions of distinct terms into any predicate or function expressions. And yet, we can still express such things as the fact that the only things that have property p are a and b. Further efficiency improvements can be obtained by "building in" the syntactic equality theory for the language of the theory. This strategy is commonly used to obtain more efficient reasoning with standard equality theories (Chang & Lee 1973; Wos, Overbeek, & Henschen 1980; Digricoli & Harrison 1986; Stickel 1986), and a similar thing can be done for syntactic equality. For any theory T and its syntactic equality theory $SEq(T)$, we can easily define an inference rule R such that $T \cup SEq(T) \models \phi$ iff $T \vdash_R \phi$. In other words, rule R has the syntactic equality axioms built into it, so we can leave them out and still derive all the same entailments. These are wonderful ideas, but unfortunately syntactic equality is not expressive enough for a transparent formalization of GB.

To see the limitation of syntactic equality, we need a slightly more complicated example. Consider the problem of expressing the fact that 0 and its successors are natural numbers. More precisely, we let $s(0)$, the successor of 0, be 1; $s(s(0))$ is 2, and so on. A first idea for expressing the simple fact that all of these successors are natural numbers is the following:

$$nn(0) \hspace{3cm} \textit{Theory HNN}$$
$$nn(X) \rightarrow nn(s(X))$$

where, here and throughout, we use such formulas to represent their universal closures, and variable names begin with uppercase letters. Then the first sentence says, under the intended interpretation, that 0 is a natural number, and the second says that, for all X, the successor of X, $s(X)$, is a natural number if X is. To illustrate the problem with syntactic equality, suppose that the language contains just one other function symbol, the constant a, and in our intended interpretation N neither a nor any of its successors names a natural number. Then our theory has the nice properties that $HNN \not\models nn(a)$, and in fact, $HNN \vdash nn(\tau)$ just in case τ names a natural number in N. That is, HNN does not entail that a is a natural number, and we can prove that τ denotes a natural number just in case it does. Obviously, though, $HNN \not\models \neg nn(a)$; we cannot prove from the theory that a is not a natural number. To get the latter entailment we need, in the first place, a necessary condition for natural numberhood like the following:

$$nn(X) \leftrightarrow (\, X = 0 \vee \exists Y(X = s(Y) \wedge nn(Y))\,) \hspace{1cm} \textit{Theory NN}$$

And then we need a theory of equality that tells us that our terms are pairwise distinct, and in particular that the term a does not have the same denotation as any other variable-free term:

$$X = X \qquad\qquad\qquad \textit{Theory SEq(NN)}$$
$$a \neq 0$$
$$a \neq s(X)$$
$$0 \neq s(X)$$
$$X \neq \tau \quad \textit{for all terms } \tau \textit{ properly containing } X \quad (\dagger)$$
$$s(X) = s(Y) \leftrightarrow X = Y$$
$$(nn(Y) \wedge X = Y) \rightarrow nn(X)$$
$$(Y_1 = Y_2 \wedge X_1 = Y_1 \wedge X_2 = Y_2) \rightarrow X_1 = X_2$$

Clearly, we now have $NN \cup SEq(NN) \models \neg nn(a)$, and $NN \cup SEq(NN) \models \neg nn(s(a))$.

$SEq(NN)$ enforces the syntactic equality restriction: distinct terms (distinct names *and* distinct variable-free function expressions generally) have distinct denotations. Notice that because we have a function symbol in the language, the syntactic equality axioms include a schema, (†), with infinitely many instances. In fact this equality theory has a form that is familiar in the logic programming literature: $NN \cup SEq(NN)$ is essentially Clark's *completion* of the definite clause theory HNN (Clark 1978; Lloyd 1984). Clark uses a completion like this in his characterization of the results that can be obtained from HNN when a certain common deductive technique is extended with the non-monotonic negation-as-failure rule, yielding a powerful but incomplete deductive strategy sometimes called SLDNF, discussed below. This approach has some problematic features, as I will mention later, and so it is reassuring to note that we need not resort to it. Classical logic gives us entailments like those mentioned, and a sound and complete (monotonic) proof method like resolution allows us to demonstrate such results.

The important point to be made about $NN \cup SEq(NN)$ is that well-known proof techniques do *not* allow us to obtain the computational advantage of syntactic equality in deductions from this theory because it contains an existential quantifier. Suppose for example, that we want to deduce results from our theory using resolution, which can be regarded as a generalization of modus ponens. The resolution method is often preferred for automatic deduction because it requires only one inference rule, but the price it pays for this is that it can only handle theories expressed in a certain form, called "clausal form." The theory must be expressed as a conjunction (or set) of universally quantified disjunctions of literals, where a literal is a simple atomic predication or the negation of a simple atomic predication. A mechanical procedure can generate this clausal form from any first order theory. When put into this form, the problem with our natural number example becomes explicit: the clausal form will contain a Skolem function for which the syntactic equality restriction cannot be presumed to hold. The specter of an unmanageable search for proofs appears again. This time, the problem is not so easily avoided, but we can make some headway. In fact, as one would expect, we can make use of the fact that we still have a subset of the variable-free terms that are known to have pairwise-distinct denotations. It is easy to design an inference rule that will exploit this fact whenever possible, and will otherwise provide the standard equality reasoning. I have described this specialized proof strategy, "SEq resolution," elsewhere, and the details need not concern us (Stabler 1988a, 1988b). The relevant point is just that it is computationally valuable to use syntactic equality wherever possible in our formalization, leaving only the required existential quantifiers as the problematic exceptions to this rule.

When one reflects on GB theories, it is easy to see that this strategy will be a minimal imposition. As in rewrite grammars, the category symbols we use are never ambiguous, and they are almost always unique. For example, we might sometimes use both *ip* and *s* to denote the same category, but there is clearly no need to do so. The matter of compositions of data structures is only slightly more clumsy. We could represent lists in terms of concatenation and difference, letting

$$[a,b,c] = [a,b] + [c] = [a,b,c] - [] = [a,b,c,d] - [d],$$

but again there is no need to do so. Instead of such concatenation and difference *functions*, we can easily use concatenation and difference *predicates*:[3]

$$append([a,b],[c],[a,b,c])$$
$$diff([a,b,c,d],[d],[a,b,c])$$

In our formalization of GB theory, the more important relations will be those that compose *trees*, but the same idea applies. We will use a unique variable-free term to represent each tree. In particular, we will use the term $a/[b,c]$ to represent the tree in Figure 1. No other term denotes this same tree. The only slightly tricky case is that we will use a and not $a/[]$ to denote the tree with no branches, but only a root labelled a. The imposition of this strategy on our formalization of GB is minimal, but the computational benefits are significant.

Figure 1

THE FORMALIZATION: EXAMPLES FROM *BARRIERS*

I have carried out, in almost complete detail, the formalization of the theory presented in Chomsky's *Barriers* and various extensions and modifications of that theory. The *Barriers* theory is of course incomplete and only partly worked out. It is a theory of movement and government – the principles of binding theory, case theory, and θ-theory are almost completely neglected. But it is one of the great advantages of logic that there is no problem with exploring the consequences of any given set of axioms, even when we know that further axioms will be required to specify the full set of relations in the domain of interest.[4] In fact, very little elaboration of the explicit principles of *Barriers* is required to allow the formal deduction of interesting results. The demonstration of this point should squelch the unwarranted but repeated rumours that GB theories are not worked out in enough detail to have many interesting empirical consequences. Furthermore, the transparency of our formalization makes modifications easy. We can change the theory and then, if we have a straightforward implementation strategy as I will explain in a moment, we can immediately explore the consequences of the change. Let me briefly present some examples to show roughly what the formalization looks like.

As we noted above, recent GB theories do not use "SD-SC" transformational rules. Rather, they propose a very general movement rule, *move-α*, which operates freely subject to the constraints of other modules of the theory. One of the main ideas of *Barriers* is that two of these modules, the theory of government and the theory of bounding, might both be based on the idea of a *barrier*. It is clear that government is a stricter locality condition than subjacency, but Chomsky says: "The intuitive idea is that certain categories in certain configurations are barriers to government and to movement (application of the general rule *move-α*).... We might...expect that one barrier suffices to block government, whereas more than one barrier inhibits movement, perhaps in a graded manner" (Chomsky 1986b). In my formalization, I follow the form of the linguistic theory exactly. A predicate move_A(Tree0,Tree) is defined as a relation between trees, where the second tree is a result of applying an arbitrary substitution or adjunction to the first:

$$moveA(Tree0,Tree) \leftrightarrow (\quad substitute(Tree0,Tree) \qquad (1)$$
$$\lor \quad adjoin(Tree0,Tree)$$
$$)$$

We can then define a relation *moveAn* which holds between two trees just in case the second tree is a result of applying *move-α* to the first tree *n* times ($n \geq 0$):

$$moveAn(Tree0,Tree) \leftrightarrow (\quad Tree = Tree0$$
$$\lor \quad \exists Tree1$$
$$moveA(Tree0, Tree1) \land$$
$$moveAn(Tree1,Tree)$$
$$)$$

We can then define the linguistically relevant properties of trees before and after movements. Subjacency, or rather, *n*-subjacency, and government are defined in terms of barriers. The definition of *n*-subjacency, as one would expect, also relies on a special "parametric" barrier. In our formalization, the different settings for this parameter are provided by having one or another short axiom defining the parametric barrier for the language being described. I will present the main parts of the formalization of the basic notions of barriers and government.[5]

In our formalization of linguistic theory, the node labels will be grammatical categories, but we must add just a little more, as we will now explain. The principal functors of the node labels will denote the major syntactic category and bar level, as in Chomsky's notation: *cp, c1, c, ip, i1, i, vp, v1, v, np, n1, n, ap, a1, a, pp, p1, p*. One special type of tree that we will need to consider below is produced by "adjoining" a subtree *sub* to another subtree *cat/seq* to produce either *cat/[sub, cat/seq]* or *cat/[cat/seq,sub]*. These trees are unusual in that we always want to treat the two nested subtrees dominated by *cat* as a single constituent composed of two *segments*. The segments of an adjunction structure will have identical root labels. In order to treat adjunction structures in this way (following May 1985; Chomsky 1986b, 92n.10), we distinguish each occurrence of a category in a tree. In our formalism this is accomplished by providing the grammatical categories with a first argument which will number the occurrence of that category in any tree. A properly numbered tree to which no adjunction has applied will have unique numbers at each node. The categories are also associated with features which are specified by a sequence in a second argument. So, for example, *np(1,[agr(sing,3),case(nom), theta(agent),index(1)])* denotes occurrence number 1 of an NP that has the agreement features singular and third person, nominative case, an agent θ-role, and index 1.

Again following May (1985), Chomsky then defines a notion of *domination* that gives a special treatment to adjunction structures (Chomsky 1986b:7):

α is dominated by β only if it is dominated by every segment of β.

In this quotation, only the second occurrence of "dominated" has the usual sense, which we have formalized with the predicate *ancestor*. Furthermore, we can take this quotation to offer a definition rather than merely a necessary condition. Chomsky's sense of *domination* can then be formalized as follows:

$$dominates(B,A,Tree) \leftrightarrow \supset Segment \tag{3}$$
$$Segment = B \rightarrow ancestor(Segment,A,Tree)$$

This notion can be used in place of the standard definition of domination in the Aoun and Sportiche (1983) variation on the idea of *c*-command (Chomsky 1986b:8):[6]

α m-commands β only if α does not dominate β and every maximal category σ that dominates α dominates β.

$$m\_commands(A,B,Tree) \leftrightarrow \neg \, dominates(A,B,Tree) \wedge \tag{4}$$
$$\supset \forall Sigma$$
$$(dominates(Sigma,A,Tree) \wedge maximal(Sigma)$$
$$\rightarrow dominates(Sigma,B,Tree) \,)$$

In treating adjunction structures, Chomsky also uses the related notion of exclusion: "α excludes β if no segment of α dominates β" (Chomsky 1986b:9). We represent this as follows:

$$excludes(A,B,Tree) \leftrightarrow \neg \exists Segment \tag{5}$$
$$Segment = A \wedge$$
$$ancestor(Segment,B,Tree)$$

This definition gives the intended treatment to the example in Figure 2. Node *ip*(3,[]) does not exclude *np*(4,[]), but *np*(4,[]) excludes *ip*(3,[]). Node *v*(2,[]) excludes and is excluded by both *ip*(3,[]) and *np*(4,[]).

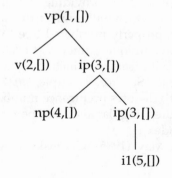

Figure 2

We also define a special notion of immediate domination between maximal projections: "so that σ immediately dominates δ in this sense even if a nonmaximal projection intervenes" (Chomsky 1986b:14-15).

$$imm\_dominates(S,D,Tree) \leftrightarrow maximal(S) \wedge \qquad (6)$$
$$maximal(D) \wedge$$
$$dominates(S,D,Tree) \wedge$$
$$\neg \exists Max$$
$$maximal(Max) \wedge$$
$$ancestor(S,Max,Tree) \wedge$$
$$ancestor(Max,D,Tree)$$

Given an axiomatization of a predicate $l\_marks(A,B,Tree)$ that holds between nodes A and B just in case A L-marks B, we can easily represent the definition of *barrier*. Chomsky provides some empirical motivation for a special treatment of IP, so he defines barriers in terms of blocking categories (BCs) as follows:

σ is a BC for β iff (σ is maximal and) σ is not L-marked and σ dominates β.
σ is a barrier for β iff either
(a) σ immediately dominates δ and δ is a BC for β, or
(b) σ is a BC for β and σ ≠ *ip*.

In case (a) σ is a barrier by inheritance; in case (b) σ is an intrinsic barrier. Our formalization is again transparent:

$$blocking\_cat(S,B,Tree) \leftrightarrow \neg \exists L \; l\_marks(L,S,Tree) \wedge \qquad (7)$$
$$dominates(S,B,Tree)$$

$$barrier(S,B,Tree) \leftrightarrow maximal(S) \wedge \qquad (8)$$
$$(\quad \exists D$$
$$imm\_dominates(S,D,Tree) \wedge$$
$$blocking\_cat(D,B,Tree)$$
$$\vee \; blocking\_cat(S,B,Tree) \wedge$$
$$\neg \exists N,F \; S = ip(N,F)$$
$$)$$

According to this definition, many nodes are barriers. Consider the following example from (Chomsky 1986b:11):

John decided [$_{cp}$e[$_{ip}$PRO to [$_{vp}$see the movie]]].

Part of this structure can be represented as in Figure 3. It now follows from our axioms that, in this tree, $cp(7,[])$ is a barrier for $np(12,[])$ but

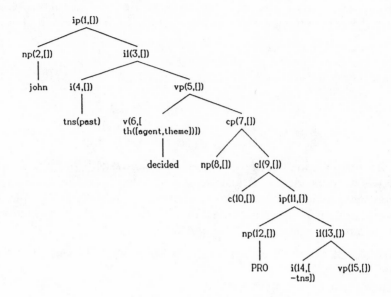

Figure 3

not for *np*(8,[]). We use this result to allow *decided* to govern the empty specifier of *cp*(7,[]) but not *PRO*.

A preliminary definition of *government* can now be formulated in terms of barriers and exclusion (Chomsky 1986b:9):

α governs β iff α m-commands β and there is no σ, σ a barrier for β, such that σ excludes α.

Again, we follow the text closely:

$$governs(A,B,Tree) \leftrightarrow m\_commands(A,B,Tree) \land \qquad (9)$$
$$\neg \exists S$$
$$barrier(S,B,Tree) \land$$
$$excludes(S,A,Tree)$$

These examples show how close the formalization is to Chomsky's own statements of the principles. They are so close as to make the formalization task nearly trivial, and to make the assessment of the adequacy of the formalization easy.[7] In this respect, the formalization differs dramatically from the formalizations used by most natural language processing systems. Typically, even in quite partial and fragmentary GB-inspired treatments of a language, the system is so complex and unmanageable that secure assessments of adequacy are not possible. The addition of new rules becomes problematic, and changes to any basic idea can require a complete reworking of the system. Of course, we have not yet discussed how our formalization might be implemented, but we turn to that point directly.

IMPLEMENTING THE FORMALIZED THEORY: EXAMPLES AND RESULTS

The formalization of *Barriers* includes only 108 first order sentences.[8] In principle, our formalization could be used directly with any sound and complete first order proof system. Furthermore, we know that if the relations formalized are computable, a sound and complete proof system will allow us to compute them.

Since our formalization respects the syntactic equality restriction and only uses existential quantifiers where required, two good proof techniques are relatively easy to apply. One is SEq resolution, mentioned above. This proof technique is monotonic, sound, and complete. There is also a much more efficient version of the strategy that is potentially incomplete, but we can design our search to avoid the potential for incompleteness whenever possible, and issue a warning whenever the risk of missing a proof is unavoidable (Stabler 1988a, 1988b).[9] Furthermore, we can collect the "answer substitutions" constructed by the proof, as is done in Horn clause programming, though the answers may be "indefinite" (i.e., they may be disjunctions). We have implemented a version of this proof strategy in a model elimination system and have applied it directly to the clausal form of the GB theory.

In order to use a resolution-based theorem prover, though, our theory must be converted to clausal form. Unfortunately, the clausal form of our initial 108 sentences includes more than 50,000 clauses. This is more than we would like, so we must move to an alternative formulation. Here again, the fact that we are using first order logic provides the enormous advantage that theory transformation strategies that are sound and complete (in a relevant sense) are well known, and for new specialized strategies the methods for establishing their soundness and completeness are well known. In this case it turns out that a trivial change in our node labels removes almost all of the clauses. If instead of labels like $np(N,F),vp(N,F),\ldots$ we use a category plus bar level notation, $x(Cat,Level,N,F)$, the definition of the X-bar categories is much simpler. Instead of $np(1,[])$, for example, we can use the only slightly less readable notation $x(n,2,1,[])$. This change requires an adjustment in only 4 of our 108 axioms, illustrating the flexibility of the formalization. Furthermore, with this change, the 108 sentences yield only 687 clauses. This clausal theory can be used directly by SEq resolution systems.

Another useful proof technique is SLDNF resolution. This is SLD resolution with the non-monotonic negation-as-failure rule (Lloyd, 1984).[10] This approach allows us to find proofs from "general programs," which are definite clause theories extended to allow negations to occur in the bodies (i.e., the antecedents) of the definite clauses (i.e., the conditionals whose consequents are exactly one positive literal). SLDNF is much faster than SEq resolution, but has some serious liabilities. SLDNF is sound in the sense that only consequences of the *completion* of the theory can be deduced (Clark 1978; LLoyd 1984). A first problem, then, is that SLDNF is sound in this sense only when the theory provides a complete axiomatization of every relation used in any proof. To enforce this restriction, it is a straightforward matter to define a *selective* SLDNF strategy, which will apply only when the relations involved are all declared to be complete in the relevant sense (Chan 1986). A related problem, though, is that the theory we want to explore is not the completion or partial completion of any general clause theory. For example, our theory contains formulas involving the equality relation which are not in the completion of any Horn theory. The completion must introduce its own equality theory, and it is not one that includes or entails all of the facts about equality that we need, though it is compatible with those facts. Our theory also contains non-Horn sentences like $p \lor q$.[11] At first one might think that a sentence like this could be expressed with general clauses like $p \leftarrow \neg q$ and $q \leftarrow \neg p$, but these do not suffice to allow SLDNF to deduce, for example, Υ from $\Upsilon \leftarrow p \lor q$. A final problem is that a single application of the negation as failure rule can fail to terminate, and so we can fail to find a proof even when there is one. These problems are difficult, but it is often possible to produce a formalization which, though radically incomplete, will suffice for a certain class of problems. The mark of a competent logic programmer is a familiarity with the delicate techniques for achieving this goal.

We have pursued both of these strategies, SEq resolution on the clausal form of our theory, and selective SLDNF resolution on a general program form of (part of) our theory. The first application developed was essentially a proof checker. As Chomsky has pointed out in a number of places, the shift away from construction-specific rules towards systems of general principles has made the determination of the properties of a structure more complicated: "Argument is much more complex, the reason being that the theory is much simpler; it is based on a fairly small number of general principles that must suffice to derive the consequences of elaborate and language-specific rule systems....[The] system of UG is an intricate and highly constrained structure; small changes in the characterization of the principles and concepts have wide-ranging and complex consequences for the languages under study and for others as well" (Chomsky 1986a:145, 148).

Given this complexity of argument, it would be useful to have implementations of GB theories that are transparent and flexible enough to allow linguists to check their analyses of particular constructions. For example, we might like to check to make sure that the principles formulated above really do entail that in the last tree we displayed, *decided* governs the empty specifier of $cp(7,[])$ but does not govern *PRO*. GB theorists do not yet have any tool that lets them do this. Analogous tools are available in other theoretical frameworks, and one prominent linguist is even purported to have suggested that these tools are *essential* for good research: "Some consequences of an entire grammar cannot be seen by the unaided human brain, just as some visual details cannot be seen by the unaided human eye."[12]

It turns out that such a tool is fairly easy to construct from our formalization. We can test to see whether consequences of interest flow from the axiomatized principles using either of the mentioned proof methods. Unfortunately, proofs from the initial formalization are still complex enough that the speed of our proof systems does not adequately compensate for their stupidity, and so we have taken the obvious step of introducing ways to guide the analysis when necessary. It turns out that guidance is not necessary too often, and so the prospects look very good for a practically useful tool. Assistance is required primarily when *moveAn* is being explored, since the proof system will then tend to search for arbitrarily many movements, a problem we will take up in detail below.[13] The various modifications of the principles explored in *Barriers* and their consequences have been formalized and the consequences have been explicitly deduced with these techniques. Remarkably few inconsistencies were found in this process. We will illustrate the value of the proof system with one error that was discovered.

Chomsky proposes that a movement of a category A to position B in a tree T is n-subjacent if there are no more than n barriers for A that are excluded by B, and the subjacency constraint is then that acceptability degrades quickly if the structure cannot be derived with movements that are *n*-subjacent for $n \leq 1$. The theory should certainly accommodate the following structure:

Who did [*ip* *John* [*vp* *see t*]]?

The two indicated constituent boundaries, though, are both barriers for the object of *see*, and so we cannot have a single wh-fronting movement without crossing more than one barrier. Chomsky suggests an alternative derivation, in which the embedded object is first adjoined to the VP and then substituted into the specifier of CP, yielding the structure in Figure 4. Chomsky suggests that this is the best case, in which even 0-subjacency is respected, but this is true only if we make a minor revision in the *Barriers* principles.

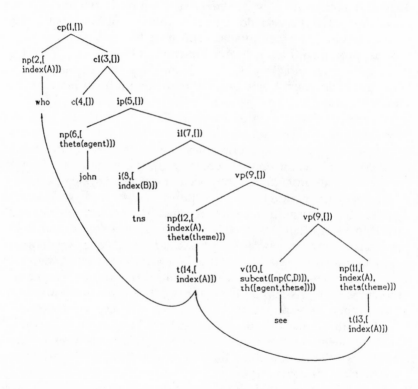

Figure 4

The problem is just that there *is* a barrier for the object of *see* that excludes the VP, viz. the VP itself. So although the adjunction to the VP would respect 1-subjacency, it is not a "best case" 0-subjacent movement unless we modify the *Barriers* definition of exclusion. Recall the previous definition: "α excludes β if no segment of α dominates β" (Chomsky 1986b:9). In the examples of exclusion discussed above, we did not note the exclusion of every node by itself, though it did follow from the definition. In particular, our proof methods can now easily establish (without any user guidance) that our theory entails $excludes(vp(9,[]),vp(9,[]),\Upsilon)$ when Υ is replaced by the term denoting the tree shown above (or when Υ is replaced by the term denoting the tree from which the structure shown above was derived).

We can easily eliminate self-exclusion, and reformalize the notion as follows:

$$excludes(A,B,Tree) \leftrightarrow \neg A = B \wedge \qquad\qquad (10)$$
$$\neg \exists Segment$$
$$Segment = A \wedge ancestor(Segment,B,Tree)$$

Given this modification of our definition of *excludes*, we can immediately prove that the movements indicated are 0-subjacent, and that the *moveAn* relation holds between the untransformed tree and this one.[14] Our formalization properly blocks the movement of $np(11,...)$ to the specifier position of $cp(1,[])$ with the 1-subjacency restriction, though it is easy to prove that this movement respects 2-subjacency.

The error in the definition of *excludes* may seem trivial, but it is really quite important to get the details right. Otherwise, the theory is just descriptively inadequate. Using guided proof techniques to explore various extensions of the *Barriers* framework, I discovered unresolved problems of essentially this kind in the recent proposals of Belletti and Rizzi on dealing with "psych-verbs" in Italian, and in that case the problems are not so easy to avoid (Stabler 1988a:sec. 10).

TOWARDS GB PARSERS

Many applications, like most parsing applications, call for drawing consequences from the theory without user guidance. For example, it would be nice to be able to prove, without user guidance, that a given string is the yield of a PF-structure that is appropriately related to a well-formed D-structure, S-structure, and LF-structure. In fact, this problem is easily formalized in logic, though we would of course have to extend our formalization of *Barriers* with the principles of the other modules of the grammar. Then we might be interested in the instances of a relation that could be formalized with a rule roughly like the following:

$$parse(String,LF) \leftrightarrow \exists DS, SS, PF$$
$$ds\_wff(DS) \wedge$$
$$moveAn(DS,SS) \wedge$$
$$ss\_wff(SS) \wedge$$
$$qr(SS,LF) \wedge$$
$$lf\_wff(LF) \wedge$$
$$pf\_trans(SS,PF) \wedge$$
$$pf\_wff(PF) \wedge$$
$$yield(String,PF)$$

Without extending the *Barriers* theory, we can consider a similar relation that could be formalized roughly as follows:

$$parse(String,SS) \leftrightarrow \exists DS$$
$$xbar(DS) \wedge$$
$$moveAn(DS,SS) \wedge$$
$$structure\_preserving(SS) \wedge$$
$$head\_movement\_constraint(SS) \wedge$$
$$n\_subjacent(1,SS) \wedge$$
$$ecp(SS) \wedge$$
$$yield(String,SS)$$

However, it is easy to see that any such instances will be practically difficult to compute without user guidance. It would be nice to show at least that every problem of this kind is decidable in principle. For example, assuming that our theory *GB* is consistent, it would be nice to show that the satisfiability of $GB \cup \{\neg parse(\text{parse}\Upsilon,X)\}$ is decidable whenever Υ is replaced with a variable-free term denoting the yield of a tree. But the prospects for such a result do not look good. On the one hand, the theory is complex enough that it does not fall into any of the well-known decidable classes (Dreben & Goldfarb 1979), and on the other hand, any attempt to establish the result with a proof-theoretic induction would be hopelessly complex. Still, I conjecture that these problems are decidable. Our systems have found lots of proofs of results of this kind, and the principles involved in the proofs do not seem to have the character that gives rise to undecidability.

Even if this conjecture is correct, it does not help with the practical problem of computing the instances of *parse*(Υ,X). Since the theory is formulated in logic, we can make use of the substantial battery of techniques known for transforming a theory to a more tractable form. Some of these techniques are rather expensive to perform, but they yield a formulation of the theory which can then provide much better runtime performance. I will briefly review three of the techniques that can be usefully applied in this case. We have not yet achieved the goal of making parsing a manageable problem with any of these strategies, for reasons that will become clear, but this work is in progress.

Data structure transformation

One of the most valuable methods for making a theory more tractable is to change the terms of the theory.[15] We have already mentioned an example of this: the change in our node labels was conceptually trivial but provided a substantial computational advantage. One other well known change that can be an enormous advantage in context-free parsing problems, is to represent strings not with lists but with a pair of "difference lists" (Tärnlund 1978; Stabler 1988a:sec.3). We will explain how this transformation can be used in the following section.

Partial evaluation and constraint satisfaction

One very valuable technique in logic programming is called "unfolding" (Sterling & Shapiro 1986; Seki & Furukawa 1987) or "partial evaluation" (Fujita & Furukawa 1988; Fuller & Abramsky 1988; Pereira & Sheiber 1987).[16] The basic idea has a natural first order generalization, where it is more often called "reduction" (Bibel, Letz, & Schumann 1987). A *reduction* is standardly defined (Dreben & Goldfarb 1979) as an effective function f such that, for some class of theories T, for every $T \in T$, T has a model iff $f(T)$ has a model. We have used two types of reduction which can be extended to preserve not only satisfiability but also "answer substitution equivalence" (Lloyd 1984). The first type, *resolution reduction*, performs a simple resolution step, adding the resolvent to the theory and discarding at least one of the parents. The second type, *simple reduction*, simply removes a clause from a theory. Thus both types of reduction are such that $f(T)$ has the same number or fewer clauses than T. It is also clear that for both of these types of reduction, if T is Horn, then $f(T)$ is also Horn. Some reductions of these types can increase the length of the shortest refutation of a theory. For example, a reduction that simply removes valuable lemmas preserves unsatisfiability and falls into our category of simple reductions, but it can obviously increase the length of the shortest refutation. We are not interested in reductions like this. Rather, we have focused on reductions F such that the shortest refutation of $f(T)$ has the same number or fewer steps than the shortest refutation of T. We call resolution reductions and simple reductions with this additional property *useful*. Many applications of "unfolding" or "partial evaluation" in Horn clause theorem proving can be regarded as the application of useful resolution reductions on finite clausal form theories.

A simple example will illustrate the idea. (Again, the technical details of this example can be skipped without losing the main argument.) Suppose a theory contains the clauses

$$answer(X) \lor \neg q(X) \lor \neg test(testX)$$
$$q(a)$$

If we also suppose that the predicate q is not used in any other clauses in the theory, then we can remove the two clauses shown and replace them by their resolvent $answer(a) \lor \neg test(testa)$. The resulting theory is obviously unsatisfiable iff the original theory is. This strategy can be generalized quite substantially, but there is one kind of case that cannot be reduced in this way. This sort of case is illustrated by a theory that includes a clausal form of the previously mentioned definition of natural numbers:

$$p(X) \lor \neg nn(X) \lor \neg test(testX)$$
$$\neg nn(A) \lor A = 0 \lor A = s(f(A))$$
$$A \neq 0 \lor nn(A)$$
$$\neg nn(A) \lor nn(f(A)) \lor A = 0$$
$$\neg nn(A) \lor B \neq s(A) \lor nn(B)$$

In this theory, we can of course still resolve the first with the third (or fourth or fifth) clauses to produce a resolvent, but we cannot replace these two sentences by that resolvent, because they may be needed for other reductions. None of the well-known useful reductions can remove all occurrences of the predicate nn from this theory. Intuitively, the problem comes from the fact that nn is recursively defined and has an infinite extension, unlike the predicate q in our previous example. More precisely (in the terminology of Seki & Furukawa 1987), the predicate nn cannot be unfolded into a finite disjunction of "primitive evaluable predicates." Also notice that, unlike many of the situations in which unfolding is most valuable, the extension of the generator nn contains simple objects (i.e., numbers) rather than sequences of some objects. Consequently, a problem like the one shown will not always be more tractable when *nn* and *test* are unfolded and their components are interleaved. For some tests, tests that depend only on part of the structure of the terms denoting the numbers (tests like "is less than 5"), unfolding and interleaving can be valuable, but for other tests that depend on more "global" properties of the numbers (like "is odd"), the strategy has no straightforward application. Unfortunately, many of the predicates in our formalization of GB are like *nn* and unlike *q*, and so, although we can get some very important gains from resolution reductions, they are not as substantial as one would like. We will discuss this further when we consider some related work, below.

There are lots of situations in which we would like to apply resolution reduction, but cannot for the reason just noted. Consider the following strategy for context-free parsing. To parse string *S*, we first prove that *T* is a derivation tree, and then we check to see if *S* is the yield of *T*. If so, we are done and *T* can be returned as a parse of *S*; if not, we try to prove that some other *T* is a derivation tree, and so on. This strategy could occur in deductions from a theory that included axioms like the following:

$$parse(S,ST) \leftrightarrow \exists ST \; s\_tree(ST) \land yield(S,ST)$$
$$s\_tree(ST) \leftrightarrow \exists NT,VT \; np\_tree(NT) \land vp\_tree(VT) \land ST = s/[NT,VT]$$

This strategy is obviously impractical. Since we have the familiar situation of a generator, *s_tree*, whose values are complex data structures (trees), it is clear that a great improvement could be obtained by, in effect, collecting the yield while the derivation tree is being computed, and requiring the appropriate correspondence between the yield and the tree at every possible point. It would be nice if we could achieve this with a resolution reduction which would unfold the *yield* predicate into its components, allowing them to be interleaved appropriately with the proof of *s_tree*. Unfortunately, the yield predicate is recursive, and this unfolding cannot be done with anything so crude as a resolution reduction. However, it is a simple matter to define new binary predicates which are like s *_tree,np_tree*, and *vp_tree*, except that they have an extra argument holding the yield of each tree:

$$parse(S,ST) \leftrightarrow s(S,ST)$$
$$s(S,ST) \leftrightarrow \exists N,NT,V,VT \; np(N,NT) \land vp(V,VT) \land append(N,V,S) \land ST = s/[NT,VT]$$

Given this formulation, we can obtain a still better theory by replacing all the string arguments by a pair of arguments, "difference lists:"

$parse(S,ST) \leftrightarrow s(S,[],ST)$

$s(S0,S,ST) \leftrightarrow \exists S1,NT,VT \; np(S0,S1,NT) \wedge vp(S1,S,VT) \wedge ST = s/[NT,VT]$

We will call this sort of strategy a "creative unfolding," since it is similar to the unfolding and reordering that can be accomplished by resolution reduction strategies, but it requires a creative redesign of some of the relations.

Now consider applying similar ideas to our GB parsing problem. Obviously, we can use a creative unfolding to, for example, constrain the computation of the S-structure SS by the components of the yield and by the constraints that apply directly to parts of the S-structure.[17] Constraining the computation of S-structure by requiring the appropriate relation to D-structure is, however, considerably more difficult. This is because the relations between parts of D-structure and parts of S-structure is quite unconstrained by *move-α*. The relations between these levels of representation is constrained when we impose not only the relation of *move-α* but also all the other constraints; but applying them all at the earliest possible points is difficult. Intuitively, the constraints on the S-structure cannot be moved back into the computation of D-structure by a resolution reduction, because of the character of the definitions of these levels. (They are like *nn* and unlike *q* in the relevant respect.) Neither is there any obvious way to use a creative unfolding to achieve the similar effect, as there was to achieve the appropriate testing of the yield in context-free parsing. This difficulty is the essential problem of GB parsing, one which it shares with many other "generate-and-test" and "constraint satisfaction problems." In fact, I think this is the computational image of the conceptual changes in GB noted in the introduction: rather than processing language with construction-specific generative rules, we must look for a structure that satisfies a small number of general constraints. Let's make the problem a little more concrete with a brief example, one part of a possible parsing problem.

Suppose we are trying to use SLD resolution (or SLDNF) to prove that there is a 1-subjacent derivation of

* *What$_i$ do you wonder how John [$_{vp}$ fixed t$_i$]?*

The attempt should fail, and of course we would like it to fail quickly. The indicated VP boundary is a barrier to the indicated movement unless the NP adjoins to it, so consider derivations that begin with this movement:

do you wonder how John [$_{vp}$what$_i$[$_{vp}$ fixed t$_i$]]?

Then we want to be able to show that fronting the NP from this adjunction site must cross more than one barrier. SLD resolution can attempt to show this by, in effect, exploring all the intermediate landing sites, all the derivations, and showing that none of them satisfies 1-subjacency. One alternative that gets explored, since nothing in the formalization of *move-α* rules it out, is the possibility that from the adjunction site, the category adjoins again to the same adjunction site. In fact, this can be done any number of times:

> *do you wonder how John* $[_{vp}what_i\ [_{vp}t_i\ [_{vp}fixed\ t_i]]]$?
> *do you wonder how John* $[_{vp}what_i\ [_{vp}t_i\ [_{vp}t_i\ [_{vp}fixed\ t_i]]]]$?
> . . .

Even if the test of other constraints are interleaved so that they apply as soon as possible after each step in the derivations explored, any system that needs to explore all of these possible derivations will never finish.

There are lots of ad hoc ways to avoid this problem. Of course it does not arise if the only movements permitted are structure-preserving substitutions. Since this restriction is too severe for most applications, sometimes a compensatory adjustment is made in X-bar theory (or whatever theory is used to define D-structures): an ad hoc provision of as many empty nodes as are required for the application. These serve, in effect, as a *finite* number of adjunction sites. This requires ad hoc changes in other parts of the grammar as well. Clearly this sort of strategy violates the spirit of the present enterprise. Furthermore, it leaves other instances of the same kind of problem untouched: cases in which an infinite or large class of structures will be searched in vain hope of satisfying a constraint that treats the whole class uniformly.

Another possible strategy for avoiding problems of the sort noted would be to establish an appropriate first order lemma. For example, we could try to show that if movement of a category from an adjunction site to some other position is blocked by 1-subjacency, a new adjunction to the current adjunction site will never make the movement possible.[18] However, results of this kind are often difficult to establish, and although the use of such results with SEq resolution is much more appealing than the elimination of adjunction altogether, it is still an ad hoc fix, because the same general kind of problem arises in lots of other situations. We would need many different special lemmas for a large, probably infinite, variety of cases. Deriving the appropriate result in response to each case also appears to be unfeasible.

Pruning the search

The previous idea suggests another related way to avoid, or at least ameliorate, the unmanageable searches in constraint satisfaction problems: to use powerful and general pruning strategies. This idea is of interest because some general pruning strategies are principled and demonstrably preserve completeness and yet are general enough to be of use in a large number of constraint satisfaction problems. Consider, for example, that Joyner (1976), drawing upon the work of Kowalski and Hayes (1969), used pruning strategies to extend resolution to a decision procedure for some simple decidable classes of first order sentences. Joyner was able to justify two kinds of restrictions on the proof search for certain classes of problems: a restriction on the number of literals in resolvents, and a restriction on the depth of nesting of the terms in resolvents. In the illustration of our problem, it is easy to see that the nesting of terms increases in the useless search. Our GB formalization does not, of course, fall into any of the decidable classes that Joyner studies, but it might be possible to justify some special pruning strategies for particular problems of interest in GB applications. Experiments with such strategies in our proof systems have shown that they can be very valuable, as one would expect.

COMPARISON WITH OTHER WORK

I think that the logical approach to GB is unique in showing promise of being able to provide anything like transparency in the implementation of GB theories. It provides the representational simplicity needed to achieve the practical goal of assessing how faithful the implementation is to the linguists' intentions, and a simple semantics that allows for rigorous assessments of transformation and proof strategies.[19] Mark Johnson (Johnson 1988a, 1988b) has done some work on showing how partial evaluation and co-routining can be used to improve the performance of a GB parsing system when the formalization is carried out in a definite clause (pure prolog) theory. As we have seen, definite clauses are not powerful enough to permit an elegant formalization of GB principles. We have also suggested that, given the complexity of linguistic theory, a formalism that does not provide substantial transparency is hopeless. But Johnson gets off this hook by explicitly disavowing any commitment to the adequacy of a definite clause representation of linguistic knowledge. Rather, he presents his work on partial evaluation and co-routining as a preliminary exploration of their potential in more adequate representational formalisms. The refutation of negative clauses from definite clause theories has a very simple proof theory, making implementation and exploration easy. Thus, although the theory transformation and co-routining techniques for such proof systems do not always carry over easily to more powerful logical systems, they can, at least sometimes, suggest valuable strategies. As we noted above, co-routining and unfolding are examples of the approaches which show the most promise in rendering proof-based parsing strategies more tractable.[20]

Verónica Dahl, together with her students and colleagues, has also developed a logic-based approach to GB formalization and implementation (Dahl 1986, 1984; Dahl & Abramson 1988; Dahl & Saint-Dizier 1986). Like the present effort, Dahl has given attention to the problem of transparency of representation. Rather than moving to a more powerful standard logic than prolog, she has defined a special powerful notation based on unrestricted rewrite grammars. Pereira (1982) provided an elegant definite clause translation for rules of the form:

$$\alpha_0, gap(X_1), \alpha_1, gap(X_2), \ldots, gap(X_k), \alpha_k \rightarrow \beta, gap(X_1), \ldots, gap(X_k)$$

where the α_i and β are sequences of categories and where the "gaps" X_i can match any sequences of categories. This rule means, roughly, "expand $\alpha_1, \ldots, \alpha_k$ to β followed by the sequence of skipped categories $gap(X_1), \ldots, gap(X_k)$."[21] Dahl generalizes this idea to allow the gaps to be eliminated or ordered in any way in the right hand sides of the rules. In effect, this allows for an easy statement of both leftward and rightward movement rules. Furthermore, the category symbols in these rules can be expressed in something like the X-bar notation mentioned above, $x(Category, Level, N, F)$, with variable category and bar level features, and so these rules can express very general principles of movement.[22] Like rewrite grammars, the system is string oriented, but derivation trees can be built and tested with constraints on movement expressed in a special notation. The constraint notation specifies configurations in which movement is to be blocked (Dahl 1986; Dahl & Saint-Dizier 1986). Subjacency is expressed in Dahl (1986) with a rule like

$$constraint(desc(b), b, a) \leftarrow bounding(a), bounding(b).$$

Dahl's work thus provides a powerful formalism for expressing general movement rules and certain kinds of constraints, a formalism that has a translation into a definite clause theory.

Dahl's work is interestingly different from ours. The notation provided for expressing linguistic generalizations is specialized and nonstandard. No doubt a precise semantics for this notation could be provided (and in fact some such semantics is implicit in the compilers for the formalism), but it is unlikely to be as simple and elegant as the semantics of first order logic. It could be that first order logic is not needed, and that Dahl's notation allows for elegant expression of just those things that one needs to formulate GB theory. Given the computational difficulty of full first order logic, this is not a bad idea. But no argument for this idea has been presented so far as I know. Dahl's notation presumably provides enough expressive power to define all of the various levels of GB representation, but it is not obvious how to do it. Nor is it clear how constraints like Lasnik and Saito's ECP could be formalized, because of the fact that it essentially involves constraints at two levels of representation. The inspiration for the approach is not, I think, that it can easily express everything we might want to. Its strength derives instead from its tie to a neat definite clause translation. As new expressive power is needed, the system is carefully extended in a way that preserves this tie. Consequently, if we could show precisely and clearly how it can formalize relations we have represented in first order logic, it might suggest valuable implementation strategies for our first order theories (or for the certain parts of them that are needed in some particular application).

CONCLUSIONS AND FUTURE WORK

The main point of this paper is that the project of implementing GB theories transparently is both manageable and worthwhile. The gulf between computational linguistics and real linguistics results from giving priority to tractability, leaving empirical and theoretical adequacy to later. But the gulf can be bridged if we reverse these priorities. On this latter approach, the completion of a parser or other application is largely in the hands of the many GB linguists, where it belongs, rather than in the hands of small groups of researchers building idiosyncratic parsing engines whose operation is often so unrelated to linguistic theory that even major theoretical developments have little or no bearing. As for the efficiency considerations, it is true that they are difficult and serious, but they can and should be taken up on an application-specific basis. Given a formalization of the knowledge to be implemented, the attempt to derive more tractable implementations can be principled and open to careful assessment.

We presented some principles of GB theory to illustrate how transparently they can be rendered in first order logic. The formalization maintains the modular structure of the GB theory exactly, and is consequently easily assessed and modified. A user-guided proof system using first order formulations of the principles of Chomsky's *Barriers* was briefly described as an example. This system has already been used to discover difficulties in linguistic theories, addressing the theoretical issues at a level of detail that is, so far as I know, unparalleled by any other GB implementation efforts. Our view is that user guidance should not be necessary, and certainly it is not an acceptable requirement in many natural language processing systems. We noted that it appears unlikely that decidability results for the problems of interest will be forthcoming, let alone guarantees of feasible computability.[23] However, aiming for a system that has reasonable computational demands on small and typical problems, even when user guidance is not available, we informally analysed some of the sources of complexity in logical approaches to GB theory. We showed how efficiency gains can be obtained by building some of the axioms of the theory into the inference rule, and by transforming the theory into a different form that is provably equivalent (in a relevant sense).[24] Essentially, we have a particularly difficult kind of constraint satisfaction problem to solve in parsing with GB theory, and it is difficult to get proof systems (or any other computational systems!) to take the best advantage of all of the available constraints. This new perspective on parsing as a constraint satisfaction problem is the computational image of the fundamental shift from construction-specific generative rules to the highly general and interactive principles and parameters of GB theory.

NOTES

* I am grateful to Verónica Dahl, William Demopoulos, and Joyce McDowell for helpful comments on an earlier draft of this paper. This research was supported in part by the Canadian Institute for Advanced Research and the Natural Science and Engineering Research Council of Canada. The material in this paper is treated in more detail in Stabler (1988b).

1 Chomsky discussed these examples in a lecture entitled "Language and Other Cognitive Systems," delivered at the University of Western Ontario, October 1987. Similar examples are discussed in sec. 6 of Chomsky (1986b) and in Lasnik and Saito (1984).

2 Some readers might prefer to skip this section on first reading; the sequel should still be intelligible. The main points of this rather technical section

are that the equality relation is essential for our task, that it poses computational difficulties unless it is handled very carefully, and that we have
designed a special proof system, "SEq resolution," that is appropriate for
the requirements of formalizations of GB theory.

3 Similarly, in arithmetic or group theory we can use either functions or
predicates. See, for example, Jane Bridge's remarks on how the two approaches compare in Bridge (1977:9-10).

4 Notice that with a nonmonotonic inference rule, we must be considerably
more careful about this point. The addition of more axioms can then
remove entailments of the partial theory. This cannot happen with standard logical approaches of the kind we are discussing here.

5 For complete details, see Stabler (1988b).

6 Notice that we interpret Chomsky's "only if" as meaning "if and only if."
Notice also that this definition allows a node to m-command itself, and it
allows the situation in which α m-commands β and α is dominated by β.
Chomsky does not rule these cases out in the text, though he notes that the
definitions could easily be modified to achieve this effect (Chomsky 1986b,
92n.11). As we will see below, the failure to enforce a non-reflexivity in
some relations can have serious consequences.

7 Although formalization is easy, it is not so easy to provide the most elegant, most computationally tractable, and most transparent formalization.
Furthermore, some relations are trickier than others. For example, we
formalize substitution and adjunction in a style suggested by tree trans-
ducer definitions. The treatment of indices and of the principles of binding
theory is also tricky. The formalization of *Barriers* required only minimal
treatment of indices (in *move-α* and SPEC-HEAD agreement).

8 This count of 108 sentences does not include the formalization of basic and
general properties of the domain. In particular, the 108 sentences do not
include the instances of an induction principle (see note 16, below), and it
does not include the infinite syntactic equality theory, which is built into
the inference rules we use. It includes the definitions of transparent representations of Chomsky's principles, together with a few structure building
and testing relations that are presupposed by those principles.

9 This is similar to the logic programmers' strategy of delaying the application of negation-as-failure as long as possible in hopes of ensuring that the
negative goal (i.e., the positive literal) will be instantiated enough to allow
safe (i.e., demonstrably sound) application. Cf. sec. 3 of Lloyd (1984).

10 This is the "pure" definition of the inference technique used by most
prolog systems. The name SLD comes from the fact that the technique uses
a Selection function in Linear resolution from Definite clauses. Lloyd
(1984) describes SLD and SLDNF and the relation of these to prolog.

11 For example, the "only if" part of axiom (1), above, is non-Horn.

12 This remark is attributed to Geoffrey Pullum in Schieber (1985).

13 An interface for users who are not experts in automated deduction is under development. When a movement is being considered, the user is asked what constituent to move and where to put it, though the user always has the option of unleashing the system on a blind and exhaustive search. We have already constructed a graphics interface that can quickly display sentence structures in their standard graphical (tree) form for reference in responding to requests for guidance, and we have built the basic interactive proof systems.

14 Later on in the text, Chomsky introduces the parametric barrier for English. When this is counted, the movement shown above satisfies 1-subjacency but not 0-subjacency.

15 This idea is familiar in computer science, where a change in data structures is one of the principal program transformation techniques.

16 As pointed out in Seki and Furukawa (1987), Naish (1985), and Smith and Genesereth (1985), certain "co-routining" strategies can be used to a achieve a similar effect, and sometimes a better effect. Co-routining can, in effect, selectively unfold clauses in a way appropriate to their instantiations at particular points in a proof.

17 This idea is applied to GB-like parsing problems in some of my earlier work (Stabler 1987a, 1987b, 1988c). See also the discussion of Johnson's work below.

18 In sub-sec. 2,11 of Stabler (1988b), I note that principles like this one are usually established by an appeal to a general principle of induction on structures. The induction principle we would like to use is second order, but since we want to restrict ourselves to first order deductions, we must instead make use of what are, in effect, the first order "instances" of the principle. Furthermore, since there are infinitely many of these, in any application we provide them only as needed, either post hoc (after noting the inability to get some result) or propter hoc (in anticipation of their usefulness).

19 I certainly do not mean to suggest that non-logical approaches to GB implementation have no interest. My suggestion is just that they have not yet shown any promise of achieving the second kind of goal that I mentioned in the introduction, that of computing all and only the properties and relations on structures that the grammar defines, including properties of ungrammatical structures, using transparent representations of GB principles.

20 Unfortunately, Johnson has not displayed his axiomatization or defined his unfolding and co-routining strategies in enough detail for me to assess their adequacy for the particular problems noted in the previous section.

21 Pereira used a sequence of dots for each $gap(X_i)$ and did not repeat them on the right hand side of the rule. This is Dahl's notation for the same idea.

22 Although general movement rules can be expressed, in the applications I

would be interesting to see whether it would be possible to prove that some set of particular instances covered all and only the movements allowed by move together with some specified constraints. This has not been attempted, as far as I know, but provides another perspective on the general idea of using reductions and other pre-computing to derive a more tractable but provably equivalent system from the general specification.

23 It is interesting to note that Chomsky explicitly and persuasively argues that there is no reason to assume that the parsing problem for natural languages must be computable in general (Chomsky 1981:11-13; Chomsky 1980:120-8).

24 Notice the contrast between our work on precomputing and building parts of the theory into the inference rules, on the one hand, and Marcus's or Berwick's and Weinberg's derivations of linguistic universals from parser architecture, on the other. Unlike the latter approach, our work maintains a clear relation between the theory and the implementation in both the levels of representation and in the properties defined over those structures; and our representation of the linguistic knowledge is not biased towards application in parsing. Marcus (1980) and Berwick and Weinberg (1984) are explicitly aiming to formulate hypotheses about the performance model, but one can imagine a performance model more similar to our implementations. Unfortunately, I must leave this idea to another paper. See Stabler (1984), and Fodor (1985, 1990) for some discussion of the relation between GB theory and these performance models.

REFERENCES

Aoun, J. and Sportiche, D. (1983). On the formal theory of government. *Linguistic Review* 2:211-36

Belletti, A. and Rizzi, L. (1986). Psych-verbs and th-theory. *Lexicon Project Working Papers* 13, Center for Cognitive Science, Massachusetts Institute of Technology, Cambridge, MA.: Forthcoming in *Natural Language and Linguistic Theory*

Berwick, R.C., and Weinberg, A.S. (1984). *The Grammatical Basis of Linguistic Performance: Language Use and Acquisition.* Cambridge, MA: MIT Press

Bibel, W., Letz, R., and Schumann, J. (1987). Bottom-up enhancements of deductive systems. In I. Plandes (ed.), *AI and Robot Control Systems.* New York: North-Holland

Bridge, J. (1977). *Beginning Model Theory: The Completeness Theorem and Some of Its Consequences.* Oxford: Clarendon Press

Brown, C.G. (1987). Generating Spanish Clitics with Constrained Discontinuous Grammars. Ph.D. thesis, Computing Science, Simon Fraser University

Bridge, J. (1977). *Beginning Model Theory: The Completeness Theorem and Some of Its Consequences*. Oxford: Clarendon Press

Brown, C.G. (1987). Generating Spanish Clitics with Constrained Discontinuous Grammars. Ph.D. thesis, Computing Science, Simon Fraser University

Chan, K.-H. (1986). Representation of negative and incomplete information in Prolog. *Procs. 6th Canadian Conf. on Artificial Intelligence*: 89-93

Chang, C.-L. and Lee, R.C.-T. (1973). *Symbolic Logic and Mechanical Theorem Proving*. New York: Academic Press

Chomsky, N. (1980). *Rules and Representations*. New York: Columbia University Press

– (1981). *Lectures on Government and Binding*. Cinnaminson, NJ: Foris Publications

– (1986a). *Knowledge of Language: Its Nature, Origin, and Use*. New York: Praeger

– (1986b). *Barriers*. Cambridge, MA: MIT Press

Clark, K. (1978). Negation as failure. In H. Gallaire and J. Minker (eds.), *Logic and Data Bases*. New York: Plenum Press

Dahl, V. (1984). More on gapping grammars. *Procs. of the Int. Conf. on Fifth Generation Computing Systems*

– (1986). Gramáticas Discontinuas: una herramienta computacional con aplicaciones en la teoría de gobierno y nexo. *Revista Argentina de Lingüística*

– and Abramson, H. (1988). *Logic Grammars*. Forthcoming

– and Saint-Dizier, P. (1986). Constrained discontinuous grammars - a linguistically motivated tool for processing language. Technical Report LCCR 86-11, Simon Fraser University

Digricoli, V.J. and Harrison, M.J. (1986). Equality-based binary resolution. *Journal of the ACM* 33(2):253-89

Dreben, B. and Goldfarb, W.D. (1979). *The Decision Problem: Solvable Classes of Quantificational Formulas*. Don Mills, ON: Addison-Wesley

Fodor, J.D. (1985). Deterministic parsing and subjacency. *Language and Cognitive Processes* 1:3-42

– (1990). Sentence processing and the mental grammar. In T. Wasow, P. Sells, and S. Shieber (eds.). *Foundational Issues in Natural Language Processing*. Cambridge, MA: MIT Press

Fujita, H. and Furukawa, K. (1988). A self-applicable partial evaluator and its use in incremental compilation. *New Generation Computing* 6:91-118

Fuller, D.A. and Abramsky, S. (1988). Mixed computation of prolog programs. *New Generation Computing* 6:119-141

Johnson, M. (1988a). Deductive parsing with multiple levels of representation. *Procs. 26th Ann. Mtg. of the Assoc. for Computational Linguistics*: 241-8

– (1988b). The use of knowledge of language. Forthcoming

Joyner, W.H., Jr. (1976). Resolution strategies as decision procedures. *Journal of the ACM* 23(3):398-417

Kowalski, R. and Hayes, P.J. (1969). Semantic trees in automatic theorem proving. *Machine Intelligence* 4:87-101. Reprinted in J. Siekmann and G. Wrightson (eds), *Automation of Reasoning 2*. New York: Springer-Verlag

Lasnik, H. and Saito, M. (1984). On the nature of proper government. *Linguistic Inquiry* 15:235-89

Lloyd, J.W. (1984). *Foundations of Logic Programming*. New York: Springer-Verlag

May, R. (1985). *Logical Form*. Cambridge, MA: MIT Press

Marcus, M. (1980). *A Theory of Syntactic Recognition for Natural Language*. Cambridge, MA: MIT Press

Naish, L. (1985). Automating control for logic programs. *J. of Logic Programming* 3:167-83

Pereira, F.C.N. (1982). Logic for Natural Language Analysis. Ph.D. thesis, University of Edinburgh, Scotland. Also available as Technical Note 275, SRI International, Menlo Park, California

– and Shieber, S.M. (1987) *Prolog and Natural Language Analysis*. Lecture Notes Number 10, Center for the Study of Language and Information, Stanford University

Seki, H. and Furukawa, K. (1987). Notes on transformation techniques for generate and test logic programs. *Procs. 1987 Symp. on Logic Programming*: 215-23

Shieber, S. (1985). Criteria for designing computer facilities for natural language analysis. *Linguistics* 23:189-211

Smith, D.E. and Genesereth, M.R. (1985). Ordering conjunctive queries. *Artificial Intelligence* 26:171-215

Stabler, E.P., Jr. (1984). Berwick and Weinberg on linguistics and computational psychology. *Cognition* 17:155-79

– (1987a). Representing knowledge with theories about theories. Technical Report 188, Department of Computer Science, University of Western Ontario, London. Forthcoming in the *Journal of Logic Programming*.

– (1987b). Restricting logic grammars with government-binding theory. *Computational Linguistics* 13(1-2): 1-10

– (1988a). Syntactic equality in knowledge representation and reasoning. *Proceedings of the First Int. Conf. on Principles of Knowledge Representation and Reasoning*, KR '89:459-66

– (1988b). *The Logical Approach to Syntax*. Forthcoming.

– (1988c). Parsing with explicit representations of syntactic constraints. In V. Dahl and P. Saint-Dizier (eds.), *Natural Language Understanding and Logic Programming II*, 15-27. New York: North-Holland

Sterling, L. and Shapiro, E.Y. (1986). *The Art of Prolog: Advanced Programming Techniques.* Cambridge, MA: MIT Press

Stickel, M. (1986). Automated deduction by theory resolution. *Journal of Automated Reasoning* 1:333-55

Tärnlund, S.-Å. (1978). An axiomatic database theory. In H. Gallaire and J. Minker (eds.), *Logic and Data Bases.* New York: Plenum Press

Wos, L.A., Overbeek, R.A, and Henschen, L. (1980). Hyperparamodulation. *Procs. 5th Conf. on Automated Deduction:* 208-19. New York: Springer-Verlag

Comment

Verónica Dahl

INTRODUCTION

Three main points have been made in Ed Stabler's chapter: that the gulf between GB theory and computational applications can be minimized; that first-order logic allows for this minimization to proceed while maintaining transparency, which in turn increases the linguist's confidence in the correspondence between intentions and results; and that first-order proof and theory transformation techniques can result in provably correct and complete applications.

These points have been supported by arguments regarding the adequacy of first-order logic and of proof and tranformation techniques for representing GB theory transparently while executably. These arguments seem to rely on two main premises:

– that first-order logic is more adequate for this task, as it is more powerful and more transparent, than either standard formalisms of formal language theory, or weaker logics such as the Horn clause logic behind Prolog;

– that the approach of using the general principles and constraints of recent GB theories to compute relations and properties of structures rather than the structures themselves holds more promise than the old approach of explicitly constructing these structures and applying transformations on them.

In this comment, I will present a complementary point of view in support of the main points made, and attempt to give further evidence of their solidity. My emphasis is on computer applications, and in providing flexible tools for linguists to use that include GB oriented primitives. How these primitives are used, as discussed more concretely later, is up to the linguistic choices they make, on which I do not make any prescriptive assumptions.

As admitted in Stabler's presentation, the computational complexities introduced in using first-order logic formulations of GB theory, while having the advantage of providing transparency and allowing feedback into the theory itself because of that transparency, make it difficult to achieve the goal of making parsing a manageable problem. The formalism presented here, as we shall see, can be used to overcome in practice some of these computational difficulties (e.g., those introduced by Skolemization in a theory with syntactic equality) and has a Horn clause equivalent which is directly runnable in Prolog.

Paradoxically, our complementation of Stabler's arguments resorts in some cases to a construction-oriented approach, as opposed to the "general principles and constraints" descriptive approach proposed by GB/Barriers theories, and followed in Stabler's presentation. I argue that these approaches are not all that opposed, and that the general principles and constraints can be used for achieving more clarity and conciseness without necessarily shifting completely away from the specificity of actual structure construction.

With respect to the third point (that first-order proof and transformation techniques make provably correct and complete applications possible), I also present a complementary point of view: that transformation techniques exist to make practical and usable applications possible. These are sophisticated versions of two of the techniques mentioned by Stabler: data structure transformations and creative unfolding, which result in automatic translation of representations of GB theory that are transparent, into Prolog ones that are not, but can be executed directly in Prolog. Thus, I agree with the first of Stabler's premises (that Horn clause-based approaches do not achieve enough transparency), but instead of resorting to other types of logic and trying to circumvent the computational problems involved in executing descriptions expressed in these logics directly, I create my own transparent formalism (specifically, Static Discontinuity Grammars) and provide processors that apply data structure transformation and creative unfolding to execute these descriptions in Prolog.

I also show some practical correspondences between this mechanization and some of Stabler's formalizations – that is, I show how some of these formalizations can be re-expressed in terms of my still transparent notations, and subsequently run by computer. As well as providing an immediate representation for these formalizations, this provides an incentive to attempt to demonstrate the theoretical equivalence between the two approaches.

Finally, I discuss related work and provide concluding remarks.

THE STATIC DISCONTINUITY GRAMMAR FORMALISM

SDGs evolved from my research on Government Binding theory and on implementing a specific GB theory application (Brown et al. 1986a; Dahl 1988 a, 1988b; Dahl 1989), as a solution to problems such as applying transformations on a tree structure without inducing a graph – as both Extraposition Grammars and Discontinuous (or Gapping) Grammars did – and without recopying the whole tree, in order in particular to allow simpler and more powerful implementations, and the straightforward incorporation of hierarchically described constraints.

In relation to Extraposition Grammars (Pereira 1981), already introduced by Stabler, SDG rules can be viewed as the same, except that

    (a) the explicit left-hand side symbols between gaps are single non-terminals instead of strings;

    (b) the skipped substrings remain in place after rewriting, instead of being repositioned at the end of the right-hand side;

    (c) a parse history is constructed automatically;

    (d) constraints can be statically described and dynamically enforced by consulting the parse history.

Instead of the Extraposition Grammar rule format:

$$\alpha_0, gap(X_1), \alpha_1, gap(X_2),..., gap(X_k), \alpha_k \rightarrow \beta, gap(X_1),..., gap(X_k).$$

we could have something like:

$$nt_0, gap(X_1), nt_1, gap(X_2),..., gap(X_k), nt_k \rightarrow$$
$$\beta_0, gap(X_1), \beta_1, gap(X_2),..., gap(X_k), \beta_k.$$

Obviously, because the skipped substrings do not change or move, we no longer need to write them explicitly, so that rules such as the above can alternatively be expressed as the conjunction of the following subrules, all affected by the same substitutions:

$$\begin{cases} nt_0 \rightarrow \beta_0, \\ nt_1 \rightarrow \beta_1, \\ \quad . \\ \quad . \\ \quad . \\ nt_k \rightarrow \beta_k \end{cases}$$

Describing movement

In all that follows, we will assume constituents with the general format:

x(Category, Level, Index, Features), where *Category* and *Index* have their usual meanings, *Level* is one of $\{ xp, \bar{x}, x^0 \}$, and *Features* is a list of features such as case, theta-role, agreement, etc.

We can now show a sample SDG rule:

{ x (Category, xp, Index, [empty | Features]) →x (Category, xp, Index, Features).

x (Category, xp, Index, Features) → x (Category, xp, Index, [trace | Features]).}

This expression of move-α accomplishes "movement" or "relating" through contextual rewriting: an empty maximal category is replaced by a maximal constituent of the same category, their indexes are unified (coindexing occurs), and the "moved" category is replaced by its trace.[1]

Such rules coexist with regular Definite Clause grammar rules, and their semantics can vary according to whether we view the subrules as a set or a list, etc. Different implementations adopt different strategies. Regardless of strategy, the core idea, that of *static discontinuity* – skipped substrings that do not move – allows the parsing derivation to be shaped as a tree rather than a graph, while maintaining type-0 power (through the fact that substitutions are shared by all subrules). GB constraints, which refer to trees, can then be directly expressed on these tree structures. No tree recopying takes place, and the recorded parse tree will contain the history of all rules applied.

Describing constraints

Because derivation trees are constructed automatically during the parse, constraints can be described in terms of a few primitives, such as "dominates(N1,N2)" (node N1 dominates node N2 in the parse tree so far). Some constraints can be expressed more transparently in terms of a primitive "constraint," which has the general form:

constraint (Path , Node, Root) :– body. [2]

where *body* is any Prolog goal relevant to describing the constraint, *Path* describes a path in the derivation, *Node* a node in that path under which no element can move out of a given zone, and *Root* is the root of that zone.

For instance, in order to describe subjacency, all we have to do is write:

constraint ([A...[B...]...], B, A) :- bounding(A), bounding(B).[3]

and define in Prolog which are considered to be bounding nodes, for
example:

bounding (x (s, xp, Index, Features)).
bounding (x (n, xp, Index, Features)).

This constraint will act as a daemon, dynamically blocking the
application of any rule that attempts to move anything under B outside of A if A and B are two bounding nodes occurring in the parse
tree so far, with A dominating B (this domination is shown in the first
argument).

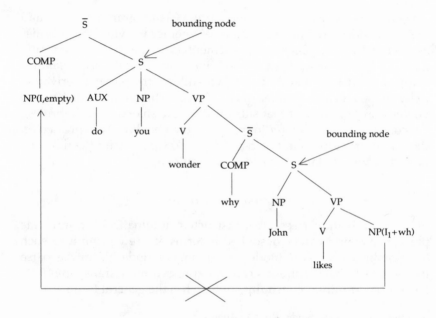

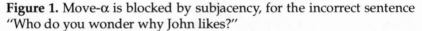

Figure 1. Move-α is blocked by subjacency, for the incorrect sentence
"Who do you wonder why John likes?"

Figures 1 and 2, respectively, show examples of blocking and allowing the above move-α rule for np. Only those constituent arguments
relevant to the movement itself are shown, and we use more compact
and traditional notation for readability (e.g., $\overline{S}$ instead of x (s, $\overline{x}$, I, F)).
Notice how the subrules provide context to each other through substi-
tution sharing, which results in the appropriate coindexing: all concerned index variables are unified. Lexical insertion of "who" is
shown after movement for convenience.

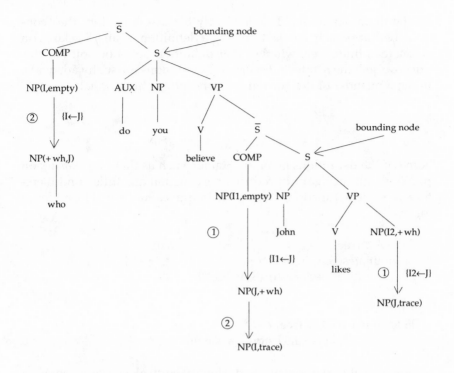

Figure 2. Two successful applications of move-α (numbered 1 and 2) for the sentence "Who do you believe John likes?"

SDG rules and constraints can be compiled into Prolog, resulting in a program that constructs the parse tree as it goes along, and checks constraints before an SDG rule application (the compiler translates all constraints into preconditions for application of movement rules).

Details about implementation are given in (Dahl & Massicotte 1988; Dahl & Popowich 1990).

OTHER GB USES OF SDG

We have already seen how SDGs can be used to transparently define rules as move-alpha and constraints such as subjacency. Here we examine some other principles Stabler formalized in first-order logic, and we argue that we can, in the context of concrete applications using SDGs, map these formalizations into Prolog with relative impunity. The Prolog definitions obtained can then be used as primitives by the grammar writer. This is mostly because we adopt the "constructive" approach, so that applying a definition means checking, on a concrete, finite tree, whether that definition holds or not. For this purpose, just the *if* side of *if and only if* definitions is usually adequate. In the remainder of this section, we concentrate on the *if* halves only.

Circumventing skolemization

Some of the definitions given by Stabler, such as that of *dominates* on p. 252, would in rigour introduce an existential quantifier, and therefore a Skolem function, during their translation into Horn clause logic:

$\forall$ B $\forall$A $\forall$Tree
  {dominates(B,A,Tree) ←$\forall$ S
        [S=B → ancestor(S,A,Tree)]}

$\forall$ B $\forall$A $\forall$Tree
$\exists$S {dominates(B,A,Tree) ←
        [S=B → ancestor(S,A,Tree)]}

However, if we simply apply the logical equivalence between $\forall$ Sp and ~ $\exists$S ~ p, we obtain:

$\forall$ B $\forall$A $\forall$Tree {dominates (B,A,Tree) ←
~ $\exists$S[S=B∧~ancestor(S,A,Tree)]}

If we now think in constructive terms, we can simply calculate the set of all segments of β in the tree that do not have α as their ancestor. If this set turns out to be empty, then we can conclude that β dominates α:

dominates(B,A,Tree): - set_of (S, (segment(B,Tree,S), not(ancestor(S,A,Tree)), Set), Set==[].

Because a concrete value for Tree, A, and B will be known at execution time and S is given a ground value by the call to 'segment,' the call to "not" (Prolog's negation as failure) will be safe.[4]

Notice that several other definitions (e.g., that of *blocking category* on p. 253, that of *governs* on p. 254, that of *excludes* on p. 259) are amenable to similar analyses, since they all involve negated existentially quantified subformulas conjoined with simpler formulas. In all these cases, we can prove that a given node does not exist by trying to find one such node in a finite, known tree, and failing.

The Empty Category Principle

One possible formulation of the ECP, as assumed in (Lasnik & Saito 1984) is as follows:

(1)   A trace must be properly governed.

(2) α properly governs β if α governs β and
      (a) α is a lexical category X^0(lexical government), or
      (b) α is coindexed with β (antecedent government)

(3) α governs β if every maximal projection dominating α also dominates β and conversely.

Clearly, if the processor constructs the tree as it goes along, and if the grammar can recognize a category as being a trace, which is merely a matter of testing straightforward definitions, we only need to use the parse tree to check computationally on the definitions of "properly governs" and "governs."

Most of this checking is straightforward in SDGs. We assume a primitive for checking node domination. Testing whether a constituent is a maximal projection is a very simple matter in our formalism: we merely need to check, through unification, that its second argument is "xp":

maxproj(x(Category,xp, Index, Features)).[5]

Similarly, the definition of proper government can test coindexing and lexical category using unification-based definitions:

lexical_category(x(_,x,_,_)).
coindexed(x(_,_,Index,_),x(_,_,Index,_)).

The definition of "governs," however, cannot directly be expressed in Horn clause terms. Its first-order logic specification, which follows, would in rigour introduce an existential quantifier, and therefore a Skolem function, undesirable from Prolog's point of view, during its translation into Horn clause logic. But if we think in constructive terms and define a predicate "mpdom $(\alpha,$Tree,M$)$" which *finds* a maximal projection M in the tree, such that it dominates α, then we can apply logical equivalences as follows, and arrive at a safe Prolog formulation:

$$\forall\alpha \; \forall\beta \; \forall\text{Tree} \; \{\text{governs} \; (\alpha,\beta) \Leftarrow \forall \; M[\text{mpdom}(\alpha,\text{Tree},M) \Rightarrow$$
$$\text{dominates}(M,\beta)] \wedge \forall M1 \; [\text{mpdom}(\beta,\text{Tree},M1) \Rightarrow$$
$$\text{dominates}(M1,\alpha)]\}\}$$

We now simply apply the logical equivalence between $\forall M$ p and $\sim\exists M \sim$p, and the equivalence between $\sim(q \Rightarrow r)$ and $q \wedge\sim r$, and obtain:

$$\forall\alpha \; \forall\beta \; \forall\text{Tree} \; \{\text{governs}(\alpha,\beta) \Leftarrow \{\sim\exists M \; [\text{mpdom}(\alpha,\text{Tree},M)$$
$$\wedge \sim \text{dominates}(M,\beta)] \wedge \sim\exists M1 \; [\text{mpdom}(\beta,\text{Tree},M1) \wedge$$
$$\sim\text{dominates}(M1,\alpha)]\}\}$$

This formulation is very near a Prolog in which the non-existence of the M and M1 in question is proved constructively: because a concrete value for Tree, α, and β will be known at execution time, we can express it as follows:

```
governs (A,B,Tree):-
        set_of (M,(mpdom(A,Tree,M), not(dominates(M,B))),S1),
        S1==[], set_of (M1,(mpdom(B,Tree,M1), not(dominates
        (M1 ,A))), S2),S2==[].
```

GB parsing and SDGs

The SDG formalization, with its automatic tree construction, its recording of movement or relation of distant constituents, and its interpretation of constraints, also in Prolog executable terms, can be seen as a sophisticated example of the data structure transformation technique mentioned by Stabler on p. 261.

In our applications for analysis, there is also some of what Stabler refers to as "creative unfolding" (p. 263): our parse is guided through contrast with the input string. The necessary "redesign of some of the relations" is automatically done by SDG processors. Similarly, in our applications for synthesis, an input semantic representation is consulted during generation. This might provide a general way out for what Stabler describes as the essential problem of GB parsing: infinite adjunctions such as those shown on p. 265 can be precluded through the simple precaution, made possible in concrete applications, of consulting what one knows (the string or its meaning).

SDGs are at the origin of two language processing applications: an automatic generator of machine error messages, and a grammar of Spanish with clitic treatment. Material related to these applications is covered in Brown et al. (1986a, 1986b); Brown (1987); Dahl (1988a, 1988b); and Brown et al. (1988). A subclass of SDGs was studied in Saint-Dizier (1988). Scattered context grammars (Greibach & Hopcroft 1969) can be considered a non-logic grammar antecedent of SDGs, in which grammar symbols have no arguments and subrules must apply simultaneously. They describe a set of context-sensitive languages, whereas in SDGs, full context-sensitive and transformational power is preserved.

Other approaches to capturing GB theory within logic programming are Sharp (1985), which uses strictly logic programming, Johnson (1987), already mentioned by Stabler, and Wehrli (1983). It is interesting to note that both Johnson's and Stabler's approaches use program transformation, although some of these uses are almost opposite: while Stabler uses them to ensure that constraints apply to a *completed* tree, Johnson uses them to automate a co-routined checking of (explicit or implicit) *partial* structures. As in our approach, Stabler's constraints are defined in descriptively general terms, such as node domination. These are then re-expressed in terms of right and left contexts. Johnson's axiomatization of move-alpha seems restricted to movement "upward" and "leftward" in the tree, and usable formulations for it do not seem easily attainable through program transformation (Johnson 1988), but these results are very preliminary and deserve further work.

The static discontinuity paradigm can also be transferred to logic programming proper, as proposed by the author in 1986. The resulting formalism, *discontinuous logic*, allows us to group several definite clause-like subrules to be applied on matching discontinuous leaves of a proof tree, all sharing the same substitutions (Dahl et al. 1986). These substitutions now apply on proof trees rather than on derivation trees. The idea of discontinuous logic was followed up in Saint-Dizier (1987), where it can be found renamed as *DISLOG*. Monteiro (1981) can be considered an antecedent of it, within the area of concurrent programming and with a fixed parallel strategy for applying the subrules.

CONCLUDING REMARKS

We have introduced a computational formalism and approach to implementing GB theory which we feel is complementary to Stabler's and strengthens his contention that transparent, while computationally useful, formulations for GB theory can be produced. This formalism is not only also transparent, but can be used to describe first-order logic formalizations and can be translated automatically into a simpler computational framework (Prolog) than those needed for full first-order logic. In discussing this formalism, we have adopted a slightly different point of view from Stabler's: that GB and Barriers do not necessarily, from a computational point of view, shift away from construction-specific rules, but the generality of their principles does make it easier to achieve transparency without giving up practicality.

We would like to stress that we are providing *tools* for executably and transparently representing general principles and constraints, but we do not presume to have an answer to the question of how to choose among the myriad of possible alternative formulations of these principles and constraints, or of how to put them all together in a completely encompassing system – assuming such a thing can be done. For instance, we have indicated how to describe two alternative definitions of government (respectively, Stabler's on p. 254 and Lasnik's & Saito's), without promoting one over the other. It is up to the linguist using these tools to decide when and how to use our primitives: Lasnik and Saito, for instance, argue that the ECP filter should apply to the output of the LF component, and that the assignment of the feature "(not) properly governed" to a trace which is (not) properly governed (with the exception of the trace of a nonargument) must be done both at S-structure and at LF. Regardless of the point at which the assignment takes place, our primitives are available for use at that point; regardless of whether the ECP filter is decreed to apply on movement at S-structure, LF, or both, we have provided a means of applying it as a *precondition* for movement, thus ruling out an explosion of unsuitable structures that are constructed only to be later discarded.

In our applications of SDGs for GB, we confess to having liberally adapted and mixed the theories in order to pragmatically suit our needs. While we had in this the blessing of the linguists in our research group, we can understand that such an approach might not meet with everybody's approval. The tools are still there for purists to attempt more faithful applications without resorting to our simplifications.

The fact that SDGs, as we have seen, can be used as a formalism into which some first-order logic specifications can be compiled opens up several possibilities: besides those mentioned in the introduction, we can imagine a hybrid system resorting to first-order logic in those cases in which SDGs are not enough, while keeping the Horn-clause translation of SDGs where this is sufficient. More generally speaking, we can consider a mixed approach in which the constructional interpretation of linguistic theory is intermingled with the general-principle-and-constraints approach.

ACKNOWLEDGMENTS

I would like to thank all the people who, as either members or visitors to my research group, have contributed in one way or another to the development and testing of various applications and processing schemes for Static Discontinuity Grammars: Michel Boyer, Charles Brown, Sharon Hamilton, Diane Massam, Pierre Massicotte, Brenda Orser, T. Pattabhiraman, Fred Popowich, and Patrick Saint-Dizier. One of these applications was supported by a SUR research contract from IBM Canada.

I am also grateful to Dan Fass, Fred Popowich, and Michael Rochemont, for helpful comments on a first draft of this paper.

Endorsement: It is the author's wish that no agency should ever derive military benefit from the publication of this paper. Authors who cite this work in support of their own are requested to qualify similarly the availability of these results.

NOTES

NB: In early reports, or early drafts of them, the SDG formalism was either unnamed (as in Dahl 1986) or was inappropriately called Constrained Discontinuous Grammars (as in Dahl et al. 1986; Brown 1987). To avoid confusion, the misnaming in these reports was corrected by the authors once a suitable name was coined, since Constrained Discontinuous Grammars is in fact a different, existing formalism (Dahl & Saint-Dizier 1986), which simply augments general Discontinuous Grammars with constraints, and does not possess the Static Discontinuity feature. Its constraints have served as ancestors of SDG constraints, but are in fact quite different, since, among other things, the latter exploit the feature of unmovable skips for achieving power that cannot be attained in Constrained Discontinuous Grammars.

1 For simplicity, we show "empty" as an explicit feature; in practice some calculation may be used.

2 ":-" stands for "if."

3 In this clause's head, the first argument's notation is in terms of a list rather than in the functional notation first used, and transcribed by Stabler on page 267. This is just a matter of convenience.

4 Calls to negation-by-failure are safe (i.e., produce no undesirable side-effects) if all their arguments are known at execution time.

5 We show all arguments with explicitly named variables as a reminder of the form of constituents; in practice, anonymous variables (noted "_") are enough, as shown in the next two definitions.

REFERENCES

Brown, C. (1987). Generating Spanish Clitics with Static Discontinuity Grammars. Ph.D. thesis, Computing Science, Simon Fraser University

– , Dahl, V., Massam, D. , Massicotte, P., and Pattabhiraman, T. (1986). Tailoring Government and Binding Theory for use in natural language translation. *Technical Report* LCCR 86 (4), Simon Fraser University

– , Pattabhiraman, T., Boyer, M., Massam, D., and Dahl, V. (1986). Tailoring conceptual graphs for use in natural language translation. *Proceedings 1986 Thornwood Conference on Conceptual Graphs*

Dahl, V. (1986). Gramaticas Discontinuas: una herramienta computacional con aplicaciones en la teoria de gobierno y nexo. *Revista Argentina de Linguistica* 2 (2)

– (1988a). Representing linguistic knowledge through logic programming. Procs. *Fifth International Conference/Symposium on Logic Programming*

– (1988b). Static Discontinuity Grammars for Government and Binding Theory. Procs. *Workshop "Informatique et langue naturelle,"* Université de Nantes

– (1989). Discontinuous Grammars. *Computational Intelligence* 5(4): 161-79

– , Brown, C., and Hamilton, S. (1986). Static Discontinuity Grammars and logic programming. *Technical Report* LCCR 86 (17), Simon Fraser University

– and Massicotte, P. (1988). Meta-programming for Discontinuous Grammars. Procs. *Meta-Programming for Logic Programming Workshop*, Bristol University

– and Popowich, F. (1990). Parsing and generation with Static Discontinuity Grammars. *New Generation Computing* 8(3): 245-74

– and Saint-Dizier, P. (1986). Constrained Discontinuous Grammars: a linguistically motivated tool for processing language. *Technical Report* LCCR 86 (11), Simon Fraser University

Greibach, S. and Hopcroft, J. (1969). Scattered Context Grammars. *Journal of Computer and System Sciences* 3:233-47

Lasnik, H. and Saito, M. (1984). On the nature of proper government. *Linguistic Inquiry* 15:235-89

Monteiro, L. (1981). Distributed logic: a logical system for specifying concurrency. *Technical Report* 5/81, Centro de Informatica, Universidade Nova de Lisboa

Pereira, F.C.N. (1981). Extraposition Grammars. *American Journal for Computational Linguistics* 7

Saint-Dizier, P. (1987). Dislog: programming in logic with discontinuities. *Technical Report* LCCR 87 (13), Simon Fraser University

Saint-Dizier, P. (1988). Contextual Discontinuous Grammars. In Dahl and Saint-Dizier (eds.), *Natural Language Understanding and Logic Programming II*. New York: North-Holland

Sharp, R. (1985). A Model of Grammar Based on Principles of Government and Binding. Master's thesis, University of British Columbia

Wehrli, E. (1983). A modular parser for French. *Proceedings 8th IJCAI 2*

CHAPTER FIVE

A Learning Model for a Parametric Theory in Phonology

B. Elan Dresher

INTRODUCTION

Much research in formal linguistics is directed at answering the two questions in (1):

(1) *Two Central Questions*
   (1) What constitutes knowledge of language?
   (2) How is it possible to acquire this knowledge?

These questions were put at the centre of linguistic theory by Noam Chomsky, who also proposed a general framework for answering them. The answer to (1), for any particular language, L, will be a specification of the grammar, G, of that language. Since languages differ, there will be many different Gs.

   A more difficult problem is to answer (2), how each G can be acquired. The nature of our problem can be illustrated schematically as follows:

(2) *The Projection Problem*

    Data of L   Universal Grammar   Grammar of L

A person, upon being exposed to data, D, from some language, eventually acquires a grammar of that language, G. This ability that humans are endowed with, that is, to acquire a grammar of a language, works for any human language: any person can learn any human language. Therefore, the cognitive principles which allow this to happen must be universally applicable. Since these principles, moreover, enable one to acquire a grammar, we may call them, collectively, Universal Grammar, or UG. Thus, while the answer to question (1) will be some particular grammar G, the answer to (2) will be a theory of UG, a set of principles which enable any person to acquire any natural language.[1]

For the past few years, I have been working, together with Jonathan Kaye of SOAS, on a project, the aim of which is to write an explicit set of procedures, of the sort that can be implemented on a computer, that could account for how someone might be able to learn the stress system of an arbitrary natural language. In other words, if D is data of some language relevant to stress, and G is the grammar of stress for that language, our aim has been to develop a working model of UG in the domain of stress, so that a computer supplied with this UG would actually be able to acquire G from exposure to D.

In keeping with the theme of this volume, I would like to consider the relation between linguistic theory and the implementation of a learning procedure of this kind. In the first part, I will look at how linguistic theory - in this case the metrical theory of stress - has influenced the implementation, and in the second part I will consider a number of ways in which the implementation might shed further light on the theory.

HOW THE THEORY INFORMS THE IMPLEMENTATION

The influence of linguistic theory on the implementation is fairly direct, since the program was specifically designed to implement a version of the metrical theory of stress. One of the reasons stress is a good area in which to experiment with learning models is that, aside from its relative independence of other aspects of grammar, there currently exists a well-developed theory of stress within a parametric framework. By way of background, I would like to briefly review some of the assumptions we make about the input data and the grammar of stress.

The data

We will begin with the data, D, which goes through several stages of preprocessing before it becomes the input to the metrical component. We assume the prior operation of rules that convert the signal into words and segments. We assume also that the various acoustic cues which indicate phonological stress are mapped into one of three degrees of stress. After this preliminary processing, the data relevant to learning word stress consists of words with vowels marked as bearing main stress (2), secondary stress (1), or no stress (0). Some sample forms are given in (3):[2]

(3) *Sample Input Data*
    (a) v a 1 n c o 2 u v e 0 r (Vancouver)   (Vàncóuver)
    (b) a 2 l g e 0 b r a 0 (algebra)   (álgebra)

Forms like those in (3) serve as the initial input into our model. However, they do not yet represent the input to the stress component. One principle that is shared by most theories of stress is that stress is sensitive to representations built on projections from syllable struc-ture. Moreover, in many languages, stress is sensitive to syllable weight, or quantity. So the first step in the analysis of the input data in (3) involves parsing the words into syllables. The parser analyzes the syllable as containing an onset and a rime. The onset contains all the material before the syllable peak (usually the vowel), while the rime is divided into the nucleus, which contains the peak of the syllable, and a coda, which contains material which follows the nucleus.

The grammar

Let us turn now to the grammar of stress: it has been fruitful to represent it in terms of metrical structures - for our purposes, we will assume metrical trees - which indicate the relative prominence of the syllables in a word:[3]

(4) *Representation of Stress in Terms of Metrical Trees*

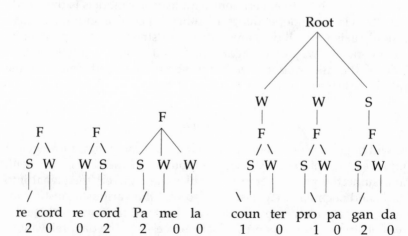

For example, in the noun *REcord*, the first syllable is more prominent, or stronger, than the second: we can represent this relation by a tree in which the left node is strong and the right node is weak. By contrast, stress in the verb *reCORD* can be represented by a tree which is right-dominant. Borrowing terms from the study of meter, we can call a group of syllables in which one syllable is more prominent than the others a foot: in the noun *REcord*, we have a trochaic foot, while the verb *reCORD* is an iambic foot. *PAmela* has the shape of a dactyl; a word like *counterpropaganda* can be represented as having three trochaic feet, of which the final one is the most prominent.[4]

Metrical theory is not just a handy representational device: it is also a theory about possible human stress systems. Observation of the stress systems of many languages reveals that certain patterns crop up over and over again, while other patterns, which from a neutral perspective appear to be just as simple, or simpler, hardly ever, perhaps never, occur.

Consider, for example, the stress system of Passamaquoddy, given in (5):[5]

(5) *Passamaquoddy Primary Stress*
  (a) If the penultimate syllable contains a full vowel, it receives stress.
  (b) Otherwise, if the antepenultimate syllable contains a full vowel, it receives stress.
  (c) Otherwise, primary stress falls on whichever one of these two syllables is separated by an odd number of syllables from the last preceding full vowel in the word, or - in the absence of a preceding full vowel - the beginning of the word.

This seems quite complex. Compare it now to the pattern in (6), which looks quite a bit simpler:

(6) *Imaginary Stress Pattern*
  (a) If a word begins with a voiced segment, stress the penultimate syllable.
  (b) Otherwise, stress the final syllable.

Nevertheless, this pattern does not, to my knowledge, occur. By contrast, patterns of the Passamaquoddy type occur quite frequently, with smaller or larger differences of detail. This sort of fact calls for an explanation. One way of accounting for this phenomenon is to suppose that metrical structures can be assembled in only a limited number of ways. We might posit, for example, that UG contains a relatively small number of parameters which control the construction of metrical structure. A learner's job is to figure out how to set these parameters for the particular language he or she is exposed to (or it, in the case of a computer).

Our model incorporates the eleven parameters listed in (7):[6]

(7) *Parameters of Metrical Theory*
    P1   The word-tree is strong on the [Left/Right]
    P2   Feet are [Binary/Unbounded]
    P3   Feet are built from the [Left/Right]
    P4   Feet are strong on the [Left/Right]
    P5   Feet are quantity sensitive (QS) [Yes/No]
    P6   Feet are QS to the [Rime/Nucleus]
    P7   A strong branch of a foot must itself branch [No/Yes]
    P8A There is an extrametrical syllable [No/Yes]
    P8   It is extrametrical on the [Left/Right]
    P9   A weak foot is defooted in clash [No/Yes]
    P10 Feet are noniterative [No/Yes]

I will briefly illustrate the effects of these parameters, starting with P1. Main stress in a word is controlled by an unbounded word tree, in which either the leftmost or the rightmost node is labelled Strong. For example, the word tree in (8a) has been constructed with P1 [Left]; this gives initial stress, as in languages like Latvian or Hungarian. Setting P1 [Right] gives fixed final stress, as in French and Farsi:[7]

(8) *P1 [Left]: Word-tree built on Rime Projections*

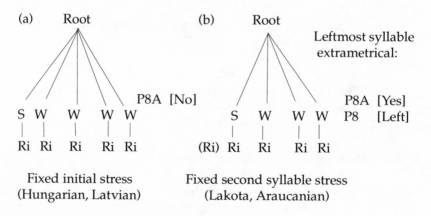

Fixed initial stress   Fixed second syllable stress
(Hungarian, Latvian)   (Lakota, Araucanian)

Main stress is not necessarily confined to a peripheral syllable, since P1 can interact with other parameters to produce different results. For example, a peripheral syllable may be designated as extrametrical by P8A and P8, meaning it does not participate in the construction of the word-tree. Extrametricality can result in main stress falling on the second or penultimate syllable; in (8b), it falls on the second syllable.

In languages such as these, only one syllable in each word is marked Strong, while all the rest are Weak. In many languages, however, syllables are first grouped together into feet, and then the word-tree is constructed on the feet. Every foot receives a stress; hence, languages with feet also exhibit secondary stresses. If a language has feet, a number of other parameters come into play.

P2 allows feet to be at most binary, or else unbounded. Suppose we choose binary feet, which give rise to an alternating pattern of weak and strong syllables. We must then choose P3, the direction of construction, which may be either from left to right or from right to left. In addition, we must select P4, which allows each foot to be left-dominant or right-dominant. We present two illustrative examples: Maranungku (Tryon 1970), in (9), has P3 [Left] and P4 [Left] - that is, left-dominant feet constructed from the left; and Warao (Osborn 1966), in (10), has left-dominant feet constructed from the right - that is, P3 [Right], P4 [Left]:

(9) *P3 [Left], P4 [Left]:*
  Left-dominant feet built from the left (Maranungku)

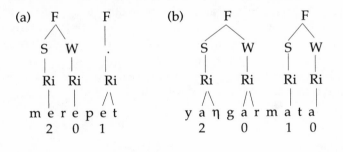

(10) *P3 [Right], P4 [Left]:*
   Left-dominant feet built from the right (Warao)

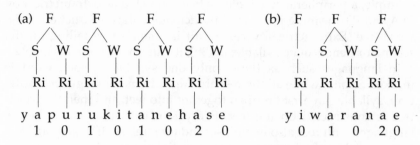

Word trees have been omitted from the examples; however, they would be constructed on the feet, with main stress devolving upon the strongest vowel in the strong foot. Depending on how various parameters are set, the strong syllable of the strong foot may be fairly far from the periphery; in this way, main stress can be quite variable, despite the limited choices in word-tree construction. Note one additional fact about the Warao word in (10b): the first syllable, being alone in a foot, ought to receive a secondary stress. Its stresslessness is due to the setting of the defooting parameter, P9, to [Yes]. Warao apparently does not tolerate stress clashes, wherein two adjacent syllables are stressed; hence, the non-branching foot is defooted, and the first syllable does not receive a stress.

The feet in (9) and (10) are not affected by the internal structure of the rimes on which they are constructed; in such languages, foot construction, and hence stress, is said to be insensitive to quantity (QI) - select P5 [No]. However, many languages have quantity-sensitive (QS) stress systems. Quantity sensitivity, in the theory being adopted here, means that a branching rime (or a branching nucleus, depending on the setting of P6) may not occupy a weak position in a foot; hence, the configurations in (11) are ill-formed:

(11) *Quantity Sensitivity (QS)*

(a) P6 [Rime]:   (b) P6 [Nucleus]:

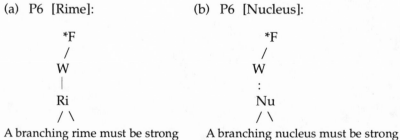

Syllables containing branching rimes or nuclei are called heavy; those that do not are called light. It follows from (11) that in quantity-sensitive stress systems, all heavy syllables are stressed. The presence of heavy syllables can considerably disrupt the smooth alternation of stresses we have observed up to here.

Finally, let's briefly consider what happens when feet are unbounded - P2 [Unbounded]. Unbounded feet have no preset limit as to their length, and an unbounded foot would propagate across an entire word unless it is stopped by something. In practice, unbounded feet are important only in quantity-sensitive stress systems, where all heavy syllables will be the heads of unbounded feet. An example of such a system is Eastern Cheremis (Kiparsky 1973), shown in (12):

(12) *P1 [Right]:*
   Main stress on the right, unbounded feet (E. Cheremis)

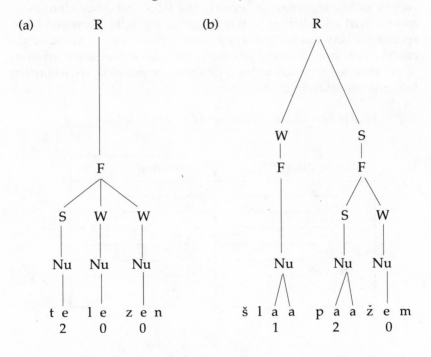

Why parameters?

Why use parameters at all to describe stress systems? A rich and highly structured theory of UG is unnecessary if the same results can be achieved by simpler means. It is therefore worth considering here some plausible alternatives which posit far less specific cognitive machinery. We can begin with the observation that stress patterns are sensitive to sequences of syllables and syllable weight. We have been assuming that there are three types of syllable that must be distinguished for purposes of stress: light syllables (L) and two kinds of heavy syllables (H) - those that branch at the level of the Rime (R), and those that branch at the level of the Nucleus (N). Let us assume that any theory of stress ought to encode at least that much information, so we would not have to consider the infinite number of possible but nonexistent rules which relate stress to other features of the phonetic string.

Imagine now a minimalist theory of stress which simply maps strings of weighted syllables (weight strings) into sequences of stresses (stress strings).[8] Consider again Maranungku: as we noted above, it has main stress on the initial syllable of a word, and secondary stresses on every odd syllable thereafter. All syllables have equal weight in Maranungku; to simplify the following discussion, let us assume that all syllables in this language are light. Now the correspondence between weight strings and stress strings in Maranungku can be summarized in the following table (note that some arbitrary upper limit to the length of the string must be adopted; we will return to this point below):

(13) *Table of Weight Strings and Stress Strings (Maranungku)*

Weight string	Stress string
S	2
SS	20
SSS	201
SSSS	2010
SSSSS	20101
SSSSSS	201010
. . . .	. . . .

In quantity-sensitive languages, such as Latin, we would have to distinguish syllable weights; again to simplify matters, let us assume only a distinction between light (L) and heavy (H) syllables. The following are tables for words up to three syllables long (Latin has no stressed light monosyllables, so the sequence L has been omitted from the tables):

(14) *Table of Weight Strings and Stress Strings (Latin)*

(a) One and two syllable words   (b) Three syllable words

Weight string	Stress string
H	2
LL	20
LH	20
HL	20
HH	20

Weight string	Stress string
LLL	200
LLH	200
LHL	020
LHH	020
HLL	200
HLH	200
HHL	020
HHH	020

Since the patterns of word stress can be listed in tables of this kind, one might be tempted to wish to reduce the whole theory of stress to the tables themselves. For any language, we would simply record the stress string corresponding to each distinct weight string; the table generated by this procedure would be the grammar of stress for that language.

A compelling argument against such a grammar has to do with the distribution of observed stress systems, as opposed to nonexistent ones. The metrical theory outlined above allows for a limited number of basic stress patterns. A grammar of tables is unable to express patterns at all. Even if supplemented with some kind of pattern seeker, we would expect to find various kinds of "crazy" stress systems:

(a) Crazy nonexistent patterns: for example, main stress on the middle syllable in odd-syllabled words, and on the right of the middle syllable in even-syllabled words. There is a general pattern, but it is unnatural and has never been observed.

(b) Systems where stress placement for individual words is not crazy, but which add up to an unnatural overall pattern: for example, stress the first syllable in words that are 2, 4, 5, and 8 syllables long, and stress the last syllable in words that are 3, 6, 7, and 9 syllables long.

(c) Finally, we would allow for systems with no discernable pattern at all.

The extent to which metrical theory cuts down on the number of possible stress systems can be seen by comparing the number of possible patterns allowed by unrestricted weight-string to stress-string mappings to those allowed by metrical theory. Weight strings range over the symbols L, R, and N; let us assume that no language distinguishes all three types, so we can restrict weight strings to L and H. With this restriction there are 2^n weight strings for a word of n syllables. Stress strings range over 2, 1, and 0, but their occurrence is not completely free, as there must be one and only one 2 in a string. Therefore, in a string of n syllables, a 2 has n possible locations; the remaining $n-1$ positions may be occupied freely by either 0 or 1, giving a total of $n \times 2^{n-1}$ stress strings for words of length n syllables. For any n, the number of possible mappings from the set of weight strings W to the set of stress strings S is S^W, that is $n \times 2^{n-1}$ raised to 2^n. The number of distinct mappings is this figure summed over all n's. The figures for $n < 6$ are given in (15):

(15) *Number of Possible Mappings from Weight Strings to Stress Strings*

Syllables n	Weight strings $W = 2^n$	Stress strings $S = nx2^{n-1}$	Mappings S^W
1	2	1	1
2	4	4	256
3	8	12	$\sim 4.3 \times 10^8$
4	16	32	$\sim 1.2 \times 10^{24}$
5	32	80	$\sim 7.9 \times 10^{60}$

The number of systems allowed by the metrical theory given in (7) is 432, that is, of the order of 10^3, which contrasts dramatically with the values shown in (15).[9] Even if we posit the existence of many more completely independent binary parameters, we will not approach the vast number of systems allowed by an unrestricted theory. If we underestimate the number of possibilities in an unrestricted mapping by eliminating secondary stress altogether, limiting the vocabulary of stress strings to 2 and 0, the solution space of the unrestricted theory comes down by many orders of magnitude, but still remains vast: $4^{16} \approx 4.3 \times 10^9$ possibilities for strings of four syllables, for example.

Another major shortcoming of the mapping-by-tables approach is that it requires us to set an arbitrary upper bound on word length. This is undesirable even for languages which happen to have relatively short words, if the upper bound is an arbitrary one. In many languages, however, the domain of word stress more closely approximates what we would call phrases, and relatively long words (nine, ten syllables, and more) are not a rare occurrence. It is clear, therefore, that the metrical theory outlined above makes nontrivial claims about the number and nature of possible stress systems.

CONSTRUCTING A LEARNING MODEL FOR METRICAL PHONOLOGY

We have now seen the sort of data that we assume as input to the stress component, and the grammar of stress we are supposing. Up to here, the model simply encodes the results of research in metrical phonology. In addition to these parameters, however, UG must also incorporate a learning theory which specifies to the learner how to set the parameters. Metrical theory is neutral as to how this is done. While learning models can be constructed without the aid of computer implementation, this is an area that is well-suited to such implementation, owing to the complexity of effects that arise from the interaction of many parameters.

Some simple learning theories

Though metrical theory is neutral as to the fine properties of a learning model for stress, we would nevertheless expect that the learning model should somehow incorporate metrical theory, assuming that it gives a correct account of the grammar of stress. Consider again the mapping-by-tables grammar discussed above: the shortcomings of unconstrained mappings of weight strings into stress strings carry over to learning systems based on such mappings. Thus, a learner could mimic the acquisition of any stress pattern by simply keeping a table of weight strings and entering the corresponding stress strings as the relevant data comes in. Though the number of possible stress systems resulting from unconstrained mappings is astronomical, the size of the table for any particular system will not be very large, being equal to the number of different weight strings encountered. Therefore, learning of stress can be modelled with recourse to only the most minimal version of UG, and without metrical parameters.

Nevertheless, this type of model is no more satisfactory than the unconstrained UG associated with it. Why should stress systems be confined to such a small part of the solution space if learning is based on unrestricted weight-string to stress-string mappings? And again, such a learner only appears to learn stress patterns; what it learns is not the pattern itself, but only a part of its extension. It would be unable to project its grammar to assign stress to weight strings not yet encountered. We conclude that such learning theories are empirically inadequate.

Let us, then, turn to learners which are confined to the space of possible grammars demarcated by the parameter set. We have shown above that limiting stress systems to those allowed by the metrical parameters results in a relatively small solution space; and this space will remain small by computational standards even if many more binary parameters are added. Therefore, the parameters demonstrate their worth over the null hypothesis as a theory of UG. But this very success might lead us to question the need for a sophisticated learning theory. Since the number of possible stress systems is small, there are any number of ways of traversing the solution space and guaranteeing that a system is found that fits the data. Two extremes that we rejected are, on one side, a brute-force learner that traverses the solution space according to a fixed schedule regardless of input; and at the other extreme, an apparently prescient learner which extracts as much information as possible from each piece of data, because it has been primed in advance with precompiled lists. There are disadvantages to both of these, some of which will arise in the following discussion.[10] Without dwelling further on these possibilities now, let us turn to the most natural assumption to make, given a system of parameters: namely, that learning is driven by cues which trigger settings of parameters.

Our project has been concerned mainly with constructing such a learning theory. For example, what in the data tells a learner that a system is quantity sensitive or not, or how to build feet? To what extent do there exist cross-parameter dependencies, and how should these be modelled? These, and many other non-trivial questions arise as soon as one attempts to build an explicit model. Let us turn now to consider some of these.

A cue-based learning theory

Appropriateness

To take one example, consider again the placement of main (word) stress, controlled by P1. This parameter may be set to [Left] (word stress left) or to [Right] (word stress right). As we noted above, the fact that this parameter has only two settings does not mean that main stress occurs invariably on the first or last syllable of a word. The direct and consistent result of this parameter setting (as well as most others in stress systems) is seen only in the production end: the construction of metrical structures. Its effects on the output forms are varied and depend on the settings of the other parameters of the system.

For example, setting P1 [Right] (main stress on the right) does result in invariable final stress in a language like Weri (Boxwell & Boxwell 1966), which has binary, quantity-insensitive, right-dominant feet constructed from the right. Sample forms are illustrated in (16):

(16) *P1 [Right]: Main stress on the right, binary feet (Weri)*

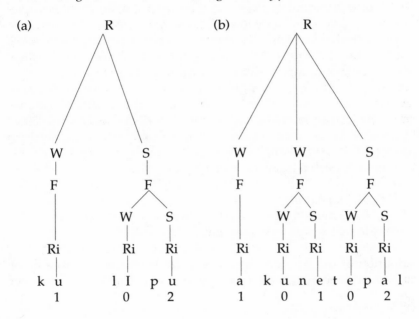

The same setting of P1 [Right], by contrast, has very different results in Eastern Cheremis, a language with unbounded, quantity-sensitive, left-dominant feet. Here, main stress appears on the last heavy syllable of words which have at least one heavy syllable (12b), and on the *initial* syllable of words with no heavy syllables (12a). Such words can be quite misleading, as they seem to indicate that main stress is on the left.[11]

It is thus a challenge to find a cue to the value of the word stress parameter that will work for all languages. The obvious naive cue - look to see if stress is on the left or right edge of the word - must be elaborated considerably, to avoid being fooled by languages like E. Cheremis. Since main stress falls upon the peripheral foot, a cue which does work requires that the learner scan a foot-sized window at both edges of the word, looking for the presence of main stress. This window varies with the values of P2 (binary vs. unbounded feet) and P5 (quantity-sensitive vs. quantity-insensitive feet); hence, main stress cannot be accurately determined until these parameters are determined.

This example illustrates that a learning theory must incorporate cross-parameter dependencies of a sort that are not apparent from the list of parameters in (7). This result is not consistent with the hypothesis of parameter independence proposed by Wexler and Manzini (1987) in their study of syntactic parameters. Also, such examples illustrate the potentially remote relationship between a parameter setting and the data which signals its presence in a grammar. We would not like this relationship to become too remote, however; in particular, we do not want to allow the learning theory to make use of "opportunistic" cues, that is, cues which happen to work in specific cases, but which have no principled basis in the system. Nor do we want the learner to engage in open-ended deductions which could lead down garden paths or become computationally intractable. Put informally, we require that cues must be appropriate to the parameters they are related to, a condition given in (17):

(17)   *Appropriateness*
        Cues must be appropriate to their parameters with regard
        to their scope and operation.

Adoption of the Appropriateness Condition ensures a desirable result, namely: no deduction or computation is permitted to the learner.

Robustness

I would now like to discuss another property that a learning theory ought to have, and that is Robustness, given in (18):

(18)   *Robustness*
        Core parameters must be learnable despite disturbances to
        the basic patterns caused by opacity, language particular
        rules, exceptions, etc.

By way of illustration, let us say we are trying to learn the pattern of Warao in (10). Suppose that the learner has already determined that it has quantity-insensitive (QI) binary feet, and let us consider how it might now arrive at the correct value of parameters P3 and P4: in other words, how could it determine that Warao has left-dominant feet built from the right edge of the word?[12]

There are four configurations generated by P3 and P4: feet can be built from the left or from the right, and the feet can be left-dominant or right-dominant. Each one of these four configurations corresponds, in its ideal form, to a characteristic pattern of alternating stresses (we can ignore the difference between 1 and 2 stresses here). Suppose, then, that we simply try to fit the stress patterns of the input words to each of these patterns in turn until we get a consistent fit. Thus, the word in (10a) is consistent also with left-dominant feet built from the left; but (10b) is not. Forms like (10b) lead the learner to reject this configuration and try another one.

The problem with this test is that the correct answer - left-dominant feet built from the right - does not match the pattern of (10b) either. The expected pattern is given in (19a):

$$/$$

(19) *Left-dominant feet built from the right (V=stressed, V=unstressed)*

(a) Basic pattern: even: V́ V V́ V V́ V   odd: V́ V V́ V V́

(b) Defooting 1: (Warao)   even: V V V́ V V́ V   odd: V V V́ V V́

(c) Defooting 2: (Garawa)   even: V́ V V́ V V́ V   odd: V́ V V V́ V

In words with an odd number of syllables, we expect the first syllable to be stressed; in (10b), it is unstressed. Now, we know why that is: it's because the initial syllable is defooted, causing the loss of its stress. This change in the pattern, though relatively minor, is enough to derail a learner looking for the pattern of (19a).

To remedy this situation, we might attempt to incorporate the effects of defooting into the test for P3 and P4. The learner, observing that there are no stress clashes in the data, could be made to assume that defooting might be at work; thus alerted, it would attempt to undo any possible effects of defooting before trying the tests for P3 and P4. This procedure would first convert (19b) to (19a), and Warao would pass the test for left-dominant feet built from the right.

Such a procedure would work for a language like Warao; we have in fact implemented it. The problem with this approach, though, is that it is extremely fragile; the learner must know in advance every factor that might cause a deviation from the ideal patterns, and must be able to correct for all of them perfectly. This is the opposite of robust: in a robust system, if you know a little, then you know a lot; but this is a situation where if you don't know something, you don't know anything. With this in mind, consider Garawa, shown in (20):

(20) *P3 [Right], P4 [Left]:*
  Left-dominant feet built from the right (Garawa)

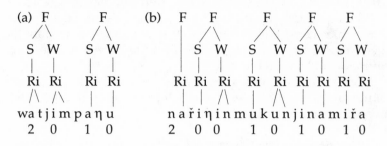

Garawa can be analysed as having the same basic pattern as Warao; however, in (20b), the expected stress clash is resolved by defooting the second foot, not the first one.[13] If the learner is unaware of this possibility, it will not succeed in learning P3 and P4.

We might therefore propose to expand the defooting parameter to include the possibility represented by Garawa. Rather than one defooting parameter, then, we may have several: it may be more correct to think of defooting as being part of a separate module containing a set of parameters which control destressing. However, if destressing is indeed the province of a whole other component of the grammar, the fragile learner must in effect embed its learning of this module inside its test for direction and labelling of trees. To the extent that destressing contains elements not entirely foreseen by UG (i.e., language particular variations that must be learned), the learner will be unable to learn P3 and P4. But even if destressing is entirely controlled by prespecified parameters, the learning strategy required is inelegant, and leads to a very complex computation, even though it may result in a solution.

Consider how this computation would go: the learner learning, say, Garawa, having determined that it has bounded quantity-insensitive feet, now wishes to figure out the values of P3 and P4. Since it has to start somewhere, say it checks first for P3L and P4L: left-dominant feet built from the left. Hence, it checks for the pattern S W S W..., and noticing an absence of stress clashes, it first sends the forms to the destressing module, which attempts to reconstruct any feet that may have been defooted. Notice there is of necessity a certain amount of guesswork involved at this stage, for there may be several ways in which to destress. Nevertheless, destressing tries something: say it does nothing to (20a), and changes the first 0 in (20b) to a 1. Now this is in fact correct. Destressing sends these forms back to the test for P3 and P4, which now attempts to match them against the pattern S W S

W.... It succeeds with (20a); however, for (20b) it finds a mismatch. So something is wrong, but the learner does not know what; in the meantime, we have generated a search tree shown in (21):

(21) *Embedded Search Paths:*
   Test for P3-P4 incorporating many-valued P9

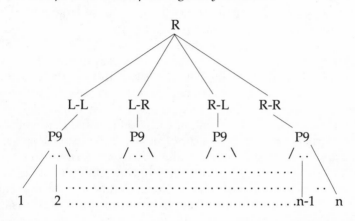

The paths under P9 represent the various possibilities allowed to destressing. So far, we have followed the path that ends at 1; when this path does not yield the correct result, the reasonable next path to try is the one that ends in 2. This follows from the search strategy which says: from the point of failure (here 1), backtrack to the lowest decision point, and then try the next possible path. This basic search logic would lead us to exhaust all possibilities of destressing for P3L-P4L first; only when these all fail do we return to the top of the tree and try another setting of P3-P4. Now, in our case, defooting was right on the first try - P3 was wrong. However, the everything-at-once learner has no way to know that, so in this case it would retreat from the correct destressing before ultimately getting everything right. Since the learner never knows in what respect it is wrong, it advances toward and retreats from the correct solution by chance.

Determinism

This sort of learning strategy has been called "nondeterministic" in the context of research on parsing (cf. Marcus 1980; Berwick & Weinberg 1984; Berwick 1985). It has been proposed that parsers should work in deterministic fashion, and it has also been proposed, by Berwick and Weinberg and also Borer and Wexler (1984), that syntactic acquisition should be deterministic. Some criteria of deterministic parsing are given in (22):

(22) *Deterministic Parsing*
      (1) No backtracking;
      (2) No undoing of created substructures;
      (3) Parsing must be at least partially data-driven.

While there are obvious computational advantages to deterministic parsing, Berwick and Weinberg argue that it also aids acquisition. Thus, suppose the parser encounters a sentence containing a new structure unknown to the parser; the parse will fail. The parser will then attempt to modify its grammar so as to accommodate the new data; but to do that successfully, it is necessary to know where the failure occurred. A nondeterministic parser, however, which routinely can make use of unlimited backtracking, will characteristically fail backwards through the whole sentence, undoing correct as well as incorrect substructures. The same is not true of a deterministic parser; as Berwick and Weinberg point out, "the effect of determinism combined with the restriction that rules refer only to bounded contexts has the effect of pinpointing errors to a 'local radius' about the point where the error is detected." The ability to keep problems local aids in the learnability of grammars.

Let us return, then, to our problems with destressing. We have seen that the attempt to learn destressing in the course of learning P3 and P4 leads to a nonrobust and nondeterministic learning path. It is interesting, therefore, that a deterministic solution exists in this case. For it turns out that we can abstract away from destressing completely. Suppose the test for direction and labelling overlooks unstressed syllables in strong positions; then, only the presence of a stressed syllable in what should be a weak position will count as a violation:

(23) *A Robust Cue for P3 and P4*
      For each setting of P3 and P4, scan across the word; the presence of a stressed syllable in what should be a weak position rules out a setting. The presence of an unstressed syllable in a strong position does not count.

This cue is restrictive enough to rule out incorrect settings of P3 and P4; but at the same time, it is robust enough to see through the defootings of both Warao and Garawa. The cue has other advantages: it works equally for non-iterated feet (P10 Yes) and quantity-sensitive feet, and it would work when faced with a language that has idiosyncratic destressing rules.[14]

This conclusion raises an empirical and a theoretical prospect. Empirically, this cue would be confounded when faced with a language-particular "footing" rule that is analogous to the sort of defooting rules that appear to be quite common. If we have indeed found the correct cue for P3 and P4, we now have grounds for excluding rules which simply stress any unstressed syllable in a certain weak position. We do find languages where certain morphemes always receive a stress; but such phenomena can be easily detected by the learner. Also we find rhythm rules, but these do not simply stress an unstressed syllable; moreover, they tend to involve alternations, and these would help the learner. To the extent that this empirical prediction holds up, it lends support to our proposed cue.

Separating out destressing, and ordering it after stressing, also accords well with the way destressing has usually been thought of, as a series of operations that apply to the output of the stress rules. It is interesting, therefore, that the parameters of stress are learnable in the absence of knowledge about the details of destressing.

On a theoretical level, the pursuit of robust cues can lead us, if successful, to a substantive notion of core grammar. It is useful to think of the grammar of a language as having a core, which is tightly constrained by UG, and a periphery, which departs in various ways from the principles of the core, and which consists of more or less idiosyncratic rules and exceptions. In any given case, however, there are few criteria for assigning any particular process to the core or to the periphery. The distinction can be bolstered by learnability considerations: the core of a grammar ought to be learnable by robust preprogrammed cues, cues which will not be misled by peripheral processes. The periphery must be learned by less principled means; the task, however, is much simplified once the core system is in place.

THE STRUCTURE OF THE LEARNING MODEL

The structure of the learning model discussed above can be schematically illustrated as in (24). The program begins with the input forms in (a). These are then parsed by the syllable parser (b). The parser outputs two types of forms (c). The first are parsed forms (rime projections) with stress numbers preserved from the input; these are the forms that are passed on to the learning system. The second type of output from the syllable parser are parsed forms with stresses removed; these are set aside, and used later by the applier.

(24) *The Structure of the Learning Model*

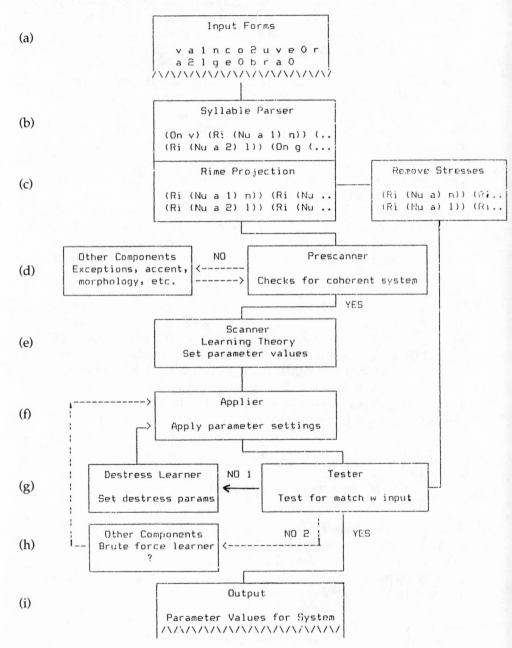

The stressed forms are then looked over (d) to make sure there are no surface contradictions in the data, that is, words with identical syllable structures but different stress patterns (e.g., *récord* and *recórd*). Such contradictions cannot be resolved by a unique setting of parameters, but indicate the influence of morphology, exceptions, lexical accent, or some other extraphonological factors. If contradictions of this type are found, it is at this point that other components (morphology, exception filters, etc.) may intervene. If the data have no obvious complications of this type, the forms are passed to the learning component proper (e). In this component, the data is scanned for a series of cues corresponding to the various parameters, and the parameters are set accordingly. For example, the scanner determines that Warao and Garawa both have binary left-dominant feet built from the right. For the reasons discussed above, it abstracts away from destressing.

The parameter values arrived at by the scanner are passed to the applier (f), which applies them to the destressed forms set aside in (c) to construct metrical structures. The structures are then interpreted to yield stress numbers, and the forms so derived are matched against the original input forms (g). If the forms match, the system assumes it has arrived at the correct grammar (i); it can then use this grammar to supply stress to new words whose stress patterns have not been given.

The criteria for what counts as a match in step (g) must allow for the fact that the applier does not have any information about destressing at this stage. To return to our example languages, we have seen (19a) that the ideal expected pattern for three-syllable words in Warao is 1 2 0 (Warao has main stress on the right), while the actual pattern (19b) is 0 2 0. Similarly, the expected pattern for a three-syllable word in Garawa (main stress on left) is 2 1 0, while the actual pattern is 2 0 0. In each case, the discrepancy (0 instead of 1 stress) is ignored by the tester, which considers the forms to match. The details of destressing can then be learned by another component dedicated to destressing. While the discrepancies between derived and input forms involved in this type of destressing are relatively minor, these examples show that the role of the tester in a cue-based learning system is not straightforward: discrepancies between input and derived forms do not necessarily indicate that the parameters are incorrectly set.

An interesting final illustration of this idea can be found in the stress system of Creek (Haas 1977), which presents the learner with an extra complication. In a large class of words, stress (actually a high tone) is computed by building binary, right-dominant quantity-sensitive feet from left to right; main stress is then assigned to the rightmost foot, as in (25a):

(25) *P1 [Right], P3 [Left], P4 [Right], QS [Rime] [Creek]*

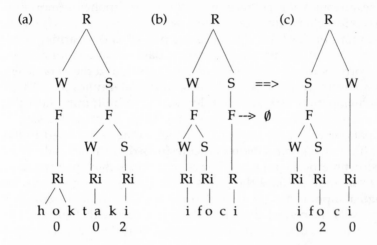

If the rightmost foot dominates only a single syllable, however, stress devolves upon the penultimate foot (25b,c). We can account for this fact by destressing a peripheral nonbranching foot in Creek (25b), as we did in Warao.[15] Creek is like Garawa, though, in that main stress appears on the same side as defooting. The result of destressing here is that the main stress, not a secondary stress, is affected by defooting: since the final foot loses its foot status, it is not eligible to receive stress, and the penultimate foot becomes the strongest in the word (25c). Unlike the other two languages, there are no secondary stresses in Creek. The result is that the expected pattern of forms like *ifoci* is 0 0 2 (0 1 2 with all secondary stresses suppressed), but the actual pattern appears as 0 2 0, which is not very close to 0 0 2. Nevertheless, the learner correctly sets the available parameters to their proper settings.

When these parameter values are passed to the applier, the applier builds metrical structures as in (25b), which yield **ifocí*. In an earlier version of the model, such forms were rejected by the tester, because of the mismatch with the input *ifóci*. The model then set off in a fruitless search for new parameter settings. But the learner was right; it was the tester that was wrong. In the current version, the tester does not reject the mismatch immediately, but refers the forms to the de-stressing learner. This learner, unlike the stress learner, has both posi-tive and negative examples of defooting (e.g., it knows there is defoot-ing in (25b) but not in (25a). When the defooting parameters have been set, the forms are returned to the applier, which makes a second pass, now taking into account destressing, and generates the correct structures (25a) and (25c). The parameter values are now confirmed by the tester.

If there are still mismatches after the second pass, the model is faced with a dilemma. While the tester can recognize a mismatch, it has no insight into its source: in a parametric system, small changes can have large effects and large changes can have small effects. Hence, it is difficult to develop a measure of closeness of fit for a parameter set based on the correspondence of an input stress string to a derived stress string. A setting that is correct in every parameter except ex-trametricality, for example, might displace every stress by one sylla-ble, resulting in no matches at all. Conversely, a parameter set that is off in a number of parameters might derive the correct stress strings in certain classes of words.

If all else fails, the model is supplied with a brute-force learner (24h) that simply cranks through the solution space, searching for more parameter settings to try. As the cue-based learner has been im-proved, however, the brute-force learner has had less and less to do, since the cue-based learner not only sets parameter values, but also rules them out. Most failures of the model now involve languages which require devices outside the universal grammar supplied to it, and which cannot be fully accounted for by any setting of the avail-able parameters.

It follows that a cue-based learning system has little alternative but to rely on its cues, and not on a tester which checks for overall correct-ness. That is, parameters set by the scanner on the basis of cues must be assumed to be correct, however great the apparent mismatch this leads to. In fact, in most cases where languages with stress systems that fall outside its UG are presented to the model, problems are detected in the first learning phase. As discussed above in connection with deterministic parsing, it is important to keep problems local. For example, when the model is given data from Cayuvava (Key 1961; Levin 1985), which has a ternary stress pattern, the learner succeeds in setting various parameters, but is unable to set parameters P3 and P4. Indeed, it is just here that the model's UG is inadequate, and it is a good sign that it is able to recognize this fact. Conversely, the success of the learning model in correctly setting the parameters of a language like Creek suggests that the current cues are on the right track, coming through robustly despite surface disturbances to the pattern.

NOTES

* This paper draws on joint research done with Jonathan Kaye. For a fuller discussion of the learning model and related issues, see Dresher and Kaye (1990), from which some of the subsequent sections have been excerpted. This research was funded in part by grants from the Social Science and Humanities Research Council of Canada (#410-84-0319 and 410-88-0729) and from IBM Canada in partnership with the Centre for Computing in the Humanities at the University of Toronto.

1 It may, of course, turn out that the principles of UG are derived from other, perhaps more basic, innate principles; or we may find that they are particular linguistic manifestations of general cognitive principles that apply to other domains as well. Until any of these are shown, however, it is prudent to assume that they are innate and language-particular; cf. Piattelli-Palmarini (1980) for debate of these issues.

2 For expository convenience we keep the ordinary English orthography in these representations; to be more precise, entries should be in phonemic form, e.g. /v æ 0 n k u 2 u v ∂ 0 r/. The use of orthography here implies no claims about the role of orthography in the acquisition of stress.

3 Metrical theory was proposed by Liberman (1975) and developed further by Liberman and Prince (1977), Hayes (1981; 1986), Prince (1983), Selkirk (1984), Hammond (1984), Giegerich (1985), and Halle and Vergnaud (1987), among others; see Hogg and McCully (1987) for an introduction.

4 These structures are intended only to exemplify the basic notions; the actual metrical structures of English words involve complications which we need not enter into here. See the references in the preceding note for detailed discussion.

5 Stowell (1979), based on work by P. Le Sourd.

6 This particular model of metrical theory is based on a modified version of Hayes (1981).

7 Many of the sample languages referred to here can be found in Hayes (1981) and Halle and Vergnaud (1987), q.v. for further details and sources.

8 I am grateful to Ken Church and Mark Liberman for comments which influenced this discussion; see Church (this volume).

9 The calculation is complicated by the fact that P9 has more than two values, as discussed below, which would lead to a higher number of

possible systems. On the other hand, it will also be shown below that we can abstract away from destressing completely in the first phase of the learning model, which results in a lower number (216).

10 See Dresher and Kaye (1990) for further discussion of these models.

11 We assume secondary stresses in E. Cheremis, though we have no information as to whether they appear on the surface. If they do not, the learning problem is more difficult, since the learner is presented with less evidence as to the distribution and relative prominence of feet. Our model can learn the correct placement of main stress in these cases whether or not there are secondary stresses.

12 Depending on how the test for extrametricality is ordered, we could also analyse Warao as having right-dominant feet built from right to left, with a final extrametrical syllable. We assume, however (contrary to Halle & Vergnaud 1987:19n), that a solution which makes no recourse to extra-metricality is preferred in this type of case.

13 Hayes (1981:54-5) proposes a different analysis which requires different parameter settings for main and secondary stress. This complexity is not required in our analysis; a similar analysis is proposed by Halle and Vergnaud (1987:19). We ignore here the difference between secondary and tertiary stresses.

14 The same principle appears in the metrical correspondence rules proposed by Halle and Keyser (1971:169f), whereby a line is deemed unmetrical if a stressed syllable occurs in a weak position, but not vice versa. We are grateful to Ray Jackendoff for calling this to our attention.

15 Hayes (1981:61) derives main stress in Creek using a word tree labelled according to the rule: label the right node strong iff it branches. This labelling convention entails a number of difficulties discussed by Prince (1983), and is not available in our parameter set. Halle and Vergnaud (1987:59-60) order destressing in Creek before the assignment of main stress.

REFERENCES

Berwick, R.C. (1985). *The Acquisition of Syntactic Knowledge*. Cambridge, MA: MIT Press

- and Weinberg, A.S. (1984). *The Grammatical Basis of Linguistic Performance*. Cambridge, MA: MIT Press

Borer, H. and Wexler, K. (1987). The maturation of syntax. In T. Roeper and E. Williams (eds.), *Parameters and Linguistic Theory*. Dordrecht: D. Reidel

Boxwell, H. and Boxwell, M. (1966). Weri phonemes. In S.A. Wurm (ed.), *Papers in New Guinea Linguistics V*. Canberra: Australian National University

Dresher, B.E. and Kaye, J.D. (1990). A computational learning theory for metrical phonology. *Cognition* 34: 137-195

Furby, C. (1974). Garawa phonology. *Pacific Linguistics Series A* (37). Canberra: Australian National University

Giegerich, H.J. (1985). *Metrical Phonology and Phonological Structure: German and English*. Cambridge, Eng.: Cambridge University Press

Haas, M.R. (1977). The tonal accent in Creek. In L. Hyman (ed.), *Studies in Stress and Accent (SCOPIL 4)*. Los Angeles: Department of Linguistics, USC

Halle, M. and Keyser, S.J. (1971). *English Stress: Its Form, Its Growth, and Its Role in Verse*. New York: Harper and Row

- and Vergnaud, J.-R. (1987). *An Essay on Stress*. Cambridge, MA: MIT Press

Hammond, M. (1984). Constraining Metrical Theory: A Modular Theory of Rhythm and Destressing. UCLA doctoral dissertation. Bloomington, IN: IULC

Hayes, B.P. (1981). A Metrical Theory of Stress Rules. MIT doctoral dissertation. Bloomington, IN: IULC

- (1987). A revised parametric metrical theory. In *Proceedings of NELS 17*

Hogg, R.M. and McCully, C.B. (1987). *Metrical Phonology*. Cambridge, Eng.: Cambridge University Press

Key, H. (1961). Phonotactics of Cayuvava. *IJAL* 27:143-50

Kiparsky, P. (1973). 'Elsewhere' in phonology. In S.R. Anderson and P. Kiparsky (eds.), *A Festschrift for Morris Halle*. New York: Holt, Rinehart and Winston

Levin, J. (1985). Evidence for Ternary Feet and Implications for a Metrical Theory of Stress Rules. Unpublished ms. University of Texas

Liberman, M. (1975). The Intonational System of English. MIT Doctoral dissertation

- and Prince, A.S. (1977). On stress and linguistic rhythm. *Linguistic Inquiry* 8:249-336

Marcus, M.P. (1980). *A Theory of Syntactic Recognition for Natural Language*. Cambridge, MA: MIT Press

Osborn, H. (1966). Warao I: phonology and morphophonemics. *IJAL* 32:108-23

Piattelli-Palmarini, M. (ed.), (1980). *Language and Learning: The Debate between Jean Piaget and Noam Chomsky*. Cambridge, MA: Harvard University Press

Prince, A.S. (1983). Relating to the grid. *Linguistic Inquiry* 14:19-100

Selkirk, E.O. (1984). *Phonology and Syntax: The Relation between Sound and Structure*. Cambridge, MA: MIT Press

Stowell, T. (1979). Stress systems of the world, unite! In K. Safir (ed.), *MIT Working Papers in Linguistics*. Vol.1:51-76

Tryon, D.T. (1970). *An introduction to Maranungku. Pacific Linguistics Series B* (14). Canberra: Australian National University

Wexler, K. and Manzini, M.R. (1987). Parameters and Learnability in Binding Theory. In T. Roeper and E. Williams (eds.), *Parameters and Linguistic Theory*. Dordrecht: D. Reidel

Comment
on Computational Learning Models
for Metrical Phonology
Kenneth Church

INTRODUCTION

Before I begin my remarks, let me say that I am basically sympathetic with the spirit of Dresher's argument, but I feel duty-bound, after having agreed to write these comments, to take a more critical perspective. These remarks are intended to point out some of the difficulties that one may run into when trying to formulate a computational theory of learning.

Sometimes it is hard to draw a line between *learning* and *training*. The statistical literature uses the term *training* to refer to simple methods such as linear regression for fitting curves (models) to data. The term *learning* has been used in a number of ways. There are some uses of the term that overlap with statistical training, but there are also (possibly) quite different uses in formal computer science, Artificial Intelligence, and Linguistic Theory. I'll mostly concentrate on trying to distinguish the statistical notions of training from the use of learning that is found in the Artificial Intelligence literature.

As a computer scientist with a background in Artificial Intelligence, I know that computers are much better at turn-the-crank tasks like parameter fitting than tasks requiring human-like behaviour, such as learning. And consequently, when I see a computer performing a task that looks like learning, I am very tempted to say that the computer is just fitting data, a task that doesn't require much intelligence (or whatever it is that distinguishes learning from training).[1] Basically, the difference between crank-turning and intelligence is that we know how to write crank-turning programs, but it can be more difficult to write "intelligent" programs. I might go so far as to distinguish the two kinds of tasks by whether or not they can be solved by a computer. Indeed, in AI, it has been said (partly in jest) that once we know how to solve a problem with a computer, we no longer think of the problem as requiring "intelligence."

By this criterion, Dresher's argument is self-defeating. In showing that a computer can solve the acquisition problem, Dresher is showing that language acquisition is not a learning problem, but rather a crank-turning problem that can be solved by simple statistical training methods. Of course, I am grossly overstating the case, but I think some readers might share at least some form of the concern. I might take a less extreme position and allow some computer programs to be considered intelligent, but only those that are sufficiently "interesting." Thus, I would want to say that linear regression and Hidden Markov Modeling do not count as learning because they are too well understood, but maybe neural networks and Dresher's program are more mystical and less well understood, and so they would count as learning.

I will attempt to argue that Dresher's program is actually more statistical than mystical. That is, I will try to show that Dresher's program is equivalent in a certain sense to a trivial program that is simply fitting data not unlike linear regression. In other words, I will attempt to show that Dresher's program doesn't actually learn anything very interesting by showing that an utterly uninteresting program can "learn" the same facts. I am basically trying to reduce Dresher's program to a trivial one, and thereby show that Dresher's program is also trivial (in a certain sense). This kind of reduction is a standard form of argumentation in computer science. Of course, it puts me in the unusual position of trying to construct a completely uninteresting program that can "learn" phonology. Normally, as a computer scientist I try to write interesting programs, but I now find myself trying to write an utterly uninteresting one.

AN UNINTERESTING "LEARNING" PROGRAM

Let me define the learning task (as Dresher does), to take a long sequence of words from language X as input, and to output a description of stress assignment for language X.

1 Input: a long sequence of words from language X

2 Output: a description of stress assignment for language X

Let me represent a *word* as a sequence of syllable weights (L or H) and stresses (0, 2). For example,[2]

record (noun) → L2H0

record (verb) → L0H2

The point is that once you have adopted this representation, learning is easy, since most of the hard problems have been encoded into the representation. This representation provides a lot of "inside information" (stipulations), so that it sidesteps a number of hard questions, including:

1 Where does the concept of syllable weight come from?

2 How do you learn the underlying representation from surface forms?

Of course, since Dresher's program assumes the same representation, I'm sidestepping the same questions that he is when I adopt this representation.

Given this representation, it is possible to learn the stress assignment facts with a trivial one-line program. Suppose the input to the learner is simply a sequence of *words* from language X

```
L2H0
L0H2
...
```

and the output is a description of the set of all possible *words* in language X. Since the set of possible *words* (weight/stress strings) is finite (in practice) and very small ($\approx$1000), it is possible (and practical) to describe the set by simply enumerating its members.

The following "trivial" Unix® program will "learn" the facts of the language very quickly:

```
sort -u
```

Surely, this program is uninteresting. Anything this program can do is probably not worth doing. If this program can learn the same facts that Dresher's program can "learn," then whatever Dresher's program is doing, it shouldn't be called learning.

Not only does my program "learn" the same facts that Dresher's program does, but, in addition, my program has a number of engineering advantages over his program:

1 There are fewer lines of code,

2 it is easier to replicate, and

3   it makes fewer assumptions (no trees, grids, etc.) so that it
     has a better chance of standing the test of time.

The main problem with my program is that it is too good; it can learn
too much. According to Dresher (in the first section, p. 300), my program can learn 4.3 billion stress systems, and yet only a few hundred
have ever been observed. Dresher argues that his program is superior
because it can learn only 432 stress systems, which is much closer to
what we find in the languages of the world.

From a computational point of view, we needn't be very concerned
with this overgeneration. Of course, it indicates that we are missing
some generalizations, but there is no pressing need to capture them
(under the terms of the learning task contract as defined above). The
"trivial learner" is a perfectly practical solution to the learning task as
defined above. If it ain't broke, don't fix it.

AN UNINTERESTING FIX

Of course, it is possible to fix the overgeneration without making my
program interesting. Recall that I am in the unusual position of trying
to avoid writing an interesting program.

So far, we have been assuming that a language could be any enu-
meration of words. The overgeneration problem can be solved "trivially" by stipulating a representation of languages. Recall that "representation" is a form of "inside information" or stipulation.

Let a *language* be an 11 bit number where

P1   The word-tree is strong on the [Left/Right]
P2   Feet are [Binary/Unbounded]
P3   Feet are built from the [Left/Right]
P4   Feet are strong on the [Left/Right]
P5   Feet are quantity sensitive (QS) [Yes/No]
P6   Feet are QS to the [Rime/Nucleus]
P7   A strong branch of a foot must itself branch [No/Yes]
P8A   There is an extrametrical syllable [No/Yes]
P8   It is extrametrical on the [Left/Right]
P9   A weak foot is defooted in clash [No/Yes]
P10   Feet are noniterative [No/Yes]

With this representation (stipulation), there are 432 possible *languages*,
according to Dresher's calculation.

Now, we can "fix" our trivial learning model by making sure that the resulting language is one of the possible 432 *languages*. One could accomplish this trivially by filtering the results at the end:

sort -u | convert_to_language

where *convert_to_language* returns an 11 bit number if the input is one of the possible *languages*, or signals an error if it isn't.

Now the trivial model no longer overgenerates. Thus, it is possible to get the job done in a completely uninteresting way. The "learning" program doesn't tell us anything about how cues interact. Therefore, learnability considerations need not tell us anything "interesting."

In general, it is hard to make strong computational arguments when the inputs and outputs are finite (and very small). If there were an infinite number of inputs and outputs (or at least a large number of them), then one could show that exhaustive uninteresting approaches such as the ones that I have been proposing would not work. But I think that it is pretty clear that stress systems are fairly small. One can talk about the possibility that a word can be arbitrarily long, but as a practical matter, it is not a bad approximation to assume that the number of output stress sequences is small and finite (especially if we limit our attention to morphemes rather than words).

THE TRIVIAL MODEL IS NOT CRAZY

For English, for example, I have found that a table with 1,024 input weight sequences and only 51 possible output stress sequences is adequate for predicting stress patterns in a large coverage Text-to-Speech system (Church 1985). This table assumes that there are no more than eight syllables in a morpheme. As far as I know, there are no exceptions in English. Another mechanism was used for stressing over morpheme boundaries since the rules are somewhat different in that case. I will not go into that question here since Dresher doesn't discuss the effects of morpheme boundaries.

The table approach has some real computational advantages for a practical real-time system. Table look-up is obviously very fast. In addition, the storage requirements are quite modest (in fact, probably less than Dresher's program, as a practical matter). The table also turned out to allow underspecified input. In the Text-to-Speech application, it is very difficult to determine underlying weight from surface spelling. It was convenient to allow variables in the input description of syllable weights.

Weight	Extrametricality	
	0 (Verb)	1 (Noun)
H	1	1
L	1	1
HH	31	10
HL	10	10
LH	01	10
LL	10	10
HHH	103	310
HHL	310	310
HLH	103	100
HLL	310	100
LHH	103	010
LHL	010	010
LLH	103	100
LLL	010	100
etc.		

In easy cases, it is possible to determine the weight directly for the orthography. For example, the weight of *torment* must be "HH" because both syllables are closed (even after stripping off the final consonant). Thus, the stress of *torment* is either "31" or "13" stress depending on whether it has 0 or 1 extrametrical final syllables:[3]

(stress-from-weights "HH" 0) → ("31"); verb
(stress-from-weights "HH" 1) → ("13"); noun

However, most cases are not this easy. Consider a word like *record*, where the first syllable might be light if the first vowel is reduced or it might be heavy if the vowel is underlyingly long or if the first syllable includes the /k/. It seems that it is impossible to say anything in a case like this. The weight, it appears, is either "LH" or "HH." Even with this ambiguity, there are only three distinct stress assignments: 01, 31, and 13.

(stress-from-weights "LH" 0) → ("01")
(stress-from-weights "HH" 0) → ("31")
(stress-from-weights "LH" 1) → ("13")
(stress-from-weights "HH" 1) → ("13")

In fact, it is possible now to use the stress to further constrain the weight. Note that if the first syllable of *record* is light it must also be unstressed, and if it is heavy it also must be stressed. Thus, the third line above is inconsistent.

I implemented this additional constraint by assigning *record* a pseudo-weight of "=H," where the "=" sign is a variable which indicates that the weight assignment is constrained to be the same as the stress assignment (either heavy and stressed or not heavy and not stressed). I can now determine the possible stress assignments of the pseudo-weight "=H" by filling in the "=" constraint with all possible bindings (H or L) and testing the results to make sure the constraint is met.

(stress-from-weights "LH" 0) → ("01")
(stress-from-weights "HH" 0) → ("31")
(stress-from-weights "LH" 1) → ("13"); No Good
(stress-from-weights "HH" 1) → ("13")

Of the four logical inputs, the "=" constraint excludes the third case, which would assign the first syllable a stress but not a heavy weight. Thus, there are only three possible input/output relations meeting all of the constraints:[4]

Weight	Extrametrical Syllables	Stress
LH	0 (verb)	01
HH	0 (verb)	31
HH	1 (noun)	13

Thus, compiling the stress assignment rules into a table has three computational advantages. In addition to improving time and space performance, the table also provides a set of constraints that can be used to reason backwards. In this case, we couldn't tell what the underlying syllable weight was from the orthography because we didn't know if the first syllable contained a schwa or a tense vowel. However, we found that we could make use of the output stress assignment in order to infer the input syllable weight. Thus, we showed that the table could be used in the backward direction to infer the input.

CONCLUSION

Dresher ultimately rejects the table-based model for two reasons: it overgenerates the space of possible languages by a factor of 4.3 billion / 432; and it places an upper limit on the size of a word.

In an earlier version of the paper, he also objected to the table-based model as "uninteresting," but this third objection seems to have been dropped in the revision, presumably because my program is intended to be uninteresting. After all, as mentioned in the introduction, it is my aim to write an uninteresting program that gets the job done. If I succeed, then I have demonstrated that the job is too easy and the intelligence is not in the learning task but somewhere else.[5]

I am not too concerned with either of Dresher's remaining criticisms. It was suggested above that morphemes are limited in length, at least in English. Even in those languages with very long morphemes, I would suspect that one could modify the representation in some way (using run-length coding or something similar) so that the table would be small and finite. Obviously, I am using the representation as "inside information," but Dresher also depends on coding a fair amount of smarts (stipulation) into the representation.

As for overgeneration, it isn't clear to me why the language learner should be concerned with the number of possible languages. The learner does not need to know *why* stress works the way that it does. All that he needs is an adequate description of one language so that he can process well-formed strings in that language. The learner might be more of a tradesman than a scholar. The learner needs to know how to turn-the-crank, but he does not need to know the best way to do so, or why turning-the-crank is the right thing to do. An adequate description is sufficient. Explanation is not required. Nor is optimality.

Of course, if you take this view of learnability, then it is unlikely that learnability arguments will tell us very much about language. It is logically possible that learnability will tell us nothing. For example, it is possible that there are only a small and finite set of languages, say 432. Perhaps all 432 languages are innately stored in the child's head so that when he hears his first word he can compute some simple function that tells him which of the 432 languages to use. The code need not have anything to do with the structure of language. It could, for example, depend on some biological or astronomical clock at the time when the child hears his first word.[6] While we are all sympathetic with the learnability approach, I have yet to see a convincing argument that demonstrates that the structure of language necessarily follows from learnability considerations.

NOTES

1 I'm not sure what the property is that distinguishes learning from training. In these remarks, I use the term "intelligence" for this purpose, but there do seem to be some forms of learning, such as learning motor control commands, which do not seem to require "intelligence."

2 It is straightforward to extend the representation in obvious ways to incorporate other facts that should be included, such as extrametricality.

3 Actually, in practice, the weight determination is complicated by the possibility that -*ment* and -*ent* might be suffixes. Note, for example, that the adjective *dórmant* does not stress like the verb *tormént* because the adjectival suffix -*ant* is extrametrical.

4 The noun should probably have the stress 10 rather than the stress 13. I assume that an extrametrical syllable has 3 stress if it is heavy, and 0 stress if it is light. The stress of the extrametrical syllable is very difficult to predict (Ross 1972).

5 I might suggest that too much has been encoded into the input representation. It was my experience when I was working on letter-to-sound rules for speech synthesis that stress assignment was the easy part. It was much harder to decide which syllables were heavy and which were light. Obviously, orthography obscures the issues. But, in addition, there are difficulties from morphology and elsewhere.

6 This argument was inspired by a casual comment by Chomsky (personal communication). I remember him arguing that learnability considerations need not tell us about language. Suppose, for example, that there were only two possible languages (as opposed to the 432 that we have in this case). It is logically possible, he argued, that the child could select the right one on the basis of something that had nothing to do with the internal structure of either one. And thus, the child could, in principle, learn a language without telling us anything about the structure of language.

REFERENCES

Church, K. (1985). Stress assignment in letter to sound rules for speech synthesis. *Association for Computation Linguistics*

Ross, J. (1972). A reanalysis of English word stress (Part I). In M. Brame (ed.), *Contributions to Generative Phonology.* Austin: University of Texas Press

CHAPTER SIX

Some Choices in the Theory of Morphology

Arnold M. Zwicky

BACKGROUND

A theory of morphology specifies what sorts of systems can associate the meanings of words to their pronunciations. The overall architecture of such a system hinges on a series of choices, seventeen of which I will discuss here. This paper has both a descriptive aim, to survey what I see as the major options, and a prescriptive one: to recommend (some variant of) one option in each case, and so to say why it is I pursue the particular variety of morphological theory that I do.[*][†]

The theorist's customary exclusions

I should make it clear at the outset that what I am engaging in here is linguistic theorizing, and not either psycholinguistic modelling or computational modelling. My concern is to find a logic connecting semantics and phonology at the word level. This logic should be linguistically appropriate, that is, its instances should be interpretable as claims about what particular people know about (certain aspects of) their languages. And it should capture generalizations; phenomena a linguist would recognize as unitary should not be treated as unconnected to one another.

But I make no claims about how the processing of language proceeds in real time, using real memories. My concern is with abstract inventories of expression types, properties of expressions, and generalizations about those properties; it makes no sense to say that such generalizations "take time." I also make no promises that this logic will fit well with existing abstract theories of computation, or of course with the computational hardware and software that happen to be available at the moment. Linguistic theorists are well advised to attend to psycholinguistics and the theory of computation – good ideas about symbolic systems are not easy to come by – but they cannot expect that questions about the way languages are organized will be reducible to problems already solved in one of these other domains. It also might well be that the current state of understanding about morphological theory would never have been reached without the spur provided by computational linguists, who find it an occupational necessity to make claims precise and get systems that run, but that wouldn't make morphological theory a branch of computational linguistics.

I will also confine myself to the theory of grammar. "Not every regularity in the use of language is a matter of grammar," Pullum and Zwicky (1987:330) observe in an article that calls for treating certain types of "morphology" (for instance, the celebrated expletive infixation in *abso-goddam-lutely*) as belonging to a domain separate from grammar – a domain of conventional regularities in language use, to be sure, and one certainly within the linguist's province, but one comprising principles that are significantly different in character from the rules of "plain morphology."

Programs, frameworks, and theories

Strictly speaking, I will not even be talking about theories here. I make a rough distinction between programs, frameworks, and theories, according to which my subject is <u>frameworks</u>, not theories.

A program comprises a few leading ideas. What I have called the Interface Program (Zwicky 1984) is indeed a program, then, since it is characterized by nothing more than the proposal that grammars are highly modular, with interactions between modules limited to certain principles of precedence. The proposal that systems of context-free phrase structure rules are sufficient for the framing of generalizations about syntactic organization constitutes a program for syntax. The proposal that the morphological rules of a language can be partitioned into a small finite number of rule-sets distinguishable on the basis of their phonological effects and the linear position of the affixes they describe constitutes a program for morphology.

To get from a program to a framework, you need a conceptual apparatus and a network of assumptions framed in terms of this apparatus. Usually when linguists talk about "theories," they're actually talking about frameworks. To get a theory, you need to fill out a framework in two ways: the set of assumptions has to be filled out so as to be complete with respect to the domain at issue, and descriptive mechanisms (that is, an interpreted formalism) must be provided. This ideal has only occasionally been approached in linguistics – so far as I know, never in morphology (as opposed to semantics, syntax, and phonology). Whenever it is approached, however, an unfortunate ambiguity can arise, as when the publication of Gazdar et al. (1985) caused the phrase "generalized phrase structure grammar" to become ambiguous as between reference to the GPSG framework and to the syntactic theory laid out in the book. (For that matter, there are probably people who think it refers to the program of phrase structure syntax in general.)

To any program there correspond an enormous number of frameworks carrying out that program, and to any framework there correspond an enormous number of theories filling out that framework. It is undoubtedly no accident that so much "theoretical" discourse is about frameworks, since these constitute a more or less manageable middle level of analysis. It is hard to say anything substantial enough about programs to allow for discussion of relevant matters of fact, and it is hard to get intellectually aroused about the details of a theory when an astronomical number of plausible alternatives come quickly to mind. In any event, my own discussion is on this middle level – not at the level of mechanisms, but at the level of properties that mechanisms must have. If you really care about the details, you're going to find it pretty thin gruel.

AGONY ABOUT "WORDS"

To reach this middle level, I'm going to have to make a rather large number of conceptual distinctions. The point is to avoid making fundamental decisions about a framework inadvertently, through the sloppy use of technical terms like "word" (and "lexical," for complaints on which see Aronoff 1989 and Zwicky 1989a, 1990b).

(Along with a rather large number of conceptual distinctions go a rather large number of pieces of terminology. I am not particularly good at devising memorable technical terms, especially by the dozen or the gross, and I have made a number of different tries at this particular set over the years. I don't suppose that the current choices are much better than their predecessors, but I do want to stress that what is at issue here is not terminology – rotten, boring, or striking – but conceptual distinctions.)

Though textbooks (like Matthews 1974) and foundational treatises (like Mel'cuk 1982) take some care to distinguish various concepts often lumped together under the label "word," in my experience most linguists have little patience with these discussions, which they view as mere philosophical quibbling. To my mind this is exactly the wrong response, roughly like rejecting the distinction between "mass" and "weight" as pointless sophistry in physics. Theoretical advances require some serious splitting, not thoughtless lumping. After the dust of splitting settles some, we of course expect to understand better the relationships between the pieces that have been split off; that is the point of the exercise.

I will be distinguishing various sorts of elementary linguistic expressions, where I understand an expression to be a pairing of semantic interpretation with phonological substance. Some of these distinctions (treated in the following section) are syntagmatic, having to do with properties of expression tokens. Others (treated in the remaining sections) are paradigmatic, having to do with properties of expression types.

Properties of expression tokens

Syntactic groupings: W, W$_{MAX}$, W$_{MIN}$

I begin with various properties of subexpressions, in particular the syntactic properties that I will label "rank" and "depth" (as in Zwicky 1990b. sec. 2). Syntactic theory requires a distinction between (at least) subexpressions of clause rank (rank C), phrase rank (rank P), and word rank (rank W).[1] Subexpressions of rank W are sometimes said to have the property of belonging to a "0-bar" or (alas) "lexical" category.

Just as subexpressions of rank P can include or be included in other subexpressions of rank P (as in the nested VPs of *must have been watching penguins*), so subexpressions of rank W can include or be included in other subexpressions of rank W (as in the nested NWs of *savings bank location information*). In such circumstances I will distinguish the most inclusive, or maximal, subexpression of a given rank from those included within it, and the least inclusive, or minimal, subexpression from those including it. Here we have one source of our inability to give a single answer to the question of how many "words" are in an expression like *savings bank location information*. There is one W$_{MAX}$ (the whole expression), but four W$_{MIN}$s (*savings, bank, location,* and *information*) and seven Ws, that is, subexpressions of rank W (the five already listed, plus *savings bank* and *savings bank location*).

Syntactic representations (hereafter, "synreps") and syntactic rules (hereafter, "synrules") are mutually characterizing. The synrep for an expression provides information about the grouping of material into constituents, which are subexpressions relevant for synrules; about the category, rank, depth, and other relevant properties of individual constituents; and about ordering, grammatical relations, and other relevant relations between pairs of constituents. A synrule is then a stipulation as to how assemblages of such properties of expressions are paired with semantic interpretation. Constituents of rank W are the building blocks for the purposes of synrules.

Prosodic groupings: w

It is well known that the grouping of linguistic material into prosodic domains, which are stretches relevant for phonological rules, is not necessarily the same as the grouping into constituents, though there are intimate relationships between the two. At least one prosodic domain, the "phonological word" w of Nespor and Vogel (1986) (they use the Greek letter omega to refer to this domain) and earlier works, is approximately co-extensive with the Ws of syntax.

The relationship between the units of morphosyntax – whether these are constituents, as in the current subsection, or tactemes, as in the next subsection – and the prosodic domains of phonology is expressed in a set of prosodic domain formation rules, which give general matchings of units (W to w, for instance) as well as matchings specific to particular items or classes of items. See Volume 4 of the *Phonology Yearbook* for further discussion of prosodic domain formation.

Properties of expression types

Inventory elements: lexemes

In *Syntactic groupings: W, W_{MAX}, W_{MIN}* I considered the grammatical analogue of the atom; now consider the grammatical analogue of the chemical element: an expression type of a language that occurs free and is an elementary object in the inventory of free expression types, in the sense that it is not a composite of other free expression types.

Like everything else I have to say here about fundamental concepts, this is a characterization, not a definition. What we mean when we say that an elementary expression type occurs free might well be as complex as what we mean when we say that a chemical element, like technetium (atomic number 43), samarium (62), or californium (98), occurs free; the properties of these elements are such as to make them extraordinarily rare in occurrence or extraordinarily short-lived or extraordinarily likely to occur only in combination with other elements, so that they are in principle free, but in practice very hard to find loose on the hoof. Lexemes are also in principle free, but their freedom is hemmed in by all sorts of considerations: a lexeme might be confined to occurrence in only a few syntactic constructions, even just one; it might occur only in a single idiom; its semantics or pragmatic values might severely restrict its distribution; it might be subject to prosodic or other phonological conditions that greatly limit where it can occur.

Indeed, similar remarks hold for being elementary. An atom of helium could be viewed as an atom of hydrogen with an electron tacked on, but that doesn't cause us to abandon the classification of helium as a chemical element. The fact that a lexeme like HAPPILY can be viewed as an instance of the lexeme HAPPY with an affix tacked on shouldn't cause us to abandon the classification of HAP-PILY as a lexeme. (Later, I will consider "superlexemes," like the unit instantiated as *cat's* in *The cat's hungry*.)

Some terminology will be necessary here; as in Zwicky (1989a, 1990a), I will engage in a certain amount of deliberate coining and stipulation of meaning. Call any free expression type in a language a "tacteme," any elementary tacteme a "lexeme" (note that nothing I have said so far would ensure that each lexeme occurs only as a single W, or that each W is an occurrence of a single lexeme), and call any other tacteme a "syntacteme." Let the (infinite) inventory of tactemes in a language be its "tacticon," partitioned into a "syntacticon" (also infinite) of syntactemes and a "morphicon" (possibly also infinite) of lexemes.[2] Generalizations about the content of the syntacticon are expressed by a special type of synrule, specifically devoted to the description of free expression types. Other types of synrules concern themselves with syntactic valency (or dependency) and with the form of syntactic constituents, and nothing guarantees that a valency set can make a constituent on its own (the subject and its predicate complement in *I am happy* and *I am in Ohio* and *I am a professor* cannot do so), or that a constituent can occur free (*they be here* in *I insist they be here* cannot do so), or that a syntacteme is a single constituent (*Flowers to the judge* can occur free, as an answer to a question, but it is demonstrably not a single constituent). Generalizations about the content of the morphicon are expressed by what I will call "morrules" – terminology intended to suggest "morphological," but without dragging along whatever further assumptions people might have about what morphology is.

It is an important factual, rather than terminological, observation that while it is reasonably common for morrules to be contingent on phonological properties of lexemes, synrules never seem to be. The latter observation, elevated to a theoretical assumption, is the Principle of Phonology-Free Syntax of Zwicky (1969) and Pullum and Zwicky (1988). I will assume it here, which means that morrules in a sense constitute the initial entry point of phonology within the grammar.

Each lexeme can be viewed as a set of properties, which will in some sense be present in all occurrences of the lexeme. These crucially include some semantic properties, some phonological properties (which I will assume can be organized into one or more "phonological representations," or phonreps, each of which is a coherent structured assemblage of phonological features), and some syntactic properties. Morrules then fall into two large classes: "cross-lexeme" rules, those having to do with generalizations relating (the properties of) distinct lexemes, and "within-lexeme" rules, those having to do with generalizations relating different properties within lexemes. There will of course be subtypes of each. For instance, garden-variety derivational rules (DRs) constitute a subtype of the cross-lexeme rules, and garden-variety inflectional rules (IRs) a subtype of the within-lexeme rules.

Forms, v-forms, p-forms, m-forms

In a very simple world, each lexeme would have constant phonological content; its pronunciation might vary according to general phonological rules (applying within domains that might be syntactic, prosodic, or even morphological), but phonological stipulation would be limited to a single phonrep for each lexeme. We live very far from this simple world.

To begin with, many lexemes in many languages have alternative phonreps (often called "forms") according to the syntactic properties of the Ws instantiating them. That is, phonologically distinct versions of a lexeme are often available to convey information about agreement ([3, SG, PRS] *jumps* and [1, SG, PRS] *jump* for the verb lexeme JUMP in English) and government ([PSP] *jumped* and [PRP] *jumping* for JUMP). The relevant syntactic properties I will call "i-features" (so as to suggest "inflectional features"). Synrules constrain the distribution of i-features on constituents of various sizes, including those of rank W. We can then consider each constituent of rank W as possessing some full coherent combination of i-features, what I will call a value set, or "v-set." Such a rank-W constituent instantiates some particular lexeme, and we can ask what phonrep corresponds to this v-set for this lexeme.

The properties of a lexeme, then, include a collection of "entries," each entry being a pairing of a v-set with a phonrep. (In the next section I will revise this characterization of the phonological properties of a form.) Note that there might be gaps in this collection, that is, there might be v-sets for which no phonrep is provided (as is the case for the English modal lexemes and all v-sets containing the i-feature [-FIN]); that there might be more than one entry for a given v-set (as is the case for the English lexeme DREAM and all v-sets containing the i-feature [PST], given the alternatives *dreamed* and *dreamt*); and that there might be more than one entry for a given phonrep (as is the case for DREAM and the v-sets containing the i-features [PRS, 1, SG] and [PRS, 3, PL], both of which correspond to *dream*).

If we are to be careful, there are in fact four distinct notions here, and linguists are not always clear as to which one they mean when they use locutions like "the (inflected) forms of a word." I would prefer to keep the unadorned term "form" for an entry, as I have already done. But we might want to refer to entries by means of their v-sets, to refer to "v-forms," so that there is a single v-form for *dreamed* and *dreamt*. And we might want to refer to entries by means of their phonreps, to refer to "p-forms," so that there is a single p-form for *run*, corresponding to v-sets containing either [PSP] or [PRS], but distinct p-forms for *dream* and *dreamt*.

And we certainly want to group entries into sets by virtue of pho-nological identities predicted by the morrules of the language, to treat [PSP] *jumped* and [PST] *jumped* as somehow the same, despite their irreconcilable difference in i-features, and to treat [PRS, 1, SG] *jump* and [PRS, 3, PL] *jump* as somehow the same, despite their irreconcil-able difference in i-features, while treating [PSP] *run* and [PRS] *run* as distinct, despite their phonological identity. The difference is that be-tween systematic (motivated, morrule-governed) and fortuitous (acci-dental) phonological identity. The full set of forms is partitioned into subsets of forms that are phonologically identical by virtue of morrule application; each such subset I will call an "m-form." It may well be that it is m-forms that linguists usually have in mind when they talk about "forms" or "inflected words."

I have to stress here that I am not proposing <u>representations</u> for a lexeme's set of entries. I am merely trying to make some essential conceptual distinctions in the underlying logic. I am not concerned here with how parochial generalizations or theoretical principles might be embedded in a system of representations, or whether sys-tems of representation can be devised that are perspicuous, efficient with respect to storage space and/or access time, or psycholinguistic-ally plausible, but rather with more fundamental issues, having to do with what sort of information should get represented in the first place.

Shapes

As if all this were not bad enough, there is another layer of lexeme-specific phonological alternation, involving not the i-features associated with Ws instantiating a lexeme, but instead the phonological and syntactic properties of the environments in which these Ws occur.

The English indefinite article lexeme has only one form (in the sense of "form" I am using here), but it still exhibits a phonological alternation between *a* and *an* (depending on the phonological environment of a W instantiating it). Welsh lexemes have various sets of forms, but for most lexemes – some are immune – each of these forms comes in a series of variants distinguished according to their initial consonants, and there seems to be no plausible way to treat this alternation (which depends on what syntactic construction the W instantiating the lexeme is in, on whether this W is initial in its constituent, and on what lexeme an immediately preceding W instantiates) as a matter of i-features. I will refer to English *a* and *an*, Welsh *cathod*, *gathod*, *chathod*, etc. (all versions of [PL] CATH "cat"), and similar examples as alternative "shapes" for the same form.

It appears that rather than associating a single phonrep with a v-set, an entry must (in general) provide an indexed set of phonreps, that is, an indexed set of shapes. The indices serve as pointers to particular shapes for the purposes of "shape rules" (SHRs),[3] which express generalizations about the association between an index and the phonology of a shape with that index. Entries are then organized in at least two dimensions, once by v-sets and once by these indices. Within-lexeme morrules of two types express generalizations about the two phonologically relevant dimensions within entries: IRs (the natural name would be "form rules"), expressing generalizations about the association between v-sets and phonology, and SHRs.

Some sort of articulation between the two dimensions, of forms and shapes, is obviously necessary. It appears that this is managed by having one special, <u>distinguished</u>, shape ("d-shape") in each set (note that I do not require that the d-shape have the same index in each entry for a single lexeme, or that d-shapes have the same index in parallel entries for different lexemes), which serves as the link between the two dimensions. IRs relate the d-shapes, and SHRs treat the d-shapes as defaults. This is (admittedly at some remove) an observation about factual matters, not a logical necessity.

Stems

In a very simple world, in the dream world of orthodox generative phonologists, for each lexeme there would be a single "stem," a single coherent collection of rudimentary information about the lexeme's phonological characteristics, a single "basic" or "underlying" phonrep, which would serve as the basis both for predicting d-shapes by IRs and for predicting the stems of other lexemes by cross-lexeme rules (so that it serves as the articulation between phonological information within lexemes and phonological relationships across lexemes). Once again, this is not the world we live in.

Indeed, there are problems with both parts of this proposal – with positing only one stem for the purposes of IRs and with positing only one stem for the purposes of cross-lexeme rules. The relevant phenomena are very familiar. In Russian, for instance, some verb lexemes have PST forms that use a stem that is one consonant (one dental stop, to be precise) shorter than the stem used by other forms (for the "place" verb, /kra/ in the PST, /krad/ otherwise). And for an Arabic verb lexeme, as discussed at length by McCarthy (1981), there is a whole series of stems, each used in one or more rules describing the phonology of related lexemes. Consequently, we must assume that for each lexeme there is an indexed set of stems, the indices serving as pointers to particular stems for the purposes of IRs and cross-lexeme rules.

Now the stem set for a lexeme is not itself an unorganized collection of phonreps. There are often systematic relationships between different stems, holding for whole classes of lexemes; these generalizations will be expressed by "stem rules" (STRs). Sometimes it is possible to hypothesize a single, perhaps strikingly underspecified, phonrep, an abstract stem (like the triconsonantal skeleton for verbs in the Semitic languages) which will serve as the basis for predicting several stems in this set, via other STRs. In general, there will one or more distinguished stems ("d-stems"), abstract or not, from which all the others can be predicted, either directly or through a series of predictions (with stem X predicted from a d-stem and stem Y predicted from stem X, for instance).

Elementary idiosyncratic lexemes

Much of the content of a morphicon is predictable, though much is not. STRs predict a lot of the stem list for a lexeme – in some instances, all of the stem list except one stem, though suppletive stems and other surprises (like the Latin verb stem *vert-* that is used in [PRF] forms and is anomalously identical to the stem used in the [PRS] and some other forms) pop up occasionally. IRs predict the association between v-sets and d-shapes – for some lexemes, in all of its details, though suppletive forms and other surprises (like the English [PSP] *run* anomalously identical to the [PRS]) pop up occasionally. SHRs predict the shape sets in forms – for some lexemes, in all of their details, though there are completely lexeme-specific alternations like the one between *a* and *an* in English.

There is at least one further type of within-lexeme rule, usually called "lexical redundancy rules" (LRRs). These express generalizations connecting different properties of lexemes, among them: syntactic subcategories to which the lexeme belongs; i-features associated with the lexeme (like gender for nouns); morphological properties, in particular "paradigm class" properties, which describe the set of IRs appropriate for the lexeme; phonological properties of some specified stem of the lexeme; and semantic properties of the lexeme. Though some of the properties of a lexeme are predictable via LRRs, some are surprises, and of course there must be some core of properties that follow from no others.

It is an important point, made in Jackendoff (1975) but insufficiently appreciated, that nothing guarantees that there is a unique minimal core of unpredictable information about lexemes, that there is only one way to reduce a redundant property structure to one that will serve for predicting the full structure by rules, cannot be further reduced without losing this first characteristic, and has no more properties stipulated than any property structure with the first two characteristics. Systems of the complexity of the typical morphicon will usually admit of multiple minimizations, thanks to the fact of mutual predictability (as when it is true both that nouns in a particular declension class are by default of the [MASC] gender and that nouns of the [MASC] gender are by default in that declension class). In fact, it seems to me that the whole project of minimization is doomed because it is ill-defined, there being no natural metric that will make comparable phonological properties (like monosyllabicity), paradigm class properties (like using a special rule for the [PSP] rather than the default), syntactic subcategory properties (like serving as a head verb in the subject-auxiliary inversion construction), i-features (like [FEM] gender), and aspects of meaning (like referring to an animal hunted for sport).

To return to rules predicting the content of a morphicon, there is also predictability via cross-lexeme rules. Some of these rules predict the entire content of certain lexemes, but again there are surprises (like the meaning of WOMAN-IZE) and again there must be some core of unpredictable lexemes, constituting the very large inventory of primary lexemes (HAPPY, KANGAROO, etc.). In fact, so much of the content of the morphicon is unpredictable that some linguists have come to look upon the morphicon as the location par excellence of idiosyncrasy. But it is clear that some lexemes are in no way (or only a bit) idiosyncratic and that many expression types with idiosyncratic associations of meaning and sound are not lexemes. (I have in mind certain affixes, like the /z/ verb suffix or the -*ness* of abstract nominals in English, and syntactic idioms, like GET NP'S GOAT or GIVE VOICE TO NP). There is simply another domain of concepts here, which has only a distant relationship to the morphicon as I have characterized it.

Much of the content of the syntacticon is unpredictable, though much is not, and the same is true of the morphicon. We might think of the unpredictable stuff as constituting distinguished subparts of the syntacticon and the morphicon (an "idiosyntacticon" and "idiomorphicon," together making up an "idiosyncraticon," along the lines of the suggestions in Zwicky 1989a), but it isn't clear to me that there is any theoretical advantage to taking this view, given my comments above about minimization. What is important is that generalizations about the morphicon are captured (this is what cross-lexeme rules, LRRs, STRs, IRs, and SHRs do), that generalizations about the syntacticon are captured (this is what syntactic rules of various types do), and that idiosyncratic associations of meaning and formal characteristics can be grounded in some finite list of elementary idiosyncratic tactemes.

The point is that the idiosyncrasies of the lexemes WOMANIZER, WOMANIZERISH, WOMANIZERISHLY, and the like should be grounded in the (partial) idiosyncrasy of WOMANIZE, and that the idiosyncrasies of the syntactemes NO VOICE BE GIVEN TO NP, NO VOICE BE LIKELY TO BE GIVEN TO NP, BE HARD FOR ANY VOICE TO BE LIKELY TO BE GIVEN TO NP, and the like should be grounded in the (partial) idiosyncrasy of GIVE VOICE TO NP, in both cases grounded via the mediation of cross-tacteme rules. The tacticon of a language is infinite, but it arises from finite collections of elementary idiosyncratic tactemes (roughly, but only roughly, what Di Sciullo and Williams 1987 call "listemes") as combined according to a finite set of cross-tacteme rules.

We might think of the full collection of elementary idiosyncratic lexemes as the "kernel" of the morphicon, the whole morphicon being predictable from this kernel via cross-lexeme rules. One way to interpret what has been called a "word-based" (as opposed to "morpheme-based") theory of morphology is that it takes this kernel as its primary object of description, consequently laying great stress on "the inheritance of irregularity, both semantic and phonological" (Aronoff 1988:768, who credits Booij 1987 with making inheritance a central matter; see also Zwicky 1987d).

CHOICES

Given this conceptual background, I turn now to various questions about how best to flesh out a framework for morphology. For some of these issues, a position has been foreshadowed in my initial discussion; for others, what I have said so far suggests no particular stand. I do not imagine that this list of issues is complete (see Zwicky 1989b, 1990a for discussion of some further choices, for the most part at a finer level of theoretical detail than the ones I consider here). No doubt the full range of morphological frameworks now under active consideration is on the order of McCawley's (1982) "thirty million theories of grammar."

In each subsection I oppose two ideas about morphology, maintaining in each case that some variant of the proposal listed first should be adopted over the other one. There are seventeen of these subsections, seven having to do with what I view as major fundamental issues in morphological theory today, ten treating subsidiary or background matters. The main points, which are so labelled in the text that follows, concern a full versus a minimal morphicon, static-condition versus derivational analyses in morphology, realizational versus combinatory morphology, autonomous morphology versus a unified morphosyntax, modular versus unitary morphology, monolayer versus layered morphology, and coanalysis of expressions versus lexemes that are coextensive with Ws.

Major issue: full versus minimal morphicon

Much of the literature on generative morphology maintains that there is a fundamental theoretical question as to whether something called "the lexicon" is full and highly redundant (so that morphological rules <u>describe</u> what is predictable within it), or minimal and redundancy-free (so that morphological rules <u>supply</u> what is predictable within it).

Now that we have cleared the conceptual underbrush a bit, it should be obvious that the two positions here are not necessarily incompatible. If "the lexicon" is the morphicon, then it is of course full; the morphicon is simply the domain of linguistic expression types that morphology concerns itself with. But there is also something that is both finite and notably less redundant than the morphicon in this sense, namely the kernel of the morphicon. The kernel is the list of lexemes that together with the set of cross-lexeme morrules provides an account of (what is predictable in) the full inventory of lexemes, and so is of some theoretical interest. But there can be no issue as to whether theorists should concern themselves with the morphicon or its kernel.

On the other hand, I can find no good place in a morphological framework for a truly minimal list of any sort. And every defense I have seen of a minimal morphicon, right up to Bromberger and Halle (1989), rests not on theoretical observations but rather on claims about the mental morphicon. Somehow, whenever theorists start talking about the morphicon they end up worrying about what people can keep in their heads.

Default-setting versus absolute rules

The morrules of a language are generalizations about the contents of the morphicon for that language. All generalizations about a particular language are, of course, subject to exceptions, and this observation is as true of morrules as of any other type. Consequently, all morrules must be seen not as placing absolute conditions on the contents of the morphicon, but rather as providing default settings. For instance, the form predicted by an IR might be pre-empted by a form predicted by a different IR rule (as when [PST] *hitted* is pre-empted by *hit*); the form might be pre-empted by some brute lexeme-particular property (as when [PST] *comed* is pre-empted by *came*); or there might be a lexeme-particular gap (as when the [PSP] for STRIDE is, for many speakers, missing).

The default-setting character of morrules leads to a methodological problem. When speakers can, without reflection, produce a series of lexemes, forms, or shapes that they have presumably neither heard nor spoken before and that conform to some generalization, then we have clear evidence that these speakers have grammars that incorporate this generalization in one way or another. We have some information about how the morphicon for such a speaker extends beyond the lexemes this speaker happens to have experienced. But there are generalizations, such as the one predicting "zero" [PST]s for a set of lexemes (HIT, SET, TREAD, etc.) with monosyllabic stems ending in /t d/, for which evidence from systematic novel creations is wanting. The methodological problem arises when we try to decide whether the weight of the evidence (and abundant counterevidence) warrants positing a morrule in situations like this one. I take this to be a question about the grammars of individual speakers, so that I take it for granted that speakers might differ considerably with respect to the generalizations captured in their grammars, but there is still the problem of deciding what the system is for any particular speaker. I believe there is no simple answer to this question, no index of rule-hood that can be calculated; the issue can be decided only by exploring the consequences that would follow from having, or not having, the rule in the grammar – which means that in many specific situations we will know of no way to remedy our ignorance.

Major issue: static-condition versus derivational analyses in morphology

Consider first an assemblage comprising syntactic and paradigm class properties, a stem, the i-features in a v-set, and a phonrep. How do IRs work to license such an assemblage, in particular to determine if the phonrep is the d-shape corresponding to the other properties? One way to view an IR is as a set of static conditions on the makeup of such assemblages. Another way is as part of a derivation; on this view, an IR is a set of conditions on the pairing of assemblages containing different phonreps, with the given assemblage licensed if it is derivable as the last in a licensed sequence of assemblages beginning with one that has the stem's phonrep as its phonrep.

Then consider the corresponding question for two lexemes, where we have two assemblages, each comprising at least syntactic and paradigm class properties, semantic properties, and a phonrep. How do DRs work to license such a pair, in particular to determine if the phonrep of the "derived" lexeme characterizes the stem corresponding to its other properties? Again, a DR can be viewed as a set of static conditions on the joint makeup of the two assemblages; or as a set of conditions on the pairing of assemblages having different phonreps, with the derived lexeme's assemblage licensed if it is derivable as the last in a licensed sequence of assemblages beginning with the other lexeme's.

Metatheoretical considerations always favour the static-condition view (though of course they yield to arguments from factual considerations). The point is that a derivational analysis has available to it auxiliary representations, representations other than those whose wellformedness is at issue. Auxiliary representations can provide "scratch space" for checking whether the given ones are licensed, but this scratch space is not available in the static-condition view. The result is that a derivational analysis cannot in general be translated into a static-condition analysis without at least loss of generalization (which arises from having to embed the conditions on one rule in another rule when collapsing them into a single rule). Derivational frameworks for IRs and DRs are thus inherently more powerful than static-condition frameworks; in the worst case, the scratch work available in a derivational framework can mimic the effect of any arbitrary

Turing machine. This is power we do not want to use unless we have to.

It appears that the power of derivational frameworks is needed in phonology (that is, for systems of rules that function merely to determine pronunciation, without also pairing semantics with phonology, as IRs and DRs do), but in morphology as in syntax I believe that a program of static conditions is at least plausible.

Martin Kay observed, in his comments on the presentation version of this paper, that since <u>reversibility</u> is a crucial consideration in computation, static-condition, or declarative, systems of description can be hard to distinguish from derivational, or procedural, systems when these are modelled computationally. Auxiliary representations vanish when two types of representations are associated via a reversible mapping, Kay pointed out. For theoretical linguists, however, there is still an issue here, which turns on matters of descriptive power and of linguistic adequacy (in particular, whether generalizations are necessarily lost when derivational descriptions are framed as static conditions).

Chained versus direct association between "basic" and "surface" phonreps

Does the phonological side of morphology involve a chain of associations between "basic" and "surface" phonreps, or will a single association suffice? The latter claim lies at the center of Koskenniemi's "two-level morphology," which has been influential in computational approaches to morphology. As Koskenniemi (1983:15) describes this proposal:

> The lexicon contains the morphophonological representations of word entries and endings. The phonemic surface level consists of phonemes, or letters of a phonemic alphabet. The essential difference between the two-level model and generative phonology is that in the former, there are <u>no intermediate stages</u> between the lexical and the phonemic representations. Instead, the two representations are directly related to each other. The relation is formulated with <u>parallel rules</u> which may refer to <u>both</u> of these two representations. Mathematically speaking, individual rules may be regarded as equations, and all rules together as a set of equations. The rules "do" nothing as such, they only test whether the correspondence is correct.

However, it seems that we cannot do without a certain number of auxiliary representations in morphology. Indeed, I have already argued that a (finite, and, one hopes, not very large) set of stems must be available for each lexeme, and these stems can serve as auxiliary representations.

Consider how we determine if [PST, MASC] /kral/ is licensed as a form of the "place" verb lexeme in Russian. The relevant IR stipulates that the suffix /l/ appears in the [PST] and that stem X is used in the [PST]. When we ask whether /kra/ is in fact licensed as stem X for this lexeme, we appeal to a STR that relates a stem Y ending in a dental stop to a stem X that lacks this consonant, so that we ask whether this lexeme has a stem Y /krat/ or /krad/ (or /kra/, on which the STR would have no effect). Indeed, the lexeme in question has a stem X /krad/, and we conclude that [PST, MASC] /kral/ is licensed. Notice that this reasoning involves an appeal to the phonrep /krad/, which is not present in the representation we were checking in the first place.

Similar remarks hold for shapes. Determining that the Welsh "soft mutation" shape *weld* represents the [INF] form of the verb lexeme meaning "see" means determining that this form has *gweld* as its d-shape, there being a SHR relating d-shapes with initial /g/ to soft mutation shapes lacking this consonant.

Such references to auxiliary representations, even if they involve invocations of several phonreps in turn, do not of course bring upon us the full power of derivational frameworks, since the auxiliary representations in question are finite in number (and supplied in the morphicon).

Static versus dynamic logic for rule interactions

In a static-condition framework, interactions between rules follow (as in Zwicky 1989c) from a logic of overrides and invocations, involving both parochial stipulations and principled predictions as to these relations between rules.

The scheme of rule interactions in Zwicky (1989c) is not in general reversible, and so is not an attractive one for computational implementation. Reversibility can be achieved, but at the cost of linguistic generalizations. Consider what it would take to make the following conditions reversible: (a) the yes-no question construction (C1) in *Had Chris clapped?* invokes (or uses) the subject-auxiliary inversion (SAI) construction exemplified in the clause *had Chris clapped*; (b) the main-clause information question construction (C2) in *When had Chris clapped?* invokes SAI; (c) the fronted negation construction (C3) in *Never had Chris clapped* invokes SAI; (d) the conjunctionless counterfactual conditional construction (C4) in *Had Chris clapped, we would have blushed* invokes SAI; (e) the subject-VP (SVP) construction in

Chris had clapped is the default with respect to SAI. It can be done; we state one condition determining SAI (if C1 or C2 or C3 or C4, then SAI) and one determining SVP (if neither C1 nor C2 nor C3 nor C4, then SVP). But of course this description refers to each of C1 through C4 twice, and so misses generalizations.

In derivational frameworks (for any component[s] of grammar), interactions between rules are a matter of applicational sequence, or ordering, and the question arises as to whether these orderings can always be predicted by universal principles or whether parochial stipulations are required in some instances. Metatheoretical considerations lead us to hope for the former, since derivational frameworks with parochially stipulated ordering are more powerful still than frameworks without it; see the discussion by Pullum (1979), who reviews the situation in syntax (building on the work of Koutsoudas and his colleagues) and concludes that the program of universally determined ordering is well supported there. Matters are none too clear in phonology (but see the survey in Zwicky 1987c, which gives hope for universally determined ordering there) or in morphology (though Zwicky 1987b suggests optimism here as well).

However, not only do almost all generative morphologists adopt a derivational framework, most of them also allow parochial ordering restrictions to get the effect of feeding and bleeding. This is true even of relatively modular frameworks, such as those of Anderson (1986) (where inflectional and derivational morphology are separate modules) and Kiparsky (1982) (where there are layers of morphology – see *Major issue: monolayer versus layered morphology*, below – that do not necessarily correspond to the inflectional/derivational division).

Rules as functions versus rules as (general) relations

Static-condition versions of morrules (of all types) can be viewed as having some directionality, of course: the logical directionality that obtains if the relation described by the rule is a function from one set of morphological objects to another.

Despite occasional claims to the contrary (in particular, by Ford & Singh 1985a, 1985b), I will maintain that morrules of most types are in fact functions, rather than merely relations of any sort whatsoever. I have already adopted this position implicitly in my discussion of DRs, IRs, SHRs, and LRRs. But I will not assume that STRs are always functions; that is, I will not assume that stem sets generally exhibit the sort of internal organization characteristic of shape sets, given the arguments in Spencer (1988) and Perlmutter (1988), among other places, that stem X can be paired with stem Y without instances of either being uniquely derivable from the instances of the other. Such demonstrations arise from situations where distinct X_1 and X_2 are systematically paired with a single Y, while a single X is systematically paired with distinct Y_1 and Y_2.

In situations like these there must be multiple d-stems (in more traditional terms, multiple underlying representations). This is a matter left open in my earlier discussion (*Stems*).[4]

I should point out that for certain types of rules the question of functionhood can be separately entertained for rules as wholes and for the phonological relationships within them.

Rules as redundancy predictors versus rules as generators of the morphicon

The issue of a full/minimal morphicon intersects with the issue of functionhood for rules, in particular cross-lexeme rules. If a full morphicon is assumed, then the purpose of morrules is to describe regularity, redundancy, predictability within it. If a minimal morphicon is assumed, then the purpose of morrules is to generate the full morphicon from this minimal object by supplying redundant or predictable properties.

Gaps in the set of lexemes have different consequences depending on which view we take. Gaps are of two types, missing sources and missing derivatives, and (as is well known) both are attested: CORRODE - CORROSION - CORROSIVE, *AGGRESS - AGGRESSION - AGGRESSIVE (missing source), INCITE - *INCITION - *INCITIVE (missing derivatives).[5] In a minimal morphicon framework, missing derivatives can be described via rule features on the input; INCITE is not subject to the DR building abstract nominals with -(*t*)*ion* or the one building adjectives in -*ive*. But missing sources can apparently be described only by some extraordinary move – via ghost lexemes like AGGRESS, via truncation or replacement rules (treating AGGRESSIVE as derived from AGGRESSION, as in Aronoff 1976), or whatever. Otherwise, the DRs in question are not functions.

The problem does not arise in a full lexeme framework, since the effect of a DR is not only to relate sources to derivatives but also to predict that the morphicon should contain lexemes with the properties of these derivatives. We would not posit a DR in the first place if there weren't <u>some</u> source lexemes, but there is no problem if some sources are missing.

Major issue: realizational versus combinatory morphology

How do phonreps get associated with meanings in morphology

(whether directly, via IRs or DRs, or indirectly, via STRs)? Is this association to be viewed as the realization of meanings via operations on stems (in a "process-based" framework), or as the combination of stems with morphemes expressing the meanings (in a "morpheme-based" framework)?[6]

There is no dispute here that suffixal and prefixal morphology is the norm. There is also no dispute that other schemes – infixes, inter-digitations, segment shifts, reduplications, metatheses, and subtractions (with various subtypes of each) – occur with respectable frequency in the languages of the world. A realizational approach to morphology, as advocated in Zwicky (1988) and Anderson (1988a), tries to assimilate concatenative morphology (that is, affixations) to the other schemes by treating them all as operations on phonreps. A combinatory approach, as advocated by McCarthy (1979, 1981), and many others since, tries to assimilate the nonconcatenative schemes to affixations by treating them all as assemblages of independently meaningful morphemes.

The frameworks are not as different as might at first appear. Realizational morphology must have its combinatory aspects; not only must prefixes and affixes be distinguished, but also, since inflectional morphology tends to have a flat structure (as Lounsbury (1957:384) observed, we often see a number of inflectional affixes in sequence but have no reason to assign internal structure to the sequence),[7] IRs that affix material must stipulate which "slot" the material fills. And combinatory morphology must have its realizational aspects, since feature operations (of copying, spreading, docking, association, reassociation, dissociation, whatever) are required to get phonological features assigned to the right segments, and these are parochially stipulated at least to the extent that one must say which rules use which operations.

There is a certain amount of morphological literature (stretching at least from Lieber 1981, Marantz 1982, and McCarthy's early work already cited, through Martin 1988) in which realizational morphology is opprobriously characterized as "transformational," presumably because for generative linguists syntactic transformations are the formal operations par excellence. The suggestion is that with a realizational framework and its formal operations (but not with a combinatory framework) comes the juggernaut of transformational grammar. Now this is simply false if the realizational framework is of the static-condition, rather than derivational, variety. Indeed, a combinatory framework with derivations must itself find a way to step out of the juggernaut's path.

Transformational doom is avoided in combinatory frameworks by three further choices, which I consider in the three following subsections. The first of these an intelligent realizational framework should make as well. The two others, which I am dubious about, together have the effect of claiming that there is no morphological component of grammar, independent of syntax and phonology. Such proposals admit that there are morphological objects of analysis, namely lexemes, and that there are rules describing them, but maintain that these rules are of exactly the same sort as the rules of (phrase structure) syntax, their phonological consequences following entirely via the operations of (automatic) phonology. Obviously some metatheoretical advantage attends proposals of this sort, since they simplify the ontology of rule types posited in a grammatical framework. The question is whether this metatheoretical simplification is justified by the facts.

A finite versus an infinite operation set

Transformational grammar lent itself to a formalization in which a "rule of grammar" was any operation describable by composing some number of elementary operations chosen from a finite kernel; crudely, a rule was anything you could represent in the formalism provided for this purpose. As a result, the set of formal operations available, that is, the set of possible rules, was infinite.

This is obviously a dangerous move metatheoretically, and virtually all modern grammatical frameworks propose to limit the set of formal operations to an effectively finite collection, via both formal and substantive restrictions. In the scheme for realizational morphology of Zwicky (1988), for instance, there is a (universally given) finite kernel of specific operations (reduplicate the first syllable, affix /d/ in slot X, etc.) that any given rule can use.[8] And there is a (universally given) finite limit on the number of operations any particular rule can use in concert; the limit follows in part from a formal incompatibility between many pairs of operations and in part from the fact that there is some universal, and not very large, upper limit on the number of slots available in inflection.

Distinct m-ops versus p-ops for both morphology and phonology

A striking difference between the realizational framework of Zwicky (1988) and most current combinatory frameworks is that I posit a set of operations (I'll call them "m-ops") used by morphological rules that is distinct from the set of operations (I'll call them "p-ops") that figure in the rules of automatic phonology, while the combinatory morphologists assume that there is only a single set here, and that it is phonological in character. (It is probably not an accident that so many of these combinatory morphologists started out as phonologists.) The latter claim is explicit in Martin (1988:236) ("The operations available in morphology are exactly the operations available in phonology"), who cites McCarthy (1979) as the source of the idea.

My position is not of course that the two sets of operations have nothing to do with one another, but rather that the m-ops are (historically) morphologized p-ops – p-ops that have come to be viewed as markers of meaning in morphology and so can be expected to exhibit the telescopings, inversions, and other reinterpretations that accompany morphologization. The two sets of operations will thus bear a family resemblance to one another, but we cannot expect every m-op to have a plausible treatment as a p-op or sequence of p-ops. In Zwicky (1988) I used umlaut in modern German and "(trisyllabic) shortening/laxing" in modern English as paradigm examples of m-ops that are not p-ops, and it would be easy to extend the list for pages, with soft mutation in Welsh, velar softening in English, and so on.

The response of combinatory morphologists in such cases is to maintain that the phonological relationships described by the m-ops at issue can always be decomposed into p-ops; see, for instance, the heroic (and quite divergent) efforts along these lines by Yip (1987) and Myers (1985, 1987) for English laxing, and the general negative answer provided by Lieber (1987) to "the question of whether phonology and morphology require two different sets of principles for dealing with sound patterns of languages" (Archangeli 1988:792). Aside from the question of whether the proposed analyses cover the facts as intended,[9] it seems to be a constant feature of these decompositions that they require parochial stipulations as to the order of application of the p-ops they appeal to. Usually this is a matter of assigning two "phonological rules" to different layers of a layered morphology (see *Major issue: monolayer versus layered morphology*, below), but that is still parochial stipulation. Presumably, with some ingenuity it will always be possible to mirror a diachronic sequence of p-ops as a synchronic one and so to translate any m-op analysis into a p-op counterpart, but I would scarcely view stipulated ordering of rules as a good trade for a bit of ontological simplification (especially if it turns out that there are other reasons not to adopt the layered framework).

Distinct morphotactics versus phrase-structure morphology-syntax

The other striking characteristic of current combinatory frameworks (Williams 1981, Kiparsky 1982, and Selkirk 1982 are representative texts) is that they import the main features of phrase-structure syntax into morphology and treat the two domains as subject to the same general principles of organization – in particular, that constructs are made up of a head of category X and an argument of category Y, that the construct belongs to the same category (X) as its head, and that the head is subcategorized for occurrence with arguments of category Y. Morphology is then, in Selkirk's words, "the syntax of words" (in my terms, the tactics of lexemes).

At least for category-changing derivational morphology in a combinatorial framework, it follows that the affixes are the heads; on this account, *-ness* is a head N sub-categorized to combine with a preceding ADJ argument. In a realizational framework, the morphological rule itself not only specifies the relationship between the category of the source and the category of the derivative, but also selects the affix; on this account, a DR relates source ADJs to derivative Ns, the phonological content of this relation being an operation appending *-ness* to the source. There is not much to choose between the two views at this level. But there are two further questions to answer: Do other syntactic principles have morphological counterparts? Do other types of morphological tactics find a natural treatment in similar terms? I believe that the short answer to both questions is no.

No other syntactic characteristics in morphology

(I'll confine myself largely to category-changing derivational morphology here, since this has been the primary domain for discussions of combinatory morphology.) The big point here is that essentially no characteristics of syntax beyond the ones already mentioned carry over to morphology, and these are simply the characteristics of what I called the "determinant" (morphological or syntactic) in Zwicky (1985a).

First, alternative orderings of head and argument are common in syntax, but there are no good parallels in morphology.

Second, syntactic constituents normally admit optional modifiers, but no (putative) morphological constituents do.

Third, syntactic heads frequently agree in various properties with their arguments, but there is no parallel property sharing between a derivational affix and its stem.

Fourth, syntactic constructions can require that some immediate constituent must contain one or more lexemes of some specified type, as the English focused negation construction does with respect to negative lexemes in its initial constituent (as in *At no time did I claim that pigs could fly*), but morphological constructions do not do so. Indeed, the very idea of "strict cyclicity" (Kiparsky 1982), according to which the morphological composition of a lexeme is not available to morphological rules building on that lexeme, presupposes that such containment conditions do not occur in morphology.

Fifth, there are special elements (including zeroes) available in syntax – sometimes filling the head position, sometimes the argument position – for the purposes of deixis, anaphora, and indefinite reference. There are no special elements (zero or otherwise) devoted to these purposes in derivational morphology. There is, for instance, no way to suppress an argument of a putative head in morphology when this head can be supplied from context, the way object NP arguments can be suppressed in syntax (as in *The deer moved to the stream and drank* or *Terry didn't know if pigs could fly, and Tracy wouldn't say*); there is nothing like *They were sad, and their-ness bothered me* (or for that matter, *Their sadness bothered me, but not their happy*, with a suppressed head).

Sixth, certain properties of syntactic constructs are normally realized as special forms of the head, via inflectional morphology (which can be nonconcatenative as well as concatenative). Derived lexemes do have inflectional forms, of course, but the properties in question are not realized by material affixed specifically to the putative head constituent, that is, the derivational affix (this would mean that the internal structure of a form like *sadnesses* would have to be SAD + [NESS + ES]) or by an operation specifically on this head, which would predict that the normal scheme for nonconcatenative inflection would be an alteration specifically in the phonology of derivational affixes.

Morphotactic phenomena not in syntax

For morphotactics of some interest, I turn to inflectional morphology, where affixes flourish. The phenomena we see there call for a descriptive scheme rather different from the combinatory rules of syntax, something more like the morpheme order charts of the structuralist morphologists (for instance, Harris 1951:Ch. 19) or the slot and filler formulas of tagmemics (Cook 1969:Ch. 1, with references to the primary literature), something very close, in fact, to the templates proposed by Perlmutter (1971) for stating conditions on the combinability and sequencing of bound word clitics. What we want is a realizational framework incorporating a "slot calculus" of the sort sketched in Zwicky (1990a).

First, while there is always default semantic content associated with a slot in an ordinary syntactic construction, the slots of inflectional morphology and of clitic groups are not necessarily characterizable in semantic terms.[10] For English verb forms, for instance, there is only one slot, which is filled by material representing either a nonfinite category ([PRP] or [GER] in *jumping*, [PSP] in *jumped*) or a finite category ([PRS, 3, SG] in *jumps*, [PST] in *jumped*); there is no common semantic content to these suffixes. For clitic groups it is commonplace for the host slot to lack any semantic characterization, as when the host is the first W of a clause, and it is reasonably common for some of the clitic slots to be characterized phonologically rather than semantically, as when Tagalog (Schachter 1974) puts its monosyllabic pronominal clitics in clitic slot 1 and its disyllabic pronominal clitics in slot 3.

Second, there are plenty of "zeroes" in inflectional morphology, by which I mean that the absence of phonological substance stands in a paradigmatic relationship to the presence of meaningful phonological substance. Consider what a combinatory framework must say about the simple fact that the English form *child* is specifically [SG] (in contrast to the [PL] *children*) and [NOM/ACC] (in contrast to the [SG, GEN] *child's* and the [PL, GEN] *children's*). I can see two sorts of analyses, neither of which is entirely satisfactory.

One possibility would be to posit that all English noun forms have two inflectional suffixes, either SG or PL immediately following the stem, and either NOM/ACC or GEN immediately after that; the morphemes SG and NOM/ACC are both stipulated to be always without phonological substance. This line of analysis requires stipulated zeroes all over the place – as Zwicky (1985b) observes, forms that are just unaltered stems are extremely common in the inflectional morphology of the world's languages – and it misses a generalization that a realizational approach captures nicely: that absence of inflectional material gains its meaning by virtue of its opposition to actually present material. A realizational approach can say that all forms use a stem, which is altered only when some rule stipulates this. Thus, given that English has a rule for the [3, SG, PRS] of verbs and no rules for the other combinations of persons and numbers in the present tense, we predict that the normal verb lexeme of the language has five [PRS] forms with shapes identical to its stem.

This first sort of analysis might be acceptable in a computational setting. The stipulation of affixes that are present in morphological analysis but are without phonological content will serve to keep the mapping between morphology and phonology reversible, and reversibility is, as I noted above, an important goal in implementations of linguistic descriptions. But, as before, the pursuit of reversibility forces a loss of linguistic generalizations.

An alternative for the number and case forms of nouns in a combinatory approach would be to stipulate that the [SG, NOM/ACC] form is identical to the stem and that the other forms are built on this form, rather than on the stem itself; *children's* would then be [CHILD, SG, NOM/ACC] + PL + GEN. This avoids the stipulation of zeroes, but at a considerable cost, namely that we have to stipulate the forms that are identical to the stem, rather than those that are not (a particularly distasteful necessity for English [PRS] verb forms, where we would have to stipulate that a form is identical to the stem if it either is not [3] or is [PL]), and we also have to give up a simple additive semantics for inflectional affixes, in favour of a scheme in which, whenever there is a conflict, the semantics of an affix overrides the semantics of the constituent with which it combines.

Third, in addition to the "zeroes" of the sort just discussed there are plenty of "zero" examples of another sort in inflectional morphology. These arise when an affix is suppressed under some phonological condition. Consider, to choose four well-known examples, the failure of the English [GEN] /z/ to appear in forms already ending in a /z/ affix (compare *kids'* and *anyone who replies' responsibilities* with *children's* and *anyone who replied's responsibilities*); the failure of the German [PL] schwa to appear for noun stems that end in schwa plus a sonorant (*das Zimmer* "the room," *die Zimmer* "the rooms" versus *das Schaf* "the sheep (SG)," *die Schafe* "the sheep (PL)"); the failure of of the Russian [PST] /l/ to appear for verb stems ending in a consonant (/pek/ "he baked" versus /pek-l-a/ "she baked"); and the failure of *ge-* to appear in German [PSP] forms for verb stems that do not begin with an accented syllable (*trompetet* "trumpeted" and *versagt* "denied" versus *ge-sagt* "said"). For the first three of these examples, a combinatory framework cannot simply block the appearance of the relevant affix under phonological conditions, for doing so would not supply a morpheme bearing the relevant semantics; apparently, these affixes must be inserted and then deleted, though so far as I know there is never any evidence that such forms in fact have any sort of affix in them.

Fourth, there are discontinuous selections of affixes in inflectional morphology. The German [PSP] forms, which combine a prefix *ge-* and a suffix *-t* or *-en* (*ge-sag-t* "said," *ge-nomm-en* "taken"), give a simple example of this discontinuity. Here it is possible to treat one of the affixes as secondary to, or parasitic on, the other – the occurrence of the prefix as dependent on the occurrence of a suffix, say – but this option does not seem to be available in the general case. Consider the expression of tense/aspect (T/A) and negation in Swahili verbs, for instance. The relevant slot template is, crudely, (NEG) - SUBJ - T/A - (OBJ) - STEM. Matters are straightforward in the future, which has *ta-* in the third slot and the negative marker *ha-* optionally in the first. For the past and perfect, however, the occurrence of *ha-* in the first slot requires the occurrence of special T/A markers in the third slot, and for the two presents, the occurrence of *ha-* requires both the absence of a marker in the third slot and the selection of a verb stem in *-i* rather than *-a* (I have capitalized the T/A markers):

wa-TA-[som-a] "they will read"	ha-wa-TA-[som-a] "they won't read"
wa-LI-[som-a] "they did read"	ha-wa-KU-[som-a] "they didn't read"
wa-ME-[som-a] "they have read"	ha-wa-JA-[som-a] "they haven't read"
w-A-[som-a]"they do read"	
	ha-wa- [som-i] "they don't read,
wa-NA-[som-a]"they are reading"	aren't reading"

The information that a form is negative thus appears in two out of three possible places within the form (which two depending on the tense/aspect in question), and no two of these three places are contiguous to one another. In a realizational framework, nothing prohibits multiple exponents of the same feature or a single exponent for a set of features; we can say in one rule that *ha-* in the first slot realizes [+NEG], and in others that *ta-* in the third slot realizes [T/A:FUT], that *li-* in the third slot realizes [T/A:PST, -NEG], that *ku-* in the third slot realizes [T/A:PST, +NEG], that the stem in *-a* is the default, that the stem in *-i* is used for [T/A:PRS, +NEG], and so on. A combinatory approach would apparently have to choose some "basic" set of fillers for the slots and map these into the actually occurring material by context-sensitive rules of replacement (replacing *li* by *ku*, say, / NEG + SUBJ + ___) and deletion (deleting *a* and *na*, say, / NEG + SUBJ + ___).

Fifth, in addition to contextually determined suppletive variants (as in the Swahili *li* - *ku* alternation), inflectional morphology occasionally exhibits portmanteau realizations of affix sequences, as when Swahili [NEG] verbs with [1, SG] subjects have *si* - where we would have expected *ha-ni-* (*sitasoma* "I won't read"); and contextually determined variant affix orders (also known as "morph(eme) metathesis"), as when the [2]-subject affixes, [SG] *u-* and [PL] *ni-*, of Swazi (Ziervogel 1952) follow the [NEG] affix in [INDIC] forms (*ka-u-vali*, *ka-ni-vali* "you don't choose") but precede it in [IMPER] forms (*u-nga-vali*, *ni-nga-vali* "choose!"). There are well known parallels in the world of bound word clitics: contextually determined suppletive variants, as when "spurious *se*" occurs instead of the first of two third-person clitics in Spanish (Perlmutter 1971); portmanteau realization, as when *kita* occurs instead of any combination of the second-person clitics *ka* and *ko* in Tagalog (Schachter 1974); and contextually determined variant orders, as when first- and second-person clitics precede third-person [ACC] clitics with [INDIC] verb forms but follow them with [IMPER] verb forms in French (*Tu me le donnes* "you give it to me" but *Donne-le-moi* "give it to me!").

Now a combinatory morphology certainly can manage to describe facts like these, but apparently only at the cost of developing a fresh – and derivational – theory of rules that replace, delete, and reorder inflectional affixes within their forms and clitics within their groups. There is nothing truly comparable in garden-variety syntax. We do not have situations where some specific verb lexeme is missing, or is replaced by some other verb lexeme, just in case a specific noun lexeme serves as its object; or where some specific combination of verb and object-noun lexemes is always replaced by a special lexeme; or where some specific combination of verb and object-noun lexemes occurs in one order in the [INDIC] but another order in the [IMPER]. (General ordering principles of this sort do of course occur, but what is notable about the inflectional and clitic facts is their item-specificity.)

Major issue: autonomous morphology versus unified morphosyntax

Most current morphological frameworks draw a sharp line between the domain of lexemes and their properties, on the one hand, and the domain of constituents and syntactemes and their properties, on the other, and for good reason. I will do the same, with the intention of having a Principle of Morphology-Free Syntax (PMFS), a Principle of Syntax-Free Morphology (PSFM), and a No Phrase Constraint (NPC) all follow from this component division.

The PMFS – variants of which are known as the Lexicalist Hypothesis (see the summary in Scalise 1984:101-2), Atomicity (Di Sciullo & Williams 1987:Ch. 3), or the Lexical Integrity Hypothesis – says that a synrule has no access to the morphological composition, or the purely morphological properties, of the lexemes instantiated by the Ws whose distribution it describes. This is the analogue, in the morphology-syntax interface, of the strictness of strict cyclicity. The PSFM says that a morrule has no access to the syntactic properties of the expressions within which the lexemes and forms it describes are instantiated. This is the analogue, in the morphology-syntax interface, of the cyclicity of strict cyclicity, according to which you can't refer to properties that are available only on a cycle external to the one you're on. The NPC (see the discussions in Scalise 1984:154-6; Bates 1988:sec. 3.5) says that a morrule builds only on objects from the morphicon (stems, lexemes, forms, or shapes), not on constituents or syntactemes.

I must point out that there are facts that might be taken as suggesting that morphology and syntax together form a single component of linguistic description (a morphosyntax, or tactics), as in early transformational grammar (Lees 1960), in some of the tagmemic literature (Elson & Pickett 1983), and in recent work by Mark Baker (1985, 1988a, 1988b). These include (a) the very common phenomenon of alternation between or co-occurrence of "particle lexemes" and inflectional morphology, as when English has alternative comparative expressions (*handsomer, more handsome*) and Swedish marks definiteness doubly (*det store huset* "the big house," with both the definite article *det* and the definite inflectional suffix *-et*); (b) the tendency for syntactic argument possibilities to be preserved in derivational morphology, as when the constituents of a clause like *The serfs rebel against the landowners* reappear within an NP, in *the rebellion of the serfs against the landowners*; (c) the reproduction of phrasal syntax to some degree within lexemes, as in the "synthetic compounds" *apple eater* and *purple-eyed*; and (d) lexeme-internal constituents that bear syntactic relations outside the Ws that instantiate their lexemes, as in the noun incorporations discussed by Sadock (1985).

Counterbalanced against these are the familiar differences between the organization of morphemes within Ws and the organization of Ws within Ps (phrases): morpheme order is nearly always fixed, whereas "free variation" in the order of Ws is common; many W-internal morphemes are bound, whereas most Ws instantiate (free) lexemes; constituents of Ws cannot be separated by interposed syntactic units, whereas constituents of Ps often can be; the principles governing prosody and segmental phonology within Ws are different from those operative within Ps; and nonconcatenative morphology frequently serves as an alternative to affixal morphology, but serves as an alternative to independent Ws within Ps only for Ws instantiating particle lexemes.

The PMFS is supported by the fact that properties of individual affixes – their phonological shapes or even their (non)occurrence – seem to be irrelevant for syntactic purposes; only the corresponding (abstract) syntactic properties of whole Ws are germane. The fact that the forms *dogs*, *cats*, and *horses* have (automatic allomorphs of) the regular [PL] suffix, that *oxen* has a special [PL] suffix, and that *sheep* has no suffix at all plays no role in English syntax, which cares only about the i-feature [PL]. Similarly, the fact that HAPPINESS has one derivational suffix, that GAIETY has another, and that JOY has none at all plays no role in English syntax, which cares only that all these lexemes belong to the syntactic category of abstract nouns. Stems in derivation and inflection are also syntactically inert; they cannot, for instance, be extracted or replaced by pro-forms of any sort (*What did you want-ists in your band?*, *I wanted people to play guitar, so I called it-ists*).

The PSFM is supported by the fact that IRs and DRs seem not to be contingent on the syntactic surroundings of the Ws instantiating the lexemes they describe, except insofar as this environment requires forms with certain i-features or lexemes belonging to certain syntactic (sub)categories. For instance, whether a noun lexeme has a [PL] form at all, or which declension class its [PL] form is drawn from, depends only upon properties of the lexeme and its stem and not upon what sort of syntactic construction it finds itself instantiated in, and similarly for the ability of a noun lexeme to serve as source in a DR describing diminutive derivatives.

Feature versus formative interface between syntax and morphology

The PMFS, PSFM, and NPC all follow automatically if synrules and morrules constitute separate components of grammar, if a realizational rather than combinatory view of morphology is taken, and if the interface between syntax and morphology is managed entirely via (abstract) features – in particular, syntactic (sub)category features, i-features, and "shape properties" (triggering SHRs and prosodic domain formation) – rather than by having syntactic formatives that correspond to the affixes of morphology.

A formative interface between syntax and morphology is one hallmark of early generative grammar, where we routinely find affixes manipulated (inserted, moved, regrouped, conflated, and deleted) by syntactic rules. Consider, for example, the famous Affix Hopping rule of English (the "Auxiliary Transformation" of Chomsky 1957), which reorders and regroups the "underlying" material PRS (HAVE + EN) (BE + ING) DANCE into (HAVE + PRS) (BE + EN) (DANCE + ING), which is to say, *had been dancing*. In Lees (1960) this rule is extended systematically to derivational morphology, where it serves to yield *dancer* from ER + DANCE and *happiness* from NML + HAPPY. But not only is the familiar Affix Hopping analysis undesirable on metatheoretical grounds, it also suffers from a number of grave difficulties in its interactions with other parts of the analysis of English (subject-auxiliary inversion, the placement of the supportive modal lexeme DO, and the description of the negator *n't*), to the extent that it has been described as "more a liability than an advertisement for transformational grammar" (Gazdar, Pullum, & Sag 1982:614, where an alternative analysis is sketched that improves on Affix Hopping on every front, including adherence to the PMFS).

Major issue: modular versus unitary morphology

Should we posit a number of subcomponents of morphology, or should morphology be viewed as a single system? I opt for a modular approach, indeed for a particular version of this approach in which at least STRs, DRs, IRs, and SHRs are distinguished. (Further subcomponents will be suggested below.)

One attractive consequence of modularity is that it allows for the prediction of huge classes of rule interactions through the "natural cyclicity" imposed by the nature of the modules themselves. Consider the particular brand of modular morphology that I am espousing here. An STR describes a stem, so it applies before any rule (IR or DR, or for that matter, another STR) that uses that stem. A DR describing derivatives that can themselves serve as sources to another DR naturally applies before it. A DR describes a stem for a derivative lexeme, so it applies before any IR describing forms of that lexeme, which in turn applies before any SHR describing shapes for certain of these forms.

One objection to this sort of modular view is that it misses the generalization that exactly the same sort of operations (m-ops, I would say, though objectors usually suppose they are p-ops) figure in all the posited subcomponents, whatever these happen to be. Admittedly, in a modular view it must be stipulated that there is a set of operations available for all types of morrules, but then something similar must be said about the kinds of features and conditions on feature distribution that play a role in synrules of various sorts. I can't see that there is a problem here.

It may be that objectors are inclined to think that each (sub)component of a grammar must constitute a representational <u>level</u>, that is, a set of representations on a symbolic inventory unique to that component. Distinctness in representational level provides a strong argument for component separation, but I can see no support for the converse reasoning, no grounds for insisting that separate components must be distinct representational levels.

Another objection, which would follow from the expectation that distinct components should be distinct representational levels, is that the line between derivation and inflection (which plays some role in nearly all modular approaches) is not a formal difference and so is hard to draw in particular instances. The line between verbs and adjectives is hard to draw sometimes, too, and so is the line between subjects and direct objects. But in all of these cases there is a clear distinction between prototypical instances – the clear instances of derivation have the function of extending the morphicon by predicting sets of lexemes from others, the clear instances of inflection provide forms of lexemes to serve as marks of syntactic constructions – and there is a set of classificational rules of thumb that either follow from the properties of the prototypical instances (as does the fact that IRs are external to DRs) or are associated with the classifications in a language-particular way (as is the fact that in English only derivation is prefixal). More than this one cannot ask for in theorizing about the facts of the world.

(Thanks to Anderson 1982 and the response by Jensen and Stong-Jensen 1984, the discussion of derivation and inflection has been framed as a subquestion under the general heading, "Where is morphology?" Is it all "in the syntax" (with or without derivation and inflection being distinguished from one another), or is it all "in the lexicon" (again, with or without derivation and inflection being distinguished from one another), or is derivation "in the lexicon" and inflection "in the syntax?" (Scalise 1988 provides a summary of this tradition.) The only way I can unpack the spatial metaphors here so as to get a coherent theoretical claim – it makes no sense, for instance, to ask whether DRs and IRs are "in" the morphicon – is to reduce these issues to the PMFS, which does not seem to be in dispute in this literature and which in any event concerns derivation and inflection equally. There may be a theoretical issue here, but I haven't found it yet.)

Modular frameworks have also been scorned because they posit several "minicomponents" or "tiny modules," as Sadock (1985:383) puts it. This might just be another variant of the objections already considered, or it might be a metatheoretical claim that unitary frameworks are in general better than modular ones. The metatheoretical issue is a complex one. On the one hand, we do not want to posit components without good reason – this was the basis for my objection above to combinatory treatments that required a set of replacement, deletion, and reordering rules for inflectional morphology – but on the other hand, we want to place as many substantive constraints as possible on rules and their interactions, and modular frameworks lend themselves admirably to this purpose. These particular metatheoretical considerations simply don't decide the question at hand, and indeed I would not want to say that metatheoretical considerations can ever be said to <u>decide</u> a theoretical question.

Major issue: monolayer versus layered morphology

Having argued in favour of modular frameworks, I now turn to a particular type of modular framework, namely the "level-ordered" morphology of Kiparsky (1982) and Mohanan (1986), which I will not adopt here.

The key claim is that each morrule, or at least each DR and IR, can be stipulated as belonging to exactly one of a small finite set of linearly ordered components of morphology, which I will call "layers" (they are known in the trade as "levels" or "strata"), and that from this assignment follow a variety of properties of the morphological configurations that the rules describe, all having to do with what is intuitively the "closeness" of affixes to their stems. The properties in question are the following: (a) how close, in linear distance, an affix is from the ultimate stem within a form (the layers of affixes nesting within one another like Russian dolls or the layers of an onion); (b) how closely bound an affix is phonologically to the stem it attaches to (the affixes of the interior layers being tightly bound to, phonologically active with, their stems, and the affixes of the exterior layers being relatively independent of, phonologically inert with respect to, their stems); and (c) to some extent, how closely bound an affix is semantically to the stem it attaches to (the affixes of interior layers tending to be tightly bound to their stems in semantically idiosyncratic combinations, the affixes of exterior layers tending to be independent of their stems in semantically compositional combinations). (For the purposes of this exposition, I am pretending that all the world is affixes, rather than translating everything into terms that are neutral as between concatenative and nonconcatenative morphology.)

There is no doubt that there is a considerable tendency for these three sorts of properties – one having to do with morphotactics, one with morphophonology, and one with morphosemantics – to co-vary. Such co-variation is the natural result of historical change; we would expect interior layers to reflect older morphological formations, exterior layers more recent ones. A certain amount of co-variation also follows from the distinction between derivation and inflection, given that derivational morphology is both internal to inflectional morphology and more likely than inflectional morphology to be semantically idiosyncratic. The question is whether the layers, insofar as they do not simply reproduce the derivation-inflection distinction (as indeed they do not in any of the detailed layered analyses in the literature), should be treated as theoretical constructs.

Note that the scheme of layers does not follow (as does the distinction between derivational and inflectional morphology) from foundational considerations in grammatical theory. Layering is posited on the basis of observations about linguistic facts. This lack of grounding in an existing theory makes layering metatheoretically suspicious, on the one hand, but exciting to theoreticians, on the other, since we have the sense of discovering an unexpected fact about language, of being surprised by a hidden orderliness in our world. Neither the suspicion nor the excitement makes an argument, of course.

There is now a considerable destructive literature on layered morphology, which argues, by reference to various paradoxes in layer assignment in particular languages, that the hypothesis of layering brings in its train more problems than it solves; see the gloomy summary in Gussmann (1988:237-9). Much of this literature – I have in mind especially Aronoff and Sridhar (1983), Zwicky (1987b), Churma (1987), and Fabb (1988) – is also constructive, in that it suggests ways in which the very real facts that layering attempts to cope with (facts like the contrast between *Mendelianism* and **Mendelismian* in English) can be described without extraordinary theoretical steps.

For example, rather than stipulating layer assignments for a morrule, in some instances we stipulate eligibility conditions on the units the rule builds on (possibly including conditions on their purely morphological properties, such as belonging to the "Latinate" or "Anglo-Saxon" class of lexemes in English). In other instances we appeal to a distinction in stem types, stipulating that the morrule uses a particular stem (and hence appealing in turn to STRs); distinctions between "inner" or "primary" morphology and "outer" or "secondary" morphology (as in Sanskrit, or in the English distinction between comparative *-er* as in *longer* and agentive *-er* as in *singer*) are then distinctions between rules using one (root-like) stem and those using another (word-like) stem. In still other instances we appeal to assignments of the "phonological" rules to distinct components of the grammar, whose interaction is governed by universal principles; for example, nonautomatic phonological alternations are described in a component or components that are presupposed by the component(s) describing automatic alternations – this is the "rules before processes" arrangement of Donegan and Stampe (1979) – with the result that the (nonautomatic) regressive voicing assimilation in *left* "precedes" and consequently bleeds the (automatic) progressive voicing assimilation in *beefed* versus *heaved*.

Overlapping versus independent accounts of phrasal and isolation phonology

Can phonological variants that appear in phrasal contexts be described together with isolation variants, or do the two sorts of phonological variation always have separate accounts?

I assume (with virtually everyone who has considered the phenomena of external sandhi) that each form of a lexeme has a d-shape that serves as the default phonrep for describing the phonology of phrases, and I assume, along with Kaisse (1985) as well as with Kiparsky and Mohanan, that nonautomatic[11] phrasal phonology (a matter of "postlexical rules," in their terms) belongs to a separate component or components from lexeme-internal and form-internal phonological alternations (a matter of their "lexical rules"). The question is whether the formal apparatus for SHRs is significantly different from the apparatus for DRs and IRs (as, I would argue, the formal apparatus for nonautomatic phonology is significantly different from the apparatus for automatic phonology), or whether the formal resources a framework makes available to SHRs – these constitute the inventory of m-ops for SHRs – are shared with those for other phonological alternations (as the formal resourses for DRs are shared with those for IRs).

The simplest assumption from a metatheoretical point of view is that there is a single inventory of m-ops, available for STRs, DRs, IRs, and SHRs. The ones that serve in SHRs as well as in morrules of other types would be said to be involved in "rules used both postlexically and lexically" in Kiparskyan terms. Such m-ops are not uncommon. The Welsh consonant mutations, for example, serve not only in a variety of celebrated syntactic contexts, but also in DRs involving prefixes; Williams (1980:sec.187) lists prefixes requiring the "soft" mutation on the stems they combine with, others requiring the "spirant" mutation, and still others requiring the "nasal" mutation.

Note that the assumption is merely that the <u>framework</u> provides a single inventory of m-ops, not that the grammar of any particular language uses the same m-ops in SHRs as in other morrules. The proposal is perfectly consistent with a language that exhibits some m-ops used only in its SHRs and others never used in its SHRs.

I have no great stake in this assumption, and it would be possible to argue that substantive differences should be expected between the m-ops of SHRs, rules primarily serving a demarcative function, and the m-ops of DRs and IRs, rules primarily serving a signifying function. Certainly the differences in their predominant functions can be expected to lead to strong preferences for certain sorts of m-ops in SHRs and for other sorts in DRs and IRs – edge mutations are "good" m-ops for SHRs, while affixations are "good" m-ops for DRs and IRs, to speak of these things in the fashion of the natural morphologists (Dressler et al. 1987) – but that does not mean that these preferences should be elevated to theoretical restrictions. Indeed, if the semiotic considerations provide a sufficient account of the way in which m-ops are deployed in the grammars of the world's languages, there is no need for the theory of grammar to say anything on the matter.

Major issue: coanalysis of expressions versus lexemes that are co-extensive with Ws

With some awkwardness, I have maintained the conceptual distinction between Ws as syntactic (and syntagmatic) tokens and lexemes as morphological (and paradigmatic) types, which has meant talking about Ws that instantiate lexemes rather than simply about "words." This is not simply the stubbornness of someone with just enough training in logic to care about such things. There are morphosyntactically problematic phenomena – including, though not necessarily limited to, some of the things that have been labelled as compounds, incorporations, serializations, phrasal affixes, bound word clitics, and (syntactic) portmanteaus – that resist any simple analysis in which each W of syntax instantiates a single lexeme and each lexeme is instantiated by a single W. Sadock (1985) and Di Sciullo and Williams (1987) make this point very clearly, though with a rather different set of conceptual distinctions and theoretical hypotheses from mine, and from each other's.[12]

First, there are lexemes whose parts act as Ws syntactically. Compounds, for instance, are lexemes built (by "compounding rules," or CORs, formally parallel to DRs) on two or more lexemes, each represented by one of its stems or one of its forms. Syntactically, compounds are Ws composed of Ws; that their parts are Ws can be seen in co-ordination examples like *plumbing and concrete repair* and *plumbing installation and repair* and in anaphora examples like *I'm the Congo representative, and you're the Togo (one)*. And (bound-word) clitic groups are lexemes built (by "cliticization rules," or CLRs, formally parallel to IRs) on two or more lexemes, one having its full set of forms and the others represented by special shapes. Syntactically, clitic groups are just sequences of Ws, not necessarily forming a syntactic constituent of any sort; this is quite clear in English Auxiliary Reduction examples like *replied's* in *The person who replied's going to be in trouble*.

Second, there are lexemes that are indivisible from the point of view of morphology but which correspond to sequences of two or more syntactic Ws. I argued in Zwicky (1987a) that this is the situation for the French portmanteaus *au* "to the [MASC, SG]," *du* "of the [MASC, SG]," *aux* "to the [PL]," and *des* "of the [PL]" (though rather different things are going on in superficially similar German and Italian examples). The portmanteau *du* corresponds to the sequence of syntactic

Ws *de le*, and I can see no evidence in favour of saying that syntax concerns itself with anything other than this sequence.

Third, there are Ws which as wholes instantiate no lexeme, though the Ws that make them up do instantiate lexemes. This is the sort of analysis I would give to French causative clause union constructions, like *fait partir* in *J'ai fait partir Jean* "I made Jean leave." Syntactically these behave like units for the purposes of object ordering (*J'ai fait Jean/le partir*, but *Je l'ai fait partir* "I made him leave"), but there is no reason to treat such a unit as instantiating a single lexeme.

There are two rather different sorts of morphological formations here, illustrated by the COR for *Congo representative* and the CLR for *replied's*. Ordinary CORs are just like DRs except for the fact that they involve more than one source lexeme. A DR or COR stipulates the syntactic and morphological properties of the derivative lexeme, describes the derivative's semantics as a function of the semantics of the source(s), and describes the phonological content of the derivative's stem(s) as a function of the phonological properties of the source(s). The phonological side of such a rule can ask for a stem, either unaltered (as in "zero derivation" and in the compound examples of the type *Congo representative*) or as modified by particular m-ops (as in ordinary affixal derivation, or in German compounds with first elements extended by *-s* as in *Arbeitszeit* "worktime" or *-en* as in *Sternenschein* "starshine" (see Lieber 1981:13, who observes that these are not inflectional affixes)). Or it can ask for a stipulated form, again either unaltered (as in the zero conversion of English [PSP] forms like *frozen* or *broken* to ADJs, or in English and German compounds with [PL] first elements, like *abstracts committee* and *Bücherfolge* "series of books" (see Lieber 1981:14f., who observes that in this set of German examples the idiosyncrasies of [PL] inflection are reproduced in full) or as modified by particular m-ops (as when French builds manner ADVs by affixation to the [FEM, SG] form of an ADJ, for instance in *faussement* "falsely").

Clear examples of CLRs are really very different. To begin with, it scarcely makes any sense to ask what syntactic or morphological properties a clitic group like *replied's* has. Such an object is not a syntactic constituent of any sort, so we can obtain no information about its syntactic properties, and it does not participate in further morphological formations, so that we have no evidence as to its morphological properties either. As for its semantics, this is supplied entirely from the syntactic constructions that the Ws *replied* and *is* participate in; the CLR contributes nothing. All the CLR provides is information about the phonology, and it does this not by stipulating stems or forms for the participating lexemes, but rather by stipulating shapes for particular participating forms. The rule responsible for *replied's* calls for two sources, the first of which is the d-shape for any form of any lexeme in the language, the second of which is (let us say) shape 2 for a finite form of an auxiliary V lexeme, which for the [PRS, 3, SG] form *is* of the lexeme BE is /z/. (The SHR in question stipulates that shape 2 is the final consonant of the d-shape, and it provides a shape 2 for only certain finite forms of certain auxiliary V lexemes – for *am, is, are, will*, and *would*, but not for *was* or *were*.)

CLRs in general are like CORs, in that they combine two or more lexemes to yield a morphological object, but (as I observed in *Morphotactic phenomena not in syntax*, above) they are also like IRs, in that they call for a single head element and specify ways in which dependent elements may, must, or must not fill various slots. They are unlike either CORs or IRs in that they build on shapes, not (stems or forms of) lexemes, and in that the objects they describe are inert so far as the rest of the morphology is concerned. I will refer to such large morphological objects (whether these are clitic groups or something else) as "superlexemes."

The description of superlexemes involves a syntactic side, a morphological side, and an account of the articulation between the two. With respect to the interface between morphology and syntax, we must at the very least require that all W_{MIN}s in an expression instantiate some lexeme, and that no W_{MIN} simultaneously instantiate two distinct lexemes, and we must provide some scheme for adjudicating conflicts between the morphicon and the inventory of syntactic constituents with respect to the properties they assign to corresponding units. I will assume (following the lead of Sadock 1985) that the universal default for negotiating such conflicts is that morphology overrides syntax, in particular, that when the morphicon and inventory of syntactic constituents disagree as to chunking for the purposes of prosodic domain formation, it is the morphicon that wins (thus, clitic groups will generally constitute prosodic domains, regardless of syntactic constituency).

But parochial stipulations are also needed. We need to be able to stipulate, for instance, whether a superlexeme in the morphicon of a language is merely an alternative (as is the clitic group *realized's* with respect to the sequence *realized is*) or whether it precludes the matching of one W to one lexeme (as *du* does in French, **de le* being unavailable as an alternative). And we need to be able to stipulate a matching between a particular morrule and a particular synrule, so as to get the effect that the expressions in question must satisfy the requirements of both rules. This is the sort of analysis implicit in Perlmutter's (1971:96) formulation of the morrule for the English "serial verb" construction in *Ronnie will go wash the dishes* versus **Ronnie goes wash(es) the dishes*: "Output condition on the *go Verb* construction: *go Verb.*" The reference to the "*go Verb* construction" invokes a particular syntactic rule combining a head V with a complement VP, and so calls up conditions that allow only a few V lexemes in the head slot (GO and COME, plus for some speakers RUN, HURRY, and a few others), that require an activity interpretation for the complement VP, that mark the construction as informal in style, and so on. The main part of the morrule itself is intended to impose at least two further conditions, that the head V lexeme be in a form whose shape is identical to the shape of the lexeme's [BSE] form, and that nothing intervene between the two Vs in this superlexeme. The point here is that other V + VP constructions of English don't have to satisfy the conditions provided by the morrule; *Ronnie helps wash the dishes* is fine, for instance, even though *helps* is not identical to the [BSE] *help*, and *Ronnie wants desperately to wash the dishes* is fine, even though it satisfies neither this condition nor the constraint against intervening material.

NOTES

* My thanks to the participants in the conference on Formal Grammar: Theory and Implementation – especially to my official discussant, Martin Kay, but also to Janet Dean Fodor, Mark Gawron, Tom Hukari, Polly Jacobson, Mary-Louise Kean, Bob Levine, and Ivan Sag – for their comments and criticisms on the presentation version of this paper. And at Ohio State to Ted Fernald and Mark Libucha, for their useful critiques of the June 1989 version, and to Gina Lee, for her aid in matters of style. This is the version of 9 September 1989.

† The following abbreviations for grammatical categories are used in the text: 1 (first person), 2 (second person), 3 (third person), ACC (accusative case), BSE (base verb form), FEM (feminine gender), FIN (finite verb form), FUT (future tense), GEN (genitive case), GER (gerund verb form), IMPER (imperative mood), INDIC (indicative mood), INF (infinitive verb form), MASC (masculine gender), NEG (negative verb form), NEUT (neuter gender), NOM (nominative case), OBJ (object marker), PL (plural number), PRF (perfect verb form), PRS (present tense), PRP (present participle verb form), PSP (past participle verb form), PST (past tense), SG (singular number), SUBJ (subject marker).

1 I adopt the term "rank" from Halliday (1961), though not of course the full conceptual apparatus of systemic grammar that goes along with it.

2 I would have preferred to use the term "lexicon" here, as in Zwicky

(1989a), and I did use this term in the oral version of this paper, but it seems to be hopelessly confusing to many linguists, for whom the word "lexicon" unavoidably calls up either a repository of idiosyncrasy – Aronoff (1989), in fact, decides to use the term unambiguously in this sense – or else what I refer to below as the "mental lexicon." Apparently the only workable solution is to avoid the word entirely.

3 SHRs as characterized here are rules describing the phonological properties of different shapes, where a particular shape is named by its index. Other types of rules distribute "shape properties," that is, the indices themselves. Some such rules are matters of syntax – shape properties often serve as marks of particular syntactic constructions, as Zwicky (1986, 1990b) points out – and others are matters of morphology in an extended sense, a topic I consider in a later section.

4 It is possible, though not necessary, to extend this treatment to situations in which one stem is suppletive (as for the Latin "be" lexeme, for which the stem /fu/, used in [PRF] forms, has nothing to do with the rest of the paradigm), and to situations where one stem is missing (as for the Latin COEP "have begun" lexeme, which lacks the stem used in [PRS] forms).

5 The significance of such facts to generative grammars was first emphasized in Lakoff (1970).

6 I assume in all of this that both synrules and morrules have a semantic side and a phonological side, that in fact what characterizes a rule of morphosyntax is the welding of the two sides into a single coin. Thus I do not explore here the proposals of Beard (1988) to treat the semantic side and the phonological side as two distinct components of grammar.

7 The idea that inflectional morphology is normally flat rather than hierarchical was rediscovered in Thomas-Flinders (1983).

8 Each operation instantiates one of a small number of universally given operation types, but that isn't relevant to the point at hand here.

9 In the appendix to Zwicky (1988) I argue that Myers's proposal does not.

10 Notice that I say merely "not necessarily" here. Particular slots are quite often characterizable in semantic terms, just as particular stems are. The point is that such a characterization is not always available, for slots or for stems, so that a general framework must allow slots and stems to be identified in an arbitrary fashion.

11 Most of the discussion of "postlexical phonology" (as in Mohanan 1986) counterposes automatic phonological alternations to the nonautomatic alternations that are the province of STRs, DRs, and IRs, but there is a growing literature on nonautomatic "postlexical" alternations, much of it the work of Ellen Kaisse (for instance, Kaisse 1986, 1987).

12 Zwicky (1987a) is the immediate predecessor of my discussion here.

REFERENCES

Anderson, Stephen R. (1982). Where's morphology? *Linguistic Inquiry* 13:571-612

Anderson, Stephen D. (1986). Disjunctive ordering in inflectional morphology. *Natural Language and Linguistic Theory* 4(1):1-3

– (1988a). Morphological theory. In Frederick J. Newmeyer (ed.), *Linguistics: The Cambridge Survey* I:146-91. Cambridge, Eng.: Cambridge University Press

– (1988b). Morphology as a parsing problem. In Karen Wallace (ed.), *Morphology as a Computational Problem*. UCLA Occasional Papers in Linguistics 7:1-21

Archangeli, Diana (1988). Review of Lieber 1987. *Language* 64(4):791-800

Aronoff, Mark (1976). *Word Formation in Generative Grammar*. Cambridge, MA: MIT Press

– (1988). Review of Di Sciullo and Williams 1987. *Language* 64(4):766-70

– (1989). Two senses of lexical. *Eastern States Conference on Linguistics* 5:13-23

– and Sridhar, S.N. (1983). Morphological levels in English and Kannada, or Atarizing Reagan. *Chicago Linguistic Society* 19(2):3-16

Baker, Mark C. (1985). The Mirror Principle and morphosyntactic explanation. *Linguistic Inquiry* 16:373-416

– (1988a). *Incorporation: A Theory of Grammatical Function Changing*. Chicago: University of Chicago Press

– (1988b). Morphological and syntactic objects. Review of Di Sciullo and Williams 1987. *Yearbook of Morphology* 1:259-83

Bates, Dawn (1988). Prominence Relations and Structure in English Compound Morphology. Ph.D. dissertation, University of Washington

Beard, Robert (1988). On the separation of derivation from affixation: toward a lexeme/morpheme-based morphology. *Quaderni di Semantica* 9:3-59

Booij, Geert E. (1987). Lexical phonology and the organization of the morphological component. In Edward Gussmann (ed.), *Rules and the Lexicon*. Lublin: Redakcya Wydawnictw Katolickiego Uniwersytetu Lubelskiego, 43-65

Bromberger, Sylvain and Halle, Morris (1989). Why phonology is different. *Linguistic Inquiry* 20(1):51-70

Chomsky, Noam (1957). *Syntactic Structures*. The Hague: Mouton

Churma, Donald G. (1987). Explaining level ordering, and how not to parse a word. *Berkeley Linguistics Society* 13:38-52

Cook, Walter A. (1969). *Introduction to Tagmemic Analysis*. New York: Holt, Rinehart & Winston

Di Sciullo, Anna Maria and Williams, Edwin (1987). *On the Definition of the Word*. Cambridge, MA: MIT Press

Donegan, Patricia J. and Stampe, David L. (1979). The study of natural phonology. In Daniel A. Dinnsen (ed.), *Current Approaches to Phonological Theory*. Bloomington: Indiana University Press, 126-73

Dressler, Wolfgang U., Mayerthaler, Willi, Panagl, Oswald, and Wurzel, Wolfgang U. (1987). *Leitmotifs in Natural Morphology*. Amsterdam: John Benjamins

Elson, Benjamin and Pickett, Velma (1983). *Beginning Morphology and Syntax*. Dallas, TX: Summer Institute of Linguistics

Fabb, Nigel (1988). English suffixation is constrained only by selectional restrictions. *Natural Language and Linguistic Theory* 6:527-39

Ford, Alan and Singh, Rajendra (1985a). Remarks on the directionality of word formation processes. *Eastern States Conference on Linguistics* 1:205-13

– (1985b). Towards a non-paradigmatic morphology. *Berkeley Linguistics Society* 11:87-95

Gazdar, Gerald, Klein, Ewan, Pullum, Geoffrey, and Sag, Ivan (1985). *Generalized Phrase Structure Grammar*. Oxford: Basil Blackwell

Gazar, Gerald, Pullum, Geoffrey K., and Sag, Ivan A. (1982). Auxiliaries and related phenomena in a restrictive theory of grammar. *Language* 58(3):591-638

Gussmann, Edmund. (1988). Review of Mohanan 1986. *Journal of Linguistics* 24(1):232-9

Halliday, Michael A. K. (1961). Categories of the theory of grammar. *Word* 17:241-92

Harris, Zellig S. (1951). *[Methods in] Structural Linguistics*. Chicago: University of Chicago Press

Jackendoff, Ray S. (1975). Morphological and semantic regularities in the lexicon. *Language* 51:639-71

Jensen, John T. and Stong-Jensen, Margaret (1984). Morphology is in the lexicon! *Linguistic Inquiry* 15(3):474-98

Kaisse, Ellen M. (1985). *Connected Speech: The Interaction of Syntax and Phonology*. New York: Academic Press

– (1986). Locating Turkish devoicing. *West Coast Conference on Formal Linguistics* 5:119-28

– (1987). Rhythm and the cycle. *Chicago Linguistic Society* 23(2):199-209

Kiparsky, Paul (1982). Lexical morphology and phonology. In Linguistic Society of Korea (ed.), *Linguistics in the Morning Calm*. Seoul: Hanshin, 3-91

Koskenniemi, Kimmo (1983). *Two-Level Morphology: A General Computational Model for Word-Form Recognition and Production*. Publication 11, Dept of General Linguistics, University of Helsinki

Lakoff, George P. (1970). *Irregularity in Syntax*. New York: Holt, Rinehart & Winston

Lees, Robert B. (1960). The grammar of English nominalizations. *International Journal of American Linguistics* 26(3), Part II

Lieber, Rochelle (1981). On the Organization of the Lexicon. Ph.D. dissertation, MIT. Bloomington: Indiana University Linguistics Club, 1980

– (1987). *An Integrated Theory of Autosegmental Processes*. Albany: State University of New York Press

Lounsbury, Floyd G. (1957). The method of descriptive linguistics. In Martin Joos (ed.), *Readings in Linguistics I*. New York: American Council of Learned Societies, 379-85

McCarthy, John J. (1979). Formal Problems in Semitic Phonology and Morphology. Ph.D. dissertation, MIT

– (1981). A prosodic theory of nonconcatenative morphology. *Linguistic Inquiry* 12(3):373-418

McCawley, James D. (1982). *Thirty Million Theories of Grammar*. Chicago: University of Chicago Press

Marantz, Alec (1982). Re reduplication. *Linguistic Inquiry* 13(3):435-82

Martin, Jack Z. (1988). Subtractive morphology as dissociation. *West Coast Conference on Formal Linguistics* 7:229-40

Matthews, Peter H. (1974). *Morphology: An Introduction to the Theory of Word-Structure*. Cambridge, Eng.: Cambridge University Press

Mel'cuk, Igor A. (1982). *Towards a Language of Linguistics*. München: Wilhelm Fink

Mohanan, K. P. (1986). *The Theory of Lexical Phonology*. Dordrecht: D. Reidel

Myers, Scott (1985). The long and the short of it: a metrical theory of English vowel quantity. *Chicago Linguistic Society* 21(1):275-88

– (1987). Vowel shortening in English. *Natural Language and Linguistic Theory* 485-518

Nespor, Marina and Vogel, Irene (1986). *Prosodic Phonology*. Dordrecht: Foris

Perlmutter, David M. (1971). *Deep and Surface Structure Constraints in Syntax*. New York: Holt, Rinehart & Winston

– (1988). The split morphology hypothesis: evidence from Yiddish. In Michael Hammond and Michael Noonan (eds.), *Theoretical Morphology: Approaches in Modern Linguistics*. San Diego: Academic Press, 79-100

Pullum, Geoffrey K. (1979). *Rule Interaction and the Organization of a Grammar*. New York: Garland

– and Zwicky, Arnold M. (1987). Plain morphology and expressive morphology. Berkeley Linguistics Society 13:330-40

– (1988). The syntax-phonology interface. In Frederick J. Newmeyer (ed.), *Linguistics: The Cambridge Survey* I:255-80. Cambridge, Eng.: Cambridge University Press

Sadock, Jerrold M. (1985). Autolexical syntax: A theory of noun incorporation and similar phenomena. *Natural Language and Linguistic Theory* 3(4):379-439

Scalise, Sergio (1984). *Generative Morphology*. Dordrecht: Foris

– (1988). Inflection and derivation. *Linguistics* 26(4):561-81

Schachter, Paul (1974). Constraints on clitic order in Tagalog. In A. Gonzales (ed.), *Parangal Kay Cecilio Lopez (Phillipine Journal of Linguistics)*, Special Monograph, 4:214-31. Also in UCLA *Papers in Syntax* 5:96-118 (1974)

Selkirk, Elisabeth O. (1982). *The Syntax of Words*. Cambridge, MA: MIT Press

Spencer, Andrew (1988). Arguments for morpholexical rules. *Journal of Linguistics* 24(1):1-29

Thomas-Flinders, Tracy (1983). Morphological Structures. Ph.D. dissertation, UCLA

Williams, Edwin S. (1981). On the notions "lexically related" and "head of a word." *Linguistic Inquiry* 12:245-74

Williams, Stephen J. (1980). *A Welsh Grammar*. Cardiff: University of Wales Press

Yip, Moira (1987). English vowel epenthesis. *Natural Language and Linguistic Theory* 5(4):463-84

Ziervogel, D. (1952). *A Grammar of Swazi (siSwati)*. Johannesburg: Witwatersrand University Press

Zwicky, Arnold M. (1969). Phonological constraints in syntactic descriptions. *Papers in Linguistics* 1(3):411-63

– (1984). Autonomous components and limited interfacing: phonology-free syntax, the Hallean syllogism, and their kin. *Chicago Linguistic Society* 20:365-86

– (1985a). Heads. *Journal of Linguistics* 21(1):1-30

– (1985b). How to describe inflection. *Berkeley Linguistics Society* 11:372-86

– (1986). The general case: basic form versus default form. *Berkeley Linguistics Society* 12:305-14

– (1987a). French prepositions: no peeking. *Phonology Yearbook* 4:211-27

– (1987b). Phonological and morphological rule interactions in highly modular grammars. *Eastern States Conference on Linguistics* 3:523-32

– (1987c). Rule interactions: another gloss on K&K. *Innovations in Linguistics Education* 5(1):91-111

– (1987d). Transformational grammarians and their ilk. *MIT Working Papers in Linguistics* 9:265-79

– (1988). Morphological rules, operations, and operation types. *Eastern States Conference on Linguistics* 4:318-34

– (1989a). Idioms and constructions. *Eastern States Conference on Linguistics* 5:547-58

– (1989b). Quicker, more quickly, *quicklier. *Yearbook of Morphology* 2:139-73

– (1989c). What's become of derivations? Defaults and Invocations. *Berkeley Linguistics Society* 15:303-20

– (1990a). Inflectional morphology as a (sub)component of grammar. In W. U. Dressler et al. (eds.), *Contemporary Morphology*. Berlin: Walter de Gruyter
– (1990b). Syntactic representations and phonological shapes. In Sharon Inkelas and Draga Zec (eds.), *The Phonology-Syntax Connection*. Stanford, CA: Center for the Study of Language and Information, 379-97

CHAPTER SEVEN

Semantics, Knowledge, and NP Modification

Stephen Crain and Henry Hamburger

INTRODUCTION

The goal of semantic theory is to provide a systematic account of the meanings of the well-formed expressions of natural language. This paper outlines a semantic theory of the workings of modifiers in English noun phrases. Our initial orientation is to pursue as far as possible a compositional, model-theoretic semantics that is independent of knowledge and psychological processing. However, we find phenomena that suggest modifications to compositionality and model theory and that require some clarification of the interaction of semantics with both knowledge and processing.

Like Montague (1970) and Keenan and Faltz (1985), our concern is with specifying how higher-level semantic constituents are synthesized from lower-level constituents. Although this compositional approach is intuitively appealing and explains many phenomena, we find two classes of data that appear to violate compositionality, at least in its simplest, most straightforward form. That simple form is one in which the basic relationship between semantics and syntax is one of correspondence, where the syntax determines the order in which the semantic constituents combine. To accommodate the observed violations of strict, simple compositionality, we briefly explore a generalized form of it. We also follow these authors in starting from a model-theoretic viewpoint. Thus, we will be concerned with the question of what object or set of objects a particular phrase can refer to, given appropriate circumstances. It is easier for both author and reader for the discussion to be in extensional terms, but it must be borne in mind that it is ultimately an intensional version of these remarks, such as that of Keenan and Faltz, that is needed. Even in their current form, the arguments we present here are sufficient to point clearly to some dilemmas for the model-theoretic approach.

The ordering of prenominal modifying expressions, an old linguistic chestnut, also receives illumination from these deliberations. For example, we explain on the basis of semantic function, rather than syntactic category why *second green ball* is preferred to *green second ball*. Nevertheless, it proves important in our account not to rule the latter form out of the language on grounds of syntactic ill-formedness, since it is indeed a part of the language. We will argue that such phrases have both a syntactic and a semantic structure, and, with certain word substitutions within a lexical subcategory, are the appropriate way to express certain concepts, such as *a happy second child*. Loosening the syntax puts some additional responsibility on semantics for selectivity. The specification of what ordering relationships are semantically possible comes as the consequence of simple and natural constraints on the semantic application rules, which are expressed extensionally in terms of set operations.

Our treatment also points to otherwise unexpected ambiguities, which we claim exist in phrases like *third tallest student* and *consecutive rainy days*. Like possible-world model-theoretic semantics, we invoke multiple models to explain these ambiguities. However, our usage differs in that the inherent structure of models are allowed to diverge (within limits) in our system. That is, the models that are assigned to different interpretations of a phrase are not simply parametric values of the valuation function that assigns entities to linguistic expressions in different models. The formalization we specify provides more internal structure than is allowed in previous model-theoretic accounts.

The construction of a model for an NP is influenced by one's knowledge of certain structural notions associated with particular nouns, such as *child*, and *home run*. This is another way in which the framework advanced here differs from many others. In our system, real-world knowledge is instrumental in the derivation of the models corresponding to the different semantic representation of NPs. Although we maintain a barrier between semantics and real-world knowledge, we have abandoned the research strategy of attempting to describe language processing without recourse to real-world knowledge, which is often viewed as a Pandora's Box of vague and unknown factors. While recognizing the existence and possible contribution of these factors to language use, many researchers have held fast to the view that admitting them into our equations would only impede investigations into the processing of linguistic information. However, our approach to semantics allows an interface with real-world knowledge in a principled way. The kind of knowledge that must be appealed to in the cases in question here can be described with precision, using only the formal mechanisms of set theory, such as sets, sequences, sets of sequences, and the like. In this respect, our approach shares features in common with recent theories of pragmatics (e.g., Stalnaker 1974; Kratzer 1981) and discourse representation (e.g., Kamp 1981; Heim 1982).

It is also a distinguishing feature of the present approach that it provides a basis for explaining why perceivers have systematic preferences for one interpretation of ambiguous phrases. Here, too, real world knowledge plays a key role. It is used to select among alternative analyses both in and out of context. In ordinary conversation, the alternatives are distinguished according to their semantic and referential appropriateness to the context. In the absence of context, principles of least cognitive effort are invoked to explain people's preferences in resolving semantic ambiguities.

In this respect our approach complements proposals about the psychological mechanisms underlying ambiguity resolution that are advanced by Crain and Steedman (1985). The same principles of least cognitive effort are also used to explain the difficulties perceivers encounter in constructing interpretations to certain well-formed expressions, such as *second first violinist*. As a final comment, from the point of view of linguistic processing our model adheres to *Processing Modularity*, since the semantic component is not instructed by real-world knowledge; rather, the semantic options for an ambiguous phrase are selected or rejected according to their fit with the perceiver's knowledge representations.

By way of introduction to our theoretical framework, the next section sets out the extensional meanings of several classes of prenominal modifiers. First we describe the effect of each type of modifier on how an NP containing it can be related to referents in a model. Then we turn to the semantic contributions of modifiers in combination.

CATEGORIZATION OF MODIFIERS

The top level cut in our categorization of modifiers is into *constrainers* and *selectors*. In the simplest cases, the distinction between the two categories is whether the smallest phrase containing the modifier has, as its extension in referential use, a set or an individual. For a constrainer, the corresponding extension is a set; for a selector, it is an individual. Take, for example, *tall* and *tallest*, as modifiers of *mountain*. *Tall* is a constrainer because there is a set of many tall mountains, but *tallest* is a selector because only one individual mountain is the tallest one. It will turn out to be necessary to elaborate this criterion to deal with selectors in the context of more complex models. The distinctions in this section will play an important part in explaining both word-order and the role of knowledge.

Constrainers: absolutes and relatives

One can distinguish absolute adjectives like *female* and *green* from relative adjectives, like *big* and *tall*. Absolute adjectives specify properties and property values with a standard of applicability that is independent of the linguistic context. In particular, no appeal is made to the head noun to determine just what is meant. Thus if X is a subtype of Y, so that all Xs are Ys, then also all green Xs are green Ys, and similarly with any other absolute adjective in place of *green*. A dog with a trace of a greenish tinge is not a green dog, even though it compares favourably to other dogs in the relevant property, most dogs not having any aspect of greenness at all. Another kind of absolute modifier is the possessive. Interestingly, the head noun also typically passes the test of absoluteness: to be a big dog, an entity must be dogsome absolutely, not only relative to big things (in addition to being big for a dog).

Relative adjectives, in contrast, are evaluated by comparison to a standard that does vary with linguistic context and often depends on the head noun of a noun phrase. Thus *a big ant* means something that (is an ant and) is big for an ant, that is, appreciably displaced toward bigness from ants of typical size, though possibly still small for an animal or physical object. Parts of the noun phrase other than the adjective under consideration and the head noun may also help determine the standard, such as *toy* (but not *red*, or *Ann's*) in *Ann's big red toy truck*, whose referent is to be big for a toy truck. Though the relative adjective itself thus modifies a subphrase of its co-constituent, its superlative form can modify its full co-constituent or even the entire rest of the noun-phrase, so that *Ann's biggest truck* is the biggest only of those trucks that are Ann's. This apparent counter-example to compositionality is explained later on, when we have extended the class of selectors to include mappable-selectors.

It is worth noting that *female* and *tall* differ along a dimension other than that of the absolute-relative distinction. To wit, *female* is dichotomous or crisp in meaning, whereas *tall* is continuous or fuzzy. Thus, an entity can be *rather tall* or *very tall*, but only with a twist in the meaning of *female* can one say *rather female* or *very female*. It has been said that this additional dimension is not independent of the first. The claim is that absolutes are always dichotomous and relatives are always continuous. We submit two potential violations of that claim, in different directions: *consecutive* as an example of a dichotomous relative and *furry* as a potential example of a continuous absolute. *Consecutive* is dichotomous because things are either consecutive or not, and it is clearly a relative, because whether things are consecutive depends not only on those things themselves but on others as well, specifically on whether those others intervene in some ordering. This is a more complex kind of relationship than the simple comparison between one entity and another that is implied by ordinary continuous relatives like *tall*. Complex relatives can also be continuous, as is the case with *frequent*, *intermittent*, and *sparse*, which indicate how densely something may occur in time or space.

Before proceeding to other categories, we should note that other adjectives can be classified as constrainers according to the criterion we have been using: they produce a set as value. Adjectives with a negative cast, like *fake* and *counterfeit*, conform to this criterion. Notice, however, that the set produced by adjectives of this type need not be a subset of the set that corresponds to the modificand: Recently a report on National Public Radio told of a forger, call him Jones, of such admirable skill that his forgeries had become collector's items. The radio announcer called them "original Jones forgeries." These original forgeries are not to be confused with non-original forgeries, which presumably can be referred to as "fake forged works." These would come into existence if someone were to deceptively simulate Jones' work. Note also that the meanings of the two modifiers *fake* and *forged*, though they both have a negative cast, do not cancel each other, but rather form a complex, composed structure.

Simple selectors

A selector, as noted, combines with a simple modificand to yield a linguistic unit that can refer to an individual entity. Ordinals and superlatives are selectors, though we have found no other groups of modifiers that are, only a smattering of individual words, including *top*, *left*, *lead*, *leadoff*, and *designated*, some of which show up in the examples below.

Beginning with ordinals, we will introduce a simple notation which will turn out to be useful for superlatives too, but will ultimately need elaboration. An ordinal, regarded extensionally, selects an element from a set, on the basis of some ordering. For felicity, this set and ordering must somehow be known to or be made known to the listener, so that the selector can do its work. For example, *the biggest bear* makes sense with respect to a finite set of bears in focus, since size is a property of bears (inherited from a supertype) and relative size is easily determined. *The second car* can make sense even though no ordering is specified and even though cars do not have a prominent default array, provided that the situation provides an ordering, say, the queue at a car wash. Selection of an appropriate element can be represented by one of a family of functions, Π_k, each of which selects from an ordered set its kth element. Thus, let Ω be a roughly linear display of objects, and suppose some ordering, say left-to-right, either is conventional or has been established in conversation. In this context, *the second object* means $\Pi_2(\Omega)$.

Superlatives resemble ordinals not only in invoking selection, but also in that the selection criterion is an ordering. A superlative, however, explicitly states the ordering by means of the gloss of its base adjective. *Biggest*, for example, means essentially *first in bigness*. To express this view requires an elaboration of the foregoing notation to allow for explicit mention of the basis for ordering. Let the ordered set Ω be replaced by the more explicit $\langle \psi, \omega \rangle$, where ω is the basis for ordering the set ψ. In the earlier example Ω was a spatially ordered array of objects; now ψ is that set of objects without regard to order and ω may be thought of as a Boolean function that for any two of the objects is true or false depending on which is to the left of the other. For a set of boxes, B, lying in a line, with LR, the left-to-right ordering understood, *the second box* is $\Pi_2(\langle B, LR \rangle)$. In this notation, *the biggest box* in the array becomes expressible as $P_1(\langle B, BIGNESS \rangle)$.[1]

Unlike the constrainers, selectors are not divided into dichotomous and continuous. Rather, they must all be dichotomous, to assure selection of a single individual. As for the relative-absolute distinction, the ordinals and superlatives are all relative, but one candidate for an absolute selector is *lead*, as in *lead singer* or *lead agency*. Something is not the lead entity by comparison (say in capacity to lead) to other entities, but rather by virtue of filling a special role, and similarly for the designated spokesperson. Against this background, consider the adjective *consecutive*, some of whose unusual nature has received attention above. On the two dimensions just noted, this modifier is again unusual. Like a superlative (and unlike an absolute), it deals with a relationship between objects rather than a property of an individual. On the other hand, like an absolute (and unlike a superlative) it has the capacity to refer to more than one element of a set, without imposing what we have called a two-dimensional structure on that set. Thus *consecutive* is a relation-based restrictor, as opposed to an individual-based restrictor (like an absolute) or as opposed to a selector (like a superlative).

We have claimed that a selector, unlike a constrainer, selects a single entity. Although this is true in many straightforward contexts, there are also cases, ignored up to now, like *the three worst pollutants*, in which the superlative apparently does not prevent its phrase from referring to more than one entity. Related examples are *two left lanes*, routinely used on highway signs, and *two leadoff singles*, used in baseball reports, even though *leadoff single* with no cardinal number refers unambiguously to a single by the first hitter in an inning. Examples like these demand some reformulation of the picture presented so far in order to state that selection of an individual is only the simplest and perhaps most common case of what a selector can do.

Note, however, that even in contexts that allow the selector to specify more than one entity, the selector is more explicit than a constrainer. This explicitness is acknowledged by the English language by the use of definiteness in the determiner. To confirm this, consider the phrases in (1) below, especially (1g-h), in reference to the times for the various runners in some race. The constrainer, *fast*, permits either a definite or indefinite determiner, as in (1a-b), and indeed the definite can occur only in case there just happens to be only one fast time. In contrast, the superlative selector, *fastest*, requires the definite, both in the singular, as shown by (1e-f), and in the plural, as shown by (1g-h). Phrases (1e) and (1g) are starred because they are semantically bizarre on their simplest readings, though in a moment we shall examine semantic rules that permit assigning them meanings by imputing structure to the set of times. Specifically, if one has in mind all times in all races of this distance by these runners, partitioned by runner, then (1g) can mean three personal bests, and (1e) can mean a personal best by Ursula. Continuing to ignore the possibility of such partitioning, we can explain the need for syntactic definiteness with superlatives even in the plural, as evidenced in (1g-h) in terms of a semantic factor. Even in a plural use, the superlative is selective in the sense that particular individuals are specified without flexibility. For example, three fast times can be any three among four fast times, but the three fastest cannot be just any old three among the four fastest, say the first, third, and fourth fastest.

(1) (a) (Ursula had) a fast time
     (b) (Ursula had) the (only) fast time

     (c) (Our team had) three fast times
     (d) (Our team had) the (only) three fast times

     (e) * (Ursula had) a fastest time (no simple reading)
     (f) (Ursula had) the fastest time

(g) * (Our team had) three fastest times (no simple reading)
(h) (Our team had) the three fastest times

Complex selectors

Our account of the semantics of selectors, using the function Π_k, is only partial, since it offers no account of a sentence like *Sandy is a second child*. The phrase *second child* in this sentence has as its extension the set of all those who are second in the birth ordering in their own brood. Since *second child* corresponds to a set, there is the potential for it to combine with another modifier, which might be either a restrictor or another selector. In particular, since second children are human beings, they can be ordered by age, so one can apply the selector *youngest* to get *youngest second child*. Notice that using *youngest* here resolves the semantic ambiguity in *second child*, between interpretation as an individual or a set. The same kind of disambiguation is the contribution of the indefinite article in *Sandy is a second child*.

When the modifier is a selector and the modificand is a partitioned set, like *child* on the child-in-a-family reading, the rule of combination is a mapping function. Each element of the top-level set – each brood in the case of *child* – is mapped by the selector to the member that the selector selects from it, for example, in the case of *second child*. To represent the semantics of these multiply applicable selectors, let MAP be a (higher order) function whose first argument is a function, f, and whose second argument is a set, S, of entities each of which is an appropriate argument for f. The value of MAP (f , S) is $\{ f(s) \mid s \, \varepsilon \, S \}$. Let BROODS be a set of ordered sets, specifically the sibling sets, each ordered by age. Then *Sandy is a second child* means SANDY ε MAP (Π_2, BROODS). This more comprehensive machinery can handle the simpler case of *the second thing* too, by conflating a one-element set and its element. Such a set is indistinguishable from its sole member from the standpoint of real world reference.

It is also possible to meaningfully apply the selectors *youngest* and *second* in the opposite order. For example, given the structured set interpretation of the noun *child*, we can apply the selector *youngest* to create the phrase *youngest child*, that is, a set of children who are last-born in their respective broods. With such a set in hand, one only needs some basis for ordering them in order to speak of *the second youngest child* in the doubly selected sense under consideration. The ordering of historical sequence provides the basis of ordering:

(2) It is rare for a youngest child to ascend the throne; indeed
     George is only the second youngest child to do so in modern
     times.

The interpretation of *second* here relies on conventional use of chro-
nology as a default ordering. The MAP notation used above must be
enriched slightly to handle this case. Specifically, the set S (the second
argument to MAP) is permitted to be ordered, and if it is, MAP (f, S)
is ordered correspondingly. Here an ordered set of ordered sets must
be evoked to correspond to *child*: a sagaful of royal broods. In the
more straightforward reading, *second youngest* is a constituent, with
an interpretation that involves Π_2.

It would seem possible, then, for *second youngest child* to have four
distinct readings, since it has two potential syntactic structures and a
two-way lexical ambiguity. One of the four is eliminated because for
two selectors to be successively applied to *child*, it must have its
set-of-sets interpretation. However, the remaining unmentioned potential interpretation can indeed be meaningful, as shown here: *(The
biblical) Joseph became the most powerful second youngest child in Egypt.*
Therefore, *second youngest child* is a three-way ambiguity: (1) the second among youngest children; (2) the next-to-youngest child; or (3)
the set of next-to-youngest children, to be selected (to yield the singular form, *child*) by other NP material, like *most powerful*. Of course,
taken out of context *second youngest child* is much more likely to receive interpretation (2), in which *second youngest* is understood as a
syntactic constituent, semantically interpreted as a (two-word) selector. (See LEAST COGNITIVE EFFORT, below, for an account of this preference.)

To allow these distinctions to be stated more succinctly we now
introduce a partial formalization. Let A be the category of adjectives
that consists of selectors. Let us say that each selector has an interpretation consisting of the capacity to make a selection, according to
some criterion, from any set for which that criterion can indeed determine selection. For example, an appropriate set for *biggest* is one with
size ordering. We posit the syntactic rule: N1 → A N2 (where the N's
are numbered, and bar-levels are omitted, for ease of reference). Two
semantic rules, R1 and R2, are associated with this syntactic rule. The
choice of semantic rule depends on the interpretation of N2. If N2
receives a simple set interpretation, then the simpler rule, R1, is applicable. Extensionally speaking, R1 has the adjective under A in the
phrase marker carry out selection from N2. For this selection to be
done, the noun under N2 must have an interpretation on which the
particular adjective's criterion can be exercised. However, if the inter-

pretation of N2 is a set of sets, each of which is appropriate according to the criterion of the adjective, then the multiple application rule, R2, is applicable. According to R2, each of the sets in the extensional interpretation of N2 is handled by R1 and the set of results becomes the extensional version of the interpretation of N1. Since N1 is a set, it may now conceivably be combined with another adjective at the next level, according to R1.

Returning to the three-way ambiguity of *the second youngest child*, we can now say that the interpretation (1) arises from successive application of R2, then R1. Interpretations (2) and (3) each involve an instance of A that syntactically dominates two words. They differ by their respective use of R1 and R2, acting respectively on the simple and structured (set of sets) interpretations of the noun *child*. Since case (3) yields a set, one must apply a further selection (like *most powerful*) to get a single element for use with the singular noun. This machinery now permits us to predict, correctly, that the plural *second youngest children*, is unambiguous, permitting only an interpretation analogous to the one in (3).

This treatment allows every selector the potential to act upon nouns in two different ways, without having to be considered ambiguous. The lexicon should not be cluttered by marking every element of a (sub)category with the same information. Nouns like *child* do get two semantic entries, but they need them in any case to account for what people know.

Iteration of modifiers: the third second first violinist

Several members of an orchestra play the part written for first violin, a part that differs from second violin. These people sit in designated chairs, referred to by order. For example, the first first violinist is usually called "the first chair first violin." This person is also typically the concert master. When the conductor is unable to perform, the concert master takes over. It is then appropriate for the second first violinist to receive a temporary geographical promotion, to fill the vacancy. The other first violins are similarly promoted. What with the flu going around, Deidre is the third second first violinist to be so promoted in the Chicago metropolitan area this month. If the phrase *the third second first violinist* is acceptable in this example, it suggests that *violinist* may be capable of referring to a three-level set.[2]

SEMANTIC PRINCIPLES OF WORD ORDER

There have been a variety of attempts to account for the order of modifiers in the noun phrases of English. We will show that syntax, semantics, and knowledge all play a role.

Limitations of lexical categories

A syntactic approach to providing an account of word order is to assign words to categories and then to specify an order among the categories. In the case of NPs, for example, positing the syntactic rules N" → Det (Adj) N', Adj → Adj (AdjP) would embody the reasonable claim that adjectives follow determiners and precede nouns (in English). Though this claim is generally true as far as it goes, a purely syntactic approach founders on the observation that there appear to be order distinctions among adjectives, that is, among members of the same syntactic class. It is not permissible, for example, to interchange the adjectives in *a helpful financial advisor*. One could try to deal with this situation by subcategorizing the adjectives on the basis of semantic properties.

This revised version of the strategy has been tried by various authors, using semantic categories like *colour, size, nationality,* and so on. Based on these semantic groupings of adjectives, the relative proximity of different adjectives to the head noun is usually described in roughly the same way: Modifiers increase in closeness to the head to the extent to which they identify an independently distinguishing property of the intended referent. For example, it has been claimed that more "specific" (Goyvaerts 1968) or "noun-like" (Bever 1970) modifiers appear closer to the head. Here are three examples of ordering relations among adjectives that have used this kind of descriptive generalization.

(3) (a) Value ⟩ Dimension ⟩ Physical Property ⟩ Speed ⟩ Human Propensity ⟩ Age ⟩ Colour (from Dixon 1982)

(b) Quality ⟩ Size,Shape, ⟩ Old,Young ⟩ Colour ⟩ Nationality ⟩ Style ⟩ Gerund (from Goyvaerts 1968)

(c) Quality ⟩ Size ⟩ Shape ⟩ Colour ⟩ Material (from Sproat and Shih 1988)

Numerous examples show, however, that it is impossible to get a solution to adjective ordering relations by simply assigning words to subcategories of adjective. Each of the counter-examples that follow consist of a phrase with a reversible pair of adjectives, that is, two adjectives that can be interchanged without destroying the grammaticality or the meaningfulness of the phrase. Admittedly, the meaning is altered in each case, in systematic ways. Additional examples are adduced with reversible pairs of modifiers in which the two modifiers need not both be adjectives.

(4) (a) military legal advisor
     (b) legal military advisor
     (c) military congressional expert
     (d) congressional military expert

First consider the examples in (4). In each case, the inner adjective, the one next to the head noun, determines the subject matter of the advice or expertise to be provided. This information provided by the adjective concerns what can be called a slot in the semantic case frame of the head noun. The earlier or outside adjectives give different kinds of information in the various examples. For *military* in (4a), the information concerns a property of the person that fills the role of *legal advisor*, so that (4a) can be paraphrased *legal advisor who is a military person*. In this case, as in (4c), (4e), and (4f), the information provided by the outer adjective concerns a slot that resides in the semantic case frame for the higher level type corresponding to *person*, and that is inherited by its subtype, *advisor* or *expert*. *Legal* as outside modifier in (4b) and *congressional* in (4d) provide still other kinds of information. The one systematic observation is that for the modifier to supply the slot information (type of advice or type of expertise), it must be adjacent to the noun, while for the non-slot meanings, adjacency is optional. More generally we find that modifiers serving to constrain the filler of a slot in the semantic case frame of the head noun either lie adjacent to that noun or are separated from it only by other such modifiers.

Keenan and Faltz (1985) state that nationality goes close to the noun. By extension, one might expect a person's continent of origin, as well as her country of origin, to go close to the noun. However, the examples in (5) show that an instance of *Asian* or *African* with a personal origin interpretation does not come so close to the noun as does the slot filler (expertise) sense.

(5) (a) African Asian expert
     (b) Asian African expert

In the next reversible pair, just one of the modifiers is a nationality. Although (5c) conforms to the Keenan and Faltz observation about nationality, (5d) does not. In phrases (5c) and (5d), there is no necessity for a shift in the kind of information that the modifiers provide, as there was in the preceding example. In each phrase, *blue* tells the colour of the (potential) referent and *Greek* presumably tells its country of origin. Here, as in (4), the position next to the head noun may carry role information. Just as an advisor has a subject-matter to advise about, so also does dye have a colour so as to dye things that colour. Colour, that is, plays a distinctive role with respect to dye. For pottery on the other hand, colour need not be important, whereas if that pottery is viewed as a cultural artefact, the cultural designation, possibly carried by nationality, attains the slot-filler status, with a consequent claim at lying close to the noun.

(5) (c) blue Greek pottery
     (d) Greek blue dye

The classification of modifiers into adjectives and participles, like that among adjectives, also fails to provide a reliable basis for predicting permissible word orders. This is another piece of evidence against the hope of explaining order by refinement of a purely syntactic approach. A glance at the examples in (6) and (7) makes it clear that the order of adjectives and participles arises from semantic considerations.

(6) (a) growing financial opportunity
     (b) decaying floral arrangement
     (c) tall touring musician
     (d) dim shooting star

(7) (a) stoical dying man
     (b) sputtering fluorescent bulb
     (c) unhappy recovering alcoholic
     (d) flashing yellow light

There are various reasons for these orders. In (6), a modifier indicating some kind of quantitative factor goes further from the head noun. The phrases in (7) raise issues of compositionality, to which we return. In each case one of the modifiers must combine with a co-constituent that either necessarily includes or necessarily excludes the other modifier. Thus, the stoicism is of interest because of the dying, and fluorescent bulbs sputter differently from other bulbs, but the recovery is only from alcoholism, not from unhappiness.

Contiguity and composition

The semantic theory we propose is like others mentioned earlier in permitting the composition of elements that are syntactically contiguous, but differs from them by also permitting composition of discontiguous elements in certain syntactically constrained ways. We consider this issue first with respect to formalisms and then again in the context of some new data.

Two potential violations of contiguous composition are the phrases *Ann's biggest ball* and *three consecutive bears*. We begin with the latter, generalized to the case of all noun phrases that contain a cardinal number, followed by the word *consecutive* and then a common noun (or something more complex but generable from N'). We consider two possible orders of semantic composition. For either composition order, it is assumed that first the noun combines with one of the other two items to form an intermediate unit with a semantic value. The latter is then combined with the remaining element. There are thus two competing orders, according to whether it is the number or the word *consecutive* whose semantic value enters into composition first. Only one of these orders conforms to a requirement of contiguous composition, namely the order that has the semantic values of the noun and of *consecutive* compose first.

To describe the range of possibilities for the semantic value that results in this case, it is useful first to define the notion of power sequence. Given any sequence, called a basis sequence, its power sequence is the set of all subsequences of that basis sequence. (Note that a power sequence is not a sequence, though its elements are.) The semantic value in question, then, lies in a subset of the power sequence of some basis sequence, the latter determined by the (head) noun in concert with the context. To take a specific example, the semantic value of *bears* lies in the power sequence of some prominent sequence of bears, say a row of them in front of the speaker and hearer. The semantic value of *consecutive bears* lies in a particular subset of that power sequence, namely the one such that each element of that subset is a sequence whose elements are successive elements of the basis sequence. Subsequent composition with the cardinal number *three* produces a semantic value that lies in a subset of the subset just described. This latter subset contains just those members of the former that have exactly the particular length, three, that the cardinal number specifies. Composition with the number first (as in *consecutive three bears*) would be just as complex as the foregoing description, except that the subsetting is done in reverse order. Therefore simplicity, per se, does not seem to favour either the contiguous or the dis-

contiguous order of composition. With either order, the cardinal behaves in a way that is consistent with its behaviour in the simpler case
where it combines directly with the head noun. Also worth noting is
that the ordinal, which is syntactically available at the same position
as the cardinal, also has a semantics that combines correctly with the
kind of (complex) semantic value posited for the combination of *consecutive* with the head noun.

   Contiguous composition is dealt something of a blow by phrases
that differ from the earlier ones by inclusion of a prenominal adjective. Before introducing an adjective, though, let us consider what
happens when a horse is placed among the bears, say as the second of
the four animals. Now the bears in positions 3 and 4 certainly do
qualify as *two consecutive bears*, but what about those at positions 1
and 3, which are consecutive among bears but not consecutive overall? The answer may depend on the practical consequences of a given
situation. Now suppose that instead of interspersing a horse among
the bears we take an array consisting of red and yellow bears. In this
context, what is the meaning of *three consecutive red bears*? The simplest possibility from a compositional standpoint would be for *red
bears* to act as a unit, playing a role equivalent to just *bears* in the
bear-and-horse discussion. The two alternative interpretations can be
paraphrased as follows.

   (8) (a) among the red bears, three successive ones
        (b) among the bears, three successive ones, each being a
             red bear

In (8b), the adjective *red*, despite its position in the midst of the noun
phrase, is apparently applied last, after all the other parts have been
composed. On this analysis, the phrase under consideration has a
noncontiguous order of composition. This result is rather a surprising
one when compared to the syntax and semantics of *the third red bear*,
where the composition respects contiguity. Applying the test of red-
ness independently of the ordinal, or possibly outside it, in violation
of contiguity, is exactly what Roeper (1972) and Matthei (1982)
claimed certain children were doing in their studies, but which gives
the erroneous interpretation (9b), below. Interpretations (9a,b) are directly analogous to (8a,b), respectively, but in the present case it is the
interpretation with contiguous composition, (8a), that is correct.

   (9) (a) among the red bears, the third one
        (b) among the bears, the third one, which is a red bear

Consider next the phrase *three consecutive rainy days*. This phrase does not appear to need a specially contrived array or other props to provide a context for its interpretation. In that sense it is semantically a more natural example than *three consecutive red bears*, our previous example with the same syntax. Here *rainy* is a restrictor (just like *red*) so that *rainy days* has the same kind of semantic value as unrestricted *days*, that is, a set of days. Since the rainy days have a natural temporal ordering in the world, just as all the days do, it is possible to take the power sequence of that sequence (of rainy days). Suppose we select from the power sequence of the rainy days the subsequences that are both of cardinality three and uninterrupted with respect to the set that forms the basis of the power sequence under consideration. The resulting incorrect semantic value can be paraphrased as *among rainy days, three consecutive ones*. Can Monday, Tuesday, and Thursday be referred to as three consecutive rainy days if it is clear throughout Wednesday? We think not. Rather, the usual understanding is that the consecutiveness is a property of the unrestricted days. Thus the semantics in this "natural" example is directly analogous to the result, (8b), that relied on a contrived context.

At the least, it takes considerable effort at creating a context, if one is to get the less usual, more straightforwardly compositional reading (we return to this point later). To do so, one needs to make the sequence of rainy days more prominent than the sequence of all days. A postnominal modifier makes this kind of interpretation easier, as the following example indicates. *Today makes three consecutive rainy days I've lost an umbrella* seems to allow the possibility of intervening non-rainy days, even in the absence of context.

To save contiguity one can move to the power sequence earlier, at *days*, instead of at *rainy days*. Then *rainy* selects day sequences that consist entirely of rainy ones, and the other two modifiers proceed as before. One objection to this approach is that the shift to a power sequence is initiated before it is warranted, that is, before we have ascended high enough in the compositional structure to encounter the word *consecutive*, which requires and hence presumably triggers the shift. However, we hold that the shift can apply anywhere, permitting an ambiguity, to be resolved by knowledge (see LEAST COGNITIVE EFFORT, below).

One view of the issue under discussion is that, strictly speaking, compositionality does not allow access to lower nodes, so that *consecutive* does not have access to *day*. The issue arises in other examples. Consider the phrase *best American compact car*. Strict compositionality does not allow *best* to see inside the *American compact car* node to find the *compact car* node to specify what it is good(est) AS. Nor does it allow *large* to go inside *large wet bird* to specify what it is large FOR (that is, for a bird, not just for a wet one).

A fix for both this last problem and that of *consecutive rainy days* is to allow each node to have a semantic value that includes not only its own semantic value (of the usual kind) but also a list of the semantic values of all the nodes it dominates. More or less equivalently, the modifier might have access to the entire structure built for its co-constituent, not just the top node. It would be necessary in either case to exclude material altered at higher levels by adjectives such as *fake*. This flexibility then necessitates the making of a selection, within the list or structure, as to which node's semantic value to use.

This move takes away some constraints on ordering, but not all, and is thus a middle ground. It takes away the constraints that would incorrectly rule out the examples mentioned above, but it leaves in place the requirement that appropriate material for a modifier to combine with must still be formed somewhere. That somewhere need no longer be the modifier's sibling but it still must be either that sibling or one of its descendants; that is, it must be c-commanded by the modifier. By loosening the compositionality constraint, it weakens some arguments about why word order must be just the way it is.

Operator-argument constraints and semantic application rules

A modifier and its modificand must be mutually appropriate. The modificand *advisor*, for example, provided a special role for modifiers specifying kinds of advice. We now consider the possibility of the modifier placing a constraint on its modificand. To begin, take the case of inappropriateness that arises with a phrase like **red biggest barn*. The noun *barn* corresponds to a type, and in a particular referential use its extension would be a set, some set of barns. The extension of *biggest barn* is not a set but an individual, the biggest one. This observation conforms to our earlier discussion of superlatives as selectors. Extensionally speaking, a selector takes a set as an argument and produces an individual. Similarly, a constrainer takes a set to a set. Failure of the starred phrase above is then accounted for by the failure of the modificand *biggest barn* (an individual) to meet the input constraint of its modifier (that its input be a set).

On the *brood-member* interpretation of *child*, the interpretation of *second child* corresponds to a set, so that another modifier can be applied. That modifier can be a selector, as in the discussion of *youngest second child* above, or it can be a restrictor, as in *crippled second child*. This last phrase sheds light on the presumed correspondence between a syntactic "flat structure" and a semantic "conjunctive reading," sometimes called an "intersective" reading. The phrase refers to a child that independently exhibits the two properties of being crippled and being second in a family. This independence contrasts with the dependence in *second crippled child*, for which the referent may be, say, the fourth child in line, so long as it is the second among the crippled children. If *crippled* is applied to the noun first (as it would be in *second crippled child*), the fact that it is a restrictor makes the mapping rule inapplicable, thereby forcing the unstructured reading of *child*, that is, a young human being. The output of *crippled child* corresponds to a (possibly fuzzy) set with no family structure. One cannot say *second crippled child* and have *second* refer to position in the brood sequence, even though the phrase is syntactically correct.

It may also be possible to get results of a related kind that rely on the subdivision, introduced above, of constrainers into absolutes and relatives. In particular, it seems that an absolute most comfortably goes between a relative and the head noun, so that it can form a category that the relative can refer to, if appropriate. For example, in *tall female giraffe*, the absolute, *female*, joins with the head noun to form a new category, female giraffes, that is to be the standard for tallness. The other possible order of modifiers is of dubious status and is certainly less preferred. Consider whether you would say of a woman sprinter that she is a *female fast runner*, meaning that she is fast among all runners, and also female.

To account for the word-order preference here, consider the following representation, which is different from the extensional one introduced earlier, but not inconsistent with it. Corresponding to a common noun there is a property or a conjunction of properties. An absolute adjective is handled similarly, and combines with a noun by conjoining the properties of both. This process can easily be repeated for additional absolutes. Relative adjectives also have properties, but they are kept separately, so that a string of adjectives followed by a noun has a representation

$$(P_1 \mathbin{\&} P_2 \mathbin{\&} \ldots Q_1 \mathbin{\&} Q_2 \ldots) \, ,$$

where the P_i are from the relatives and the Q_i are from the absolutes and the head noun. The Q_i need to be kept together because each of the P_i has an interpretation that hinges on the Q_i collectively. This reasonably simple account is adequate on condition that all the relatives precede all the absolutes. If that condition is violated, as by the dubious example above, the price is keeping track not just of two separate collections of properties but of their specific intercalation. Notice that this approach deals successfully with phrases like *Ann's biggest truck*, in which the possessive, despite being pulled by syntax out of the compositional order, belatedly contributes its properties to the list of Q_i. In sum, intercalation in the semantic representation would be complex, hence is to be avoided, so the ordering in the sentence should correspond to that (keeping absolutes, including the head noun, together), except where syntax dictates otherwise, as when a possessive determiner participates in modification.

Semantic structure ambiguity

A phrase can have two meanings despite having no syntactic or lexical ambiguity. This is because semantic ambiguity can arise at the phrase level from alternative available semantic relationships between/among the constituents of the phrase. For example, it is clear from the earlier discussion that *military advisor* has two meanings, with *military* describing either the topic of advice or the occupation of the person. The ambiguity must be traced either to a lexical ambiguity in *military* or to a semantic structure ambiguity that is a consequence of there being two possible rules of semantic combination. Since the only wisp of distinction between the two putative readings of *military* has to do with suitability for use in one or the other of the two ways of modifying *advisor*, we regard this as a case of semantic structure ambiguity.

The case is perhaps stronger and clearer with a carefully chosen participle. Thus, *travelling circus* is ambiguous, for the same kinds of reasons, this time with a participle as modifier, rather than an adjective. As (10 a,b) suggest, *travelling* can modify *circus* with information about its inherent characteristics, in which case the two words must be adjacent to each other, or else information about the current condition, with adjacency optional. There is a single meaning of *travelling* here, as can perhaps be best seen from the two relative clause paraphrases of the respective meanings, *circus that travels* and *circus that is travelling*. Since the meaning distinction that is involved can be expressed by alternative aspects of the verb, it should certainly not take up space in the lexicon. A further move for the nonproliferation of lexical readings occurs with our treatment of certain complex uses of ordinals, discussed earlier.

(10) (a) (momentarily) stationary travelling circus
      (b) (once again) travelling travelling circus

The possibility of semantic ambiguity of the type under discussion should not come as a surprise altogether, since a somewhat similar phenomenon arises for individual words in synecdoche, the use of a part for the whole or vice versa, or the special for the general (token/type) or vice versa. The *Random House Dictionary* gives as examples *ten sail* for *ten ships* and *a Croesus* for *a rich man*. Synecdoche is thus another phenomenon in which words don't need multiple meanings to be read in multiple ways in use, here even in the case of single words. Specifically, *sail* doesn't need to have an alternative reading in which it means *ship*, since part-to-whole synecdoche applies to its base and only meaning. Of course, it will have to be possible to determine what particular type of entity *sail* is related to by the part-whole relation, but that knowledge must be available anyway. It is one of several interactions between knowledge and semantics that will be touched upon in the next section.

LEAST COGNITIVE EFFORT

We have introduced several semantic category distinctions for adjectives. These distinctions explain the existence of semantic ambiguities that are otherwise mysterious. Many of these ambiguities go unnoticed, however, in the absence of special contexts favouring a particular interpretation of the modifier. A noteworthy feature of the framework advanced here is the use of real-world knowledge in resolving semantic ambiguities that arise in modified NPs. The purpose of this section is to show how the same knowledge representations can be invoked to explain people's preferences in interpreting semantic ambiguities both in ordinary conversation and in the so-called null context.

We have appealed to real-world knowledge in several instances already to point out the unexpected interpretations of certain NPs, such as *second youngest child*. To illustrate the ambiguity of this phrase we constructed a context that is appropriate for the unusual interpretation on which *second* is a simple selector that picks the second of the contextually-established set of youngest children. As part of the perceiver's knowledge representation, this context is used to resolve the ambiguity. It is worth noting, however, that the interaction of syntactic and semantic parsing and the knowledge representations of the perceiver may be "weak" in the sense that it is strictly limited to the evaluation of the relative fit of the alternative analyses that are made available by these other components of language processing. This brings our views in line with *Processing Modularity*, as well as with *Representational Modularity* (see Hamburger & Crain 1984, 1987 for discussion).

We would contend that knowledge representation also plays a

prominent role in explaining how ambiguities are resolved when there is no prior context at all. In this respect we follow the Referential Theory of Crain and Steedman (1985). Crain and Steedman propose that in the absence of context, perceivers actively attempt to construct a mental representation of a situation that is consistent with the utterance of the sentence in question. In addition to the characters and events depicted by the sentence itself, the construction of a mental model sometimes requires people to represent information that a sentence (more accurately, a speaker) PRESUPPOSES, not just what it ASSERTS. The process of augmenting one's mental model to represent the presuppositional content of sentences has been called "the accommodation of presuppositional failure" by Lewis (1979), "extending the context" by Stalnaker (1974) and Kartunnen (1974), and the "addition of presuppositions to the conversational context of an utterance" by Soames (1982). In the following paragraphs, we will refer to this process as the accommodation of presuppositional failure.

The accommodation of presuppositional failure plays a critical role in the Referential Theory. The process of adding information to one's mental model is used to explain which interpretation of an ambiguous phrase or sentence will be retained. In interpreting linguistic material out of context, as soon as an ambiguity is encountered perceivers attempt to construct model-based representations corresponding to all of the alternative analyses. Due to limited working memory resources, however, they rapidly weed out all but a single analysis. According to this account, perceivers settle on the interpretation that requires fewest modifications in establishing a coherent semantic representation. In other words, they favour the interpretation that carries the fewest presuppositions. Crain and Steedman (1985) call this the Principle of Parsimony.

> **The Principle of Parsimony:** If there is a reading that carries fewer unsatisfied but consistent presuppositions than any other, then that reading will be adopted and the presuppositions in question will be incorporated in the perceiver's mental model.

This principle of interpretation is used "on-line," that is, on a word-by-word basis, so that all but one analysis of a local ambiguity can be rapidly discarded, making room in working memory for subsequent linguistic material. The next two subsections discuss the use of this principle in resolving semantic ambiguity, both in and out of context.

Simple contexts

We restrict attention first to some particularly simple contexts, of the sort used in certain experiments on child language. In this way we both control the context and render world knowledge irrelevant for the moment.

Consider the ambiguous lexical item *child*. It can mean, roughly, either *offspring* or *young human being*. The *offspring* sense is associated with family structure. We restrict attention to a simple nuclear family containing a couple and their brood. The existence of a birth sequence among the members of any brood, along with the fact that each human belongs to a sex category, makes terms like *older brothers* meaningful. The fact that our shared knowledge includes the notion of a birth-ordered brood makes it unnecessary to have any special conversational context to speak of *the second child* in such a family and be understood as meaning the second oldest one. Shared knowledge also permits us to speak of *a second child* out of context; compare (11a,b).

(11) (a) John is a second child.
      (b) ? Texas is a second state.

Although (11a) means that there is a family in which John is the second oldest child, and although a corresponding interpretation is available for (11b), it is nevertheless not appropriate to say (11b) without a special context. In other words, there is indeed a country in which Texas is in second position on a prominent ordering (area), but that ordering is not accorded the special status enjoyed by the birth order of children in a family. This is true despite the further analogy that while states are subject to other orderings – population, entrance to statehood – so, too, does one order children on other criteria, such as height.

Now we can see how the Principle of Parsimony attempts to explain the resolution of semantic ambiguities. Consider the interpretation of the phrase *second child* in (12).[3]

(12) A second child walked through the door.

The preferred interpretation of *second child* in (12) would have the reader suppose that there is some set of children already under discussion, and that one member of this set had previously walked into the room. While this sentence is slightly odd out of context, the cost associated with the accommodation of these presuppositions is not so great as to render the sentence anomalous. In fact it seems that the process whereby presuppositions are accommodated is less costly than recovering the alternative interpretation of *second child* when this phrase appears with the indefinite article, as in (11a).

Complex contexts: "consecutive"

Escalating slightly in complexity, let us reconsider the use of the modifier *consecutive* in phrases such as *three consecutive rainy days*. The different interpretations that are assigned to this phrase are illustrated in (13) and (14):

(13) That's three consecutive rainy days.
(14) That's three consecutive rainy days that I forgot my umbrella.

Recall that the preferred reading of *three consecutive rainy days* is non-compositional, with the interpretation on which it has been [rainy [three [consecutive days]]]. The following figure illustrates this interpretation:

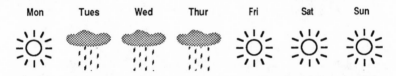

On the alternative, compositional interpretation, the consecutive rainy days on which the speaker forgot his umbrella need not have been successive days. This is depicted in the following figure.

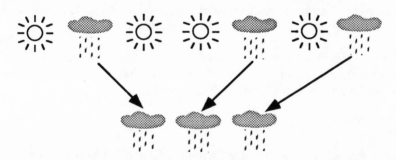

The Principle of Parsimony can be invoked to explain why the structured set interpretation of ambiguous phrases like *second child* and *consecutive rainy days* is less preferred. Simply put, it takes greater cognitive effort to construct a structured set interpretation, because this interpretation requires a greater number of modifications to one's mental model of the domain of discourse. It should be pointed out, however, that this "least effort" principle of ambiguity resolution, although quite powerful in the null context, is easily overruled in context. The construction of a structured set interpretation from scratch, however, is a task of significant proportions, as attested by semantic anomalies such as *Texas is a second state* and *Hugh is a biggest child*, as compared to their conventional counterparts, such as *Sandy is a second child* and *Hugh is a youngest child*. But even when a structured set reading of a noun can be accommodated, because of its availability as part of our background knowledge, this reading often remains as the dispreferred interpretation. In other words, there is a default preference for unstructured sets over structured sets. Evidence of this was given earlier, in examples like *second youngest child* and *consecutive rainy days*.

It is worth pointing out that this preference can be overridden if the unstructured set interpretation requires the accommodation of a number of unmet presuppositions. For example, in (15) the NP *a fourth finger* can either be used with the presupposition that three fingers have already been found (an unstructured set), or it might refer to the structured set of "pinky fingers" that an archaeologist has collected, for instance.

(15) That (fossil) is a fourth finger.

The world of sports provides a great many nouns that give rise to structured set interpretations. One example is given in the seemingly contradictory sentences (16) and (17). Example (16) exhibits the usual, default preference for the unstructured set reading of *homers*. Here, *three consecutive homers* means consecutive at-bats by different players. However, the same phrase is given a structured set reading in (17). There the homers under discussion are a subset of Reggie Jackson's at-bats. The difference between the unstructured set and structured set interpretations explains why (16) and (17) are not contradictory (for people who know the rules of baseball).

(16) There have never been three consecutive homers in a
      world series game.

(17) Reggie Jackson hit three consecutive homers in the third
      game of the 1978 world series.

It is worth mentioning an important difference between this example and the earlier example of *consecutive rainy days*. Recall that in the preferred reading of the earlier example, the modifier *rainy* was interpreted as outside the scope of *consecutive*, resulting in a non-compositional meaning. In the present case, compositionality is not at issue because *consecutive* is adjacent to the lexical item *homers*. Nevertheless the same preference for the unstructured set interpretation arises here as well.

As a final example, note that *quarters*, as in the quarters of a basketball game, refers to a structured set, whereas *quarters* in the monetary sense refers to an unstructured set. This explains why it is reasonable to say *That was a dirty fourth quarter* (which one might hear at a basketball game in Detroit, for instance), but it is difficult to accommodate the presuppositions of the alternative reading, just as it is difficult to interpret the sentence *That was a dirty fourth dime*.

PSYCHOLOGICAL REALITY

As a default principle for resolving semantic ambiguities, we proposed that unstructured set interpretations are favoured over those that call for structured sets. This followed from a "least effort" principle, the Principle of Parsimony. This same principle has been invoked in the literature on adult sentence processing to explain the systematic preferences perceivers exhibit in resolving syntactic ambiguities that arise with so-called Garden Path sentences, due to Bever (1970), such as *The horse raced past the barn fell*.

As with semantic ambiguities, this example shows that people exhibit systematic preferences for resolving structural ambiguities, and they often find it difficult to identify the dispreferred interpretations. The purpose of this section is to indicate how the Principle of Parsimony can be extended to structural ambiguity resolution: to explain the analysis that perceivers assign to ambiguities as a function of the cognitive effort that is required in constructing discourse representations corresponding to the alternative meanings.

The Principle of Parsimony has been applied to syntactic ambiguity resolution by Ni and Crain (1990) in research focussing on the same structures that characterize the classic Garden Path sentences. The existence of a garden path effect in *The horse raced past the barn fell* has been taken as evidence of our tendency to assign the simple past form of morphologically ambiguous verbs such as *raced*; the past participial form (*cf. ridden*) is strongly dispreferred. Choosing the simple past form incurs a cost, however, since the result is that the subsequent verb *fell* cannot be incorporated into the analysis; hence, a garden path effect results.

Previous research has found, however, that people's judgments of sentence grammaticality can be manipulated experimentally by creating minimal semantic changes in the subject NP of the sentences, while holding syntactic structure constant. For example, Ni and Crain found that garden path effects do not occur when the definite determiner in (18) is replaced by *only*, as in (19).

(18)   The students furnished answers before the exam received high marks.

(19)   Only students furnished answers before the exam received high marks.

Another contrast is between sentences like (19), with *only* followed directly by the noun, and sentences like (20), which also contain an adjective:

(20)   Only dishonest students furnished answers before the exam received high marks.

Based on the Principle of Parsimony, Ni and Crain predicted that sentences (18) and (20) should evoke garden path effects, but sentences like (19) should not. For purposes of exposition, it will be useful to explain the reasoning behind this prediction within the theory of discourse representation proposed by Heim (1982), called FILE CHANGE SEMANTICS.

In file change semantics, a semantic representation is conceived of as a box of file cards. Certain file cards can be accessed at any time: these represent the background knowledge or "common ground" that participants bring to any discourse. But in addition, the discourse participants may add new file cards or write on old ones, as demanded by the current discourse. A new card is added whenever a new entity is introduced. This is done, for example, in response to indefinite NPs such as *a student* or *some student*. We can contrast this with definite descriptions like *the students*, in (18). Here the use of the definite determiner suggests that a file card should already exist, either in the background knowledge or in the set of file cards that have been created during the current discourse. In this case, if no card can be located corresponding to the entity in question, then a new file card must be added. This process is one instance of accommodation of a presuppositional failure.

Other types of modifiers introduce further complications in effecting modifications to files to accommodate unsatisfied presuppositions. In discussing modifiers such as *even* and *only*, Karttunen and

Peters (1979) propose that these words carry an "existential implica-
tion" that there are other individuals under consideration besides the
one(s) mentioned by the head noun. For instance, the sentence *Even
President Bush thinks Dan is an idiot* carries the presupposition that
there are other people besides Bush that think the same thing, namely,
that Dan Rather is an idiot.

Now consider sentences that begin with *only*, followed by a noun,
such as (19) above. The initial NP in (19), *only students*, presupposes
that there are other individuals under consideration that are being
contrasted with students. Suppose, then, this phrase is encountered in
the null context. This requires the perceiver to create a new file card
for *students*, and to extend the current file cards to meet the additional
presupposition that there are other individuals under consideration,
being contrasted to students. This extension requires the creation of a
CONTRAST SET. Following the Principle of Parsimony, the perceiver attempts to make the minimal modifications to files. One change is
clear, a new file card must be created, corresponding to students. But
with this card in place, there are several ways to introduce the contrast set. One way to accommodate this presupposition would be to
add another new file card, identifying the contrast set. The problem
with this alternative is that no properties of the contrast set have been
identified: it could be teachers, people in general who are not students, and so on. A second possibility is to partition the file card that
has just been created for students. It would be eminently reasonable
to take this tack, for example, if information is available for forming
the contrast set somewhere in the sentence itself. In example (19), the
morphological ambiguity of the verb *furnished* allows the words following *only students* to be analysed as a modifying phrase. And this,
in turn, allows the perceiver to partition the file card corresponding to
students into ones who have been "furnished the answers..." and a
contrast set of students who have not. Ni and Crain propose that, as a
pragmatic default, perceivers favour the modification of currently
available discourse referents over the creation of new ones. This simple "least effort" principle is a straightforward adaptation of the Principle of Parsimony.

Notice what should happen, according to the Principle of Parsimony, if the initial NP also contains an adjective, as in example (20),
repeated here.

(20) Only dishonest students furnished the answers before the
      exam received high marks.

Encountering this phrase out of context causes the perceiver to create a new file card representing dishonest students. In addition, the determiner *only* requires a contrast set. This contrast set is already available if, following the pragmatic default we just mentioned, the newly created card corresponding to dishonest students is subdivided so as to create a new discourse referent, namely a set of individuals who are students, but not dishonest ones. This results in the expectation that people will once again misanalyse the ambiguous phrase *furnished the answers*. In sum, the prediction is that sentences beginning with NPs with both *only* and an ADJ should evoke garden path effects, just like sentences whose initial NP contains the definite determiner, as in (18) above.

These predictions were investigated in the Ni and Crain study using a self-paced reading task. As predicted, they found that there was a significant difference between sentences like (18) and (20), and the *only* sentences with no adjective. The former clearly induced garden path effects, in the form of increased reaction times at the critical word (for example, *received* in example [20]). By contrast, sentences like (19), with *only* without an ADJ, patterned exactly like unambiguous control sentences. These findings offer strong presumptive support for the Principle of Parsimony.

CONCLUSION

Three important modules for human processing of natural language are syntax, semantics, and world knowledge. The semantic module has been our specific concern here. In trying to formulate an adequate semantic representation for phrases we are pushed to the realization that it is intertwined with both syntax and world knowledge in interesting and unsuspected ways. The results of these deliberations have clear consequences for the design of natural language interfaces.

NOTES

1 Instead of making ω a boolean comparison of two arguments, one might think of having it simply be a one-argument function, taking each element of ψ to an integer corresponding to its position in the ordering. Then Π_k would simply return whichever element of ψ, call it ψ^*, the ordering ω mapped to ψ. That is, $\Pi_k (\langle \psi, \omega \acute{O} \rangle) = \psi^*$, where $\omega(\psi^*) = k$. This move, however, has the undesirable consequence of requiring an adjustment of the values assigned by ω to the elements of ψ whenever an element is added to or removed from ψ. A further advantage of the chosen representation is that if ψ_1 is a subset of ψ_2 then the two corresponding ωs are

identical over ψ_1. Thus if Pat is a taller representative than Barbara, she is also a taller person.

2 One might object that *first* does not have its usual, ordinal sense in *first violinist, first lieutenant, first base,* and so on. One does, after all, say *lead guitar* (not *first guitar*) and the fourth base is home plate. Still, first lieutenants do give orders to second lieutenants, not vice versa, and it is required to touch first base en route to second. So the ordinality is valid, but apparently it applies at the level of the type, to form a new type.

3 In (11a), the predicate phrase is interpreted as a characteristic of individuals (i.e., an individual level predicate), rather than as a property of specific individuals (i.e., a stage-level predicate). In (12), the finite tense signals the simple-selector interpretation of *second*.

REFERENCES

Bever, T. (1970). The cognitive basis for linguistic structures. In J.R. Hayes (ed.), *Cognition and the Development of Language.* New York: John Wiley & Sons

Crain, S. and Steedman, M. (1985). On not being led up the garden path: the use of context by the psychological syntax processor. In D. Dowty, L. Karttunen, and A. Zwicky (eds.), *Natural Language Parsing.* Cambridge, Eng.: Cambridge University Press, 320-58

Dixon, R.M.W. (1982). Where have all the adjectives gone? In *Where Have All the Adjectives Gone?* Berlin: Walter de Gruyter & Co.

Goyvaerts, D.L. (1968). An introductory study on the ordering of a string of adjectives in present-day English. *Philologia Pragensia* 11:12-28

Hamburger, H. and Crain, S. (1984). Acquisition of Cognitive compiling. *Cognition* 17:85-136

– (1987). Plans and semantics in human processing of language. *Cognitive Science* 11:101-36

Heim, I. (1982). The Semantics of Definite and Indefinite Noun Phrases. Ph.D dissertation, University of Massachusetts, Amherst MA

Kamp, H. (1981). A theory of truth and semantic representation. In J. Groenendijk, Th. Janssen, and M. Stokhof (eds.), *Formal Methods in the Study of Language, I.* Mathematisch Centrum, Amsterdam, 277-322

Karttunen, L. (1974). Presupposition and linguistic context. *Theoretical Linguistics* 1:181-94

– and Peters, S. (1979). Conventional implicature, In C-K Oh, and D.A. Dinneen (eds.), *Syntax and Semantics, Vol. XI: Presupposition.* New York: Academic Press

Keenan, E.L. and Faltz, L.M. (1985). *Boolean Semantics for Natural Language.* Dordrecht: D. Reidel

Kratzer, A. (1981). Partition and revision: the semantics of counterfactuals. *Journal of Philosophical Logic* 10:201-16

Lewis, D. (1979). Scorekeeping in a language game. *Journal of Philosophic Logic* 8:339-59

Matthei, E. (1982). The acquisition of prenominal modifier sequences. *Cognition* 11:301-32

Montague, R. (1970). In R. Thomason (ed.), *Formal Philosophy*. New Haven: Yale University Press

Ni, W. and Crain, S. (1990). How to resolve structural ambiguities. In *NELS 20*, Amherst, MA

Roeper, T.W. (1972). Approaches to a Theory of Language Acquisition with Examples from German Children. Unpublished doctoral dissertation. Harvard University.

Soames, S. (1982). How presuppositions are inherited: a solution to the projection problem. *Linguistic Inquiry* 13:483-545

Sproat, R. and Shih, C. (1988). Prenominal adjectival ordering in English and Mandarin. In J. Blevins and J. Carter (eds.), *NELS 18*, Amherst, MA

Stalnaker, R. (1974). Pragmatic presuppositions. In M.K. Munitz and P. K. Unger (eds.), *Semantics and Philosophy*. New York: New York University Press

CHAPTER EIGHT

On the Development of Biologically Real Models of Human Linguistic Capacity

Mary-Louise Kean

A formal linguistic theory which accurately characterizes the average human being's capacity to acquire and maintain knowledge of the language of his/her speech community is of necessity a biological theory, a theory of the functional structure of components of the human brain. Linguistic theories which attempt to characterize human linguistic capacity are, in this respect, no different from theories which attempt to characterize visual cognition. On this view, a formal linguistic theory must be both psychologically and biologically real. An elegant theory of language structure which comports neither with the exigencies of structural processing as carried out on-line by people nor the computational structure of human brain mechanisms may be of interest and importance for a host of reasons, but it is not a theory of human linguistic capacity.

This view does not entail rampant reductionism from formal linguistics to neurobiology. It does, however, limit the class of formal grammars which are of interest to the study of human cognition. Specifically, it requires that there be some explicit algorithm(s) through which the linguistic theory is related to the theories of language production and comprehension and (possibly via processing theories) to the analysis of the functional organization of language relevant brain systems. While the issue of psychological reality has engaged a considerable amount of scholarly energy since the 1960s, the issue of biological reality has not. It is, however, not a new issue; arguments against biological reality are encountered in the nineteenth century literature on aphasia. In 1878, Hughlings Jackson argued that "we must not classify [in aphasia] on the basis of a mixed method of anatomy, physiology and psychology any more than we would classify plants on a mixed natural and empirical method, as exogens, kitchen-herbs, graminaceae, and shrubs" (cited in Jakobson 1972).

This position goes through only if one accepts certain assumptions: (a) that there is a significant scientific distinction between what is natural and what is empirical, and either (b) that anatomy, physiology and psychology are merely arbitrary levels in the description of linguistic capacity or (c) that the botanical categories cited by Jackson are significantly distinct levels of generalization. As far as I can see, assumption (a) simply makes no sense. As for assumption (b), the best evidence is that anatomy, physiology, and psychology are not arbitrary levels in the conceptualization of linguistic capacity, and therefore that assumption must be rejected. Assumption (c) fares no better; the categories cited are natural-kind terms, perhaps, but they are arbitrary-kind terms of distinct levels of analysis and not analytic levels themselves of a parity with anatomy, physiology, and psychology (e.g., whether sorrel is a kitchen herb or a vegetable is cuisine-specific but botanically irrelevant, whereas exogens are exogens). The position taken here is, then, a complete rejection of Jackson's (and Jakobson's) position with respect to aphasiology and other domains of inquiry relevant to the biology of language, while it concurs with Jackson on the matter of practice of botany.

Whereas language structure (grammar), language processors for comprehension and production, and the neuroanatomy and neurophysiology of language are all conceptually distinct, the study of the aphasias and other disorders of language is not itself a conceptually distinct domain in the sense that there could ever be a theory of aphasia (or more generally deficits) that would be a characterization of an independent level of conceptualization and representation of human linguistic capacity. The theoretical interest in studying language disorders lies in the fact that in dealing with functional analyses of disorders one is dealing with the interface of conceptually distinct characterizations of human linguistic capacity. Research on language disorders provides a test for and a means of revelation of the nature of relations among systematic levels of representation of linguistic capacity. Present research typically focuses on the grammatical and psycholinguistic analyses of disorders (e.g., the articles which regularly appear in journals such as *Brain and Language* and *Cognition*). Neurobiological considerations as yet play no significant role in the conceptualization and analyses of disorders. This is largely due to the incomparable states of development of neurobiology and linguistics and psycholinguistics and is not necessarily a consequence of any "in principle" theoretical argument. A variety of arguments, however, have been developed to provide reason for the disregard of neurobiology by linguists and psycholinguists, including those who support the claim that a theory of human linguistic capacity must be biologically real. Three types of arguments have the greatest currency: the "scientific," the "conceptual," and the "methodological."

"Scientific" arguments often take the following form: Linguistic theory has been developed to a significant extent; however, neurobiology has not advanced sufficiently for there to be any meaningful relation drawn between brain structure and linguistics. It is certainly the case that the functional structure and operating principles of significant aspects of the brain are still ill understood. The fact that our understanding of neurobiology is far from complete is not, however, sufficient to license the wholesale disregard of what is known; after all, how are we to ever know when neurobiology and linguistic theory have developed to a point where meaningful relations can be established if we systematically ignore it? Many design characteristics of the nervous system are coming to be well-understood, and, while the precise relation of these to formal linguistic theory is as yet unknown, they offer many intriguing possibilities for the development of our understanding of the biology of language. What may at best be analogies today, may be the bases for explanations in the future.

Essential to all learning is the connectivity between neurons. Neuronal transmission takes place at the synapse, where the output of one neuron is transmitted to the next. Considerable attention has been given to the synapse, in particular to the development of synaptic efficacy as it is critical to learning. A phenomenon central to the study of synaptic efficacy and how it is enhanced is "long term potentiation" (LTP) (see Seifert 1984 for several reviews and discussion). Three characteristics of LTP are of note. First, the efficacy of a system is supported by multiple overlapping inputs. Change in synaptic efficacy can be effected for a period of time by a single event, while long term change is supported by recurrent positive information. Second, LTP provides for cumulative activation. Rather than activation proceeding in a linear sequence, because of feedback properties of a system, even one exposure to a stimulus allows for iterated activation. The third defining feature of LTP is that it is selective. These three features – multiple positive inputs, iterated activation, and selectivity within a system – are exactly the class of general physiological principles which would be expected on the basis of linguistic and psycholinguistic theories of language acquisition. Thus, while the detailed circuitry underlying linguistic capacity remains to be elucidated, critical physiological principles which explain learning in neural circuits are coming to be well-understood and provide a biological basis for many general claims which have been made about language acquisition.

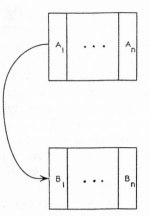

Figure 1. Schematic illustration of mapping system between two functional loci. In such situations there is a loss of information as the output of A is mapped onto B.

In grammatical theories components of the grammar form a partially ordered set. Schematically, the set can be represented as in Figure 1, with the nodes A-B associated with particular components of the grammar. Typically, in studies of language deficits, from the nineteenth-century work on aphasia to the present, language deficits are characterized in terms of an impairment to one component or another; thus, for example, I have argued that a symptom often associated with Broca's aphasia is a phonological deficit, while others have argued that it is a syntactic or semantic deficit (Kean 1977). Characteristic of such arguments is the assumption of a direct translation of some (sub)component of a linguistic theory onto some brain system(s). In the extreme this view leads to the localization of specific components of linguistic capacity in specific anatomical regions of the brain. Consideration of the general principles of anatomical organization cast doubt on such approaches.

The representational systems which are exploited in behaviour are autonomous, of necessity distinctly characterized; that is, I am trusting that no one will dispute that both psychologically and neurally our capacities for voice recognition and face recognition are distinct in significant respects, as are knowledge of one's native language and the spatial layout of one's house. Based on what is known from clinical aphasia research, there are several non-contiguous areas of the left hemisphere which are involved in supporting normal linguistic capacity. If there were simply successive and/or parallel inputs from one system to another, then it might be possible that the components of grammatical theory could be conveniently mapped onto brain areas. However, while such connections do exist, another sort of connection also exists. A mapping between two functional systems, A and B, can be effected if the output of the components of A, or some proper subset of them, is projected onto a third system, an A-B system, which in turn projects onto the components of B, or some proper subset (Figure 2). In this case there is a convergence of A representations on A-B, which in turn projects to B. In such a process there will be a loss of information; if A were replicated in A-B then A would be non-autonomous and indistinguishable from A-B. It is the function of A-B to re-represent information in a form appropriate for input to B. Taking A-B to be a functionally combinatorial system, its output is distributed across B (or some proper subset of B); at the same time, the output of A-B will also be distributed back across A. A cortical structure could serve as an A-B system, as could subcortical structures; various subcortical structures are eminently well-placed and connected to involve candidate A-B systems of the type just described. For example, all inputs to the cortex come through the thalamus and cortical areas project back to the thalamus.

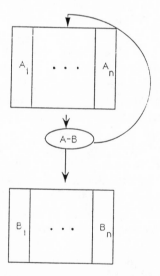

Figure 2. Schematic illustration of a mapping system between two functional loci that is mediated by an intervening combinatorial system. The input to A-B involves a convergence of information from the subcomponents of A; the output of A-B is a representation which distributes across (some proper subset of) B and feedsback as an input to A.

To date, analyses of linguistic deficits have not seriously taken into account the potential existence of A-B type systems as well as direct mappings systems from A to B. However, postulating the existence of both types of systems in the support of linguistic capacity has great neuroanatomical plausibility. It comports with the facts of there being cortico-cortico connections, significantly among functionally and anatomically distinctive cortical loci, and with there being a complex array of ascending and descending pathways between various cortical systems and various subcortical structures. That is, the anatomical design features of the brain seem hardly functionally interpretable unless one assumes something on this order. Schematically, then, the neural system underlaying human linguistic capacity is probably more akin to Figure 3 than to Figure 1.

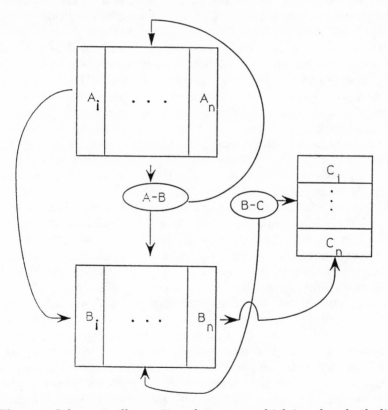

Figure 3. Schematic illustration of a system which involves both direct mapping systems between functional loci and indirect mappings which are mediated by combinatorial systems which feed both forward and backward.

The neural plausibility of a model such as that illustrated in Figure 3 requires that we re-evaluate the interpretations of data from deficit research as well as more generally reconsidering what we expect to learn from such research. Functional organization of the brain along the lines I have outlined suggests that there will be no trivially direct mapping from components of a grammatical theory onto brain systems. At the same time, it provides the basis for a potential explanation of why attempts to characterize particular aphasias as "syntactic," "phonological," etc., disorders have all failed; if the components are not discretely represented in the brain then it stands to reason they won't be found. What has been found, however, is of interest. Specific disorders seem to involve disturbances in multiple components of the grammar and processors, but never the annihilation of any specific component; this is just the sort of situation one could expect under the model outlined here. Broca's aphasics, for example, have difficulties with at least some derivational and inflectional morphemes, with various syntactic constraints, and with lexical retrieval. The task for neurolinguistics becomes one of describing in detail the range of disorders associated with specific syndromes, and then using those data to model how language is organized in the human brain, a task far beyond the traditional clinical mapping of symptoms onto anatomy. Such modelling is not simply of interest for enhancing our understanding of human brain systems, it also has the potential for making significant contributions to our understanding of processing. The real-time processing of language cannot be carried out independently of how the brain organizes linguistic capacity.

Neither the brief discussion of LTP nor the discussion of the neuroanatomical organization of linguistic capacity provides any biological explanation for any linguistic phenomenon. In the case of LTP, however, we can see the emergence of physiological principles which can provide a neural explanation for language acquisition. In the case of the neuroanatomical organization of the brain, the issue is one of introducing considerations of neuroanatomical plausibility to inform the study of acquired language disorders. In both cases I see cause to take heart that we may be on the right track in developing a biologically real theory of linguistic capacity. Thus, I reject as unfounded "scientific" arguments to the effect that there is nothing to be gained at this juncture from taking cognizance of developments in neurobiology.

"Conceptual" arguments against biological realism take a different form from "scientific" ones. They are often based on the assumption that how the brain implements human linguistic capacity is irrelevant to cognitive sciences. This view explicitly rejects biological reality as a criterion for a theory of human linguistic capacity. Such arguments are often based on analogy. A software program can be implemented on a variety of hardware systems; therefore, the specific hardware, the brain, which supports human linguistic capacity, is not all that important. This view, of course, overlooks the fact that the specific hardware system of a computer does greatly influence how and what information is processed. There are, to take a trivial example, a host of word processing programs available, but one would hardly say that they can be identically implemented on *any* machine. What is at issue is how human beings process and represent language and not how some beings might achieve those functions.

There are insufficient neurobiological data to say anything of substance at this time about the real-time processing of language. There is, however, evidence from other domains which can serve to illustrate the point that neurobiology has potentially a very potent role to play in the analysis of behaviour. A recent and important case in point involves the relation between thought and emotional response. It is the common view that an emotional response to an event is based on some cognitive assessment of the situation, that is, cortical analysis. Thus, the idea is that if you see someone who you dislike, you first recognize the face, identify the individual, and, given that identification, have an emotional response. The neuroanatomical interpretation of this view has been that sensory information is relayed through the thalamus to the cortex and from the cortex to some structure in the limbic system, a set of subcortical structures, and the limbic system then causes the emotional response. Recent work by LeDoux has shown, however, that this view is not correct. He has found that in addition to pathways from the cortex to the amygdala, a limbic system structure involved in learning and emotion, there are also direct pathways from the thalamus to the amygdala. Because of the time required for synaptic transmission, the consequence is that an emotional response gets elicited milliseconds in advance of cognitive registration (the amygdala being only one synapse from the thalamus whereas cognitive registration involves multiple synapses). These research results have profound implications for both psychology and psychiatry, and they offer a potent illustration of how neurobiology can significantly effect our understanding of behaviour. Language processing takes place in real-time. The time required to carry out the various computations involved in on-line structural sentence processing is a function of the neuroanatomical organization of language, ceteris paribus. Given the combined neural and computational complexity of sentence processing it is sheer hubris to imagine that psycholinguistic processing will be fully understood on the basis of behavioural data alone.

The third class of arguments used against taking neurobiology into consideration in the study of human linguistic capacity, at least at this time, is essentially methodological and turns on the messiness of human brain damage data. There can be no disputing the fact that human lesion data are very messy. The precise geography of the lesions of any two individuals who have had similar strokes is, for example, variable; the details of an individual's vascular architecture can have significant consequences for the scope (depth and/or area) of a lesion caused by a cerebro-vascular accident. Additionally, there are individual differences in human brains; the scope and consequence of such differences are not known. Developmental dyslexics have diffuse anomalies of neural ontogeny involving the language areas of the brain (Geschwind & Galaburda 1987), and in-development anomalies in phonological processing are evident (Mann 1986); psycholinguistic studies of adult developmental dyslexics have, however, failed to provide any evidence of significant linguistic anomalies (Kean 1989). At present there are no data on the extent to which such individual differences have consequences for the behavioural deficits which arise consequent to brain damage. A third factor complicating the situation is that very small and discrete lesions can have profound effects; in the majority of reported cases, aphasic patients do not have such small and relatively well circumscribed lesions. To give an indication of the behavioural ramifications of a very small restricted lesion, due to an aeschemic attack during surgery, a patient, R.B., had a profound chronic global amnesia; histological analysis of his brain after death revealed that the damage was restricted to bilateral destruction of a single subcomponent of the hippocampus, a limbic structure (Squire et al. 1989). With relatively large lesions such as those encountered in aphasiological research, deficits may be due to damage to a structural processing centre, destruction of fibers of passage from one processing centre to another, and so on. Such observations about brain damage indicate the difficulty inherent in much of the data for studying the detailed neuroanatomy of language, but that is all; they do not provide reason to dismiss neuroanatomy from consideration. The methodological complexity required to carry out an analysis is not a scientifically acceptable argument for rejecting the potential relevance of the analysis.

A twist on the line of argument based on the messiness of much brain damage data is encountered in studies which do present anatomical data. At issue are patients who seemingly have the same disorder but distinct lesions. There is a disorder known as deep dyslexia in which patients have very specific reading disorders: In reading major category items, deep dyslexics make semantic and visual substitution errors (e.g., reading *symphony* as "orchestra" or as "sympathy"), and they have extreme difficulty in reading any function words and cannot read legal non-words (e.g., *flist*) (Marshall & Newcombe 1980). Deep dyslexics cannot exploit the phonological route to reading, i.e., read through mapping graphemes onto phonemes. In a study of the CAT scans of five deep dyslexics, Marin (1980) found variability in the lesions; no specific area of brain damage is seemingly responsible for this disorder. In all cases there was extensive subcortical damage as well as cortical damage with varying areas of involvement. From such an example one might argue that the human brain is very plastic and that within broad parameters functions can be localized most anywhere. But before jumping to that conclusion two questions must be raised:

(1) Would one expect to find a localized centre for phonological reading?
(2) Do deep dyslexics have the same set of disorders?

In response to the first question, it should be apparent that the capacity to read phonologically turns on the integration of two complex and quite distinct processing systems, visual and linguistic, the former of which is demonstrably quite complex neuroanatomically and neurophysiologically and the latter of which surely is also. Thus, phonological reading must entail systems, and hence there is every reason to anticipate that it can be disrupted in consequence to brain damage to a variety of areas. Put somewhat differently, to expect a function such as a phonological reading to be discretely localized is to retreat to the tradition of Spurzheim, the most extravagant of all the nineteenth-century phrenologists.

Coltheart (1980) presents behavioural data on twenty-two deep dyslexics; the data are inadequate to address the question of how behaviourally similar the specific patients discussed by Marin are, but they do provide sufficient data to answer the second question. Many, but not all deep dyslexics are clinically classified as having Broca's aphasia; as would be expected, only some of those patients show agrammatism of speech (the tendency to omit function words and bound morphemes). Some deep dyslexics have anomia (difficulty in naming objects), but not all. As would be expected, some patients are agrammatic and anomic, while others have one or the other symptom and yet others have neither in any appreciable degree. One patient in the sample had "a very severe case of presenile dementia" and "had numerous other deficits (for example, no spontaneous speech at all)." Thus, the population of deep dyslexics is not uniform; rather it is a group of individuals who are classed together on the basis of a single symptom. Interesting as deep dyslexia is, it is far from clear that deep dyslexics should be treated as a single group. Variability of lesions within any population defined on a single symptom viewed in isolation from all other behaviour is neurobiologically unexceptional; by the same token, as clinical syndromes are defined on arbtrary sets of symptoms, they too should not be expected to be neuroanatomically uniform.

In the absence of a neurolinguistic agenda which is concerned with the biological reality of linguistic theory, two neurally neutral approaches to the study of deficits have emerged. On one view it is appropriate to study some specific aspect(s) of linguistic capacity in groups of patients. One value in this approach is that it allows one to consider whether some deficits are shared by all patients with aphasia. It also is a ready avenue for the investigation of double dissociations, the situation where one group of patients has impairment in some area X but is sparing of function in some area Y, while another group shows the reverse pattern. Deep dyslexia can serve in an example of a behavioural double dissociation: while deep dyslexics show a selective loss of the ability to phonologically read with a sparing of the capacity to carry out "whole word" reading, another group, surface dyslexics, show the reverse pattern of impairment which renders them impaired in the reading of phonologically irregular words (Patterson, Coltheart, & Marshall 1985). Behaviourally it has long been hypothesized that skilled normal readers employ both phonological and whole word routes to reading (Taylor & Taylor 1983); the contrast between deep and surface dyslexia provides evidence for the biological reality of that hypothesis. Thus, there is no question that group studies of classes of patients have the potential for providing valuable data for a biologically real theory of linguistic capacity; in principle such studies can provide critical evidence for deciding among competing theories of human linguistic capacity.

Group studies, however, investigate isolated facets of linguistic performance across populations of patients. In a typical experiment the performance of a group of Wernicke's aphasics might be compared with that of a group of Broca's aphasics on a specific task; whether or not the two populations differ with respect to whatever variable is being tested is a statistical finding and not necessarily a finding which holds for each pair of patients from the two populations. There is linguistically and psycholinguistically noteworthy variability within clinical populations. With respect to spontaneous speech, Broca's aphasics, for example, fall into three distinct groups: speakers of one-to-two word utterances, agrammatic speakers who tend to leave out function words, and speakers whose utterances are anomalous for their shortness but whose utterances are grammatical sentences or sentence fragments. Thus, while there may be linguistically significant communalities among all Broca's aphasics, superficial observation indicates that there will also be differences. Because statistical analyses can obscure important data about variability in performance within a patient group, the second common approach to the study of deficits has emerged, the single case study.

The single case study approach to aphasia research has a long history in clinical neurology, but until relatively recently has played a limited role in the linguistic and psycholinguistic analysis of deficits. In a single case study, the investigator(s) carry out extensive research on one particular patient. These studies can be very enlightening; deep dyslexia, for example, gained prominence because of the single case study work of Marshall and Newcombe, which first appeared in 1966 and gave rise to the notion of deep dyslexia in 1973, and their work led to the study of other cases. There are, however, a number of problems with single cases studies. Because attention is focused on a single individual, there is no a priori basis for assuming the generalizability of findings to the normal population at large. The fact that in much of the research done on single cases there is little attention to neuroanatomy provides an additional limitation on the role for such research in developing a biologically real theory of human linguistic capacity.

In practice, though not out of necessity, research on single cases tends to focus on isolated symptoms. In consequence, single case research has the potential for being very misleading. An individual might, for example, be a deep dyslexic for a variety of reasons, such as a limitation in phonological processing or a limitation in the mechanisms involved in the integration of phonological and visual information. If one's focus is solely on the reading aloud of single words in studying the impairments of deep dyslexics, then important data may be missed. For example, patients with an impairment in integration should be able to repeat nonsense words whereas a group of patients with limitation in phonological processing might be able to repeat known lexically represented words but not nonsense words. One of the virtues of single case studies is that they allow for the investigation of the co-occurrence/interrelation of complex symptomatologies within a single patient. This potential has yet to be significantly exploited.

Research on the biological foundations of language and the development of a biologically real theory of linguistic capacity has made relatively little progress to date. This is the result of a variety of factors. In part this is due to the current level of understanding which exists in neurobiology and the fact that we have limited access to the study of the human brain, and in part it is due to disregard for what is known in behavioural neurobiology. At the same time, methodological practice in the study of individuals with aphasias has limited the ability of that area to contribute to the development of psychologically as well as biologically real theories of human linguistic capacity. A practical agenda for neurolinguistics which has the promise for making meaningful contributions has three components:

(1) attention advances in neurobiology which can shed light on mechanisms of learning, response to brain damage, and principles of neural organization;
(2) repeated studies of various aspects of linguistic capacity on the same populations of patients so that both individual and group data can be systematically analysed; and
(3) given (1) and (2), efforts be made to develop biologically real models of linguistic capacity.

REFERENCES

Coltheart, M. (1980). Deep dyslexia: a review of the syndrome. In M. Coltheart, K. Patterson, and J.C. Marshall (eds.), *Deep Dyslexia*. London: Routledge & Kegan Paul

Geschwind, N. and Galaburda, A.M. (1987). *Cerebral Lateralization: Biological Mechanisms, Associations, and Pathology*. Cambridge, MA: MIT Press

Jakobson, R. (1972). *Child Language, Aphasia, and Phonological Universals*. The Hague: Mouton

Kean, M.L. (1977). The linguistic interpretation of aphasic syndromes: agrammatism in Broca's aphasia, an example. *Cognition* 5:6-46

– (1989). Grammatical capacity and developmental dyslexia. In C. von Euler (ed.), *Brain and Reading*. London: MacMillan

Mann, V.A. (1986). Why some children experience reading problems: the contribution of difficulties with language processing and phonological sophistication in early reading disability. In J.K. Torgesen and B.Y. Wong (eds.), *Learning Disabilities: Some New Perspectives*. New York: Academic Press

Marin, O.S.M. (1980). CAT scans of five dyslexic patients. In M. Coltheart, K. Patterson, and J.C. Marshall (eds.), *Deep Dyslexia*. London: Routledge & Kegan Paul

Marshall, J.C. and Newcombe, F. (1966). Syntactic and semantic errors in paralexia. *Neuropsychologia* 4:169-76

– (1973). Patterns of paralexia. *Journal of Psycholinguistic Research* 2:175-99

– (1980). The conceptual status of deep dyslexia. In M. Coltheart, K. Patterson, and J.C. Marshall (eds.), *Deep Dyslexia*. London: Routledge & Kegan Paul

Patterson, K.E., Marshall, J.C., and Coltheart, M. (eds.) (1985). *Surface Dyslexia: Neuropsychological and Cognitive Studies of Phonological Reading*. London: Lawrence Erlbaum Associates

Seifert, W. (ed.) (1984). *Molecular, Cellular, and Behavioral Neurobiology of the Hippocampus*. New York: Academic Press

Squire, L.R., Shimamura, A.P., and Amaral, D.G. (1989). Memory and the hippocampus. In J. Byrne and W. Berry (eds.), *Neural Models of Plasticity*. New York: Academic Press

Taylor, I. and Taylor, M.M. (1983). *The Psychology of Reading*. New York: Academic Press

CHAPTER NINE

Properties of Lexical Entries and Their Real-Time Implementation

Lewis P. Shapiro

INTRODUCTION

This paper is about lexical properties and the sentence processing devices that implement them in both normal and brain-damaged subjects.[1] I will first summarize some work that has to do with the organization of the lexicon, particularly representations involving strict subcategorization, argument structure (a-structure), thematic information, and lexical conceptual structure (lcs). I will then discuss a series of psycholinguistic experiments that examines the real-time processing of some of these properties in normal subjects. Within this discussion I will also describe some recent work that suggests that lexical access involves the serial activation of multiple interpretations of polysemous nouns. Yet for a particular type of brain damaged subject who has incurred damage to the left anterior cortex – agrammatic Broca's aphasia – this normally fast-acting serial activation appears to be protracted. I will then show how protracted lexical access might not extend to the activation of thematic information in agrammatic Broca's aphasia, and will discuss some on-going work that attempts to resolve this apparent discrepancy. Finally, I will discuss a recent study that appears to make contact with the notion that thematic roles are part of (a non-grammatical) lcs, and that lcs entries are shaped by the form in which visual information is parsed.

THE ORGANIZATION OF THE LEXICON

Lexical entries appear to consist of, at least, a word's syntactic category, subcategorization frame, a-structure, and its meaning/lcs. As approximations to such entries, consider:

(1) *write*   V
                      [NP]
                      (x(y))
                      [cause (x,y) [by means of language]]

(2) *give*   V
                      [NP PP]
                      (x(y(z)))
                      [cause ([x], [go ([y], [path from x to z]]])) or 'x
                      gives y to z'

Note that thematic role labels appear to be missing from this organ-
izational scheme. This view of the lexicon (from Grimshaw, 1990; see
also Rappaport & Levin 1986, Jackendoff 1987, Levin 1990) claims that
a-structure and thematic roles are rather different objects, that a-structure makes reference to thematic role labels only insofar as to use the
thematic hierarchy to govern the relative prominence of one argument over others in a structured a-structure. That is, the only information in a-structure is the relative prominence each argument bears,
and not what theta-role might be assigned to each argument. So, for
example, the a-structure for *write* shows that the x-argument (the
"external" argument) is more prominent in the hierarchy than the
y-argument (the "internal" argument).

On this view theta role labels are read off from the lcs of a predicate,
not from its a-structure. In (2), the lcs states that "x causes y to go
along a PATH from x to z" (Jackendoff 1983) or in less formal terminology, "x gives y to z." In terms of thematic roles, however, *give* takes
three obligatory ones: (AGENT THEME GOAL). Within this account
of the lexicon, thematic role labels are simply epiphenomenal; they
fall out naturally from an lcs representation. That is, the function these
thematic role labels play in the grammar are registered within the
internal structure of lcs, not within an independent level of thematic
representation (this also means that lcs is the level of representation
responsible for theta-assignment). However, for simplicity's sake I
will use, when necessary, the more standard thematic role labels instead of a more richly specified lcs when describing verb representations in this paper.

It turns out then, that lcs is the representation responsible for verbs
idiosyncratically selecting for different sets of thematic roles, not a-
structure, since a-structure does not contain the vocabulary necessary
for such selection. But not only do verbs lcs-select for different sets of
"simple" thematic roles, they also select for complements having

more complex semantic realizations (Grimshaw 1979, 1990; Pesetsky 1983):

(3) Some people claim [that Duke was a Zombie]
     PROPOSITION (P)
(4) It's amazing [how weird Duke was]!
     EXCLAMATION (E)
(5) They wondered [whether Duke had been zombified]
     INTERROGATIVE (Q)
(6) They attempted [to zombify Duke]
     INFINITIVE (I)

And while some verbs select for only one of these semantic realizations, others select for many:

(7) Some people knew [that Duke was a Zombie]
(8) We knew [how weird Duke was]!
(9) (Only) we knew [whether or not Duke had been zombified]

We can thus represent *know* in the following way:

(10) *know*   V (category)
                    [__S'] (strict subcategorization)
                    (x(y)) (structured a-structure)
                    x 'knows' y → (y a P) (lcs subentries)
                                  (y an E)
                                  (y a Q)

Notice in this framework that *know* has several lcs subentries, each corresponding to a different semantic realization of its syntactic frame.

As Grimshaw (1979) points out, these lexical properties can help disambiguate clauses with initial *wh*-phrases:

(11) It's amazing how fat Opus is
(12) I'll ask how fat Opus is

In (11), the complement *how fat Opus is* can only be interpreted as an exclamation given that *amazing* only selects for E (and not Q):

(13) *amazing*(x,y) → y an E

and, in (12), *how fat Opus is* can only be interpreted as an interrogative given that the verb *ask* only selects for Q (and not E):

(14) *ask* (x,y) → y a Q

That verbs have different subentries, each associated with a particular lcs, is obeyed in morphology. For example, consider the verb *manage*, which allows both an NP and an S' as syntactic realizations:

(15) Reagan managed the budget
(16) Reagan managed to stay awake

The word formation rule (WFR) that allows *mis*-prefixation picks out the NP realization, and not the S' realization:

(17) Reagan mis-managed the budget
(18) *Reagan mis-managed to stay awake

So, the question is: Why does *mis*-prefixation pick out the NP from the subcategorization complex of verbs like *manage*? Carlson & Roeper (1980) claim that WFRs act only on the unmarked subcategorization of a complex – in this case the [NP] version. On their account, (17) is grammatical and (18) is not because the rule-derived form takes an unmarked subcategorization.

Grimshaw argues for another possibility: that there are two cases of *manage*, with one roughly meaning "to keep things under control" – the NP version – and the other meaning something like "to succeed in" – the S' version. Given the lexical organization shown in (10), these two versions can be partially represented as subentries:

(19) *manage* (x,y) → y a THEME
              (x,y) → y an INFINITIVE

Now the input and the output of the WFR will be the same: *mis*-prefixation will act on the version of *manage* that takes a THEME, and will yield a verb with the same lcs and strict subcategorization as its base.

One piece of evidence for this subentry hypothesis comes from "concealed" constructions (Grimshaw 1984) – syntactic NPs that are interpreted as complex semantic types. For example:

(20) Mitzi managed *to keep things under control* and I managed *it* too.

The NP - *it* - is interpreted explicitly as "to keep things under control," thus the INFINITIVE semantic type can be realized as an NP as well as an S'. But the other version of *manage*, the version allowing a THEME, only selects for an NP. So, the lexical entry for *manage* needs to be changed to reflect this information:

(21)   *manage* (a)   [__NP]
                        (x,y) → y a THEME

       manage (b)   [__NP
                         S']
                        (x,y) → y an I

Carlson and Roeper's Unmarked Subcategorization Hypothesis would predict that, since WFRs consider only the NP, the concealed form of the NP should also allow *mis*-prefixation, regardless of which version of *manage* is involved. Sentence (22), embedded with *manage* (a), and sentence (23), embedded with *manage* (b), show that this is not the case; *mis*-prefixation acts only on the NP realization of *manage* (a):

(22)   Mitzi *managed* the budget but I mis-managed *it* hopelessly
(23)   *Mitzi managed *to keep things under control* but I mis-man-
       aged *it* hopelessly

The same case can be made for *re*-prefixation. So, for example, the verb *claim* allows an NP and S' realization:

(24)   Mitzi claimed the missing treasure
(25)   Mitzi claimed that the treasure was missing

Re-prefixation acts on the NP version, not the S' version:

(26)   Mitzi re-claimed the missing treasure
(27)   *Mitzi re-claimed that the treasure was missing

Claim can be represented in two subentries, with one meaning something like "to take possession of y" and the other meaning some-thing like "to assert a proposition":

(28)   *claim*   (a)   [__NP]
                        (x,y) → y a THEME

       claim   (b)   [__NP
                         S']
                        (x,y) → y a P

And *re*-prefixation acts only on the NP realization of *claim* (a), shown in the "concealed" construction in (29), and not *claim* (b), shown in (30):

(29) Mitzi claimed *the missing treasure* but the pirates re-claimed *it* first

(30) *Mitzi claimed *that the treasure was missing* but the pirates re-claimed *it* first

So, WFRs, like *mis*- and *re*-prefixation, pick out subentries of verbs, subentries organized by lcs. And when a WFR applies to a subentry of a particular verb, the derived version will have the same lcs as its subentry.

In summary, lexical entries for verbs include strict subcategorization, argument structure, and lcs. Verbs with the same strict subcategorizations can have different lcs representations, and these can be represented with different subentries. An individual verb can also have the same lcs representation realized differently in the syntax.

Before I examine how some of these lexical properties might influence sentence processing, I first need to take a slight detour and describe some work on the lexical access of nouns with multiple interpretations. This detour will turn out to be informative about the operating characteristics of lexical activation, with implications for the activation of some of the more "linguistic" properties I have just described.

LEXICAL ACCESS OF NOUNS WITH MULTIPLE MEANINGS

Normal subjects

It is by now fairly well established that normal subjects, when listening to a sentence for meaning and encountering a noun with potentially multiple interpretations, access at some point all these interpretations (e.g., Swinney 1979; Seidenberg, Tanenhaus, Leiman, & Bienkowski 1982; Jones 1990). So, for example, consider the following:

(31) "It was such a nice day for fishing that Jack headed down to the *bank* # with his gear # ..."

If subjects are asked to decide, right after the noun "bank," whether or not "SHORE" and "MONEY" are words, reaction times (RTs) are faster (i.e., primed) than when they are asked whether or not the unrelated "NOISE" is a word. But when the sentence is tapped well past "bank," priming for the contextually irrelevant meaning "MONEY" diminishes to the baseline – to that of "NOISE" (Swinney 1979). Note also that context here has little effect on this exhaustive access of multiple meanings; though the context of the sentence might be biased toward only one of the multiple possibilities for an ambiguous noun (in this case, biased toward "SHORE"), all are still primed. This latter result has been taken as evidence for the contextual impenetrability – or modularity – of lexical access.

Though it appears that all the interpretations for polysemous nouns are activated in parallel, some evidence suggests that they may actually be considered serially in order of their frequency-of-occurrence (e.g., Simpson & Burgess 1989). There is an RT advantage for more frequent meanings over others. So, in (31), normal subjects prime "MONEY" (a word reflecting "bank's" most frequent meaning) more quickly than they prime "SHORE" (a word reflecting "bank's" secondary meaning).

Aphasic subjects

Priming results are not so clear-cut for aphasic subjects, however. Recently, Swinney, Zurif, and Nicol (1989) found that both normal elderly subjects, and aphasic subjects who were classified as "fluent" and who had suffered posterior cortical damage, normally accessed both the most frequent and less frequent meaning of a polysemous noun regardless of context. Of more interest, however, was that found for a group of agrammatic Broca's aphasic subjects, those subjects who primarily suffered anterior frontal lobe cortical damage near what is known as "Broca's area."

Taking a lead from the work of Milberg and Blumstein, who found that Broca's aphasic subjects do not prime in an isolated word condition (e.g., Milberg, Blumstein, & Dworetzky 1987), Swinney et al. found that, unlike normals and fluent aphasic patients, their agrammatic Broca's aphasic subjects prime only for the most frequent interpretations of polysemous nouns in sentences. So, taking (31) as an example, these subjects would prime only "MONEY" when the sentence is tapped immediately after the noun "bank" (though, interestingly, the context is biased toward the secondary interpretation "SHORE" – meaning that the lexical access "module" is still intact).

Swinney et al. surmised that the anterior lesions responsible for agrammatic Broca's aphasia result in a protracted rise-time for lexical access. That is, the normal operating characteristics of lexical access is such that all meanings for a polysemous noun are accessed quickly and serially in terms of frequency of occurrence. But because lexical access is slowed after anterior cortical damage, agrammatic Broca's aphasic subjects prime only the first or most frequently occurring meaning for a polysemous noun in the immediate vicinity of the noun, and that only when tested "downstream" from the polysemous noun would other meanings prime.[2]

This account – a protracted time-course of information access – might even explain other aspects of linguistic impairments common to agrammatic Broca's aphasia; aspects that at first blush seem to have little to do with each other (Zurif 1990): the inability to process the closed class vocabulary normally (e.g., Bradley, Garrett, & Zurif 1980; Shapiro, Zurif, Carey, & Grossman 1989), and the apparent inability of these patients to understand sentences that involve moved constituents and traces (Grodzinsky 1990). On this account, the relevant information necessary to process sentences in real-time (be they closed class items, associative aspects of noun interpretations, traces and their antecedents) is not made available at the right time in the processing "stream."

In any event, given the possibility that the time-course of information access is protracted subsequent to the anterior cortical damage underlying agrammatic Broca's aphasia, it is of interest to investigate the time-course of access with other information types. But first we need to examine the time-course of lexical activation in normal subjects.

Activation of verb properties

Normal subjects: background

The last few years have seen a proliferation of work investigating how the notions a-structure and thematic roles enter into theories of sentence processing. Many of these theories rest on the possibility that something like multiple theta-grids become available once the verb is encountered during a parse. The most direct evidence for this exhaustive activation comes from some of the work I and others have been associated with (Shapiro, Zurif, & Grimshaw 1987, 1989; Shapiro & Levine 1990; for similar claims see also Rayner, Carlson, & Frazier 1983; Tanenhaus & Carlson 1990). But this work, in other guises, has a history that dates back to the 1960s.

In the first of these earlier investigations, Fodor, Bever, and Garrett (1968) argued that verbs can be classified in terms of the number, or type, of deep structure configurations (from Chomsky's *Aspects* 1965) they can dominate. In terms expressed here, this means that the more subcategorizations associated with the main verb of a sentence, the

wider the range of hypotheses generated about the type of constructions a verb phrase can dominate. As a consequence of this complexity metric, Fodor et al. proposed that a sentence with a verb phrase
headed by a verb that allows more subcategorization possibilities is
more complicated than a sentence headed by a verb that allows fewer
possibilities.

Corroborating their thesis, Fodor et al. found that sentences containing verbs with the potential to accept two kinds of complements,
an NP and an S', were more difficult to "process" than those containing verbs allowing an NP and not an S'. Moreover, they found this to
be so even though the two different verb types were inserted in sentences that only contained direct object NP constructions. For example, consider the following sentences used in their experiment:

(32) The janitor hit the tenant who complained about the high
      rent
(33) The janitor reported the tenant who complained about the
      high rent

The verb *hit* in (32) has the potential of accepting only an NP complement. The verb *report* has the potential of accepting both an NP, as in
(33), and a sentential complement:

(34) The janitor reported that the tenant complained about the
      high rent

Though in both (32) and (33) only the NP complement was realized,
sentence (33) – inserted with the more complex verb – proved more
difficult than (32).

There was a methodological limitation to this study: Subjects were
asked, in one experiment, to restate the test sentence in their own
words. In another experiment, subjects were asked to reconstruct a
sentence from a scrambled set of words. It has become clear in the last
several years that the luxury of conscious reflection permitted by such
tasks cannot be directly related to the unconscious devices that sus-
tain real-time sentence analysis. That is, allowing subjects to interpret
a sentence at some point *after* having heard it won't tell much about
the processes that actually guided that interpretation.

Later studies have seemed to avoid this methodological limitation.
Several innovations have been developed that purport to tap into the
sentence comprehension system as the sentence unfolds over time,
presumably reflecting the output of the operations of the sentence
processor. Two such methodological innovations involve either forcing the processing system to its limit (e.g., via the rapid serial presen-

tation of words in a sentence (RSVP), or via time-compressed speech), or introducing a secondary task while subjects are attempting to understand a sentence. This latter approach turns on the assumption that as aspects of sentence processing increase in complexity, processing capacity for the secondary task decreases. This decrease in capacity is then reflected in longer reaction times (RTs) to the secondary task. And the secondary task can be introduced at various points during the temporal unfolding of the sentence so that processing complexity can be measured on-line, that is, during the course of sentence comprehension, not after-the-fact.

Just such an approach using phoneme monitoring as the secondary task was undertaken by Hakes (1977). Hakes had subjects monitor for a target phoneme either within the verb of interest or within the noun that was head of the NP complement. The prediction was that a sentence containing a verb that was more complex, allowing both an NP and an S', would yield longer phoneme monitoring times than a sentence containing a verb that was less complex, allowing an NP complement and not an S'.

Hakes failed to find the complexity effect reported by Fodor et al. He suggested two possible reasons for the results: (1) that verb representation does not affect on-line processing, but only processing acting on the already-comprehended sentence (as measured by, for example, paraphrasing); or (2) the failure to find the complexity effect was due to seeking it in the wrong place. It has been pointed out that phoneme monitoring is fragile: it has been shown to be confoundable with a variety of variables, including the phonological "shape" of the preceding word, the similarity between the to-be-monitored phoneme and the initial phoneme of the preceding word, etc. (Seidenberg et al. 1982).

In any event, two other "on-line" studies have shown an effect of verb complexity on sentence processing. Both made use of techniques that placed heavy demands on the listener. Holmes and Forster (1972) used RSVP – requiring subjects to report sentences that were rapidly presented on a screen, word-by-word. They argued that RSVP forces the viewer to process each word as it occurs, pushing the sentence processing system to its limit without degrading the input.

Holmes and Forster found that one-clause sentences containing so-called "simple" verbs – those that did not allow sentential complements – were easier to report than sentences with verbs that had the further potential of accepting sentential complements. They thus argued that their data supported Fodor et al.'s original contention that verb complexity – defined in terms of a verb's potential to enter into different complement types – affects the processing of sentences.

In another on-line study, Chodorow (1979) used the auditory analog of RSVP, time-compressed speech, to assess the effect of verb
structure on sentence processing. Subjects were required to remember
word lists presented after the sentence. Once again, sentences with
verbs that did not allow sentential complements were more easily
processed than those that did allow such constructions, even though
both verb types were embedded in sentences without sentential complements.

Some cautionary notes concerning the use of RSVP and time-compressed speech must be entered, however. It is possible that these two
studies showed the desired effect of verb complexity only because
they by-passed the normal input system by encouraging back-up processing strategies used to recover from perceptually problematic circumstances. After all, both produced their effects by depending on
faster-than-normal presentation rates. And these studies used techniques that were inherently unable to tap into the sentence processing
system locally. Since subjects were required to report *after* sentence
presentation, one could argue that conscious reflection permeated the
comprehension process.

But perhaps more importantly, all these studies included target
verbs with varying subcategorization frames:

(35)   *attack*   [∅]
                        [NP]

(36)   *attend*   [NP]

(37)   *give*   [NP PP]
                        [NP NP]

From my perspective, if Fodor et al.'s verb complexity thesis is to be
taken seriously, then an attempt should be made to ensure that verbs
of any given type should be relatively homogenous so far as their
subcategorization frames are concerned. This was obviously not the
case, for even the so-called "simple" verbs of (35) - (37) can be claimed
to differ among themselves so far as complexity is concerned. For
example, *attend* – allowing only an NP – should be considered less
complex than *give* because the former allows fewer hypotheses to be
generated about the type of constructions the VP can dominate than
the latter. Yet these verbs were considered as comprising a homogenous class only because they did not allow sentential complements.

In summary, those studies that have shown a relation between verb
complexity and sentence processing have not been without their

problems. But even if there is a link between representations and processing complexity, to what aspect of verb representation ought it to be attributable? Each of these previous studies begs the distinction between lcs/thematic possibilities and strict subcategorization frames. That is, though it might be true that verbs that allow an NP and an S' have more subcategorization frames than verbs that allow an NP and not an S', it is also the case that the former might allow more lcs subentries than the latter. So there is a confound between the number of strict subcategorization frames and lcs subentries. And, as I have shown previously in this paper, Grimshaw's work on the lexicon details verbs that select sentential complements that differ from one another in terms of the specific semantic types they select. So, it is certainly not clear that the strict subcategorization representations of verbs influence sentence processing.

We attempted to disentangle this confound by separating the effects of strict subcategorization from lcs/thematic representations, and by using a task – a cross-modal lexical decision – that does not rely on faster-than-normal input.

LCS/thematic activation

We (Shapiro, Zurif, & Grimshaw 1987) exploited the fact that verbs select both for different sets of lcs/thematic subentries and for different syntactic realizations or strict subcategorization complexes. We tested whether or not these lexical properties would have an influence on real-time sentence processing.

We looked at verbs that accommodated only one obligatory two-place entry, an (AGENT THEME) as in *fix*, verbs that allowed only one obligatory three-place entry, an (AGENT THEME GOAL) as in *give*, and verbs that accommodated both two- and three-place subentries, an (AGENT THEME) and an (AGENT THEME GOAL) like *donate* and *send* (that is, verbs that allowed an optional third argument).

This notion of "subentries" is different from the notion characterized in the section *The Organization of the Lexicon*. That is, the subentries stipulated for verbs like *send* and *donate* do not have to do with different meaning representations, but instead have to do with more "complex" entries, one entry having two arguments, another having three (see also, Williams 1980 and Pinker 1989 for a similar representational framework). It will turn out that even this notion of "subentry" – a notion that does not have much in the way of independent evidence from linguistic theory – will nevertheless affect real-time sentence processing.

These four verb types differ also in terms of their strict subcategorizations. So, the obligatory two-place verbs allow just one syntactic realization, an NP, the obligatory three-place verbs allow one realization, an NP PP, our "nonalternating datives" allow two realizations, an NP and NP PP, and our "alternating datives" allow three realizations, an NP, NP PP, and a double-NP. We placed these verbs in identical NP-V-NP-PP sentences (with embedded subject relatives) like the following:

The boy who was tall *fixed* the toy in the park yesterday
The boy who was tall *gave* the toy to the girl yesterday
The boy who was tall *donated* the toy to the girl yesterday
The boy who was tall *sent* the toy to the girl yesterday

We also gathered verbs that, in addition to selecting a simple (AGENT THEME) subentry, selected among a corpus of complex semantic types. So, for example, we examined verbs that we called two-complements, those that allowed both a simple two-place lcs/thematic subentry (AGENT THEME) and another subentry containing one of these complex semantic types (PROPOSITION) (e.g., *accept*). And we looked at four-complement verbs, those that allowed, again, a simple two-place structure (AGENT THEME) but also allowed three other subentries, each consisting of one of the three complex semantic types: (PROPOSITION), (EXCLAMATION), and (INTERROGATIVE) (e.g., *discover*). Unlike the subentries stipulated for verbs like *fix, give, donate,* and *send*, these subentries are directly related to the linguistic evidence described in the introduction. That is, these subentries have to do with different lcs representations, and the more subentries a verb accommodates, the more complex the verb.

These two verb types, though differing in terms of lcs complexity – allowing different lcs/thematic subentries – nevertheless had the same strict subcategorization complexes: each allowed an NP and an S'. We placed these two- and four-complement verbs into NP-V-S' sentences like the following:

The woman *accepted* that the key was missing
The woman *discovered* that the key was missing

We presented these sentence types embedded with the target verbs to normal listeners. Immediately after encountering the verb in the sentence, a probe was presented visually on a computer monitor, the probe consisting of a series of letters either forming a morphologically complex word in English, or a non-word. The probes, when forming English words, were not related to the sentence in any way, and were controlled for frequency of occurrence, mean number of letters, and number of syllables. The subject, while listening to the sentence for meaning, had to decide as quickly and as accurately as possible whether the probe indeed formed a word in English; reaction times were recorded. The sentence always continued to play in the normal manner.

The assumption here was that as the sentence became more complex in the immediate vicinity of the verb (or rather, as the verb became more complex in terms of either the number of lcs/thematic subentries each entailed, or in terms of the number of different syntactic realizations), the reaction time taken to make the secondary cross-modal lexical decision on the unrelated visual probe would increase.

That is indeed what we found. Moreover, it was the number of lcs/thematic subentries that counted in this respect, not syntactic realizations. So, verbs that allowed one thematic possibility, with either two or three thematic roles within that structure (e.g., *fix*, *give*), yielded significantly faster RTs on the secondary task than verbs that allowed two thematic frame possibilities, one with two roles and another with three (e.g., *donate*, *send*). And complement verbs that allowed two subentries (e.g., *accept*) yielded faster RTs than complement verbs that allowed four subentries (e.g., *discover*). Consider, again, that these RT differences occurred in the immediate vicinity of the verb in sentences that were virtually identical in form.[3]

We interpreted these findings as evidence for the momentary exhaustive activation of multiple lcs/thematic information in the immediate temporal vicinity of the verb. That is why verbs that allowed four possibilities resulted in greater interference than verbs that allowed only two, for example. This interpretation bears similarity to the work of Swinney and colleagues just discussed (that multiple information about a lexical item is activated momentarily).

To a certain extent, these data are not so surprising. From a representational perspective, it appears from the morphology data that I presented earlier that lcs/thematic information has a certain representational privilege over strict subcategorization – that WFRs act on subentries organized by lcs representations, not strict subcategorization (Grimshaw 1984). And from a psycholinguistic perspective, it is not so surprising that multiple lcs/thematic information is activated in the immediate temporal vicinity of verbs in NP-V-NP-PP sentences (or even NP-V-S' sentences). When the verb is encountered in such neutral sentence contexts, any one of several thematic possibilities might be appropriate to the sentence being heard (e.g., (AGENT THEME), (AGENT THEME GOAL), etc.; (AGENT PROPOSITION), (AGENT INTERROGATIVE) etc.). So, given the verb *discover*, for ex-

ample, the listener could not tell at the point of having to make a
lexical decision at the verb whether the sentence would be "John
discovered the key," "John discovered that the key was missing, " and
so forth. Thus it could be argued that the processor needs all possibilities available to it at the point where the verb is encountered in
neutral sentence contexts, so it can assign these roles onto argument
positions.

But the similarity between this work with lcs/thematic activation
and Swinney's work with the activation of polysemous nouns extends even to the issue of contextual impenetrability. In a more recent
study (Shapiro, Zurif, & Grimshaw 1989), we sought to determine
whether or not the apparent exhaustive activation of multiple lcs
subentries would be observed when verbs were embedded in sentences that were not neutral, in sentences that were structurally biased
toward one particular subentry.

The same secondary lexical decision task used in our previous
work was used here, with the probes presented immediately after the
main verb in each sentence. Biasing was accomplished by moving an
argument having the interpretation of a THEME (the indirect object
NP) into a pre-verbal position via passivized cleft constructions, and
moving an argument having the interpretation of a PROPOSITION (a
sentential clause) into a pre-verbal position via passive constructions.
In this way, by the time the verb (and lexical probe) was encountered,
only one lcs/thematic possibility would be "evident" to the processor,
the one relevant to the entire sentence being heard. The sentences
were like the following:

It was [for the boy] that [the bike] was *fixed* yesterday
It was [to the boy] that [the letter] was *sent* yesterday
[That the answer was wrong] was *accepted* by the boy
[That the answer was wrong] was *discovered* by the boy

So, for example, though a two-complement verb like *accept* allows
both an (AGENT THEME) and an (AGENT PROPOSITION), and a
four-complement verb like *discover* allows an (AGENT THEME),
(AGENT PROPOSITION), (AGENT EXCLAMATION), and an
(AGENT INTERROGATIVE), the sentence would be biased toward
only the (AGENT PROPOSITION) structure – signalled by a "that"
clause. The device that activates the verb and all its lcs/thematic
possibilities then could, in principle, ignore activating all possibilities
except the one indicated in the pre-verb sentence context. If this were
to happen, no RT differences should then occur between any verb
types differing in lcs/thematic complexity, since by the time the verb

is encountered only one subentry need be active for any verb – the one stipulated in the pre-verb context.

However, that possibility turned out not to be the case. For example, those "dative" verbs that allowed both an (AGENT THEME) and an (AGENT THEME GOAL) yielded longer RTs on the secondary task than those obligatory two-place verbs that allowed only an (AGENT THEME), even though the sentences in which the verbs were embedded were biased toward only an (AGENT THEME) interpretation. And the four-complement verbs yielded longer RTs than the two-complement verbs, again, even though the sentences in which these verbs were embedded were biased toward only one of multiple possibilities, an (AGENT PROPOSITION) interpretation. Thus, the device that activates the verb and its multiple lcs/thematic representations does so even when faced with contexts that could simplify its operation. That is, the activation device is so "dumb" and data-driven (driven only by the phonological form of the verb) that it ignores the pre-verb sentence information. These data then attest to the modularity of lexical access over an initial phrase structure parse.[4]

Aphasic subjects

We know then, from these data, that lexical activation makes available in the verb's immediate temporal vicinity a verb's multiple lcs/thematic possibilities, regardless of sentence context. The next step was to investigate whether agrammatic Broca's aphasic subjects show a normal time-course of lcs activation, or whether they show a protracted rise-time reminiscent of Swinney et al.'s results with noun access. We (Shapiro & Levine 1990) again used the cross-modal lexical decision interference task, and presented to a group of independently assessed agrammatic Broca's aphasic patients, a group of fluent aphasic patients, and a group of normal elderly controls NP-V-NP-PP and NP-V-S' sentences over headphones. The verbs filling the verb slot in these sentences again differed in terms of their lcs/thematic possibilities. The probes for the secondary lexical decision were placed immediately after the verb in one set of sentences, and, in another set of sentences, the probes were placed further downstream, immediately after the preposition.

We found the following: when the probes were placed immediately after the verb, our normal control subjects seemed to activate all thematic possibilities for a verb, corroborating our earlier findings. Yet when the probes were placed downstream from the verb, no effects of thematic activation were observed, that is, no differences were observed among the different verb types. There are (at least) two explanations for this last result. It might simply be that the effect associated with activating multiple lcs/thematic subentries dissipates over time, so that when the preposition is encountered, the effects have disappeared. But it might also be the case that by the time the preposition is encountered in the sentence, all thematic roles have been assigned onto the argument positions in the sentence. We are presently testing these two accounts.

Importantly, the same normal patterns were observed for the agrammatic Broca's aphasic subjects (the fluent subjects' data, as a group, were difficult to interpret). So, why is it that these agrammatic Broca's aphasic subjects appear to show a normal time-course of lcs/thematic activation, yet as Swinney et al. (and Prather) has shown, these patients have a putative protractive rise-time of lexical access when the domain is limited to the referential interpretations of polysemous nouns? A perhaps more parsimonious story would have shown that these patients also exhibit a slower rise-time in thematic activation. But that did not happen.

We have considered two explanations for this discrepancy. The first suggests that the lexical decision interference task that we have used to assess verb activation taps a different, perhaps later, stage of perceptual processing than does the lexical decision priming task used to chart the activation of polysemous nouns. On this account, the exhaustive activation of multiple lcs/thematic possibilities in the vicinity of the verb could be more apparent than real for the agrammatic Broca's aphasic subjects because the task itself is more attuned to later-occurring processing. If this explanation turns out to be correct, then these patients would be expected to show a slower rise-time for any limited representational domain – including lcs subentries – with any task that taps earlier aspects of processing. We are presently testing this possibility.

There is another possible explanation, however. It might be that to access the interpretation of a polysemous noun, one must go from the acoustic/phonetic information to the noun's form in the lexicon, and that the activation of this form is then passed on to other nodes in the network, where those nodes represent items that are associatively related. Thus, either through a search or spreading activation – both directed by frequency of occurrence considerations – the various interpretations associated with a polysemous noun are accessed.

But activation of thematic information about a verb might be a different story: it does not have to do with searching through a network; rather, once the phonological form is mapped onto the verb's entry in the lexicon, the lcs/thematic possibilities become available all at once (at a certain computational cost). Thus, rather than a time-dependent process, thematic activation is associated with the so-called "effort" required to activate indivisible information chunks of various sizes. On this account, then, the putative slower-than-normal rise-time of lexical access in Broca's aphasia is irrelevant when considering the apparently normal thematic activation of these patients. That is, the sensitivity that these patients show for lcs/thematic entries may have nothing to do with a time-based activation of linked referential units. We are testing this possibility as well.

Finally, I'd like to end with a summary of a recent study (Canseco-Gonazalez, Shapiro, Zurif, & Baker 1990) that examines the fact that the configurations of lcs entries are sensitive to the form in which visual information is parsed and translated for the linguistic system (see also Jackendoff 1987, for similar claims). So, for example, just as a dative verb requires two subentries to accommodate a GOAL or potential possessor whether or not the argument linked to the thematic role actually appears in a sentence, so, too, the activity that the verb refers to will also implicate a potential possessor whether or not the visual system provides any information concerning that possessor.

An "artificial" language study

This study, then, asked the following questions: Could it be that brain damage known to otherwise impair grammatical capacity actually spares the representation of thematic roles, given that they might fall out from lcs, a non-grammatical notion? And would lcs/thematic information in this case be represented even in the absence of a natural language medium?

To address these questions, we tested a severely impaired Broca's aphasic patient on an artificial visually-based language called c-ViC. The c-ViC system is a computerized visual communication system designed for the rehabilitation of severely aphasic patients (Steele, Illes, Weinrich, & Lakin 1985; Steele, Weinrich, Kleczewska, & Carlson 1989). It allows the user to display, select, and arrange graphic symbols into meaningful patterns on the computer screen. Most important, for present purposes, it allows the user to arrange symbols to describe depicted events.

We focused on the c-ViC symbols that refer to pictured *actions*. We theorized that the ease with which these symbols could be learned would be predictable in terms of the number of lcs/thematic subentries for natural language verbs that could equivalently refer to the pictured actions. We assumed here that lcs/thematic subentries refer to information that is not uniquely linguistic, but rather are responsive to information provided by the way in which we parse the world of visual experience, that is, in terms of categories like agent of actions, goals of actions, paths of actions, and so on (Jackendoff 1983,

1987). On this account, pictured activities (and what they refer to) would directly influence the difficulty of learning c-ViC "predicate" symbols, and this difficulty would be directly equivalent to that provided by natural language verbs. This hypothesis involved another assumption: that though other grammatical capacities are affected by damage within the language region of the brain (see, for example, Grodzinsky 1990), operations involving lcs/thematic activation might be spared (possibly because, whatever its linguistic function, thematic information mirrors forms of organization that are not particularly linguistic).

Skirting most of the major details, our test involved presenting pictures to our subject. The subject had to describe the pictures by using *non-iconic* symbols he had been trained to associate with different "predicates." Sometimes these pictures could be described with a two- or three-argument sentence embedded with a "pure transitive verb" (a verb accommodating only one entry, an (AGENT THEME)), as in "the man *fixed* the tire," and "the man *fixed* the tire in the garage." Sometimes the pictures could be described using a two- or three-argument sentence embedded with a "dative verb" (a verb accommodating two subentries, one with (AGENT THEME), the other, (AGENT THEME GOAL)), as in "the man *served* the milk," and "the man *served* the milk to the woman." Consider here that the third argument associated with the pure transitive "verb" was an adjunct, and did not form part of the "verb's" lexical entry. The third argument of a dative verb was always an argument of the verb.

There was a training phase and a test phase. During the training phase, the subject was presented with each picture and a corresponding c-ViC "sentence." The sentence contained noun and verb slots, with the noun slots filled with iconic symbols (e.g., in "the man served the milk," a picture of a man for "the man" and a picture of milk for "the milk" were present) but with the "verb" slot left unfilled. From a corpus of non-iconic symbols (several 6-line figure drawings without any known relation with real-world objects), the trainer provided a correct symbol to occupy the unfilled verb slot. Critically, sometimes the same symbol was associated with the "verb" in a "sentence" with two arguments and in a "sentence" with three arguments; sometimes a separate and *different* symbol was associated with the "verb" in a "sentence" with two arguments than in a "sentence" with three arguments. This training session continued until all the pictures, c-ViC "sentences" and non-iconic "predicate" symbols were presented.

The test phase consisted of presenting the subject with each of the pictures with its c-ViC "sentence." Again, each "sentence" had the nouns correctly depicted but the "verb" slot was left unfilled. For each picture-sentence combination, the subject was presented with the entire corpus of non-iconic "predicate" symbols and was required to provide the correct symbol – that is, that which was previously trained to correspond to the action in the pictured activity. Trials continued until a criterion of 100 per cent correct responses was reached, that is, until the subject learned the correct symbol for the missing "verb" in each of the presented c-ViC "sentences."

We found the following: for the C-ViC "verbs" that had as their English equivalent verbs that accommodated only one lcs/thematic entry (AGENT THEME), it was significantly more disruptive to have to learn two different symbols – one for the predicate in a two-argument "sentence" without the adjunct and one for the predicate embedded in a three-argument "sentence" with the adjunct – than it was to learn the same symbol for both versions of the predicate. The opposite was true for c-ViC "verbs" that have as their English equivalent verbs that accommodated two lcs/thematic subentries, (AGENT THEME) and (AGENT THEME GOAL): it was significantly less disruptive to have to learn two different symbols – one for the predicate in a two-argument sentence without the GOAL, the other for the predicate in a three-argument "sentence" with the GOAL – than it was to learn one symbol for both versions of the predicate.

Correspondingly, symbols associated with verbs that allowed only one subentry were easier to learn when they were embedded in two-argument sentences (where the adjunct was not made explicit); yet symbols associated with verbs that accommodated two subentries were easier to learn when they were embedded in three-argument sentences (where the GOAL or "possessor" was explicitly indicated).

In effect, this subject represented verbs that had only one subentry with only one symbol, regardless of whether that predicate occurred in a two- or three-place sentence; and represented verbs that had two subentries with two different symbols depending on whether the verb was embedded in a two- or three-argument sentence.

These data go hand-in-hand with the notion that the lcs/thematic representation for a verb like *fix* contains only one entry, and thus it is easier to associate a single c-ViC symbol with it's c-ViC equivalent, yet a verb like *serve* has two subentries, one without the GOAL represented and a second with it represented. It is thus easier to associate two distinct symbols for the verb, one for each subentry.

Importantly, this severely language-impaired patient appeared sensitive to these lcs/thematic facts, even in the context of learning a visually-based artificial language. There is a caveat here, however. Our patient, though severely impaired in speech, was not so impaired in comprehension. Thus, at this point we can not claim that this patient had so much brain damage as to impair his grammatical capacity. However, this does not detract from the finding that even in a visually-based artificial language, the description of actions seem to be rooted in lcs representations.

SUMMARY

To summarize, I have tried to make the following points: (1) the lexicon is organized in such a way as to make distinctions between various levels of representation, including strict subcategorization, argument structure, and lcs. And it might be the case that thematic role labels are not part of the argument structure representation of verbs, but are instead epiphenomenal and are read off lcs; (2) any individual verb can have several lcs subentries, each either corresponding roughly to a different meaning (e.g., *discover* allows, in one subentry, a PROPOSITION, and in another, an EXCLAMATION, etc.), or each subentry having different sets of thematic roles (e.g., *send* allows, in one subentry, an AGENT THEME, and in another, an AGENT THEME GOAL); (3) an operating characteristic of lexical activation is such that multiple information is exhaustively activated in the immediate temporal vicinity of the lexical item, even in contextually-biased sentence contexts; (4) lcs/thematic information, and not strict subcategorization, appears to be the information contacted during this on-line lexical activation; (5) agrammatic Broca aphasic patients appear to have protracted activation of, at the very least, nouns with multiple interpretations, but so far, this may not extend to verbs and their multiple lcs/thematic possibilities (though we are testing such a possibility); and, finally, (6) I presented a study that suggests that lcs/thematic entries, representing the way in which we parse the world, can extend to the use of predication in a visually-based, artificial language.

NOTES

1 The work reported here was supported in part by NIH (NIDCD) Grant # DC00494.
2 Prather, Zurif, Stern, and Rosen (1990) recently presented data from a study investigating the time-course of lexical priming using a continuous lexical decision task with words presented in lists. Varying the time between word presentations (inter-stimulus intervals, or ISIs), they found that though normal and elderly control subjects prime at ISIs of 500 ms.,

an agrammatic Broca's subject only primed at an ISI of 1500 ms. These results support an inference of protracted lexical access for this patient.

3 Recently, Schmauder (1990) has reported a failure to "replicate" the work done by Shapiro et al. (1987). However, we (Shapiro, Brookins, Gordon, & Nagel 1991) recently discovered what we believe to be the locus of this "failure": Schmauder's probes were all morphologically simple – homogenous, thereby not allowing the secondary lexical decision task to do its proper work – to allow significant interference to occur between the primary and secondary tasks. Indeed, by using Schmauder's probes, but perceptually altering them and making them more difficult to read, we obtained thematic complexity effects.

4 It seems that these data have been used as evidence for lexically-driven (as opposed to phrase structure-driven) parsers since thematic information is available very early on during sentence processing. Certainly the data reported in Shapiro et al. (1987) are neutral in this regard. But even the the contextual impenetrability results of Shapiro et al. (1989) do not speak to this issue. Consider the following scenario: A partial phrase structure parse of the sentence is computed and then the verb is encountered and its lcs/thematic entries are activated. The partial parse – an argument – is then compared to the lexical subentries, activating the one subentry relevant to the partial parse. Thus, the greater the number of subentries that need to be compared to the argument set up by the first-pass parse, the longer the RTs on the secondary task presented right after the verb. Is this a lexically-driven parser? No; it is a deterministic and data-driven parser, but nothing lexical guides anything.

REFERENCES

Bradley, D., Garrett, M., and Zurif, E.B. (1980). Syntactic deficits in Broca's aphasia. In D. Caplan (ed.), *Biological Studies of Mental Processes*. Cambridge, MA: MIT Press

Canseco-Gonzalez, E., Shapiro, L.P., Zurif, E.B., and Baker, E. (in press). Predicate-argument structure as a link between linguistic and non-linguistic representations. *Brain and Language*

Carlson, G. and Roeper, T. (1980). Morphology and subcategorization: case and the unmarked complex verb. In H. van der Hulst, T. Hoekstra, and M. Moortgaat (eds.), *Lexical Grammar*. Dordrecht: Foris

Chodorow, M. S. (1979). Time-compressed speech and the study of lexical and syntactic processing. In W. Cooper, and E. Walker (eds.), *Sentence Processing*. Hillsdale, NJ: Lawrence Erlbaum Associates

Chomsky, N. (1965). *Aspects of the Theory of Syntax*. Cambridge, MA: MIT Press

Fodor, J.A., Garrett, M., and Bever, T. (1968). Some syntactic determinants of sentential complexity: verb structure. *Perception and Psychophysics* 3:453-60

Grimshaw, J. (1979). Complement selection and the lexicon. *Linguistic Inquiry* 10:279-326

– (1984). Word Formation and the Structure of Lexical Entries. Unpublished manuscript, Brandeis University

– (1990). *Argument Structure*. Cambridge, MA: MIT Press

Grodzinsky, Y. (1990). *Theoretical Perspectives on Language Deficits*. Cambridge, MA: MIT Press

Hakes, D.T. (1971). Does verb structure affect sentence comprehension? *Perception and Psychophysics* 10:229-32

Holmes, V.M. and Forster, K.I. (1972). Perceptual complexity and underlying sentence structure. *Journal of Verbal Learning and Verbal Behavior* 11:148-56

Jackendoff, R. (1983). *Semantics and Cognition*. Cambridge, MA: MIT Press

– (1987). On beyond Zebra: the relation between linguistic and visual information. *Cognition* 26:89-114

– (1987). The status of thematic relations in linguistic theory. *Linguistic Inquiry* 18:369-411

Jones, J. (1989). Multiple access of homonym meanings: an artifact of backward priming? *Journal of Psycholinguistic Research* 18:417-32

Levin, B. (1990). Where syntax and semantics meet: the view from unaccusatives. Paper presented to the CUNY Conference on Human Sentence Processing, New York, NY

Milberg, W., Blumstein, S., and Dworetzky, B. (1987). Processing of lexical ambiguities in aphasia. *Brain and Language* 31:138-50

Pesetsky, D. (1983). Paths and Categories. Unpublished doctoral dissertation, MIT, Cambridge, MA

Pinker, S. (1989). *Learnability and Cognition: The Acquisition of Argument Structure*. Cambridge, MA: MIT Press

Prather, P., Zurif, E.B., Stern, C., and Rosen, J. (1990). Effects of focal brain damage on access of lexical and visual information. Paper presented to the CUNY Conference on Human Sentence Processing, New York, NY

Rappaport, M. and Levin, B. (1986). What to do with theta-roles. *Lexicon Project Working Papers* 11. Center for Cognitive Science, MIT

Rayner, K., Carlson, M., and Frazier, L. (1983). The interaction of syntax and semantics during sentence processing: eye movements in the analysis of semantically biased sentences. *Journal of Verbal Learning and Verbal Behavior* 22:358-74

Schmauder, R. (In press). Argument structure frames: a lexical complexity metric? *Journal of Experimental Psychology: Learning, Memory, and Cognition*

Seidenberg, M.S., Tannenhaus, M.K., Leiman, J.M., and Bienkowski, M. (1982). Automatic access of the meanings of ambiguous words in context:

some limitations of knowledge-based processing. *Cognitive Psychology* 14:481-537

Shapiro, L.P., Brookins, B., Gordon, B., and Nagel, N. (In press). Verb effects during sentence processing. *Journal of Experimental Psychology: Learning, Memory, and Cognition*

Shapiro, L.P. and Levine, B.A. (1990). Verb processing during sentence comprehension in aphasia. *Brain and Language* 38:21-47

Shapiro, L.P., Zurif, E.B., Carey, S., and Grossman, M. (1989). Comprehension of lexical sub-category distinctions by aphasic patients: proper and common, and mass and count nouns. *Journal of Speech and Hearing Research* 32:481-8

Shapiro, L.P., Zurif, E.B., and Grimshaw, J. (1987). Sentence processing and the mental representation of verbs. *Cognition* 27:219-46

Shapiro, L.P., Zurif, E.B., and Grimshaw, J. (1989). Verb processing during sentence comprehension: contextual impenetrability. *Journal of Psycholinguistic Research* 18:223-43

Simpson, G. and Burgess (1985). Activation and selection processes in the recognition of ambiguous words. *Journal of Experimental Psychology: Human Perception and Performance* 11:28-39

Steele, R., Weinrich, M., Wertz, R., Kleczewska, M., and Carlson, G. (1989). Computer-based visual communication in aphasia. *Neuropsychologia* 27:409-26

Swinney, D. (1979). Lexical access during sentence comprehension: (re)consideration of context effects. *Journal of Verbal Learning and Verbal Behavior* 18:645-59

Swinney, D., Zurif, E.B., and Nicol, J. (1989). Lexical processing during sentence comprehension in agrammatic and Wernicke's aphasia. *Cognitive Neuroscience* 1:25-37

Tannenhaus, M. and Carlson, G. (1989). Lexical structure and language comprehension. In W. Marslen-Wilson (ed.), *Lexical Representation and Process*. Cambridge, MA: MIT Press

Williams, E. (1984). Argument structure and morphology. *The Linguistic Review* 1:81-114

Zurif, E.B. (1990). The neurology of language. Seminar presented to the CUNY Conference on Human Sentence Processing, New York, NY

Contributors

Bob Carpenter, Department of Philosophy, Carnegie Mellon University

Kenneth Church, AT&T Bell Laboratories, Murray Hill, New Jersey

Stephen Crain, Department of Linguistics, University of Connecticut

Verónica Dahl, School of Computing Science, Simon Fraser University

B. Elan Dresher, Department of Linguistics, University of Toronto

Janet Dean Fodor, Linguistics Department, City University of New York

Mark Gawron, Hewlett-Packard Laboratory, Palo Alto, California

Henry Hamburger, Department of Computer Science, George Mason University

Pauline Jacobson, Department of Cognitive and Linguistic Sciences, Brown University

Mary-Louise Kean, Department of Cognitive Science, University of California, Irvine

Richard T. Oehrle, Department of Linguistics, University of Arizona

Lewis P. Shapiro, Department of Psychology and the Center for Complex Systems, Florida Atlantic University

Edward P. Stabler, Jr., Department of Linguistics, University of California, Los Angeles

Arnold M. Zwicky, Department of Linguistics, Ohio State University